Get the eBook FREE!

(PDF, ePub, Kindle, and liveBook all included)

We believe that once you buy a book from us, you should be able to read it in any format we have available. To get electronic versions of this book at no additional cost to you, purchase and then register this book at the Manning website.

Go to https://www.manning.com/freebook and follow the instructions to complete your pBook registration.

That's it!
Thanks from Manning!

Flutter in Action

ERIC WINDMILL
FOREWORD BY RAY RISCHPATER

MANNING
SHELTER ISLAND

For online information and ordering of this and other Manning books, please visit
www.manning.com. The publisher offers discounts on this book when ordered in quantity.
For more information, please contact

> Special Sales Department
> Manning Publications Co.
> 20 Baldwin Road
> PO Box 761
> Shelter Island, NY 11964
> Email: orders@manning.com

Manning Publications Co.	Acquisitions editor:	Brian Sawyer
20 Baldwin Road	Development editor:	Susanna Kline
PO Box 761	Technical development editor:	John Guthrie
Shelter Island, NY 11964	Review editor:	Aleks Dragosavljević
	Production editor:	Anthony Calcara
	Copyeditor:	Tiffany Taylor and Frances Buran
	Proofreader:	Melody Dolab
	Technical proofreader:	Gonzalo Huerta-Cánepa
	Typesetter:	Gordan Salinovic
	Cover designer:	Marija Tudor

ISBN 9781617296147
Printed in the United States of America

brief contents

iii

contents

foreword

One of the things the Flutter team is deeply grateful for is the supportive community of Flutter developers. For nearly any question you may have, you can find an answer on Stack Overflow, Medium, or even someone's GitHub account. Many answers come with fully working sample code with a license that lets you use the code right in your application. We see this spirit of cooperation and camaraderie as crucial to making you successful with Flutter.

Until now, though, there's been little material that you can actually hold in your hands and work through at your desk or in the evenings as you learn how to use Flutter. While blogs, Medium, and online documentation have been a paradigm shift for book publishers, especially in computing, there's still a need for long-form material on topics, and Flutter is no exception.

This is why this book is so important. There are things you can't get from a five-hundred-word Medium post or a snippet of code on Stack Overflow. Thinking deeply about things like how your application manages its state requires you to understand the platform deeply. In this book, you'll not only see how to use Flutter, but you'll understand why using Flutter in the ways Eric and people online say to actually works in practice.

Eric covers many of the things that developers have found challenging when moving to Flutter. Between these pages you'll learn about how layout works, how to build widgets that interact with users, and how to build complex applications that span multiple pages and carry complex application sate. For users new to Dart, there's an entire chapter on how Dart handles asynchronicity. Because today's mobile applications are communicating applications, you'll also see how to handle JSON with HTTP backends, and as a bonus, how to use Firestore to manage data storage. And, to wrap things up, there's a whole chapter on testing.

Throughout, Eric's taken the time to explain not just what, but why. I urge you to do the same—while you can dip in and out of a chapter to get just the morsel of information you need, why not pause for a minute and savor the experience of actually holding this book and going deeper? Doing so will make you a better programmer with Flutter and pay dividends elsewhere in your life as you slow down and remember how to not just learn, but master a new technology.

I and the entire Flutter team are excited to see what you build with Flutter. Thank you for trusting us with your ideas.

—RAY RISCHPATER
TECHNICAL PROGRAM MANAGER, FLUTTER
GOOGLE

preface

When I started using Flutter in September 2017, it was in an alpha stage. I started using it because my boss told me to. I had no opinions about it because I had never heard of it. I hadn't even heard of Dart, which had been around for nearly a decade by then. But—and this probably isn't a spoiler— I got hooked immediately. Not only is the end product of the highest quality, but the development process is perhaps the most enjoyable of any SDK that I've used. The tooling, the community, the API, and the Dart language are all a joy to participate in.

That's why I've written this book. I legitimately believe that Dart and Flutter are the near-future, gold-standard of application development. And I've written a book that I think will get any developer from zero to one with Flutter. This book is half tutorial, half spreading-the-good-word.

Nearly two years after starting to use Flutter, I'm now working at my second job that lets me build a Flutter app everyday, and my enthusiasm hasn't wained. Flutter is the truth.

In those two years, Flutter has grown quite a bit. It went from alpha to beta to version 1, and it's now stable. Dart went from version 1 to 2, and is now putting a lot of effort into making it an ideal language to write modern UIs in. And now, at the time of this writing, Flutter for web is in technical preview. It looks like it'll only get more exciting.

Flutter is going to keep improving, but the foundation is now set. And that's why I think this book can really help. No matter how it grows, this book will get you started and build your Flutter foundation.

There is no shortage of resources for learning Flutter. My goal with this book, however, is to cover the process in one go. You'll learn about Dart a bit, and you'll learn about Flutter a lot. By the end of the book, you'll have experience writing a mobile app from scratch. This book covers all of the foundational knowledge you need to write beautiful, buttery-smooth mobile apps with Flutter. I'll cover UI and layout, animations and styling, network requests, state management, and more.

acknowledgments

This is the first book I've written. One of the things I've learned in the process is just how many people are involved. I am truly only one of many, many people who put a lot of work into this.

First, I'd like to thank two of my former bosses and colleagues, Matthew Smith and John Ryan. When they hired me at AppTree, I hadn't heard of Flutter or Dart. And more, I still had (and continue to have) a lot to learn about building software. They taught me everything I know, and were patient the entire time. It is the best job I've ever had, and it allowed me to fall in love with Dart and Flutter.

I'd like to acknowledge my editor at Manning, Susanna Kline, for two reasons. First, I had no clue about how to write a book. Susanna has been patient, yet persistent. She's also been kind, yet honest. All those qualities certainly allowed me to write the best book I could. And secondly, she really let me explore and write the book I wanted to write. Which is why, at the end of this process, I'm still loving it.

I'd like to thank all the reviewers, colleagues, and friends who've read the manuscript and given feedback. This includes those who've commented over at the Manning book forum. I can say with 100% certainty that the book would've suffered without the feedback. Specifically, I'd to thank all the reviewers: Andy King, Damian Esteban, David Cabrero Souto, Edwin Kwok, Flavio Diez, Fred Heath, George Onofrei, Godfred Asamoah, Gonzalo Huerta-Cánepa, Jacob Romero, Joel Kotarski, Jose San Leandro, Kumar Unnikrishnan, Martin Dehnert, Nitin Gode, Paul Brown, Petru Bocsanean, Pietro Maffi, Samuel Bosch, Sander Zegvelt, Serge Simon, Thamizh Arasu, Willis Hampton, and Zorodzayi Mukuya.

Of course, I have to thank everyone who works on Flutter and Dart, as well as the Flutter community online. This community has been by far the most pleasant, uplifting, and friendly tech community I've ever been a part of.

Lastly, I want to thank the following dogs and cats that I know, who I used as examples through out the book: Nora, Odyn, Ruby, Doug, Harper, Tucker, Yeti, and Rosie. (If you own one of these animals and you're reading this, you get no royalties. Thank you.)

about this book

Flutter in Action is a book about empowering everyone (and anyone) to create mobile applications with the Flutter SDK and the Dart programming language. It focuses first on understanding the who, what, why, and how of Flutter. Over the first few chapters, I hope to convince you that Flutter is worth your time, and ease you into the basics. Following that, I take a deep dive into the UI: layout, routing, animations, and more. And then I spend time on state management and the tougher concepts, like asynchronous programming with Flutter in Dart. I finish with some short chapters about HTTP and Firebase, as well as testing.

Importantly, this book is focused on Flutter-specific contents. I will not use third-party resources to develop niche apps or solve niche problems. This entire book uses only a handful of libraries outside of Flutter.

Who should read this book

This book is for application developers that want to write Flutter apps. Whether you have experience with writing web apps, native mobile apps, Xamarin, or something I don't even know about yet, this book is for you. The important thing for you to understand is how modern applications work. I don't expect you to know how to write code across the whole stack, only that you know what a modern stack consists of.

There are a ton of resources and blog posts out there that contain much of this information. The point of this book is to bring everything together in one easy-to-follow format.

How this book is organized

This book has eleven chapters over four sections.

Part 1 is meant to prepare you to dive in:

- Chapter 1 explains what Flutter is and why we, mobile developers, should care. It also gets into the basics of Flutter.
- Chapter 2 departs a bit and covers (briefly) the Dart programming language, as well as an intro into object-oriented programming (OOP). If you know about Dart, or are comfortable picking up a new language, you can skip this chapter.
- Chapter 3 takes a dive into how Flutter works under the hood and the basics of writing Flutter code. By the end of this chapter, you will have your environment set up, as well as have a basic understanding of writing a Flutter app.

Part 2 covers all things UI. It uses a dumb, stateless app to cover forms, animations, and more:

- Chapter 4 covers all the basic widgets in Flutter. This chapter is all about the base features that you'll likely use in every Flutter app you ever write.
- Chapter 5 is about forms and gestures. In short, this chapter explains how the user interacts with the app you're writing.
- Chapter 6 is about making the app beautiful. It covers painting to the canvas and takes a deep dive into animations in Flutter.

Part 3 is all about state management. Some of this section is where many of the toughest concepts come into play. It uses an e-commerce app as the example:

- Chapter 7 is all about routing. It includes passing state from one route to another, as well as routing animations.
- Chapter 8 is about state management. It's the first chapter to cover some concepts that aren't exactly Flutter-specific. It includes new widget types, like the `InheritedWidget`, as well as using the bloc pattern to manage state.
- Chapter 9 is my favorite, I think. It covers asynchronous Dart concepts like streams and how to incorporate those concepts into Flutter. Spoiler: Flutter supports those features as first-class citizens.

Part 4 is called "Beyond the Foundation" because it's about moving out of your IDE and into subjects that can apply to any SDK: network calls, Firebase, working with JSON, and testing:

- Chapter 10 is all about using outside resources. It covers HTTP, Firebase, and JSON serialization.
- Chapter 11 is about everyone's favorite topic: testing. It includes Flutter's built-in testing framework, as well as mockito and the Flutter driver.

In general, this book is meant to build up from one chapter to another. It's a tutorial-style book, which means if you "choose your own adventure," there may be important pieces missed.

About the code

This book contains (mostly) large blocks of code, rather than short snippets. Therefore, most of the examples are annotated and explained for each code listing. Because this book is about writing entire apps, the code for each section is highly reliant on the entire app. So, at the beginning of most code snippets, I've left a comment, following // on the top line, of where you can find the code snippet in the source code of the app.

You can find the source code for these example apps by downloading it from the publishers website at https://www.manning.com/books/flutter-in-action.

liveBook discussion forum

Purchase of *Flutter in Action* includes free access to a private web forum run by Manning Publications where you can make comments about the book, ask technical questions, and receive help from the author and from other users. To access the forum, go to https://livebook.manning.com/#!/book/flutter-in-action/discussion. You can also learn more about Manning's forums and the rules of conduct at https://livebook .manning.com/#!/discussion.

Manning's commitment to our readers is to provide a venue where a meaningful dialogue between individual readers and between readers and the author can take place. It is not a commitment to any specific amount of participation on the part of the author, whose contribution to the forum remains voluntary (and unpaid). We suggest you try asking the author some challenging questions lest his interest stray! The forum and the archives of previous discussions will be accessible from the publisher's website as long as the book is in print.

about the author

Eric Windmill is a software engineer, who's focused largely on client-side applications. He's been lucky enough to work with Flutter since its very early days, at multiple companies now. He is the author of FlutterByExample.com. He is passionate about helping open the doors and removing barriers into tech.

about the cover illustration

The figure on the cover of *Flutter in Action* is captioned "Femme Tattare de Kazan," or "Kazan Tattar Woman" in English. The illustration is taken from a collection of works by many artists, edited by Louis Curmer and published in Paris in 1841. The title of the collection is *Les Français peints par eux-mêmes*, which translates as *The French People Painted by Themselves*. Each illustration is finely drawn and colored by hand and the rich variety of drawings in the collection reminds us vividly of how culturally apart the world's regions, towns, villages, and neighborhoods were just 200 years ago. Isolated from each other, people spoke different dialects and languages. In the streets or in the countryside, it was easy to identify where they lived and what their trade or station in life was just by their dress.

Dress codes have changed since then and the diversity by region, so rich at the time, has faded away. It is now hard to tell apart the inhabitants of different continents, let alone different towns or regions. Perhaps we have traded cultural diversity for a more varied personal life—certainly for a more varied and fast-paced technological life.

At a time when it is hard to tell one computer book from another, Manning celebrates the inventiveness and initiative of the computer business with book covers based on the rich diversity of regional life of two centuries ago, brought back to life by pictures from collections such as this one.

Part 1

Meet Flutter

The first section of this book is in three chapters, and it's meant to prepare you to build full-blown Flutter apps. In particular, this includes three subjects.

First, I'll introduce all things Flutter in chapter 1. This includes the whos, whats, whys, and hows: how it works, why it's worth investing in, and the mental model needed to use the SDK. This chapter is largely conceptual and involves little code.

I also devote a chapter to Dart, the programming language that Flutter uses. I like to call Dart *Java Lite*. And I mean that in a great way. If you're comfortable with object-oriented and strongly typed languages, you can probably just skim this chapter.

Then, in chapter 3, we'll explore Flutter itself. This chapter uses a simple Flutter example app to explain how Flutter works, both from the perspective of how you write code, as well as some more explanations of how the engine works. By the end of chapter 3, you'll be set up, comfortable with the SDK, and ready to start building a Flutter app. If I did a good job, you'll also understand what's under the hood.

Meet Flutter

This chapter covers

- What is Flutter?
- What is Dart?
- Why does Flutter use Dart?
- When is Flutter the right tool (or the wrong tool)?
- A brief intro to how Flutter works

Flutter is a mobile SDK, built and open sourced by Google; and at its core, it's about empowering everyone to build beautiful mobile apps. Whether you come from the world of web development or native mobile development, Flutter makes it easier than ever to create mobile apps in a familiar, simplified way. Flutter is special in that it makes it truly possible to "write once, and deploy everywhere." As of this writing, Flutter apps will deploy to Android, iOS, and ChromeOS. In the near future, Flutter apps will also run as web apps and desktop apps on all major operating systems.

In short, Flutter is a truly complete SDK for creating applications. It's a platform that provides everything you need to build applications: rendering engine, UI components, testing frameworks, tooling, router, and many more features. The consequence is that you get to focus on the interesting problems in your app. You can focus specifically on the domain functionality, and everything else is taken care of. The value that Flutter provides is astonishing.

In fact, that's how I found myself here, writing this book. I had to learn Flutter because of my job, and I loved it from the moment I started. I effectively became a mobile developer overnight, because Flutter felt so familiar to my web development background. (The Flutter team has said that they were influenced by ReactJS.)

Flutter isn't only about being easy, though. It's also about control. You can build exceptional mobile apps using Flutter with a shallow knowledge of the framework. But you can also create incredible and unique features, if you so choose, because Flutter exposes everything to the developer.

This is a book about writing a (relatively) small amount of code and getting back a fully featured mobile app that works on iOS and Android. In the grand scheme, mobile app development is new. It can be a pain point for developers and companies alike. But I believe Flutter has changed that (and that's a hill I'm willing to die on).

This books has one goal: to turn you into a (happy) Flutter (and Dart) developer.

1.1   *Why does Flutter use Dart?*

Flutter apps are written in the programming language called Dart. I'll describe Dart in depth throughout the book, but for now, just know that all the code you write in a Flutter app is Dart code. In fact, to us, the mobile developers, Flutter appears to be nothing more than a Dart library.

Dart is also owned and maintained by Google. This may give you pause. There are reasons to be skeptical of this choice: it's not one of the hot languages of today, few companies use it in production, and the community must be small. What gives? Is Google just using it because it's Google's language? I imagine that played a role, but there are practical reasons, too:

- Dart supports both just-in-time (JIT) compiling and ahead-of-time (AOT) compiling:
  - The AOT compiler changes Dart into efficient native code. This makes Flutter fast (a win for the user and the developer), but it also means that (nearly) the entire framework is written in Dart. For you, the developer, that means you can customize almost everything.
  - Dart's optional JIT compiling allows hot reloading to exist. Fast development and iteration is a key to the joy of using Flutter.
- Dart is object-oriented. This makes it easy to write visual user experiences with Dart, with no need for a markup language.
- Dart is a productive, predictable language. It's easy to learn, and it feels familiar. Whether you come from a dynamic language or a static language, you can get up and running with ease.

And I think Google owning Dart *is* an advantage. In the last few years, Dart has made great strides to be a nice language specifically for writing modern UIs. The type system and object orientation make it easy to reason about writing reusable components for the UI. And Dart includes a few functional programming features that make it easier to turn your data into pieces of UI. Finally, asynchronous, stream-based programming features are first-class citizens in Dart. These features are used heavily in reactive programming, which is the paradigm of today.

Lastly, Dart excels at being a language that's easy to learn. As a coworker of mine said about hiring, "We don't have to find Dart people, only smart people."

1.2   On Dart

Besides explaining Flutter in depth, I will also introduce the basics of Dart. Dart is a programming language. And programming languages can be, as it turns out, hard to learn. The fundamentals of Dart are similar to all higher-level languages. You'll find familiarity in Dart syntax if you're coming from JavaScript, Java, or any other C-like language. You'll feel comfortable with Dart's object-oriented design if you're coming from Ruby or Python.

Like all languages, though, the devil is in the details (and, as they say, doubly in the bubbly). The joys of Dart and the complexity of writing good Dart code lie not in the syntax, but in the pragmatics.

There's good news, though. Dart excels at being a "safe" language to learn. Google didn't set out to create anything innovative with Dart. Google wanted to make a language that was simple and productive and that could be compiled into JavaScript. What Google came up with works well for writing UIs.

The fact that Flutter can compile to JavaScript is less relevant for Flutter development, but it has had interesting consequences for the language. Originally, Dart was created as a language for web development. The stretch goal was to include a Dart runtime in the browser, as an alternative to JavaScript. Eventually, though, Google decided to write a compiler instead. This means nearly every feature in Dart must fit inside JavaScript semantically.

JavaScript is a unique language, and it isn't necessarily feature-rich. It accomplishes what it needs to accomplish, without any extraneous bells and whistles (which is a plus, in my opinion). So, in the past, Dart has been limited by what JavaScript can do. The result is a language that feels more like Java but is less cumbersome to write. (I like to jokingly call it "Java Lite," which is a compliment.)

There is nothing particularly exciting about its syntax, and no special operators will throw you for a loop. In Dart (unlike JavaScript), there is one way to say true: `true`. There is one way to say false: `false`. If (3) { would make Dart blow up, but it's coerced to `true` in JavaScript.

In Dart, there are no modules (like C# and the like), and there is really only one dynamic in which people write Dart code: object-oriented. Types are used in Dart, which can be a hurdle if you're coming from Ruby, Python, or JavaScript, but the type system is not as strict as in many typed languages.

All this is to say that Dart is a relatively easy language to learn, but you should take the time you need to learn it. Writing an app in Flutter is writing Dart. Flutter is, underneath it all, a library of Dart classes. There is no markup language involved or JSX-style hybrid language. It'll be much easier to be a productive Flutter developer if you're comfortable writing effective Dart code. I'll cover Dart in depth in chapter 2.

1.3   Who uses Flutter?

At the time of writing, Flutter is used in production by big and small companies alike. I've been lucky enough to use Flutter at work since September 2017, when the technology was still in its alpha stage. By the time you read this, Flutter will be in (at least) version 1.9.0, and my previous company will have migrated all of our clients off of our native apps and onto our Flutter app.

While this isn't a book about me, I am going to tell you a bit about what I do, because I want you to know that I'm confident in the future of Flutter. The company that I previously worked for is in the enterprise space. Its product is used by some big companies like Stanford University, Wayfair, and Taylor Parts. The core product is a BYOD (bring your own database) platform that lets customers plug in a few options and press a few buttons, and it spits out mobile and web apps to manage work flows and business-related enterprise issues. The mobile app supports offline usage, Esri maps, and real-time feedback. We did all this with Flutter (on mobile) and Dart on the server side. The point is this: don't be afraid of the limitations of this cross-platform tool.

We weren't the only ones using Flutter in production. As of this writing, Google AdWords and Alibaba are both using Flutter in production. You can see more examples of who's using Flutter (including an app I worked on for two years) on Flutter's website on the showcase page.[1]

1.4   Who should be using Flutter?

Regardless of your role at your company, or even if you're building apps for fun, everyone should consider Dart for their next project.

1.4.1   Teams, project leads, and CTOs

Flutter has proved, in front of my own eyes, that it increases productivity and collaboration by orders of magnitude. Before Flutter, each time a new feature was introduced to a product at my former company, it had to be written and maintained three times by three different teams—three different teams that could hardly collaborate because they had different skill sets.

Flutter solved that problem. Our three teams (web, iOS, and Android) became one unified clients team. We all had the same skill set, and we could all collaborate and lend helping hands.

---

[1]You can find the showcase at https://flutter.dev/showcase.

At my current job, we're rewriting a native iOS client in Flutter for the same reason. It allows us to be flexible and productive while offering users both iOS and Android apps. After a failed attempt at a different, unnamed cross-platform solution, Flutter has proven to be the ideal tool.

1.4.2 Individual developers

As developers, we often get starry-eyed and want to start a new project that will change everything. The key to success with this sort of work is busting out the project quickly. I can't count how many times I was ready to start a new project and quit before I began because of JavaScript build tools and setup. If you need to build an MVP fast, and iterate quickly, Flutter just works.

1.4.3 Code school students and recent CS grads

Code schools are quite popular, and unfortunately for the graduates, that means there are many grads fighting for the same junior-level jobs. My advice to anyone looking for their first job is to build a portfolio that sets you apart. Having a published mobile app with actual users will do that, and it's easier than ever to achieve with Flutter.

1.4.4 Open source developers

Flutter is open source. Dart is open source. The tools and the libraries are open source.

1.4.5 People who value speed

Flutter is for people who want to build an app quickly that doesn't sacrifice performance. By *speed*, I mean the speed at which you can write code and iterate, and the speed at which Flutter builds. Thanks to hot reloading, Flutter rebuilds your application in sub-second time as you're developing.

I would also argue that Dart makes you more productive, adding more speed. Dart is strictly typed and fully featured. Dart will save you from having to solve problems that are already solved, and the syntax and tooling make debugging a breeze.

1.4.6 People who are lazy

I'm a lazy developer. If a problem is solved, I don't want to waste time solving it again. Flutter comes with a massive library of Material Design widgets that are beautiful and ready to use out of the box. I don't have to worry myself with designing and building complicated pieces of a mobile app (such as a navigation drawer). I want to focus on the business logic that makes my app unique.

1.4.7 People who value control

Although I'm lazy, I do want to know that if I need to, I can change anything about my app. Flutter exposes every layer of the framework to the developer. If you need to write some custom rendering logic, you can do that. You can take control of animations between frames. Every high-level widget in Flutter is a string that can be unspooled and followed to the inner workings of the framework.

1.5   Who this book is for

This book assumes that you've developed an application before. That could be a web app, a native mobile app, Xamarin, or something I don't even know about. The important thing for you to understand is how a modern application works. I don't expect you to know how to write code across the whole stack, only that you know what a modern stack consists of. This book will focus on writing a mobile application in Flutter, and I will throw around common terms like *state, store, services,* and so on.

If you meet those criteria, I can assume that you're familiar with the common threads across all programming languages. You don't need to know Dart, but you do need to know about basic data structures (`Map`, lists, and so on) and features of all high-level languages (control flow, loops, and so on).

Finally, this book assumes that you know some high-level information about software engineering in general. For example, Dart and Flutter operate completely in the camp of the object-oriented paradigm.

This book is perfectly suitable for you if you're a junior developer, a senior developer, or anywhere in between. The prerequisites are simply that you've worked on large code bases before and you're interested in learning Flutter.

1.6   Other mobile development options

Before I offer up unsolicited opinions on your other options, I want to make this crystal clear: good developers think critically about which tools and technologies should be used in every different situation. And Flutter is not the answer 100% of the time. (But I will try hard to convince you otherwise.)

1.6.1   Native development (iOS and Android)

Your first choice is to write native apps for iOS and Android. This gives you maximum control, debugging tools, and (potentially) the best performance. At a company, this likely means you have to write everything twice: once for each platform. You probably need different developers on different teams with different skill sets, and those developers can't easily help each other.

1.6.2   Cross-platform JavaScript options

Your second option: cross-platform, JavaScript-based tools such as web views and React Native. These aren't bad options, either. The problems you experience with native development disappear. Every frontend web developer on your team can chip in and help; all they need are some modern JavaScript skills. This is precisely why large companies such as Airbnb, Facebook, and Twitter have used React Native on core products.

Of course, there are some drawbacks. (You knew there would be drawbacks.) The biggest is called the *JavaScript bridge.*

The first "mobile apps" to be built cross-platform were simply web views that ran on WebKit (a browser rendering engine). These were literally embedded web pages. The problem with this is basically that manipulating the DOM is very expensive and doesn't perform well enough to make a great mobile experience.

Some platforms have solved this problem by building the JavaScript bridge, which lets JavaScript talk directly to native code. This is much more performant than the web views, because it eliminates the DOM from the equation, but it's still not ideal. Every time your app needs to talk directly to the rendering engine, it has to be compiled to native code to "cross the bridge." In a single interaction, the bridge must be crossed *twice*: once from platform to app, and then back from app to platform, as shown in figure 1.1.

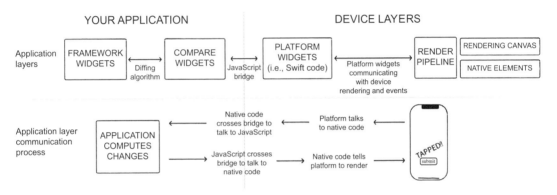

Figure 1.1 The JavaScript bridge is a major bottleneck to mobile frameworks in JavaScript. The JavaScript isn't compiled to native code and therefore must compile on the fly while the app is running.

Flutter compiles directly to ARM code when it's built for production. (ARM is the processor used in modern mobile devices, wearables, internet of things [IoT] devices, and so on.) And Flutter ships with its own rendering engine. Rendering engines are outside the scope of this book (and my knowledge, for that matter). Simply, though, these two factors mean that your app is running natively and doesn't need to cross any bridge. It talks directly to native events and controls every pixel on the screen directly. Compare the JavaScript bridge to figure 1.2, which represents a Flutter app.

The JavaScript bridge is a marvel of modern programming, to be sure, but it presents two big problems. First, debugging is hard. When there's an error in the runtime compiler, that error has to be traced back across the JavaScript bridge and found in the JavaScript code. The second issue is performance. The JavaScript bridge is expensive: each time a button in the app is tapped, that event must be sent across the bridge to your JavaScript app. The result, for lack of better term, is jank.

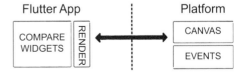

Figure 1.2 The Flutter platform, in the context of the JavaScript bridge

Many of these cross-platform problems are solved with Flutter. Later in this chapter, I'll show you how.

1.7 The immediate benefits of Flutter

I'm going to make an assumption about you. Since you're reading this book (and this section), it follows that you're curious about Flutter. It's also likely that you're skeptical.

The reasons you have for being skeptical are fair. It's a new technology, and that means breaking changes in the API. It means missing support for important features. It seems possible that Google could abandon it altogether one day. Not to mention the fact that Dart isn't widely used, and many third-party libraries that you want may not exist.

Now that I've pinned you, let me change your mind. The API likely will not change, as the the company that's developing Flutter and Dart uses Dart internally on major revenue-generating apps such Google AdWords.

Dart has recently moved into version 2.5, which means it will be a long time until it changes much. In the near future, there likely won't be many breaking changes.

Finally, features are indeed missing, but Flutter gives you the complete control to add your own native plugins. In fact, many of the most important operating system plugins already exist, such as a Google Maps plugin, camera, location services, and device storage. And new features are being added all the time. By the time you read this, this paragraph may be irrelevant.

1.7.1 No JavaScript bridge

The JavaScript bridge, used in most cross-platform options, is a major bottleneck in development and in your application's performance. Scrolling isn't smooth, applications aren't always performant, and they're hard to debug.

Flutter compiles to actual native code and is rendered using the same engine that Chrome uses to render (called Skia), so there's no need to translate Dart at runtime. This means apps don't lose any performance or productivity when running on a user's device.

1.7.2 Compile time

If you're coming from native mobile development, one of your major pains is the development cycle. iOS is infamous for its compile times. In Flutter, a full compile generally takes less than 30 seconds, and incremental compiles take less than a second thanks to hot reloading. At my day job, we develop features for our mobile client first because Flutter's development cycle allows us to move so quickly. Only when we're sure of our implementation do we write those features in the web client.

1.7.3 Write once, test once, deploy everywhere

Not only do you get to write your app one time and deploy to iOS and Android (and soon, web!), you also only have to write your tests once. Dart unit testing is quite easy, and Flutter includes a library for testing widgets.

1.7.4 Code sharing

I'm going to be fair here: I suppose this is technically possible in JavaScript as well. But it's certainly not possible in native development. With Flutter and Dart, your web and mobile apps can share all the code except each client's views. You can use dependency injection to run an AngularDart app and a Flutter app with the same models and controllers. (And, in the very near future, Flutter will be able to target Web and Desktop, too.) And obviously, even if you don't want to share code between your web app and your mobile app, you're sharing all your code between the iOS and Android apps.

In practical terms, this means you are super productive. I mentioned that we develop our mobile features first at my day job. Because we share business logic between web and mobile, once the mobile feature is implemented, we only have to write views for the web that expect the same controller data.

1.7.5 Productivity and collaboration

Gone are the days of separate teams for iOS and Android. In fact, whether you use JavaScript in your web apps or Dart, Flutter development is familiar enough that all your teams will be unified. It's not a stretch by any means to expect a JavaScript web developer to also effectively develop in Flutter and Dart. If you believe me here, then it follows that your new unified team will be three times more productive.

1.7.6 Code maintenance

Nothing is more satisfying than fixing a bug once and having it corrected on all your clients. Only in very specific cases is there a bug on the Flutter-produced iOS app and not the Android one (and vice versa). In 100% of these cases, these bugs aren't bugs, but cosmetic issues, because Flutter follows device OS design systems in its built-in widgets. Because these are issues like text size and alignment, they are trivial in the context of using engineering time to fix them.

1.7.7 The bottom line: Is Flutter for you?

You can spend all day listening to people tell you the benefits or downfalls of any technology. At the end of the day, though, it's all about the tradeoff. So *should you care about Flutter*? I've sprinkled in the answer to this already, but let me give it to you straight.

Are you an *individual developer* working on a side project or new product? Then the answer is simple: yes. This is absolutely for you. The amount of time you'll spend getting up to speed with Dart and Flutter will pay off big time in the long run.

Are you a *CTO* deciding if your company should adopt the technology? Well, this is a little more nuanced. If you're starting a new project and trying to use the skills of web developers, then absolutely. You'll get better performance and a more cohesive team, and all your developers (mobile and web), will be able to pick it up quickly. However, if you have a big team of iOS and Android engineers, then probably not. If you have the resources to not be concerned with keeping parity between your clients, then why rewrite them? Why gamble on a new technology? Flutter is about empowering anyone to build native quality apps, but if you're *already* empowered to build native apps, it's probably not for you. (This is why Airbnb famously abandoned React Native.)

My final comment is this: you can be up and running with a new Flutter app in about an hour from a standing start. If you already do iOS or Android development on your machine, you likely have most of the tools needed already, and you can be up and running in a matter of minutes. You might as well give it a try.

1.8   *Future benefits of Flutter: Web apps and desktop apps*

As of this writing, the Flutter team has officially announced Flutter for the web (also known as Hummingbird). This project is extremely exciting. When it's stable, Flutter will be the first framework that is *truly* "write once, deploy everywhere." Flutter is working on the functionality to deploy applications not only to iOS and Android, but also ChromeOS, browsers, macOS, Windows desktop apps, and Fuchsia.

As of Google I/O 2019, Flutter web is in technical preview. Right now, you can experiment with it and make web apps. That being said, I will not be talking about Flutter web in this book. There are two reasons for this:

- As I mentioned, the project is currently in the *technical preview* stage. That means everything you learn about it is likely to change.
- More important, the goal of Flutter web is that it "just works." So, in theory, if you learn everything in this book, once Flutter web becomes stable, you'll already know everything you need to write a web app with Flutter.

1.9   *A brief intro to how Flutter works*

At a high level, Flutter is a reactive, declarative, and composable view-layer library, much like ReactJS on the web (but more like React mixed with the browser, because Flutter is a complete rendering engine as well). In a nutshell, you build a mobile UI by composing together a bunch of smaller components called *widgets*. Everything is a widget, and widgets are just Dart classes that know how to describe their view. Structure is defined with widgets, styles are defined with widgets, and so are animations and anything else you can think of that makes up a UI.[2]

> **WARNING** "Everything is a widget" is a potentially misleading statement that you'll see everywhere on the internet, including in the official documentation. This doesn't mean there aren't other objects in Flutter. Rather, it means that every piece of your app is a widget. Styles, animations, lists, text, buttons, and even pages are widgets. For example, there isn't an object called "App" that defines the root of your application. The root of your application can technically be any widget. To be sure, there are other objects in the Flutter SDK (such as *elements*), which we'll discuss later.

---

[2] A brief intro to widgets from the docs: http://mng.bz/DNxa.

Suppose you're building a shopping cart app. The app is pretty standard: it'll list products, which you can add to a cart via Add and Remove buttons. Well, the list, the products, the buttons, the images, and everything else are widgets. Figure 1.3 shows how some of these widgets would be coded. Other than widgets, the only classes you're likely to write are your own logic-specific classes, which aren't related to Flutter.

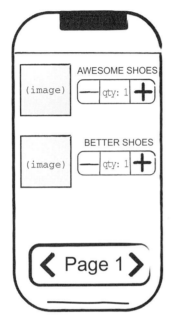

```
build(BuildContext context) {

    return Column(

        //...

            Image(),

            Text("BETTER SHOES"),

        //...

            IconButton(

                icon: Icon(Icons.chevron_left),

            ),

            Text("Page $page_num"),

        //...

    ); // column

}
```

Figure 1.3 Everything is a widget.

Everything is widgets inside widgets inside widgets. Some widgets have state: for example, the quantity widgets that keep track of how many of each item to add to the cart. When a widget's state changes, the framework is alerted, and it compares the new widget tree description to the previous description and changes only the widgets that are necessary. Looking at our cart example, when a user presses the + button on the quantity widget, it updates the internal state, which tells Flutter to repaint all widgets that depend on that state (in this case, the text widget). Figure 1.4 shows a wire frame of what the widgets might look like before and after pressing the "+" IconButton.

Figure 1.4 `setState` updates the displayed quantity.

Those two ideas (widgets and updating state) are truly the core of what we care about as developers. For the remainder of this chapter, I want to break down, in depth, what's *really* happening.

1.9.1 *Everything is a widget*

This is a core idea in Flutter. Everything is a widget. Again, this doesn't mean that there aren't other object types in Flutter—there are. Later in this book, I explore these other objects in depth, but as a developer you'll rarely care about anything other than widgets. The point is that there aren't `models` and `view models` or any other specific class type in Flutter.

A widget can define any aspect of an application's view. Some widgets, such as `Row`, define aspects of the layout. Some are less abstract and define structural elements, like `Button` and `TextField`. Even the root of your application is a widget.

Using the shopping cart example again, figure 1.5 shows how you might code some of the layout widgets, while figure 1.6 shows some structural widgets. To be sure, though, there are a lot more widgets than we can see, because they define layout, styles, animations, and so on.

For context, these are some of the most common widgets:

- *Layout*—Row, Column, Scaffold, Stack
- *Structures*—Button, Toast, MenuDrawer
- *Styles*—TextStyle, Color
- *Animations*—FadeInPhoto, transformations
- *Positioning and alignment*—Center, Padding

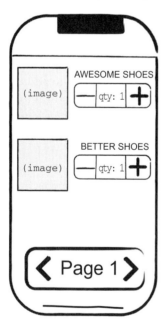

```
build(BuildContext context) {
    return Column(
        //...
            Row(),
            Padding(),
        //...
            Row(
                children: [
                    IconButton(),
                    //...
                ],
            ), // row
    ); // column
}
```

Figure 1.5 Examples of common layout widgets

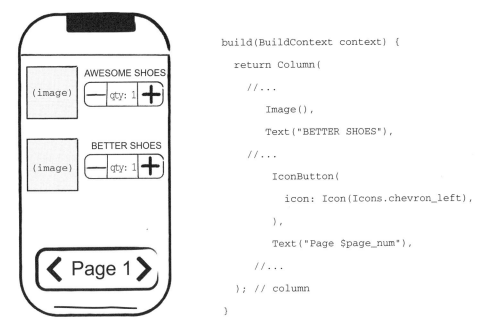

Figure 1.6   Examples of common structural widgets

1.9.2   *Composing UI with widgets*

Flutter favors composition over class inheritance, which allows you to make your own unique widgets. A majority of widgets are combinations of smaller widgets.[3]

In practice, that means that in Flutter you aren't subclassing other widgets in order to build custom widget. This is wrong:

```
class AddToCartButton
 extends Button {}
```

Rather, you *compose* your button by wrapping the Button widget in other widgets:

```
class AddToCartButton extends StatelessWidget {
  // ... class members
  @override
  build() {
    return Center(              This widget will center this
      child: Button(            AddToCartButton forever.
        child: Text('Add to Cart'),
      ),                        Pass text in, and now you
    );                          have a custom component.
  }
}
```

---

[3]Composition over inheritance from the Flutter docs: http://mng.bz/dxov.

If you're coming from the web, this is similar to how React favors building small, reusable components and combining them.

Widgets have a few different life-cycle methods and object members. The most important method, though, is `build()`. The `build()` method *must* exist in every Flutter widget. This is the method in which you actually describe your view by returning widgets.

1.9.3 *Widget types*

Most widgets fall under two categories: *stateless* and *stateful*. A `StatelessWidget` is a widget that you (as the developer) are okay with being destroyed. In other words, no information is kept within it that, if lost, will matter. All of the widget's state or configuration is passed into it. Its only job is to display information and UI. Its life depends on outside forces. It doesn't tell the framework when to remove it from the tree, or when to rebuild it. Rather, the framework tells *it* when to rebuild. (If this seems confusing, keep reading. It will make sense when contrasted against `StatefulWidget` types.)

In our shopping cart example, the `AddToCartButton` widget is stateless. It doesn't need to manage state, and it doesn't need to know about any other part of the tree. Its job is just to wait to be pressed and then execute a function when that happens.

This doesn't mean the Add to Cart button will never change. You may want to update it at some point to say Remove from Cart: some other widget will pass in the `String` that represents the text to display on the button (like "Add" or "Remove"), and it will be repainted when the word being passed to it changes. It *reacts* to new information.

A `StatefulWidget` in the shopping cart application, on the other hand, is the `QuantityCounter` widget, because it's managing a piece of stateful data that tracks the number of items you wish to add to your cart. A `StatefulWidget` object has an associated `State` object. The `State` object has special methods such as `setState` that tell Flutter when it needs to think about repainting.

`State` objects are long-lived. They can tell Flutter to repaint, but it can also be told to repaint because the associated stateful widget has been updated by outside forces.[4]

Let's consider our shopping cart app again. So far, we know there are quite a few components on the screen. These components are composed together via a combination of stateful and stateless widgets. Importantly, there is a `StatefulWidget` called `QuantityCounter`: a custom widget that I created by combining a variety of built-in widgets. Figure 1.7 shows a wireframe of this custom widget.

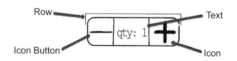

Figure 1.7 **The quantity widget is composed of buttons, text fields, and layout widgets.**

---

[4]Check out this detailed introduction to Widgets from the docs: http://mng.bz/rPae.

The build method for this would look something like the following. I've pointed out the parts you should care about right now.

Listing 1.1 Example build method for the custom QuantityCounter stateful widget

```
Widget build(BuildContext context) {            build always
  return Container(                     ◄────    returns a widget.
    child: Row(
      children: List<Widget>[
        IconButton(
          icon: Icons.subtract,                 Built-in property on a button widget
          onPressed: () {          ◄────        that listens for user interaction
            setState(() {
              this.quantity--;
            });
          }),
        new Text("Qty: ${this.quantity}"),  ◄──  The widget will be repainted at this
        new IconButton(                          point in the tree every time the
          icon: Icons.add,                       state object's quantity is called.
          onPressed: () {          ◄────         This callback will call setState,
            setState(() {                        which increases the state's
              this.quantity++;                   quantity counter.
            });
          }),
      ],
    )
  );
}
```

Decreases the state's quantity counter → (points to `setState(() { this.quantity--;`)

To be sure, there's a lot of layout and styling missing there, but that's the markup you need. The important information in that code block, though, is what's going on inside the IconButton and Text widgets.

This widget has access to several methods from the base State object class. The most important is setState. Every time the + or - button is pressed, the app will call setState. This method will update whichever part of the widget's state you tell it to, and will tell Flutter to repaint the widgets that rely on the state change. Figure 1.8 shows wireframes of how the quantity widget might be updated when the "+" button is tapped.

This process of building and updating widgets is called its *life cycle*. We'll explore life cycles in depth throughout the book, but figure 1.9 and the following list give an overview of a StatefulWidget's life cycle.

Figure 1.8 User interaction can trigger the framework to re-render using setState.

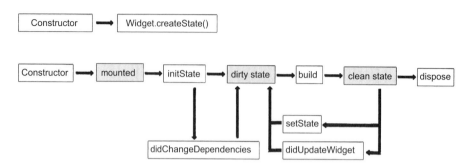

Figure 1.9 **The stateful widget is actually two objects: the widget and a State object.**

Looking at the QuantityWidget again, its life cycle may look something like this:

1 When you navigate to the page, Flutter creates the object, which creates the State object associated with this widget.

2 As soon as the widget is mounted, Flutter calls initState.

3 After the state is initialized, Flutter builds the widget (and, as a consequence, renders it; you'll see that process in the next section).

4 Now, the quantity widget is sitting and waiting for three possible events:

- The user navigates to a different part of the app, in which case the state can be disposed.

- Widgets outside of this one in the tree have updated and changed some sort of configuration that this widget relies on. In that case, this widget's state calls didUpdateWidget and repaints if necessary. This may happen if an item sells out and a widget higher in the tree tells this widget to disable itself, since you can no longer add the item to the cart.

- The button is tapped, which calls setState and updates the widget's internal state. This also tells Flutter to rebuild and re-render.

1.10 *Flutter rendering: Under the hood*

The real superpower of Flutter is the process it does one million times every day—the process by which Flutter builds (and rebuilds) your app. At any moment, your Flutter app is composed of a giant widget tree. Figure 1.10 shows a contrived example of what one page of the shopping cart's widget tree might look like. (In reality, it's much larger than this tree.)

Take a look at one of the CartItem widgets. This widget is Stateful, and each of its children likely relies on the state of that widget. When the state of the CartItem widget is updated, the rendering process in the subtree from this point begins.

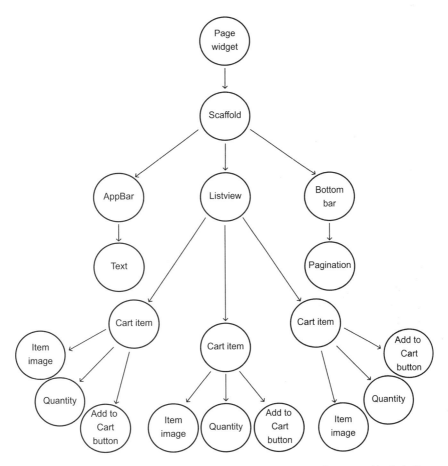

Figure 1.10 **This represents a widget tree, but in reality there are far more widgets in the tree than I can show.**

Flutter widgets are reactive. They respond to new information from an outside source (or setState), and Flutter rebuilds what it needs to. This is the high-level process:

1 A user taps a button.
2 Your app calls setState in the Button.onPressed callback.
3 Flutter knows that it needs to rebuild, because the Button state is marked dirty.
4 The new widget replaces the old one in the tree.
5 Flutter renders the new tree.

Now that Flutter has its new widgets, it's ready to render. The render step is itself a series of steps. Figure 1.11 shows an overview of the rendering steps that Flutter takes, with an emphasis on step 3.

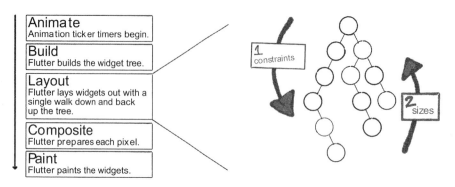

Figure 1.11 The high-level steps of the rendering process

Flutter kicks off the render by starting any animation tickers. If you need to repaint—for example, because you're scrolling down a list—the starting position of any given element on the screen is incrementally moved to its ending location, so that it's a smooth animation. This is controlled by animation tickers, which dictate the *time* that an element has to move. This effectively controls how dramatic the animations are.

During an animation, Flutter rebuilds and repaints on every frame (which is a lot). Later in this book, we'll take a deep dive into animations in Flutter.

1.10.1 *Composing the widget tree and layout*

Next, Flutter builds all the widgets and constructs the widget tree. By *widgets,* here I mean the data and configuration that dictate how elements on the screen will look. When it builds a button for the tree, it's not actually building a blue rectangle with text in it; that's a later step. Widgets just handle the configuration of elements that will eventually be painted on the screen.

After the widget tree is composed, Flutter can start thinking about layout. Flutter walks down the tree—only once—in linear time. (If you aren't familiar with Big O notation, *linear time* means *fast.*) On the way down, it's collecting information about the position of widgets. In Flutter, layout and size *constraints* are dictated from parent to child.

On the way back up the tree, every widget now knows its constraints, so the widget can tell its parent its *actual* size and position. The widgets are being laid out in relation to each other.

In the shopping cart example, this could mean that when the \+ button is tapped on the `QuantityWidget`, and the state is updated with a new quantity, Flutter walks down the widget tree, and `QuantityWidget` tells the buttons and text fields their constraints (not actual size). Then the buttons will tell the widgets representing the \+ and \- icons *their* constraints, and so on down the tree. Once the algorithm bottoms out at the leaf-node widgets, then all the widgets know their size constraints. On the way back up they can all safely take up the right amount of space at the correct position.

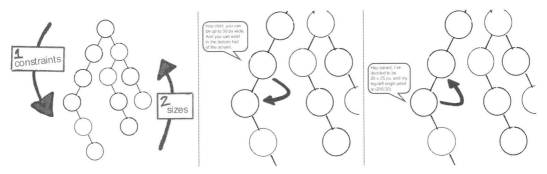

Figure 1.12   Flutter lays out all the widgets in one walk down and back up the tree, because widgets dictate their children's size constraints in Flutter.

Figure 1.12 illustrates this process (on a tree much smaller than any Flutter app would really be).

This single traversal of the widget tree is powerful. In contrast, in a browser, layout is controlled by the DOM and CSS rules. Because of the cascading nature of CSS and the fact that an element's size and position can be controlled by its parents or itself, it takes many walks down the DOM tree to position all elements. This is one of the biggest performance bottlenecks on the modern web.

1.10.2 Compositing step

Now that each widget is laid out and knows it isn't conflicting with any other widgets, Flutter can paint the widgets. It's important to note here that the widgets still aren't *rasterized*, or physically painted to pixels on the screen. That's coming up.

The compositing step is next. This step is when Flutter gives widgets their actual coordinates on the screen. Now they know the exact pixels they'll take up.

This step is purposefully and importantly separate from the painting step. Because the steps are separate, the widgets that have been composited can be reused if needed. This is useful, for example, when you're scrolling through a long list, as shown in figure 1.13. Rather than rebuilding each of those list items every time a new one scrolls on or off the screen, Flutter already has them built and painted, and can plug them in where they need to go.

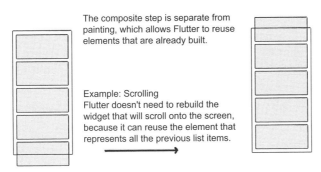

The composite step is separate from painting, which allows Flutter to reuse elements that are already built.

Example: Scrolling
Flutter doesn't need to rebuild the widget that will scroll onto the screen, because it can reuse the element that represents all the previous list items.

Figure 1.13   The composite step is separate from the painting step, to increase performance.

1.10.3 *Paint to the screen*

Now the widgets are ready to go. The engine combines the entire tree into a render-able view and tells the operating system to display it. This is called *rasterizing*, and it's the last step.

We just covered an entire framework in a couple of paragraphs. It was a lot. You shouldn't be concerned yet if you don't know exactly how Flutter works, because I'll beat this dead horse throughout this entire book. These are the three main ideas I want you to keep in mind as we dive deeper into Flutter, because they're what matters to us as developers:

- Flutter is reactive.
- Everything is a widget.
- State objects are long-lived and are often reused.
- Widgets' constraints are dictated from their parents.

If you'd like more information about how Flutter renders, check out this hour-long Google Tech Talk explaining the rendering engine: http://mng.bz/xlvg. It's a few years old, but the information is still relevant.

1.11 *Final note*

If I can leave you with one impression at the end of this chapter, it's this: Flutter is simple to use and a powerful tool, but it does take effort to use well. It is, especially if you're not a ReactJS web developer, a new paradigm of approaching the UI. If you find yourself frustrated while learning from this book, don't assume it's your fault. In fact, there are only two possible explanations. First, and most likely, you are just like every other human being: programming is hard, and learning takes time. Reread material, take a nap, and get back to it. You will get it. The only other explanation is that I have done a poor job of making the material digestible, and I welcome you to berate me on your choice of platform. I'm @ericwindmill everywhere.

Summary

- Flutter is a mobile SDK written in Dart that empowers everyone to build beautiful, performant mobile apps.
- Dart is a language made by Google that can compile to JavaScript. It's fast, strictly typed, and easy to learn.
- The advantages of using Flutter are that it compiles to native device code, making it more performant than other cross-platform options. It also has the best developer experience around, thanks to Dart's JIT and Flutter's hot reload.
- Flutter is ideal for anyone who wants to make a highly performant cross-platform app quickly. It's probably not the best choice for a large company with existing native teams.

- In Flutter, *everything* is a widget. Widgets are simply Dart classes that describe their view. A UI is created by composing several small widgets into complete widget trees.
- Widgets come in two main flavors: stateless and stateful.
- Flutter provides state management tools, such as widget life-cycle methods and special `State` objects.

A brief intro to Dart

2

This chapter covers

- Dart's Hello, World!
- Anatomy of a Dart program
- Basic Dart syntax such as control flow, loops, and functions
- Object-oriented programming in Dart
- Using I/O Dart libraries

This book is about building mobile apps with Flutter. But you can't write a Flutter app without learning a bit about the Dart programming language first. The good news is that Dart is also quite easy to pick up. If you're already comfortable enough with Dart that you understand the following code block, you can skip this chapter:

```
class CompanyContext extends StateObject {
  final bool isLoading;
  String _companyId;

  CompanyContext({
    this.isLoading = false,
  });
```

```
  String get companyId => _companyId;
  void set companyId(String id) {
    _companyId = id;
    _initApp();
  }

  factory CompanyContext.loading() => CompanyContext(isLoading: true);

  @override
  String toString() => 'CompanyContext{isLoading: $isLoading, _companyId:
➡ $_companyId}';
}
```

The command line

Many instructions in this book will involve running commands in your machine's terminal. I'm a big fan of GUIs, and I don't use the command line much. You don't need to be a command-line wizard to use this book. Just know that anytime you see a line of code that starts with a $, it's a command for your terminal. The following => shows the return value (if any). For example, the command `which dart` in most Unix system terminals returns the file path to your Dart SDK. You can use it to ensure that you have Dart installed:

```
$ which dart
=> /usr/local/bin/dart
```

Before proceeding, make sure Dart is installed on your machine. Installation instructions can be found in appendix A.

2.1 *Hello, Dart!*

Like all good programming books, we're going to start with a program that prints "Hello, World" (kind of) to your console. In your favorite text editor, create a new file in the hello_world directory called hello_world.dart. Write this code in the file:

```
void main() {
  print('Hello, Dart!');
}
```

Now, back in your terminal, you can execute Dart code with the CLI command `dart`. To follow along with these instructions, make sure you're in the right project directory where your hello_world.dart file lives. Then, run the "Hello, Dart" example:

```
$ dart hello_world.dart
// => Hello, Dart!
```

If "Hello, Dart!" did in fact print, congrats! You wrote your first Dart program, and you're officially a Dart programmer!

2.1.1   Anatomy of a Dart program

Dart programs of all shapes and sizes have a few things in common that must exist: most important, a main function in the entry file of your program. This is the first piece of the puzzle. Figure 2.1 shows a Dart function definition.

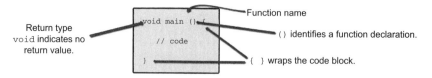

Figure 2.1   The main function in Dart

All Dart functions look like this, but main is special. It's always the first code that's executed in a Dart program. Your program must contain a main function that the Dart compiler can find.

Notice the word void in the example. void is the return type of this function. If you haven't used typed languages, this may look strange. Types are a core part of writing Dart code. Every variable should have a type, and every function should return a type (or void). void is a keyword that means "this function doesn't return anything." We'll dive deeper into the type system when we have more robust examples to walk through. But for now, just remember: all functions return a type (or void).

Next in this example is the line that contains the print function:

```
print('Hello, Dart!');
```

print is a special function in Dart that prints text to the console.

On that same line, you have a String ('Hello, Dart!'), and you have a semicolon (;) at the end of the line. This is necessary at the end of every statement in Dart. That's all you need to write a Dart program.

This section will introduce the basics of setting up and running a Dart program. It will also introduce some common Dart syntax. Finally, we'll use the dart:io package to learn about importing libraries, and standard-in and standard-out.

2.1.2   Adding more greetings

I want to expand on the greeter example so I can talk about some of Dart's basic syntax. In general, a lot of Dart syntax is similar to many languages. Control flow, loops, and primitive types are as you'd expect if you come from almost any language.

Let's write a program that will output this to the console:

```
Hello, World!
Hello, Mars!
Hello, Oregon!
Hello, Barry!
Hello, David Bowie!
```

There's a lot to learn in simple examples. To start, refactor the old example to create a separate function that prints. Your file will look like this:

```dart
void main() {                    To call a function, add ()
  helloDart();        ◁———       to the end, with no body.
}

void helloDart() {      ◁——      A second function
  print('Hello, Dart!');         declaration
}
```

Next, the `helloDart` function needs to be told what to print, because you don't want it to print "Hello, Dart!" forever. You'll do this by passing in a name to replace "World." You pass in arguments to functions by putting a type and variable name in the `()` in the function signature:

```dart
                                    This function now expects a name argument.
void helloDart(String name) {  ◁—   Trying to call this function with anything other
  print('Hello, $name');            than exactly one argument, of the type String,
}                                    is an error.
```

You don't just want to print one name, though; you want to print a sequence of names. The names will come from a hard-coded `List`, Dart's basic array-like data structure. A `List` manages its own size and provides all the functional programming methods you expect for an array, like `map` and `forEach`.

For now, you can create a list with the list-literal constructor using square brackets: `var myList = [a,b,c]`. Add a list of names to your `main` function:

```dart
void main() {
  List<String> greetings = [  ◁—   Defines a collection type, which has objects in it that
    'World',                         have a type: in this case, a List filled with Strings.
    'Mars',                          Another example would be Map<int, String>.
    'Oregon',
    'Barry',
    'David Bowie',
  ];
  helloDart();
}
```

Right now, there's an error in the program. This sample calls `helloDart()` without a string as an argument. We need to be passing each of those individual greetings in to the call to `helloDart()`. To do so, loop over the `greetings` variable and call the `helloDart()` function inside every iteration of the loop:

```dart
void main() {
  List<String> greetings = [
    'World',
    'Mars',
    'Oregon',
    'Barry',
    'David Bowie',
```

```
    ];
    for (var name in greetings) {        ◁──┐   A for..in loop is similar to other languages. It
      helloDart(name);            ◁──────┐  │   hits each member of the list once, in order,
    }                                    │  │   and exposes it as a variable in the code block.
  }          Passes the variable exposed by the
}            for..in loop in to the helloDart call
```

Finally, update the `helloDart` method to print "Hello" followed by the specific greeting. This is done with *interpolation*. String interpolation in Dart uses the `${}` syntax for expressions, or just a `$` for single value. Here is the full example.

Listing 2.1   Dart `for-in` loops

```
void main() {
    List<String> greetings = [
    'World',
    'Mars',
    'Oregon',
    'Barry',
    'David Bowie',
  ];
  for (var name in greetings) {
    helloDart(name);
  }
}

void helloDart(String name) {
  print('Hello, $name');
}
```

That's all it takes. This should work now.

2.1.3   *I/O and Dart libraries*

The final feature in this example is interacting with a user. The user will be able to say who they want to greet.

The first step is importing libraries. The Dart SDK includes many libraries, but the only one that's loaded in your program by default is `dart:core`. Some common libraries in the Dart SDK are `dart:html`, `dart:async`, and `dart:math`. Different libraries are available in different environments. For example, `dart:html` isn't included in the Flutter SDK, because there's no concept of HTML in a Flutter app. When writing a server-side or command-line application, you'll probably use `dart:io`. Let's start there.[1]

To import any library, you only need to add an `import` statement at the top of a Dart file:

```
import 'dart:io';
```

---

[1]For more information on the `dart:io` library, check out the official docs at http://mng.bz/5AmZ.

We won't use standard input and outputs in this book much, if at all, after this, so don't get bogged down in the details of the io library right now. This program asks for a name from the user on the command line and then greets that person.

Listing 2.2 I/O in Dart

Again, main is the start of the program.

```
import 'dart:io';

void main() {
    stdout.writeln('Greet somebody');
    String input = stdin.readLineSync();
    return helloDart(input);
}

void helloDart(String name) {
    print('Hello, $name');
}
```

stdout.writeln is functionally the same as print but can also be used to write text to files.

readLineSync is a blocking function that stops execution and waits for the user to respond in the command line.

You could improve this program by looping over everything and repeatedly asking for a name, or make it a number guessing game that exits when you guess the write number. I'll leave that for you to do on your own.

2.2 Common programming concepts in Dart

If all programming languages can be described in terms of the Beatles catalogue, Dart is like the Beatles' greatest hits. Everyone loves the Beatles, because the Beatles are great. And everyone knows the song "Hey Jude." But when you're listening to the Beatles' greatest hits at a fun, upbeat party, you're never worried that you're going to suddenly be listening to the song "Within You Without You." I love that song, but it's not for everyone, and it's certainly not a party song. When writing Dart code, you're never scared that you're going to run into unexplainable syntax or behavior: it's all expected and, in the worst-case scenario, easy to grok when you look at the docs.

There are a few important concepts you should keep in mind while writing Dart code:

- Dart is an object-oriented language and supports single inheritance.
- In Dart, *everything* is an object, and every object is an instance of a class. Every object inherits from the Object class. Even numbers are objects, not primitives.
- Dart is typed. You cannot return a number from a function that declares it returns a string.
- Dart supports top-level functions and variables, often referred to as *library members*.
- Dart is *lexically* scoped.

And Dart is quite opinionated. In Dart, as in all programming languages, there are different ways of getting things done. But some ways are right and some are wrong. This quote from the Dart website sums it up: "Guidelines describe practices that should always be followed. There will almost never be a valid reason to stray from them."

> **Just in time: Typed programming languages**
>
> A language is *typed* if every variable's type is known (or inferred) at compile-time. In human English, a language is typed if you, as the developer, can (or must) explicitly assign types to variables in your code. A language is *dynamic* if the types are inferred at runtime. JavaScript, Python, and Ruby are dynamic languages. (Under the hood, though, all languages are typed to some degree.)
>
> Types are used because they make your code *safer*. Your compiler won't let you pass a string to a function that expects a number. Importantly, in Dart, this type check is done at *compile time*. This means you'll never ship code that crashes because a function doesn't know what to do with a different type of data than it expects.
>
> The biggest benefit of using a type system is that it reduces bugs.

2.2.1   *Intro to Dart's type system*

The type system in Dart is something I'll discuss throughout the book. The type system is straightforward (as far as type systems go). That said, it has to be briefly examined before I can talk about anything else. It's more complicated than many subjects, such as `if` statements, but it must be learned first. I encourage you to circle back to this section at any time throughout the book if you need a type-system refresher.

Before I became a Dart developer, I wrote Ruby, Python, and JavaScript, which are dynamic. They have no concept of types (to the developer). When I started writing Dart, I found using types to be the biggest hurdle. (But now, I don't want to live in a world without them.)

There are a few key places that you need to know about types for now, and the rest will be covered in time. First, when declaring variables, you give them a type:

```
String name;        ◁──┐  The type always comes before
int age;               │  the value it describes.
```

Using types prevents you from assigning values to variables that aren't compatible:

```
int greeting = 'hello';
```

If you try to compile that file by running it in your terminal, you'll get this error:

```
Error: A value of type 'dart.core::String' can't
    be assigned to a variable of type 'dart.core::int'.
Try changing the type of the left hand side,
    or casting the right hand side to 'dart.core::int'.
```

First, that's a pretty darn good error message, as error messages tend to be in Dart. (Thanks, Dart team.) But also, this is what's called *type safe*. Types ensure at compile time that your functions all get the right kind of data. This reduces the number of bugs you get at runtime.

> **TIP** If you're using one of the IDEs suggested in the appendix and have installed the Dart plugin, you won't even get that far. The linter will tell you you're using the wrong type straight away. This is, in a nutshell, the value of type systems.

COMPLEX DATA TYPES

When using data structures like a List or Map, you use < and > to define the types of values within the List:

```
A list of strings
  └─▷ List<String> names;
      List<int> ages;      ◁─┐
      Map<String, int> people;  ◁─┘
```

A list of integers

A map whose keys are strings and values are integers

TYPES IN FUNCTIONS

Recall from earlier that the main function has a return type of void. Any function that's being used for its side effects should have this return type. It means the function returns nothing.

Other functions, though, should declare what they're going to return. This function returns an int:

```
int addNums() {
  // return an int
}
```

The second place you use types in functions is when you define arguments:

```
int addNums(int x, int y) {
  return x + y;
}
```

DYNAMIC TYPES

Dart supports dynamic types as well. When you set a variable as dynamic, you're telling the compiler to accept *any* type for that variable:

```
dynamic myNumber = 'Hello';
```

Technically, you could just mark everything as dynamic, which makes Dart *optionally typed*. And to that, I'd say "Good luck!" This would remove the benefits of using types, but still force you to write the word dynamic everywhere. I point that out because there are some instances in which you don't *explicitly* assign a type:

```
var myString = 'Hello';
```

This works, but if you then tried to set `myString` to 3, the compiler would throw an error. Once a variable is given a type, that's its type forever. Also, functions don't have to be annotated with a return type:

```
myPrint() {              ◁——— Notice the lack of return type.
    print('hello');
}
```

This works, but the type is still inferred. Trying to assign the return value of `myPrint` to a variable would throw an error:

```
// doesn't work
var printer = myPrint();
```

This doesn't work, because there is no return value.

SHOULD YOU EVER USE DYNAMIC TYPES?

`dynamic` comes in handy. It's pretty common to use `dynamic` in maps. Perhaps you're working with JSON:

```
Map<String, dynamic> json;
```

If you're converting some JSON to a Dart object, you know the keys of the `Map` are going to be strings, but the values could be strings, numbers, lists, or another map.

As for the `var` keyword, its usefulness is a matter of code style. The `var` keyword can only be used to define variables and cannot be used to define a type, unlike `dynamic`. In other words, this isn't valid:

```
Map<String, var> json;   ◁——— Invalid use of var!
```

So, the scope of where `var` *can* be used is small. In the cases where it's valid, you should prefer to use the actual type of the variable you're defining (if the variable is reassignable). If the variable shouldn't be reassignable, it's common to use `final`, without any type definition. This is almost always done in the bodies of functions, and not as class members. Otherwise, you're better off using types.

2.2.2   Comments

Dart supports three kinds of comments:

```
// Inline comments

/*
Blocks of comments. It's not convention to use block comments in Dart.
*/

/// Documentation
///
/// This is what you should use to document your classes.
```

Generally, documentation comments with three slashes are used for documenting your code. Anything you think will stay in the code forever should use this style of comments. Inline comments are used for brief insights into something on a specific line.

2.2.3 *Variables and assignment*

Variables are used in Dart to tell an object or class to hold onto some local state. Establishing a variable in Dart is as you'd expect. This is a variable definition:

```
String name;
```

That line simply tells your program that there will be a value called `name`, but the value is yet to be determined (but, in this case, it will be a `String`). At this point, `name` hasn't been assigned to a value, so its value is `null`. All unassigned variables in Dart are `null`. `null` is a special value that means "nothing." In Dart, `null` is an object, like everything else. That's why `ints`, `Strings`, `Lists`, and everything else can be assigned to `null`. Technically, you could do this:

```
int three = null;
```

According to the Dart style guide, you should avoid explicitly assigning objects to `null` (see http://mng.bz/om52).

FINAL, CONST, AND STATIC

These three keywords "extend" the type of the variable. The first two, `final` and `const`, are similar. You should use these keywords if you want to make a variable *immutable* (in other words, if you never intended to change the value of the variable). The difference in the two is subtle.

`final` variables can only be assigned once. However, they can be declared *before* they're set at the class level. Or, in English, a `final` variable is almost always a variable of a *class* that will be assigned in the *constructor*. If those terms aren't familiar, don't worry. They'll be covered in depth later.

`const` variables, on the other hand, won't be declared before they're assigned. Constants are variables that are always the same, no matter what, starting at compile time.

This is acceptable:

```
const String name = 'Nora';
```

But this is not acceptable:

```
const String name = 'Nora $lastName';
```

That value in the second example could change after compile time. For example, it could be "Nora Smith" or "Nora Williams." Therefore the variable `name` is not allowed to be marked `const`.

const variables should be used whenever possible, as they boost performance. In Flutter, there are special tools to help make your classes and widgets const. I'll cover that later.

Lastly, there is a modifier called static. static methods are used solely in classes, so I'll discuss them later as well.

2.2.4 Operators

There aren't any big surprises in Dart operators, as you can see in table 2.1.

Table 2.1 Dart operators

Description	Operators
Arithmetic	* / % ~/ + -
Relational and type test	>= > <= < as is is!
Equality	== !=
Logical and/or	&& ||
Assignment	= *= /= ~/= %= += -= <<= >>= &= ^= |= ??=
Unary	expr++ expr-- . ?. -expr !expr ~expr ++expr --expr

I'd like to point out a couple of these operators that are used often but may not be familiar to you:

- ~/ is the symbol for *integer division*. This never returns a decimal point number, but rather rounds the result of your division to the nearest integer. 5 ~/ 2 == 2
- as is a keyword that *typecasts*. This has everything to do with classes and object orientation, so I'll cover it later.
- is and is! check that two objects are the same type. They are equivalent to == and !=.
- In the unary row, ignore the word "expr." That's only used to make the operators readable.

2.2.5 Null-aware operators

Null-aware operators are one of my favorite features in Dart. In any language, having variables and values fly around that are null can be problematic. It can crash your program. Programmers often have to write if (response == null) return at the top of a function to make asynchronous calls. That's not the worst thing ever, but it's not concise. I use Go quite a bit, and it isn't a robust language. (That's not a judgment, it's a statement of fact.) About once in every 10 lines of code, there's an if statement checking for nil. This makes for some robust functions.

Null-aware operators in Dart help resolve this issue. They're basically ways to say, "If this object or value is `null`, then forget about it: just cut out here, but don't throw an error."

The number one rule of writing Dart code is to be concise but not pithy. Anytime you can write less code without sacrificing readability, you probably should. The three null-aware operators that Dart provides are `?.`, `??`, and `??=`, and I'll explain them next.

THE ?. OPERATOR

Suppose you want to call an API and get some information about a `User`. And maybe you're not sure whether the user information you want to fetch even exists. You can do a standard null check like this:

```
void getUserAge(String username) async {
  final request = new UserRequest(username);
  final response = await request.get();
  User user = new User.fromResponse(response);
  if (user != null) {
    this.userAge = user.age;
  }
  // etc.
}
```

> `await` is syntactic sugar for writing async code. We'll go over it in depth later.

> A standard null check without null-aware operators

That's fine. It works. But the null-aware operators make it much easier. The following operator basically says, "Hey, assign `userAge` to `user.age`. But if the `user` object is `null`, that's okay. Just assign `userAge` to `null`, rather than throwing an error":

```
void getUserAge(String username) async {
  final request = UserRequest(username);
  final response = await request.get();
  User user = new User.fromResponse(response);
  this.userAge = user?.age;
  // etc.
}
```

> Delightfully shorter null check

If `user` is indeed `null`, then your program will assign `userAge` to `null`, but it won't throw an error, and everything will be fine. If you removed the `?.` operator, it would be an error to call `age` on a `null` `User` object. Plus, your code is more concise and still readable. That's the key: clean, concise code.

> **NOTE** It's worth pointing out that if any code below the line `this.userAge = user?.age;` relied on `useAge` *not* being `null`, the result would be an error.

THE ?? OPERATOR

The second null-aware operator is perhaps even more useful. Suppose you want the same `User` information, but many fields for the user aren't required in your database. There's no guarantee that there will be an age for that user. Then you can use the double question mark (`??`) to assign a "fallback" or default value.

This operator says, "Hey program, do this operation with this value or variable. But if that value or variable is null, then use this backup value." It allows you to assign a default value at any given point in your process, and it's super handy:

```
void getUserAge(String username) async {
  final request = new UserRequest(username);
  final response = request.get();
  Useruser = new User.fromResponse(response);
  this.userAge = user.age ?? 18;      ⟵
  // etc.                              | If user.age is null, defaults to 18
}
```

THE ??= OPERATOR

This last null-safe operator accomplishes a goal pretty similar to the previous one, but the opposite. While writing this, I was thinking about how I never use this operator in real life. So I decided to do a little research. And wouldn't you know it? I should be using it. It's great.

This operator basically says, "Hey, if this object is null, then assign it to this value. If it's not, just return the object as is":

```
int x = 5
x ??= 3;
```

In the second line, x will not be assigned 3, because it already has a value. But like the other null-aware operators, this one seeks to make your code more concise.[2]

2.3   *Control flow*

The strangest thing about technology is that we treat computers like they're smart, but they're actually really dumb. They only know how to do roughly two or three things. You can expect a human, or even a dog, to react appropriately to any given number of situations. Dogs know that if they're hungry, they need to eat to survive; and they know what's food and what isn't. They aren't going to accidentally eat a rock and hope it works out.

Computers aren't as nice to work with. You have to tell them everything. They're quite needy, actually. So we have to take great pains to ensure that *no matter what* situation arises, the computer knows how to handle it. This is basically why we have *control flow*, which is the basis for pretty much all logic.

Control flow in Dart is similar to most of the high-level languages. You get if statements, ternary operations, and switch statements.

---

[2]To learn more, read Seth Ladd's blog post "Null-Aware Operators in Dart" at http://mng.bz/nvee.

2.3.1 *if and else*

Dart supports if, else if, and else, as you'd expect. Here's a standard if statement:

```
if (inPortland) {
  print('Bring an umbrella!');
} else {
  print('Check the weather first!');
}
```

Inside your conditions, you can use && for "and" and || for "or":

```
if (inPortland && isSummer) {
  print('The weather is amazing!');
} else if(inPortland && isAnyOtherSeason) {
  print('Torrential downpour.');
} else {
  print ('Check the weather!');
}
```

Finally, Dart is sane, and a condition must evaluate to a Boolean. There is only one way to say "true" (true) and one way to say "false" (false). In some languages, there is a concept of "truthiness," and all values coerce to true or false. In such languages, you can write if (3) {, and it works. That is not the case in Dart.

2.3.2 *switch and case*

switch statements are great when there are many possible conditions for a single value. These statements compare ints, Strings, and compile-time constants using ==. In other words, you must compare a value to a value of the same type that cannot change at runtime. If that sounds like jargon, here's a simple example:

```
int number = 1;
switch(number) {
  case 0:
    print('zero!');
    break;
  case 1:
    print('one!');
    break;
  case 2:
    print('two!');
    break;
  default:
    print('choose a different number!');
}
```

The switch statement must be told to exit, or it will execute every case. Cases should always end in a break or return statement. More on this in a bit.

That's perfectly valid. The variable number could have any number of values: it could be 1, 2, 3, 4, 66, 975, -12, or 55. As long as it's an int, its a possible value for number. This switch statement is simply a more concise way of writing an if/else statement. Here's an overly complex if/else block, for which you should prefer a switch statement:

```
int number = 1;
if (number == 0) {
    print('zero!');
} else if (number == 1) {
    print('one!');
} else if (number == 2) {
    print('two!');
} else {
    print('choose a different number!');
}
```

That's what a `switch` statement does, in a nutshell. It provides a concise way to check for any number of values. It's important, though, to remember that it only works with runtime constants. This is not valid:

```
intfive = 5;
  switch(five) {
      case(five < 10):        ◁———  five < 10 isn't definitely constant at compile time and therefore
      // do things...                cannot be used. It could be true or false. You cannot do
  }                                   computation within the case line of a switch statement.
```

2.3.3   *Advanced switch usage*

In `switch` statements, you can fall through multiple cases by not adding a `break` or `return` statement at the end of a case:

```
intnumber = 1;
switch(number) {
  case -1:
  case -2:
  case -3:
  case -4:
  case -5:
    print('negative!');
    break;
  case 1:
  case 2:
  case 3:
  case 4:
  case 5:
    print('positive!');
    break;
  case 0:
  default:
    print('zero!');
    break;
}
```

In this example, if the number is between -5 and -1, the code will print `negative!`.

EXITING SWITCH STATEMENTS

Each case in a `switch` statement should end with a keyword that exits the switch. If it doesn't, you'll get an error:

```
switch(number) {
  case 1:
    print(number);
    // ERROR!
  case 2:
  //...
```

Most commonly, you'll use break or return. break simply exits out of the switch; it doesn't have any other effect. It doesn't return a value. In Dart, a return statement immediately ends the function's execution, and therefore it will break out of a switch statement.

In addition to those, you can use the throw keyword, which throws an error. (More on throw in a bit; it will always exit a function as well.) Finally, you can use a continue statement and a label if you want to fall through but still have logic in every case:

```
Stringanimal = 'tiger';
switch(animal) {
  case 'tiger':
    print('it's a tiger');
    continue alsoCat;
  case 'lion':
    print('it's a lion');
    continue alsoCat;
  alsoCat:
  case 'cat':
    print('it's a cat');
    break;
  // ...
}
```

This switch statement will print it's a tiger and it's a cat to the console.

TERNARY OPERATOR

The ternary operator is technically that: an operator. But it's also kind of an if/else substitute. And it's also kind of a ??= alternative, depending on the situation. I use ternaries in Flutter widgets quite a bit. The ternary expression is used to conditionally assign a value. It's called *ternary* because it has three portions—the condition, the value if the condition is true, and the value if the condition is false:

```
                    Is this condition true or false?    If true, return       If false,
                                                        this first option.   return this option.

var nametag = user.title == 'Boss' ? user.name.toUpperCase() : user.name;
```

This code says, "If this user's title is 'Boss,' change her name to uppercase letters. Otherwise, keep it as it is."

2.3.4   *Loops*

You can repeat expressions in loops using the same keywords as in many languages. There are several kinds of loops in Dart:

- Standard `for`
- `for-in`
- `forEach`
- `while`
- `do while`

Each of these works exactly as it does in every programming language I've come across. So, I'll just provide some quick examples.

FOR LOOPS

If you need to know the index, your best bet is the standard `for` loop:

```
for (var i = 0; i < 5; i++) {
  print(i);
}
```

If you don't care about the index, the `for-in` loop is a great option:

```
List<String> pets = ['Odyn', 'Buck', 'Yeti'];
for (var pet in pets) {
  print(pet);
}
```

An alternative, and probably the preferred way to loop if you don't care about the index, is using the method on iterables called `forEach`:

```
List<String>pets = ['Abe', 'Buck', 'Yeti'];
pets.forEach((pet) => pet.bark());
```

`forEach` is special in two ways. First, it's a function that you call on a `List`. The practical implication is that it creates a new scope. Any value you have access to in the `forEach` loop is not accessible thereafter.

Second, the logic in `forEach` blocks can only provide side effects. That is, you cannot return values. These loops are generally useful for mutating objects, but not for creating new ones.

> **NOTE**   `forEach` is a *higher-order function*. That topic will be explored shortly.

WHILE LOOPS

Again, `while` loops behave exactly as you'd expect. They evaluate the condition *before* the loop runs—meaning it may never run at all:

```
while(someConditionIsTrue) {
  // do some things
}
```

do-while loops, on the other hand, evaluate the condition *after* the loop runs. So they *always* execute the code in the block at least once:

```
do {
  // do somethings at least once
} while(someConditionIsTrue);
```

BREAK AND CONTINUE

These two keywords help you manipulate the flow of the loop. Use continue in a loop to immediately jump to the next iteration, and use break to break out of the loop completely:

```
for (var i = 0; i < 55; i++) {
  if (i == 5) {
    continue;
  }
  if (i == 10) {
    break;
  }
  print(i);
}
```

This loop will print the following:

```
0
1
2
3
4
6
7
8
9
```

2.4 Functions

Functions look familiar in Dart if you're coming from any C-like language. We've already seen a couple examples of this, via the main function. Now we'll dig deeper into functions and see how they're written in Dart. Here's a basic function:

```
void main() {

}
```

2.4.1 Anatomy of a Dart function

The anatomy of a function is pretty straightforward:

```
String makeGreeting(String name) {      ◁——— Function signature
  return 'Hello, $name';          ◁——┐
}                                       └ Return type
```

The function *signature* follows this pattern: `ReturnType functionName(ArgumentType arg)`. And every function that uses `return` must have a return type—otherwise, its return type is `void`.

It's important to note that Dart is a true object-oriented language. Even functions are objects, with the type `Function`. You can pass functions around and assign them to variables. Languages that support passing functions as arguments and returning functions from functions usually refer to these as *higher-order functions*. We'll explore higher-order functions in depth when we start writing Flutter apps.

Dart also supports a nice shorthand syntax for any function that has only one expression. In other words, is the code inside the function block only one line? Then it's probably one expression, and you can use this syntax to be concise:

```
String makeGreeting(String name) => 'Hello, $name';
```

In this book, we'll call this an *arrow function*. Arrow functions implicitly return the result of the expression. `=> expression;` is essentially the same as `{ return expression; }`. There's no need to (and you can't) include the `return` keyword.

2.4.2 *Parameters*

Dart functions allow positional parameters, named parameters, and optional positional and named parameters, or a combination of all of them. Positional parameters are simply what we've seen so far:

```
void debugger(String message, int lineNum) {
  // ...
}
```

To call that function, you *must* pass in a `String` and an `int`, in that order:

```
debugger('A bug!', 55);
```

NAMED PARAMETERS

Dart supports named parameters. *Named* means that when you call a function, you attach the argument to a label. This example calls a function with two named parameters:

```
debugger(message: 'A bug!', lineNum: 44);
```

Named parameters are written a bit differently. You wrap any named parameters in curly braces (`{ }`). This line defines a function with named parameters:

```
void debugger({String message, int lineNum}) {
```

Named parameters, by default, are optional. But you can annotate them and make them required:

```
Widget build({@required Widget child}) {
  //...
}
```

In order to annotate variables with the `required` keyword, you must use a Dart library called `meta`. More on this when we get into the Flutter work.

The pattern you see here will become familiar when we start writing Flutter apps. For now, don't worry too much about annotations.

POSITIONAL OPTIONAL PARAMETERS

Finally, you can pass positional parameters that are optional, using [ ]:

```
int addSomeNums(int x, int y, [int z]) {
  int sum = x + y;
  if (z != null) {
    sum += z;
  }
  return sum;
}
```

You call that function like this:

The third parameter is optional, so you don't have to pass in anything.

You can pass in a third argument, since you've defined an optional parameter.

```
addSomeNums(5, 4)
addSomeNums(5, 4, 3)
```

2.4.3   *Default parameter values*

You can define default values for parameters with the = operator in the function signature:

```
addSomeNums(int x, int y, [int z = 5]) => x + y + z;
```

2.4.4   *Advanced function concepts*

Functions are the bread and butter of reusable code because they let us define our own vocabulary in our programs. In a robust app, there are likely thousands of lines of code. It's easy to get lost. When used correctly, higher-order functions help add a layer of abstraction to our code that makes it easy to reason about. Consider these two examples that do math:

```
List<int> nums = [1,2,3,4,5];

int i = 0;
int sum = 0;
while (i < nums.length) {
  sum += nums[i];
  i+=1;
}
print(sum);

List<int> nums = [1,2,3,4,5];

print(addNumbers(nums));
```

It's possible that the addNumbers function (not shown here) is implemented *exactly* the way the first example adds the numbers. But the second example adds a nice layer of abstraction and tells you exactly what it's doing, as if you're reading English. You don't have to read each line of code to understand what's happening. And as a bonus, you know that if the addNumbers function is bug-free, it will remain bug-free every time you use it in an app. This is a simple example, of course, but breaking up functions into single-responsibility chunks of logic makes them much easier to get right.

Creating your own vocabulary by breaking up functions is called *abstraction*. Remember, computers are dumb. We have to tell them exactly what we want them to do. But humans are smart. We use abstraction to write low-level, explicit instructions for the computer, and then we wrap it up in nice little functions for future programmers who will be reading our code.

In Dart, abstracting away logic is possible because it supports these higher-order functions. A function is higher-order if it accepts a function as an argument or if it returns a function. In other words, higher-order functions operate on other functions. If you aren't sure about higher-order functions, you've likely seen them before in a different language:

```
List<int> nums = [1,2,3];
nums.forEach((number) => print(number + 1));
```

forEach is a higher-order function because it takes a function as its argument. Another way to write that would be like this:

```
void addOneAndPrint(int num) {
  print(num +1);
}

nums.forEach(addOneAndPrint);
```

> **NOTE** The first forEach example uses an *anonymous function*, which means it doesn't have a name. It's defined right there in the argument to forEach, and after it's executed, it's gone forever.

Earlier, I mentioned that functions are just objects, like everything in Dart. That's why you can use functions like you can any other object, including passing them around as variables and return values.

In reality, you can get away without writing your own logic that uses higher-order functions. But you'll likely come across them in the wild when processing Iterable objects. (List, for example, is an Iterable, because you can iterate over it.) Iterable objects (and Map objects, to an extent) provide functions like forEach, map, and where, which are higher-order functions that perform some task on every member in the list. I've already discussed forEach, but let's look at an example using map.

List.map is the same as forEach in that it takes a function as an argument, and that function is called with each member of the list as an argument. It's different from forEach in that it returns a value from each function call, and the return values are added to a new list. For example:

> **List.map takes a function as its argument. Each time the inner function is called, it's passed a member of the smallNums list as an argument.**

```
List<int> smallNums = [1,2,3];
Iterable<int> biggerNums = smallNums.map((int n) => n * 2);
```

This code looks at each member of smallNums and calls a function on it. In this case, that function is (int n) ? num * 2. So it's going to call the function once for 1, once for 2, and once for 3. The list biggerNums is [2, 4, 6]. Even though you *can* get away with not using too many higher-order functions, you'll see how useful they can be in Flutter development.

2.4.5 *Lexical scope*

Dart is *lexically scoped*. Every code block has access to variables "above" it. The scope is defined by the structure of the code, and you can see what variables are in the current scope by following the curly braces outward to the top level:

```
String topLevel = 'Hello';

void firstFunction() {
  String secondLevel = 'Hi';
  print(topLevel);
  nestedFunction() {
    String thirdLevel = 'Howdy';
    print(topLevel);
    print(secondLevel);
    innerNestedFunction() {
      print(topLevel);
      print(secondLevel);
      print(thirdLevel);
    }
  }
  print(thirdLeve);
}

void main() => firstFunction();
```

This is a valid function, until the last print statement. The third-level variable is defined outside the scope of the nested function, because scope is limited to its own block or the blocks above it. (Again, a block is defined by curly braces.)

2.5 *Object-oriented programming (in Dart)*

Modern applications basically all do the same thing: they give us (smart humans) a way to process and collaborate large data sets. Some apps are about communication, like social media and email. Some are about organization, such as calendars and note taking. Some are simply digital interfaces into a part of the real world that's hard for programmers to navigate, like dating apps. But they all do the same thing. They give users a nice way to interact with data.

Data represents the real world. All data describes something *real.* That's what object-oriented programming is all about: it gives us a nice way to model our data after real-world objects. It takes data, which dumb computers like, and adds some abstraction so smart humans can impose our will onto the computers. It makes code easy to read, easy to reason about, and highly reusable.

When writing Dart code, you'll likely want to create separate classes for everything that can represent a real-world "thing." *Thing* is a carefully chosen word, because it's so vague. (This is a great example of something that would make a dumb computer explode but that a smart human can make some sense of.)

Consider if we were writing a point-of-sale (POS) system used to sell goods to customers. What kinds of classes do you think you'd need to represent "things" (or data)? What kind of "things" does a POS app need to know about? Perhaps we need classes to represent a Customer, Business, Employee, Product, and Money. Those are all classes that represent real-world things. But it gets a bit hairier from here.

Ponder some questions with me:

- We may want a class for Transaction and Sale. In real life, a transaction is a process or event. Should this be represented with a function or a class?
- If we're selling bananas, should we use a Product class and give it a property that describes what *type* of product it is? Or should we have a Banana class?
- Should we define a top-level variable or a class that has only a single property? For instance, if we need to write a function that simply adds two numbers together, should we define a Math class with an add method, or just write the method as a static, global variable?

Ultimately, these decisions are up to you, the programmer. There is no single right answer.

2.5.1   *Classes*

My rule of thumb is, "When in doubt, make a new class." Recall those previous questions: Should a transaction be represented by a function of Business or its own class? I'd say make it a class. And that brings me all the way back to why I used the vague word *thing* earlier. A thing isn't just a physical object; it can be an idea, an event, a logical grouping of adjectives, and so on. In this example, I would make a class that looks like this:

```
class TransactionEvent {
  // properties and methods
}
```
⟵ **Uses the class keyword to define a new class**

And that might be it. It might have no properties and no methods. Creating classes for events makes the type safety of Dart that much more effective.

The bottom line is that you can (and, I'd argue, should) make a class that represents any "thing" that isn't obviously an action you can do or a word you'd use to describe some detail of a "thing." For instance, you (a human) can exchange money with someone. It makes sense to say, "I exchange money." It doesn't make sense to say, "I transaction," even though a transaction is an idea. Having a `Transaction` class makes sense, but an `ExchangeMoney` class doesn't.

Nearly all the code you write in Dart will be contained in classes. And a class is a blueprint for an `object`. That is, a class describes an object that you can create. The object itself is what holds any specific data and logic. For example, a `Cat` class might look like this:

```
class Cat {
    String name;
    String color;
}
```

This class describes an object that can be created, like this:

```
Cat nora = new Cat();
nora.name = 'Nora';
nora.color = 'Orange';
```

A note about the (lack) of the new keyword

If you're coming from many other object-oriented languages, you've probably seen the new keyword used to create new instances of a class. In Dart, this new keyword works the same way, but *it isn't necessary*. In Dart 2, you don't need to use new or const to create an object. The compiler will infer that for you. More on the motivation behind this language feature in chapter 3.

From here on out, I will not use the new keyword, as it's considered bad practice in Dart.

The `Cat` class itself doesn't have any information. It's a blueprint. The `nora` object, though, is a `Cat` *instance*. It has a name and color, and those aren't related to any new instances of `Cat` that are made in the future. You could, later in the code, create a new cat:

```
Cat ruby = Cat();
nora.name = 'Ruby';
nora.color = 'Grey';
```

`nora` and `ruby` are completely separate. They are instances of the class. After writing the class, you generally don't interact with the class itself, but rather the instances of (aka objects created by) the class.

NOTE There are a couple of caveats when you want to interact with the class directly, which I'll cover as we go.

2.5.2   *Constructors*

You can give classes special instructions about what to do as soon as a new instance is created. These functions are called *constructors.*

Often, when creating a class, you'll want to pass values to it or perform some initialization logic. You can use the constructor to assign those values to properties of an instance of that class:

```
class Animal {        Declares properties of this
  String name;    ◁──┘ class (they are null to start)
  String type;

  Animal(String name, String type) {   ◁──── Default constructor
    this.name = name;              ◁──┐
    this.type = type;                 │ Passes in arguments to the constructor
  }
}
```

A default constructor is written as a function that shares a name with the class. Any arguments that need to be passed in to the function, to be assigned to the properties of the class, are defined just like function arguments. You can pass in arguments to the constructor and assign them to the instance properties of the same name.

In some languages, you have to explicitly assign each property to the variable you passed to the constructor, like the previous example (for example, calling `this.name = name` in the constructor body). Dart provides some nice syntactic sugar to make the code less verbose. You can achieve the same thing like this:

```
class Animal {
  String name, type;
                                   Automatically assigns arguments
  Animal(this.name, this.type);  ◁──┘ to properties with the same name
}
```

You can put whatever code and logic you want in a constructor. It's just a plain ol' function:

```
class Animal {
  String name, type;

  Animal(this.name, this.type) {
    print('Hello from Animal!');
  }
}
```

Earlier, I referred to a constructor as a *default constructor.* There are other types of constructors, and classes can have multiple constructors. I will cover those later in this book. But first, I want to talk about the next important topic in object-oriented programming: inheritance.

2.5.3 *Inheritance*

In object-oriented programming, *inheritance* is the idea that a class can *inherit* or *subclass* a different class. A cat is a specific kind of mammal, so it follows that a cat will have all the same functionality and properties as all other mammals. You can write a Mammal class once, and then both the Dog and Cat classes can *extend* the Mammal class. Both of those classes will then have all the functionality of the Mammal class:

```
class Cat extends Mammal {}
class Eric extends Human {}
class Honda extends Car {}
```

⊲⎯⎤ **Uses extends to inherit all of**
    ⎥ **a superclass's functionality**

When a class inherits from another class (called its *superclass*), it's essentially a copy of the superclass, and you can add extra functionality—whatever you define in the class itself. (For example, Cat is a copy of the Mammal class, but you can also add a function called meow.) Let's look at a small, concrete example:

```
// superclass
class Animal {
  String name;
  int legCount;
}

// subclass
class Cat extends Animal {
  String makeNoise() {
    print('purrrrrrr');
  }
}
```

In this example, if we made an instance of Cat, then it would have properties called name and legCount:

```
Cat cat =  Cat();
cat.name = 'Nora';
cat.legCount = 4;
cat.makeNoise();
```

Those are all perfectly valid expressions. You can set the cat's name, because it's also an Animal. This is not valid, however:

```
Cat cat =  Animal();
cat.makeNoise();
```

Animal is the superclass and has no concept of or relationship to any of the subclasses that extend it.

To expand on inheritance, consider if we made a class that's almost exactly the same, but for a Pig:

```
class Pig extends Animal {
  String makeNoise() {
    print('oink');
  }
}
```

It's now perfectly valid to do this:

```
Pig pig =  Pig();
pig.name = 'Babe';
pig.legCount = 4;
pig.makeNoise();
```

Since Pig *extends* Animal, like Cat, it has a name property and a legCount property. Finally, inheritance is like a tree. If Pig inherits from Mammal, which inherits from Animal, which inherits from Life, then Pig has access to all the members of *all* those classes. Every object in Dart inherits, eventually, from Object, as illustrated in figure 2.2.

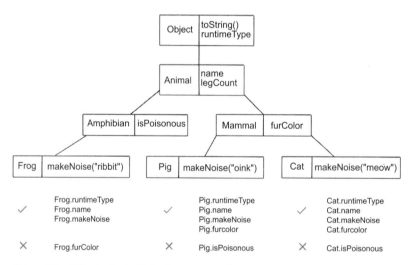

Figure 2.2   Object-oriented inheritance example

2.5.4   *Factories and named constructors*

Right now, one of the great challenges that humans are facing is creating renewable energy. There's a common thread between all the possible sources of energy: it all ends up as energy in the end. But for a brief moment, the wind is just wind, not yet turned into energy; and sunbeams are just sunbeams. Science needs to know how to turn these different substances into energy.

> **TIP**   I don't know anything about physical science. Please go easy on me.

This is what factory and named constructors do. They're special constructor methods of classes that create an instance of that class, but with predetermined properties.

Named constructors always return a *new* instance of a class. `factory` methods have a bit more flexibility: they can return cached instances or instances that are subtypes. In code, that `Energy` class might look like this:

```
class Energy {
  int joules;                         Default constructor

  Energy(this.joules);        ◄───┘
                                              Using "Energy." syntax and returning
                                              an instance of that class makes this a
                                              named constructor.
  Energy.fromWind(int windBlows) {     ◄──
    final joules = _convertWindToEnergy(windBlows);
    return  Energy(joules);            ◄──
  }                                         All constructors must return
                                            an instance of the class.

  factory Energy.fromSolar(int sunbeams) {            ◄──────
    if (appState.solarEnergy != null) return appState.solarEnergy;
    final joules = _convertSunbeamsToJoules(sunbeams);
    return appState.solarEnergy =  Energy(joules);
  }
}
               The factory will potentially return an existing instance of
               Energy. Otherwise, it will create a new instance, assign
                                     it, and return it.
```

2.5.5 *Enumerators*

Enumerators, often called *enums*, are special classes that represent a specific number of constants. Suppose you have a method that takes a `String` and then does some magic and changes the color of text in an app:

```
void updateColor(String color) {
  if (color == 'red') {
    text.style.color = 'rgb(255,0,0)';
  } else if (color == 'blue') {
    text.style.color = 'rgb(0,0,255)';
  }
}
```

This is great, unless you pass "macaroni," "crab cakes," "33445533," or any other string into `updateColor`. You can use an enum to buy yourself some type safety without the verbosity of a class. At the end of the day, that's what an enum is about: it makes your code harder to break and easier to read.

So your `Color` enum can look like this:

```
enum Color { red, blue }
```

In your code, you can access colors like this: `Color.red`. Variables and fields can now have `Color` as a type, and it must be assigned to either `Color.red` or `Color.blue`. And as an added bonus, `switch` statements can switch on an enum and demand that you have a `case` statement for every type in the enum (or a default at the end).

Now your function can look like this:

```
enum Color { red, green, blue }

void updateColor(Color color) {
  switch(color) {
    case Color.red:
      // do stuff
    case Color.green:
      // do stuff
    case Color.blue:
      // do stuff

  }
}
```

Then, when you call the function, it must be passed a `Color`:

```
updateColor(Color.red);
updateColor(Color.green);
updateColor(Color.blue);
```

If you try to pass in "macaroni," the code will throw an error.

A note about more Dart features

This chapter is meant to be an overview of the crucial pieces of Dart that you'll need to write Flutter apps—but there's much more. Some of the features of Dart that will be discussed later in this book are asynchronous features, type generics, abstract classes (also known as *interfaces*), and generator functions. These features are cool and important but need a lot of context to be described accurately. So, I will discuss them in depth when the time comes. For now, the only requirement is that you understand the foundation of Dart.

Summary

- Dart's syntax is familiar if you know any C-like language.
- Dart is an object-oriented, strictly typed language.
- All Dart programs begin with a main function as the entry point to the application.
- Types are used to ensure that code is using the correct values at the correct time. They can seem cumbersome, but they're helpful for reducing bugs.
- Functions must return types or `void`.
- Most operators in Dart are like operators in other languages, but there are a few special operators, such as ~/, is, and as.
- Null-aware operators are useful for performing null checks, which ensure that values are not `null`.

- For control flow, Dart supports `if/else` statements, as well as `switch` statements and ternary operators.
- Using an enum with a `switch` statement enforces accounting for all possible cases.
- Loops in Dart should be familiar if you come from most other languages. There are `for` loops, `for-in` loops, `while` loops, and `do while` loops.
- Dart functions are objects and can be passed around like any other value. This is called a *higher-order function* in many languages.
- Dart is a true object-oriented programming language, and your code will make heavy use of classes, constructors, and inheritance.
- There are multiple types of constructors: the default constructor, `factory` constructors, and named constructors.
- An enum is a special kind of class that gives additional type safety when there is a predetermined number of options for a property or variable.

Breaking into Flutter

This chapter covers
- Dissecting Flutter basics via the Increment app
- Flutter widget classes
- BuildContext, the widget tree, and the element tree
- Flutter development environment and tips

I imagine, because you're reading this, that you're at least intrigued by Flutter. By the end of this chapter, I hope you'll be *excited* about it. In this chapter, I'll walk you through the ins and outs of Flutter. I'll show you how to use it and how it works under the hood. The goal of this chapter is to build a foundation. This is the plan for doing so:

1. Take an in-depth look at the counter app, which is the app that's generated when you start a new Flutter project with the CLI.
2. Make the counter app more robust by adding some basic widgets.
3. Spend some time talking about `BuildContext`, the widget tree, and elements. Understanding how this works is 90% of debugging Flutter errors.
4. Learn tricks and tools that the Flutter team has built in to the SDK that makes development enjoyable.

NOTE   If Flutter isn't installed on your machine yet, you can find installation instructions in the appendix. If you have trouble setting it up, look for additional help in the docs at https://flutter.dev/get-started.

3.1   *Intro to the counter app*

Getting started with Flutter (after you have it installed on your machine) is as easy as running a command in your terminal. Anytime you start a new Flutter project, you'll do so by running `flutter create` in your terminal. This generates the starting code for your project.

WARNING   If you didn't notice the note in the previous section, please make sure your environment is set up before proceeding! You can find instructions for downloading Flutter and all its dependencies in appendix A of this book or at https://flutter.dev/get-started.

Let's fire up that first Flutter app. Navigate in your terminal to the location you want this app to live:

```
$ cd ~/Desktop/flutter_in_action/
$ flutter create counter_app
$ cd counter_app && flutter pub get
$ flutter run
```

The pub get command gets package dependencies in Dart. It must follow flutter if you're building a Flutter app.

Now run your app. Figure 3.1 shows what you should see in your simulator.

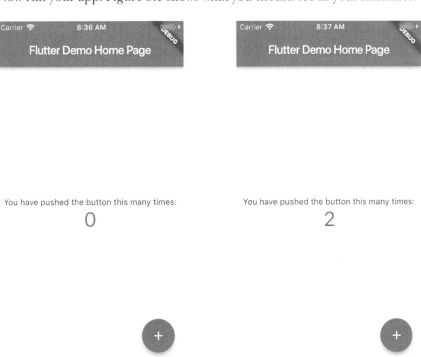

Figure 3.1   The Flutter counter app

You can press that button, and the counter will increase. It's a hoot. The app doesn't do much else, but it's worth noting how easy it is to get started with Flutter!

This is called the "counter app" around the internet. It's the "hello world" equivalent in Flutter. Anytime you start a new project, you'll have this as your starting point.

3.1.1   Flutter project structure

A Flutter project, when first created, is a big directory. The good news is that most of it doesn't matter to us right now. In fact, much of it won't ever matter to you. This is what your directory should look like:

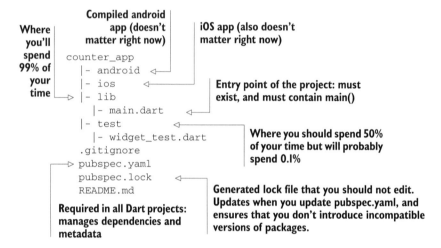

At this point, the main takeaway is that lib is where you'll be adding code for a Flutter project, and main.dart is the app's entry point.

3.1.2   Anatomy of a Flutter app

The majority of the counter app lives inside the main.dart file. The generated starting code in main.dart is beautifully commented by the Flutter team, and you can get a ton of information out of those comments alone. But I want to break down the most important parts and tease out those comments. Starting from the top of the file:

```
import 'package:flutter/material.dart';    ◁——— Imports the material library
```

A large portion of Flutter that we interact with is just a Dart library. This library includes everything you need to write a Flutter app, including all the widgets included with the SDK by default. In this case, the app is importing the material library, which includes all the base widgets, plus the ones that follow Google's Material Design system. There's also flutter/cupertino.dart, which provides iOS-styled components. We'll use Material in this book.

NOTE   The Material and Cupertino libraries come with the same core features and differ only in the widgets that are included by default. The Material library is more robust at this point, and most examples, documentation, and tutorials on the internet use it. I'll use it only for that reason. Neither Material nor Cupertino is better or worse.

APPLICATION ENTRY POINT

At the top of the counter app, you'll see a `main` function:

```
void main() => runApp(MyApp());
```

Like all Dart programs, a Flutter app uses the `main` function as the entry point. In Flutter, you wrap your top-level widget in a method called `runApp`. At the least, your app will contain a line like this one. In a more robust app, you might do more in your `main` function, but you must call `runApp` with your top-level widget passed as an argument.

Remember, everything is a widget. That includes the root of your application! There is no special object or class for this.

3.1.3   *Again, everything is a widget*

In Flutter, (nearly) everything is a widget, and widgets are just Dart classes that know how to describe their view. They're blueprints that Flutter will use to paint elements on the screen. The widget class is the only view model that Flutter knows about. There aren't separate controllers or views.

NOTE   As I've stated before and will go into in more depth soon, there are other object types in Flutter. But widgets are the model class that tell those other objects what to do. As developers, all we care about is writing models that Flutter knows how to turn into a UI. Widgets are declarative in nature, which is nice. We don't have to worry about actually rendering the screen. We don't (often) care about individual pixels. Widgets abstract those pain points away for us. This is one reason that we say "everything is a widget": because everything we care about is a widget.

In most other frameworks, especially on the web, widgets are called *components*, and the mental model is similar. A widget (or component) is a class that defines a specific piece of your UI. To build an app, you make a ton of widgets (or components) and put them together in different ways to gradually compose larger widgets.

A difference, though, between components and other frameworks (like ReactJS) and widgets is that a widget can define any aspect of an application's view. Some widgets, such as `Row`, define aspects of layout. Some are less abstract and define structural elements, like `Button` and `TextField`. The theme that defines colors and fonts in your app is a widget. Animations are defined by widgets. In a component-based framework from the web, you *can* build a component that has a singular job of adding padding to a child widget, but you don't have to. You could use CSS to add padding to whichever component you want. In Flutter you can *only* style widgets with other widgets. To add padding, you use a `Padding` widget.

The point is that every piece of your UI is a widget. Even the root of your app is a widget. There isn't a special object called `App`. You define your own widget, such as `MyApp`, which returns yet another widget in its `build` method.

The Flutter library is full to the brim with built-in widgets. When you start creating your own widgets, you'll do so by composing these built-in widgets together. These are some of the most common widgets:

- *Layout*—`Row`, `Column`, `Scaffold`, `Stack`
- *Structures*—`Button`, `Toast`, `MenuDrawer`
- *Styles*—`TextStyle`, `Color`, `Padding`
- *Animations*—`FadeInPhoto`, transformations
- *Positioning and alignment*—`Center`, `Padding`

3.1.4 *The build method*

Every widget that you create must have a `build` method, and that method must return another widget. In most cases, it can be any widget. Here's a bare minimum `StatelessWidget`:

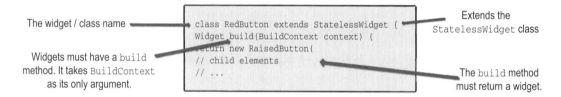

The widget / class name

Extends the `StatelessWidget` class

Widgets must have a `build` method. It takes `BuildContext` as its only argument.

The `build` method must return a widget.

```
class RedButton extends StatelessWidget {
  Widget build(BuildContext context) {
    return new RaisedButton(
    // child elements
    // ...
```

Back in the app, take a look at this top-level widget, `MyApp`. `MyApp` in this counter app example is your top-level widget, but it's not special—it's a widget like anything else:

An annotation (decorator, in other frameworks) that tells Dart this class's superclass (StatelessWidget) has a build method, but this method should be called instead

MyApp is a widget, like everything else in Flutter.

Every widget has a build method that returns another widget.

MaterialApp (a built-in widget) wraps your app to pass Material Design-specific functionality to all the widgets in the app.

Widgets are classes that have constructors that take arguments. MaterialApp takes optional, named parameters: title, theme, and home, which take a String, ThemeData, and Widget, respectively.

```
class MyApp extends StatelessWidget {

  @override

  Widget build(BuildContext context) {
    return MaterialApp(
      title: 'Flutter Demo',
      theme: ThemeData(
        primarySwatch: Colors.blue,
      ),
      home: MyHomePage(title: 'Flutter Demo Home Page'),
    );
  }
}
```

3.1.5 *The new and const constructors in Flutter*

In Flutter, you'll create many instances of the same widgets. Many built-in widgets have both regular constructors and const constructors. Immutable instances of widgets are more performant, so you should always use const when you can. Flutter makes this easy by letting you omit the new and const keywords altogether. The framework will infer which one to use and always use const when it can:

```
Widget build(BuildContext context) {
    return Button(                        ◁────  Neither the Button class nor the Text
        child: Text("Submit"),                   class is created with the new keyword.
    );
}

// compared to
Widget build(BuildContext context) {
    return new Button(                    ◁──────  Uses the new keyword
        child: new Text("Submit"),
    );
}
```

In practice, this means you don't have to consider which widgets can be constant and which can't. Flutter will take care of that for you. A bonus benefit is that your build methods look cleaner. Also, you can leave off the new keyword anywhere in your app anytime you create an instance of any class. It doesn't have to be a widget. As of Dart 2.3, this feature can be used in any Dart environment, not just in Flutter.

3.1.6 *Hot reload*

Hot reload is one of Flutter's greatest selling points to native mobile developers. If this section doesn't excite you, I don't know how to help you.

A fun fact about Dart is that is has both an ahead-of-time (AOT) compiler and a just-in-time (JIT) compiler. In Flutter, when you're developing on your machine, it uses JIT. It's called "just in time" because it compiles and runs code as it needs to. When you deploy the app in production, Flutter uses the AOT compiler. For us developers, that means you can develop and recompile code quickly in development, but you don't sacrifice non-native performance in production.

Let's test out how hot the hot reload really is. In the counter app, on line ~15, change the text passed in to the MyHomePage title argument:

```
// chapter_3/counter_app/lib/main.dart -- line ~15
home:  MyHomePage(title: 'Flutter Home PageDemo'); // old

home:  MyHomePage(title: 'Hot Reload Demo'); // updated
```

Fire that hot reload. You should see the change happen instantly. And that's just a tiny example. You could have added new widgets and changed the theme color, and it would have reloaded just as quickly. Let's check out one more example.

> **Using hot reload**
>
> Depending on your environment, you can trigger a hot reload a number of ways:
>
> - In Intellij, Visual Studio Code, or Android Studio, there's a Hot Reload button, and the shortcut is Cmd-S (Ctrl-S on machines running Windows or Linux). This comes as a feature of the Flutter plugin for these IDEs.
> - If you used `flutter run` in your terminal, type `r` in that terminal to hot reload.

On line ~12, in the `ThemeData` constructor, update the `primarySwatch` argument to a different color:

```
// chapter_3/counter_app/lib/main.dart -- line ~12
theme: ThemeData(
    primarySwatch: Colors.blue,        // old
),

theme: ThemeData(
    primarySwatch: Colors.indigo,      // updated
),
```

Hit that hot reload again. If everything went okay, your top app bar and the button should have changed colors in subsecond time. Pretty amazing stuff.

3.2   *Widgets: The widget tree, widget types, and the State object*

In the Flutter library, there are a ton of built-in widgets. Almost all of them are made from two different widget types: `StatelessWidget` and `StatefulWidget`. There are a couple more high-level widget types, which we'll see throughout the book. But 95+% of the time, you'll be using these two.

The general goal when developing a UI with Flutter is to compose a ton of widgets together to build the *widget tree*. A Flutter app is represented by a widget tree, similar to how the DOM on the browser is a tree structure. The widget tree is an actual tree data structure in code built behind the scenes by Flutter, but it's also a useful way to talk about the structure of your Flutter app. While learning Flutter, whether throughout this book or elsewhere, you'll encounter the widget tree quite often.

In short, the tree is a collection of nodes, where each node is a widget. Every time you add a widget in a `build` method you're adding a new node the tree. The nodes are connected by their parent-child relationship.

Figure 3.2 shows a simplified visual representation of the widget tree for the counter app. In reality, there are a few more widgets in there, but don't worry about specifics right now. And don't get bogged down in the different widgets in that tree. For now, you only need to know that the widget tree is how Flutter apps are structured.

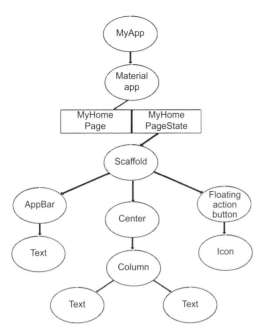

Figure 3.2 Counter app widget tree

The process of composing widgets together into this tree is done by telling widgets that their child(ren) are more widgets. A simple example is styling some text:

```
return Container(
    child: Padding(
        padding: EdgeInsets.all(8.0),
        child: Text("Padded Text")
    ),
);
```

The Container widget has a property called child, which takes another widget.

The Padding widget also has a property called child, which takes a widget.

In the widget tree, `Container` is the parent of `Padding`, which is the parent of the `Text` widget.

Not every widget has a `child` property, though. Other common properties in Flutter that allow you to pass widgets into widgets are `children` and `builder`, both of which we'll see later (and often) in this book.

3.2.1 Stateless widgets

The difference between `StatefulWidget` and a `StatelessWidget` is right in the name. A `StatefulWidget` tracks its own internal state. A `StatelessWidget` doesn't have any internal state that changes during the lifetime of the widget. It doesn't care about its configuration or what data it's displaying. It could be passed configuration from its parent, or the configuration could be defined within the widget, but it *cannot change its own configuration*. A stateless widget is immutable.

NOTE When it comes to learning about widgets, you'll see the word *configuration* often. It's kind of vague, but basically it encapsulates everything within your widget: the variables passed in and its size constraints, as well as meta information used by Flutter internally.

Imagine you've created a custom button widget in your app. Perhaps it will always say Submit, as shown in the next listing.

Listing 3.1 An example button widget

```
class SubmitButton
 extends StatelessWidget {
  Widget build(context) {
    return Button(
      child: Text('Submit'),
    );
  }
}
```

This is fine, but perhaps you want the button to say Submit in some cases and Update in others. In order to make the button class more usable, you can tell Flutter to render the button based on its configuration and data, as the following listing shows.

Listing 3.2 A widget with configuration

```
class SubmitButton extends StatelessWidget {
  final String buttonText;
  SubmitButton(this.buttonText);

  Widget build(context) {
    return Button(
      child: Text(buttonText);
    );
  }
}
```

Any data passed into the widget is part of its configuration.

You can omit useless constructors in Dart, so this constructor wasn't in the last example. Now it's needed so the button knows to expect an argument when it's built.

Passes in a variable rather than a string literal. Flutter now knows to re-render this button whenever the variable passed in is different.

Either way, this widget is static and void of logic because it can't update itself. It doesn't care what the button says. Its configuration relies on parent widgets. It doesn't know how to ask to be rebuilt, unlike a stateful widget (which we'll see soon).

When I say "void of logic," I don't mean a stateful widget can't have methods and properties like any other class. It can. You can have methods for your stateless widget, but a stateless widget is destroyed entirely when Flutter removes it from the widget tree. We'll talk more about the widget tree and context later in this chapter, but it's important to understand that a stateless widget shouldn't be responsible for any data you don't want to lose. Once it's gone, it's gone.

3.2.2 *Stateful widgets*

A stateful widget has internal state and can manage that state. All stateful widgets have corresponding state objects. Figure 3.3 shows the simplified widget tree again.

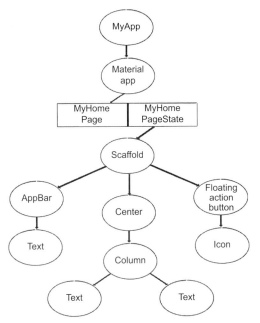

Figure 3.3   Example widget tree

Notice the MyHomePage tree node is connected to the MyHomePageState tree node. I designed this to visually represent that all StatefulWidget instances actually have two classes involved. This is the anatomy of every stateful widget in code:

Overrides the superclass method createState

```
class MyHomePage extends StatefulWidget {      ◁────── Inherits from StatefulWidget
    @override
    _MyHomePageState createState() => _MyHomePageState();      ◁─┐  Every stateful
}                                                                │  widget must have a
                                                                 │  createState method
                                                                 │  that returns a State
class _MyHomePageState extends State<MyHomePage> {      ◁─┐      │  object.
    @override                                             │
    Widget build(BuildContext context) {                  │
        // ..                         Your state class inherits from
    }                                 the Flutter State object.
}
```

**StatefulWidget's
required build method**

If you remember, earlier I said that every widget class must have a build method. As you can see, the StatefulWidget class doesn't have a build method. But every stateful widget has an associated state object, which does have a build method. You can think of the pair of StatefulWidget and State as the same entity. In fact, stateful widgets are immutable (just like stateless widgets), but their associated state objects are smart, mutable, and can hold onto state even as Flutter re-renders the widgets.

Private values in Dart with an underscore

In the previous example, notice that the class name is _MyHomePageState. It begins with an underscore, which is used to mark the class as *private*. All statements can be private. A top-level value that's private, such as this class, is only available within the current file. If a class member, such as a variable or function, is marked private, it's only available to use within that class itself.

Consider this Cat class:

```
class Cat {
    String name;
    String _color;

    void meow() => print("meow");

    void _pur() => print("prrrr");
}
```

Then, consider interacting with it:

```
Cat nora = Cat();
nora.name = "Nora";        // Okay
nora._color = "Orange"; // Invalid!
nora.meow();               // Okay
nora._pur();               // Invalid!
```

Private variables and class members are used quite a bit in Dart programming, solely to make your class APIs more readable.

MyHomePage is a stateful widget because it manages the state of the counter in the center of the app. When you tap that button, it fires a method called _incrementCounter:

```
void _incrementCounter() {
  setState(() {          One of the methods a Flutter State
    _counter++;          object uses to manage internal state
  });
}
```

3.2.3   setState

setState is the third important Flutter method you have to know, after build and createState. It exists only for the state object. It more or less says, "Hey Flutter, execute the code in this callback (in this case, increase the counter variable by one), and then repaint all the widgets that rely on this state for configuration (in this case, the number on the screen in the middle of the app)" (see figure 3.4). This method takes one argument: a VoidCallback.

In this example, the state object is the _MyHomePageState widget, and its children interact and rely on the state. When you press the button, it calls a method passed to

Counter app functionality

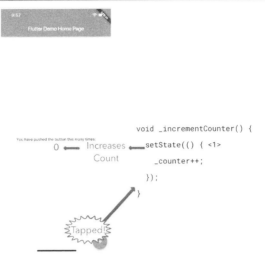

Figure 3.4 `setState` **tells Flutter to repaint.**

it from `_MyHomePageState`. That method calls `setState`, which in turn calls the `_MyHomePageState.build` method again, repainting the widgets whose configurations have changed (see figure 3.5).

There isn't much more to `setState` than that, but it's worth noting that `setState` can't execute async code. Any async work should be done before calling `setState`, because you don't want Flutter to repaint something before the data it's meant to display has resolved. For example, if you're fetching a GIF from a GIF API on the internet, you don't want to call `setState` before the image is ready to be displayed.

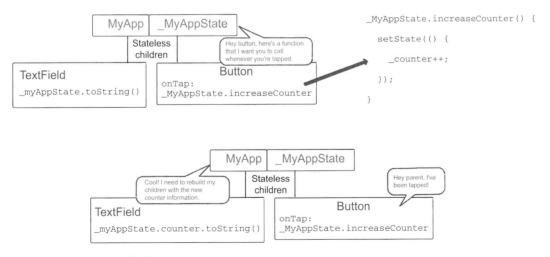

Figure 3.5 `setState` **visual**

3.2.4   *initState*

The state object also has a method called initState, which is called as soon as the widget is mounted in the tree. State.initState is the method in which you initialize any data needed *before* Flutter tries to paint it the screen. For example, you could subscribe to streams or compute some data into a human-friendly format.

When Flutter builds a stateful widget and its state object, the first thing it's going to do is whatever logic is in the initState function. For example, you may want to tell ensure that a String is formatted properly before the widget's build method is called and anything is rendered:

```
class FirstNameTextState extends State<FirstNameText> {
    String name;

    FirstNameTextState(this.name);

    @override
    initState() {
        super.initState();
        name = name.toUpperCase();
    }

    Widget build(BuildContext context) {
        return Text(name);
    }
}
```

> The State.initState method is marked as **mustCallSuper** in the superclass. So, you must call the superclass implementation of initState in your overridden method.

There are a few other *lifecycle* methods on the state object, and in a later chapter I'll discuss a widget's lifecycle in depth, including more on initState. Figure 3.6 shows all the methods and the order in which they're called.

There is a lot in this figure, and you shouldn't get bogged down in it. I'll spend a ton of time on it later! For now, though, it's important to know that initState and setState exist, and when to use them. initState is called once every time a state object is built. setState is called by you, the developer, whenever you want Flutter to re-render.

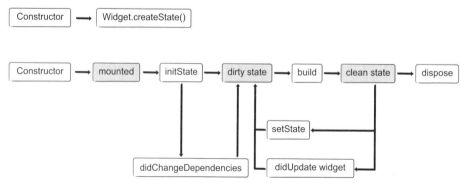

Figure 3.6 StatefulWidget lifecycle

3.3 *BuildContext*

BuildContext is another concept in Flutter that's crucial to building apps, and it has everything to do with tracking the entire widget tree—specifically, where widgets are located in the tree. When you update the theme in your ThemeData, as we did to change the color of the counter app, it updates child widgets throughout the widget tree. How does this work? It's tied to the idea of BuildContext.

Every build method in a widget takes one argument, BuildContext, which is a reference to a widget's location in the widget tree. Remember, build is called by the framework itself, so you don't have to manage the build context yourself, but you will want to interact with it often.

A concrete example is the Theme.of method, a static method on the Theme class. When called, Theme.of takes a BuildContext as an argument and returns information about the theme at that place in the widget tree. This is why, in the counter app, we can call Theme.of(buildContext).primaryColor to color widgets. That gets the Theme information for *this point in the tree* and then returns the data saved at the variable primaryColor in the Theme class.

Every widget has its own build context, which means that if you had multiple themes dispersed throughout your tree, getting the theme of one widget could return different results than another. In the specific case of the theme in the counter app, or other of methods, you'll get the nearest parent in the tree of that type (in this case, Theme; see figure 3.7).

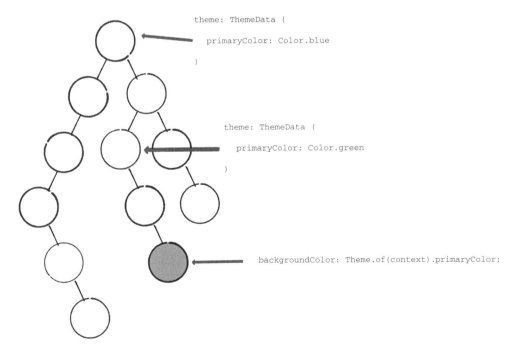

Figure 3.7 Using Theme in Flutter

The build context is used in various ways to tell Flutter exactly where and how to render certain widgets. For example, Flutter uses the build context to display modals and routes. If you wanted to display a new modal, Flutter needs to know where in the tree that modal should be inserted. This is accomplished by passing in `BuildContext` to a method that creates modals. We'll see this in depth in the chapter on routing. The important point about the build context, for now, is that it contains information about a widget's place *in the widget tree*, not about the widget itself.

Widgets, state, and context are arguably the three cornerstones of the foundation for developing a basic app in Flutter. Let's put them in action now.

3.4   *Enhancing the counter app with the most important widgets*

The default counter app isn't useful right now. You can't even reset your count. In this section, we'll extend the functionality of the counter app and explore some of the most important widgets in Flutter. According to the documentation, the absolute basic widgets are the following:

- Container
- Row
- Column
- Image
- Text
- Icon
- RaisedButton
- Scaffold
- AppBar

Figure 3.8   Finished counter app 2.0

Of these widgets, Column, Text, Icon, Scaffold, and AppBar are already in the counter app. We'll add the rest to make the counter app a bit more fun. Your improved counter app will look like figure 3.8 in the end.

3.4.1   *RaisedButton*

First, let's add a button to decrease the counter. All of this functionality will live in the _MyHomePageState class. To decrease the counter, we need

- A button to click
- A function that decrements _counter by one

RaisedButton is one of the Material Design-based buttons, and it appears slightly elevated. Raised buttons are used to add dimension to your layout, as opposed to a Flat-Button. To add the button, let's start in the build method of _MyHomePageState in the next listing.

> ### Listing 3.3 Adding a raised button to `_MyHomePageState.build`

```
// _MyHomePageState
Widget build(BuildContext context) {
    return  Scaffold(
      // ...
      body:  Center(
        child:  Column(
          mainAxisAlignment: MainAxisAlignment.center,
          children: <Widget>[
            // ...
            RaisedButton(
              child: Text("Decrement Counter"),
              onPressed: _decrementCounter,
            ),
          ])),
      // ...
```

Adds a RaisedButton ⟶

onPressed is a property on a button that expects a callback. By passing in a callback, we can manage state in this parent widget (another common pattern).

To finish up that functionality, we need to write the _decrementCounter method:

```
void _decrementCounter() {
  setState(() => _counter--);
}
```

setState takes a callback as an argument, which should solely update pieces of state in the widget.

Interaction is largely handled by callbacks in Flutter, like onPressed. In widgets provided by Flutter and that you'll write, you'll use callbacks to execute some function when a user interacts with your app. In built-in widgets, you'll see onPressed, onTapped, onHorizontalDrag, and many more. Chapter 5 is devoted to user interaction, where I'll cover these further.

3.5 *Favor composition in Flutter (over inheritance)*

> *Designing object-oriented software is hard, and designing reusable object-oriented software is even harder.*

This is the opening line of *Design Patterns: Elements of Reusable Object-Oriented Software*, by Erich Gamma et al., published in 1994. In all object-oriented programming, one of the hardest design issues is establishing relationships between your classes. There are two ways to create relationships between classes. The first, inheritance, establishes an "is a" relationship. Composition establishes a "has a" relationship. For example, a Cowboy *is a* Human, and a Cowboy *has a* Voice. Inheritance tends to have you designing objects around what they are, and composition around what they do.

3.5.1 *What is composition?*

What if you wanted to make a game where you're a cowboy and you have to protect the wild west from aliens? Maybe you have classes like this:

```
Human
  .rideHorse()

  Cowboy
```

```
      .chaseOutlaws()
      .fightAliens()

  Rancher
      .herdCattle()

Alien
    .flySpaceship()
    .invadeEarth()
```

Great. You got to reuse the `rideHorse` method because cowboys and ranchers both, in fact, ride horses. You're well into making this killer game when you have the wild idea that the aliens learn the ancient art of horse riding. Well, that's a problem. An alien *isn't* a human, so you shouldn't have `Alien` inherit from `Human`. But you also don't want to rewrite `rideHorse`.

This could have been avoided by using composition from the beginning, rather than inheritance. You could have a `HorseRiding` class, which could be added as a member to any class. It'd look more like this:

```
HorseRiding
    .rideHorse

Cowboy
    HorseRidingInstance.rideHorse()
    .chaseOutlaws()
    .fightAliens()

Rancher
    HorseRidingInstance.rideHorse()
    .herdCattle()

Alien
    HorseRidingInstance.rideHorse()
    .flySpaceship()
    .invadeEarth()
```

This is great. No matter how many objects need to ride a horse, you have an easy, decoupled way to add that functionality.

The curious among you might be asking, "Why not just make all the actions into their own classes and inherit everything?" Well, that's not a bad idea. Maybe the rancher learned how to fly a spaceship. So now how do we think about our objects that have these methods?

Well, a `Cowboy` is a `HorseRider` and `AlienFighter` and `OutlawChaser`. Similarly, the alien and rancher are combinations of what they can do:

```
Alien = HorseRider + SpaceShipFlyer + EarthInvader
Rancher = HorseRider + CattleHerder
Cowboy = HorseRider + OutlawChaser + AlienFighter
```

If you made classes that represent HorseRider, EarthInvader, and the like, then you could *implement* those actions into your classes. This is what composition is.

(If you're thinking, "That sounds a lot like the idea behind *abstract classes*," you're correct. We'll explore those deeply in the part 3 of this book.)

3.5.2 *An example of composition in Flutter*

The example in listing 3.3 with a RaisedButton uses composition:

```
//...
RaisedButton(
  child: Text("Decrement Counter"),
  onPressed: () => _decrementCounter(),
),
//...
```

To make a button that says Decrement Counter, you *pass in* another widget (Text) that handles the responsibility of setting text.

In Flutter, always favor composition (over inheritance) to create reusable and decoupled widgets. Most widgets don't know their children ahead of time. This is especially true for widgets like text blocks and dialogs, which are basically containers for content.

A more robust example of a button may look like this:

```
class PanicButton extends StatelessWidget {
  final Widget display;
  final VoidCallback onPressed;

  PanicButton({this.display, this.onPressed});

  Widget build(BuildContext context) {
    RaisedButton(
      color: Colors.red,

      child: display,

      onPressed: onPressed,
    );
  }
}
```

This widget's configuration is passed in to it, including the widget to display. Imagine the display passed in is Text("Panic").

Sets the button's background color to red

This text widget is passed in from the parent. This is key!

The callback is passed in as well. This makes it as flexible as possible. It doesn't care about the callback and isn't tied to any certain functionality. All it cares about is displaying a button and telling its parent when that button is pressed (via the callback).

Here, using composition, I'm saying "This button *has* text," rather than "This text *is a* button." What if you want the button to display an icon instead of text? It's already set up to do that. All you need to do is pass in an Icon instead of Text. The button doesn't care about its child, it only knows that it has one.

You could kick that up a notch and pass in the color if you wanted to. The button doesn't even care about that, only that it will be told what color it is.

Anyway, back in your app, you should now have a button that you can use to decrement the counter by one. Next, we'll keep adding more to the app.

3.6   *Intro to layout in Flutter*

The most common questions from those working in Flutter for the first time are about layout. Flutter's rendering engine is unique in that it doesn't use one specific layout system. Way down on the low level, it doesn't consider the screen a Cartesian graph (at first). It doesn't force the developer to use flex layout, a Cartesian graph, or other common systems like width in, height out (WIHO). It leaves that up to us. And often, we mix and match those systems to achieve the layout we want.

Widgets, as we now know, are high-level classes that describe a view. There are lower-level objects that know how to paint these widgets onto the screen. In practice, that means the layout system is abstracted away for the developer, which opens up the possibility of using several different paradigms together. There are widgets that use the flexible layout, commonly known as FlexBox on the web. And there are widgets that allow us to explicitly place widget on the screen at given coordinates. In this section, I want to explore some of the most common layout widgets.

Besides layout widgets, I'll also talk about *constraints* in Flutter. Constraints are a core part of understanding layout. In a nutshell, though, constraints tell widgets how much space they *can* take up, and then the widgets decide what they will take up. In section 3.6.2, I talk about constraints in depth.

3.6.1   *Row and Column*

The most commonly used layout style in Flutter is known as the *flexible* layout, just like FlexBox. You can use flex layouts with `Column` and `Row` widgets. The counter app already has a `Column` widget in it, as shown in the next listing.

Listing 3.4   Column widget in the counter app

```
// _MyHomePageState
body: Center(                          Aptly named column that lays
    child: Column(                     out all its children in a column
        mainAxisAlignment: MainAxisAlignment.center,    Alignment property
        children: <Widget>[                             similar to FlexBox in
            Text('You have pushed the button this many times:'),   CSS. It tells Flutter
            Text(                                       how to lay out the
                '$_counter',                            Column children in
                style: Theme.of(context).textTheme.display1,   relationship to each
            ),                                          other ("each other"
            RaisedButton(                               is key!).
                child: Text("Decrement Counter"),
                onPressed: _decrementCounter,
            ),
        ],
    ),
),
```

Some widgets (mainly layout widgets) take a list of widgets as children, rather than a single child.

The Row widget behaves like the Column but on a horizontal axis. It will take all its children and lay them out, one by one, next to each other, from left to the right.

> **TIP** In some languages (as in speaking languages, not programming languages), words are written right-to-left. In this case, Flutter supports RTL settings and would change the behavior of the Row widget. This is outside the scope of this chapter. If you aren't developing an app that will be localized to one of these RTL languages, then this shouldn't concern you.

I want to wrap the decrement button in Row in the example app so I can add a second button beside it. In that same code block, start by adding Row around RaisedButton.

Listing 3.5 Wrapping widgets in a Row

```
// _MyHomePageState.build

Row(                            // new
  children: <Widget>[    // new
    RaisedButton(
      color: Colors.red,
      child: Text(
        "Decrement",
        style: TextStyle(color: Colors.white),
      ),
      onPressed: _decrementCounter,
    ),
  ],                            // new
),                              // new
```

When you hot-reload your app, the Decrement button is now aligned to the left side of the screen (see figure 3.9). This is because flexible widgets try to take up as much space as they can on their *main axis*. The Row widget expands as much as it can horizontally, which in this case is as wide as the whole screen, constrained by its parent (the column).

You have pushed the button this many times:

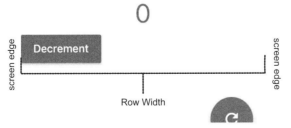

Figure 3.9 **Row widget with single child and no alignment**

3.6.2 *Layout constraints in Flutter*

Layout and constraints are monumentally important in Flutter. Flutter is, after all, mainly a UI library and a rendering engine. Understanding how widgets determine their sizes will save you headaches in the future. You will certainly, at some point, get some errors when you're using `Row` and `Column` and other layout widgets. These are layout-constraint errors. When developers are learning Flutter for the first time, they'll certainly see a `flutter layout infinite size` error.

This is an error that can be a headache to correct, unless you know how constraints work. I need to take a conceptual aside to discuss how Flutter knows what pixels to paint on the screen, thanks to constraints.

3.6.3 *RenderObject*

I've said many times that there are a couple of objects in Flutter other than widgets. One of the most important to understand is `RenderObject`. This class is mainly used internally. You'll rarely have to use it directly.

Render objects are responsible for the actual painting to the screen done by Flutter. They are made internally by the framework, and all the render objects make up the *render tree*, which is separate from the widget tree. The render tree is made up of classes that implement `RenderObject`. And render objects have corresponding widgets.

As developers, we write widgets, which provide data (such as constraints) to a render object. The render object has methods on it like `performLayout` and `paint`. These methods are responsible for painting the pixels on the screen. They're concerned with *exact* bits of information for controlling pixels. All styling and layout work done in widgets is largely an abstraction over the render objects.

These render objects are also without any state or logic. By design, they know some basic data about their parent render object, and they have the ability to visit their children, but they don't coordinate with each other on the scale of the whole app. They don't have the ability to make decisions—they only follow orders.

Importantly, widgets build child widgets in their `build` method, which create more widgets, and so on down the tree until it bottoms out at a `RenderObjectWidget` (or a collection of `RenderObjectWidgets`). These are the widgets that create render objects that paint to the screen.

Consider a `Column` widget, which would not be a leaf `RenderObjectWidget` in a widget tree. A column is an abstract layout idea; it isn't an actual thing you can see. Text and colors are concrete objects that can be painted. The job of a column is to provide constraints, not to paint anything on the screen.

> **NOTE** `RenderObjects` aren't of much concern to us as developers, but they're an important piece of the relationship between your widgets and how Flutter actually works. The render object API is exposed to us, but it's unlikely you'll need to use it.

3.6.4 *RenderObject and constraints*

Render objects are closely tied to layout constraints. While you can set your own constraints on widgets using constraint widgets, render objects are ultimately responsible for telling the framework a widget's true, physical size. Constraints are passed to a render object, and that object eventually decides, "Okay, given these constraints, I will be this size and in this exact location."

In other words, constraints are concerned with `minWidth`, `minHeight`, `maxWidth`, and `maxHeight`. `Size`, on the other hand, is concerned with actual `width` and `height`. When a render box is given its constraints, it then decides how much of that allotted space it will actually take up (its *size*).

Different render objects behave differently. The most common render object subclass, by far, is `RenderBox`, which calculates a widget's size using a Cartesian coordinate system. In general, there are three kinds of render boxes:

- Those that try to take up as much space as possible, such as the boxes used by a `Center` widget
- Those that try to the same size as their children, such as the boxes used by an `Opacity` widget
- Those that try to be a particular size, such as the boxes used by an `Image` widget

Thus far in the discussion about render objects, those three styles are the most important thing to remember. At this point in the book, I won't discuss actually writing render objects; I'm only giving a foundational explanation. It's important to remember, though, that different widget's `RenderObject`s behave in one of those three ways.

3.6.5 *RenderBoxes and layout errors*

Back to the original layout problem: the `flutter layout infinite size` error. This error happens when a widget's constraints tell it that it can be infinitely large on either the horizontal or vertical access. This has everything to do with the constraints that are passed to it, and the way its render object behaves.

Sometimes the constraints that are given to a box are *unbounded*. This happens when either the `maxHeight` or `maxWidth` given to a render box is `double.INFINITY`. Unbounded constraints are found in `Row`, `Column`, and widgets that are scrollable. That makes sense, because a row can be—in theory—infinitely wide (depending on its children). But the render engine can't actually paint an infinitely wide widget, because we're human beings constrained by time and the computer is constrained by processing power and memory.

`Row` and `Column` are special because they're flex boxes. Their render objects don't, by default, fit into one of those three categories of render object behavior that I mentioned earlier. They behave differently based on the constraints passed by their parents. If they have bounded constraints, they try to be as big as possible *within those bounded constraints*. If they have unbounded constraints, they try to fit their children in the direction of their main axis. For example, a column full of images that has unbounded constraints will try to be as tall as the combined height of all the images.

The constraint passed to the column's children is determined by the constraints passed to the column. If you don't know to look for it, this can lead to a pesky error. Let me try to make this more concrete with an example. Here's how Columns within Columns can cause infinite height:

The outer Column gives its children unbounded height.

The inner Column now has an unbounded constraint, so it will try to fit its children.

The Expanded widget tells its children to take up as much space as they can on the main axis of the flex box.

```
child: Column(
    children: <Widget>[
        Column(
            mainAxisAlignment: MainAxisAlignment.center,
            children: <Widget>[
                Expanded(
                    child: Text(
                        'You have pushed the button this many times:',
                    ),
                ),
            ],
        ),
    ],
),
```

In this case, the inner column is going to try to be whatever size its child tries to be, and is unbounded by its own parent. The Expanded will say, "Great! I have no height constraint, and it's in my nature to try and be as big as possible, so I'm going to expand forever." That'll throw an error.

Also, it's worth noting that flexible widgets, as well as some scrolling widgets, always try to take up as much space as possible on their *cross axis*. A column will always try to be as wide as its parent, and a row will always try to be as tall as its parent.

Because widgets pass constraints *down* the tree, there can be some degrees of separation between nested flex boxes, and you'll end up with an infinitely expanding child somewhere. This often leads to that pesky error mentioned before. This is often solved by ensuring that you aren't using a widget that tries to be as big as possible in nested flexible widgets.

It's quite common to have nested flexible widgets, such as rows of widgets within a column. There isn't one go-to fix for this problem because the constraints vary depending on what widgets you're using. In general, though, if you know how flexible widgets behave, this problem is easier to tackle.

3.6.6 *Multi-child widgets*

Now that you have a bit of information about constraints and dealing with flexible widgets, let's put it into practice in the following listing. Back in the app, let's add this second button to the row, which will increment the counter (see figure 3.10).

Listing 3.6 Adding a second button to the Row

```
Row(
  children: <Widget>[
    RaisedButton(
      color: Colors.red,
      child: Text(
        "Decrement",
        style: TextStyle(color: Colors.white),
      ),
      onPressed: _decrementCounter,
    ),
    RaisedButton(               ⟵——— The newly added widget
      color: Colors.green,
      child: Text(
        "Increment",
        style: TextStyle(color: Colors.white),
      ),
      onPressed: _incrementCounter,
    ),
  ],
),
```

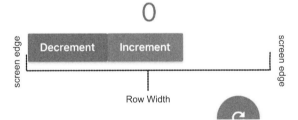

Figure 3.10 Row **widget with multiple children and no alignment**

Now there are two buttons, both aligned to the left side. To make that a little more pleasing to look at, we need to add an alignment to the Row. Flexible widgets can be told how to space their children with a few different alignment options that can be passed to the mainAxisAlignment property:

```
Row(
  mainAxisAlignment: MainAxisAlignment.spaceAround,   ⟵ Uses the
  children: <Widget>[                                      spaceAround
    RaisedButton(                                           alignment option
      color: Colors.red,
  // ...
```

If you come from the web, spaceAround may look familiar (see figure 3.11). The Axis Alignment options are the same as the FlexBox and CSS Grid properties for justification and alignment. Figure 3.12 shows all the flexible layout alignments from a real-life example.

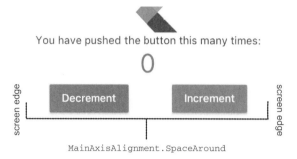

You have pushed the button this many times:

0

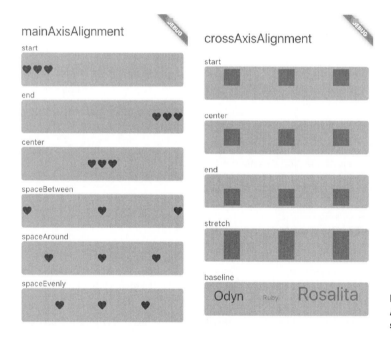

MainAxisAlignment.SpaceAround

Figure 3.11   **Row widget with spaceAround alignment**

Figure 3.12 Alignment styles in Flutter

That's the basics of using multi-child `Row` and `Column` widgets. You'll find yourself using a lot of them, so it's worth understanding the basics.

3.6.7   *Icons and the FloatingActionButton*

In Flutter, all the Material Design icons are built in and available as constants. Compared to my experience on the web, this is a real blessing. Icons are a core part of building mobile interfaces where space is limited. In Flutter, you don't have to find an external library or upload images if you're happy using the Material Design style icons. There are several icons, and they can all be seen and searched through at https://material.io/tools/icons. Table 3.1 lists the icons I use most often.

In the counter app right now, an `Icon` is used in the `FloatingActionButton`: the Add icon. Since `Icons` is a constant, you can access `Icons` anywhere in your app

Table 3.1 Common Material Design icons

Icon	Const name	Icon	Const name
+	`Icons.add`	✓	`Icons.check`
▼	`Icons.arrow_drop_down`	▲	`Icons.arrow_drop_up`
→	`Icons.arrow_forward`	←	`Icons.arrow_back`
‹	`Icons.chevron_left`	›	`Icons.chevron_right`
✕	`Icons.close`	≡	`Icons.menu`
♥	`Icons.favorite`	↻	`Icons.refresh`

(passed in to the `Icon` widget). The `Icon` widget is, as you probably guessed, a widget. You can use it anywhere.

The `FloatingActionButton` button is a prime example of a widget that Flutter gives you, styled and all, for free. According to the `FloatingActionButton` documentation (http://mng.bz/079E), "A floating action button is a circular icon button that hovers over content to promote a primary action in the application. Floating action buttons are most commonly used in the `Scaffold.floatingActionButton` field." When used in a `Scaffold` (as it is in our app), it's placed where it needs to be, with no work necessary on your part. You can use it anywhere you'd like, though, if you want a circular button that has styles that make it look "elevated" with a box shadow.

Back in the app, we want the `FloatingActionButton` (FAB) to reset the counter, not increase it. Easy enough! What are the steps to get this done?

1 Write a new method `resetCounter`, and pass it to the FAB's `onPressed` argument.
2 Change the icon used in the FAB.

First, let's write the method. All we want to do is set _counter back to 0. Also, don't forget that we need to tell Flutter to repaint:

```
void _resetCounter() {
  setState(() => _counter = 0);
}
```

That's a simple enough method. Now we have to update the FAB itself.

Step 1 is choosing the right `Icon`. I choose `Icons.refresh`, which will be passed into the FAB. In the FAB, change the icon and the function passed into the `onPressed` callback:

Calls _resetCounter on tap,
rather than _incrementCounter

```
floatingActionButton: FloatingActionButton(
  onPressed: _resetCounter,
  tooltip: 'Reset Counter',
  child: Icon(Icons.refresh),
),
```

Tooltip that reflects what the button does to make the app more accessible

The Icon widget's unnamed, required argument expects IconInfo. All Material Design icons are available as constants on the Icons class.

When you hot-reload the app, it should now reflect the changes with the different icon and functionality.

3.6.8   *Images*

Flutter makes it easy to add images to your app via the `Image` widget. The `Image` widget has different constructors, depending on the *source* of your image: that is, whether the image is saved locally in the project or you're fetching it from the internet.

The quickest way to add an image is the with `Image.network` constructor. You pass it a URL as a `String`, and it takes care of everything for you. An example is `Image.network("https://funfreegifs.com/panda-bear")`. Any URL that resolves to an image can be passed.

In your app, though, it's more likely that you'll need some images hosted locally. In this case, you use the `Image.asset` constructor. This constructor works the same way: you pass in a path to an image in your project, and it resolves it for you. However, you have to tell Flutter about it in your pubspec.yaml file first.

In this counter app, let's put a Flutter logo at the top of the app. There's already a Flutter logo image in the GitHub repository for book. The image also needs to be added to the pubspec.yaml file. I'll take this opportunity to briefly walk through the pubspec.yaml of a basic Flutter app. (If you start a new Flutter project, the pubspec.yaml file has in-depth comments, which you may find helpful.)

Listing 3.7   Adding an image to your Flutter pubspec.yaml file

```
name: counter_app
description: A new Flutter project.    Metadata describing
version: 1.0.0+1                       your project

environment:                           Refers to your Dart SDK version,
  sdk: ">=2.0.0-dev.68.0 <3.0.0"       which should be 2 or higher

dependencies:              Dependencies needed in the
  flutter:                 production version of your app
    sdk: flutter
    cupertino_icons: ^0.1.2      Gives you access to iOS style
                                 icons, if you want to use them

dev_dependencies:                Dependencies used in
  flutter_test:                  development only
    sdk: flutter

flutter:                         Flag that ensures you have access to Material Icons
  uses-material-design: true
  assets:
    - flutter_logo_1080.png      The important part, where you declare your assets
```

Where you configure Flutter

Any assets that you need in your app must be listed under the `assets` header in your spec file. It *must* follow this format. YAML is sensitive to whitespace. The assets themselves should be listed as a path from the lib folder in your project. I just happened to put mine directly under lib, but if it was in a folder called images, that line would say images/flutter_logo_1080.png.

Now that you've added flutter_logo_1080.png to your assets, you're going to have to restart your app. Hot reload doesn't work if you change your spec files. But hot restart does work, and it should be much faster than stopping and starting your app. You can perform a hot restart by typing R into the terminal in which you ran `flutter run`.

Now you can access that image in the counter app by adding an `Image` widget to the `Column` widget's children, as shown in the next listing.

Listing 3.8 Adding an image to your Flutter app

**The first argument to Image.asset expects
the exact name you listed in pubspec.**

```
children: <Widget>[
  Image.asset(
    'flutter_logo_1080.png',
    width: 100.0,
  ),
  Text(
    'You have pushed the button this many times:',
  ),
```

**The Image widget allows you to explicitly set the width
and height of an image. If you don't, the image will be
as large as its true size in pixels.**

Now, if you hot reload, you'll see an image in your app.

3.6.9 *Container widget*

The image doesn't look great right now. It's just sitting there on top of the text, without any spacing. Let's clean it up with the `Container` widget. Figure 3.13 shows what we're going for, and it can all be done with the `Container`.

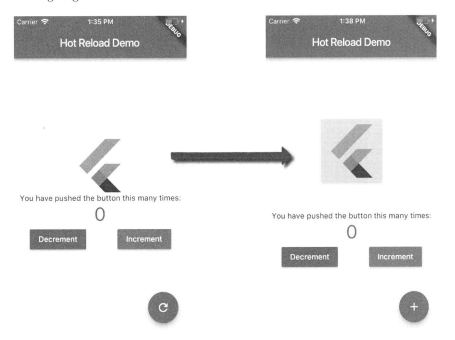

Figure 3.13 Transforming the Flutter logo with the `Container` widget

Some widgets, such as Container, vary in the way they size themselves based on their constructor arguments and children. In the case of Container, it defaults to trying to be as big as possible; but if you give it a width, for instance, it tries to honor that and be that particular size.

The Container widget is a "convenience" widget that provides a slew of properties that you would otherwise get from individual widgets. For example, there is a Padding widget that solely adds padding to its child. But the Container widget has a padding property (among others).

You will likely get a *lot* of use out of the Container widget. Look at all these optional properties you can take advantage of (and these aren't all) from the constructor of the Container widget:

```
// From Flutter source code
  Container({
    Key key,
    this.alignment,
    this.padding,
    Color color,
    Decoration decoration,          ◁——┐  Here, you can set all kinds of other
    this.foregroundDecoration,             properties like Border, BorderRadius,
    double width,                          BoxShadow, background images, and more.
    double height,
    BoxConstraints constraints,
    this.margin,
    this.transform,
    this.child,
  })
    ...
```

We'll explore all of these in time, but the point is that if you need to style a widget in some way, you should reach for a Container. Wrap your Image.asset in a Container, and then add the following properties to it.

Listing 3.9 Adding a `Container` widget

Puts space between widgets. The EdgeInsets.only constructor tells Flutter where to add the margin (in this case, 100 pixels of margin below this widget).

Adds space around the current widget. The EdgeInsets.all constructor puts space on all sides. Figure 3.13 illustrates margin vs. padding.

```
    Container(
┌——▷  margin: EdgeInsets.only(bottom: 100.0),

      padding: EdgeInsets.all(8.0),          ◁————┐  Passes decoration a class
                                                       called BoxDecoration,
      decoration: BoxDecoration(          ◁————      which decorates boxes

        color: Colors.blue.withOpacity(0.25),   ◁———  Sets the background color

        borderRadius: BorderRadius.circular(4.0),  ◁——┐  BorderRadius has multiple constructors:
      ),                                                  use circular when you want to curve all
                                                          four corners of the box.
```

```
child: Image.asset(
  'flutter_logo_1080.png',
  width: 100.0,
),
),
```

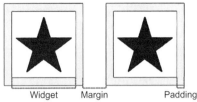

Passes the image in to the child property, as usual

Hot-reload one more time. Your app should look like the original goal from figure 3.14. And, more importantly, you've learned about all of the foundational concepts of wrangling UI in Flutter.

Figure 3.14 Using the `margin` property versus the `padding` property

3.7   The element tree

Now that you've seen a handful of widgets, I'd like to take one last opportunity to explore Flutter under the surface. If you've tried messing with Flutter before this book, you've likely seen the graphic floating around that discusses the "layers" of the framework. It looks like figure 3.15.

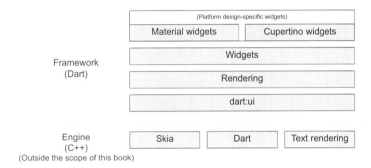

Figure 3.15   A simplified look at the layers of abstraction in the Flutter SDK

About 99.99% of the time, we developers get to live in the top layers of that table: in the Widgets layer and Material/Cupertino layer. Below those layers are the Rendering layer and the `dart:ui` library. Dart UI is the most low-level piece of the framework written in Dart. This library exposes an API to talk directly with the rendering engine on device. Dart UI allows us to paint directly on the screen using the `canvas` API, and lets us listen for user interaction with `hit testing`.

> ### The element tree and its importance to the developer
>
> For the rest of this section, I'm going to explain what `Element` objects are and how they are relevant to you, the developer. That said, you'll rarely use elements directly. This section is meant to give you an understanding of how the framework operates. It is a tough concept to grok, but it doesn't have any bearing on your ability to move through this book.

(continued)
Understanding the inner workings of Flutter comes in handy in a few "gotcha" situations. This understanding may help you debug your apps in the future, but you shouldn't get hung up on it. It's good to be aware of now, but it's not necessary for you to completely understand it. That will come with time.

The long and short of that library is that it'd be an extreme slog of a process to write an app with it, but you could. You'd have to calculate coordinates for every single pixel on the screen and update the screen with every single frame. That's why Flutter has widgets, the high-level abstractions that give us a declarative approach to building a UI. We don't have to worry about working with pixels or low-level device hit testing.

Looking at figure 3.15, this just leaves the layer in between the widgets and `dart:ui`: rendering. It turns out that there's yet another tree in your Flutter app: the *element tree*. The element tree represents the structure of your app, in much the same way the widget tree does. In fact, there's an element in the element tree for every widget in the widget tree.

Earlier in the book, I described widgets as blueprints that Flutter will use to paint elements on the screen. When I said *elements* in that sentence, I literally meant the Flutter `Element` class. Widgets are configurations for elements. Elements are widgets that have been made real and mounted into the tree. Elements are what are actually displayed on your device at any given moment when running a Flutter app.

Each Element also has a `RenderObject`. All of these render objects make up the render tree. Render objects are the interface between our high-level code and the low-level `dart:ui` library. With that in mind, you can think of the element as the glue between the widget and render trees (see figure 3.16).

You *can* use render objects directly as a Flutter developer, but I doubt you'll ever want to. Render objects do the actual painting to the screen and are therefore quite

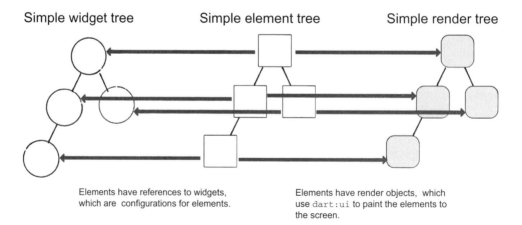

Simple widget tree   Simple element tree   Simple render tree

Elements have references to widgets, which are configurations for elements.

Elements have render objects, which use `dart:ui` to paint the elements to the screen.

Figure 3.16   The Flutter framework manages *three* threes, which interact via the element tree.

complex and expensive. That's why there are three trees in Flutter. They give the framework the ability to internally be smart about reusing expensive render objects while being careless about destroying inexpensive widgets.

With this in mind, I'd like to talk more about elements, but we shouldn't worry about the render tree anymore. The relationship between elements and widgets, however, is worth investigating.

3.7.1 Elements and widgets

Elements are created by widgets. When a new widget is built, the framework calls `Widget.createElement(this)`. This widget is the initial configuration for the element, and the element has a *reference* to the widget that built it. The elements that are created are their own tree, as well. The element tree is, in the simplest explanation, like the skeleton of your app. It holds the structure of the app, but none of the details that widgets provide. It can look up configuration details via those references to its corresponding widget.

Elements are different than widgets because they aren't rebuilt; they're updated. When a widget is rebuilt, or a different widget is inserted at some place in the tree by an ancestor, an element can change its *reference* to the widget, rather than being re-created. Elements can be created and destroyed, of course, and will be as a user navigates around the app. But consider an animation. The animation calls `build` after every frame change—which is a lot! (Up to 60 times per second, in fact.) During an animation, the widget at every frame is the same type but varies slightly in configuration. (That is, some display properties have changed. For example, a widget's color might be a slightly different shade in each frame of the animation.) In this case, the element itself doesn't have to rebuild, because the tree is still structurally the same. The widget gets rebuilt on every frame, but the element only updates its reference to that widget.

And this is how Flutter gets away with rebuilding widgets constantly, but remains performant. Widgets are just blueprints, and it's cheap to replace widgets in the tree without disturbing the tree that's *actually* displayed on the screen, because it's handled by elements.

There's one last important detail I'd like to touch on: state objects are actually managed by elements, not widgets. In fact, under the hood, Flutter renders based on elements and state objects and isn't as concerned with widgets. In the next section, we'll look deeper into how the state object interacts with elements and widgets.

This is all necessary (and optimal), because widgets are immutable. Because they're immutable, they can't change their relationships with other widgets. They can't get a new parent. They have to be destroyed and rebuilt. Elements, however, are mutable, but we don't have to update them ourselves. We get the speed of mutable elements, but the safety of writing immutable code (via widgets).

> **NOTE** Again, elements, like render objects, are rarely of concern to the developer, but you can create your own. You'll likely always stick to writing widgets.

3.7.2   *Exploring the element tree with an example*

To add a bit more flair to the app (and demonstrate how the element tree works), I want to swap the increment and decrement buttons each time the Reset button is pressed. To start, let me point out some relevant code in the counter app.

Listing 3.10   `_MyHomePageState` configuration

**This boolean will be used to determine
if the buttons should be swapped.**

**These keys are going to be
important, but for now just
know that they exist.**

```
class _MyHomePageState extends State<MyHomePage> {
  int _counter = 0;
  bool _reversed = false;
  List<UniqueKey> _buttonKeys = [UniqueKey(), UniqueKey()];
  // ... rest of class
}
```

To make this easier, I made a widget called `FancyButton`, shown in the next listing. This is a stateful widget that manages its own background color, as well as calling a callback passed into it when the button is pressed.

Listing 3.11   The `FancyButton` custom widget

```
class FancyButton extends StatefulWidget {
  final VoidCallback onPressed;
  final Widget child;

  const FancyButton({Key key, this.onPressed, this.child}) : super(key: key);

  @override
  _FancyButtonState createState() => _FancyButtonState();
}

class _FancyButtonState extends State<FancyButton> {
  @override
  Widget build(BuildContext context) {
    return Container(
      child: RaisedButton(
        color: _getColors(),                    // This button manages its own color.
        child: widget.child,
        onPressed: widget.onPressed,
      ),
    );
  }

                                                 // Manages color for
                                                 // all fancy buttons
  Color _getColors() {
    return _buttonColors.putIfAbsent(this, () => colors[next(0, 5)]);
  }
}
```

```
Map<_FancyButtonState, Color> _buttonColors = {};
final _random = Random();
int next(int min, int max) => min + _random.nextInt(max - min);
 List<Color> colors = [
  Colors.blue,
  Colors.green,
  Colors.orange,
  Colors.purple,
  Colors.amber,
  Colors.lightBlue,
];
```

Helper methods, used to allow the
buttons to manage their own state, but
also ensure that they're never the same
color. This code is contrived and not
important to the lesson at hand.

The getColors method manages color for *all* the fancy buttons by using the putIfAbsent method on Dart Map objects. This method says, "If this button is already in the map, tell me its color. Otherwise, put this in the map with this new color, and return that color."

The FancyButton widget is used in the _MyHomePageState.build method (shown in the next listing). The buttons are first created as variables and will be used in the widget tree in the *returned* portion of this build method.

Listing 3.12 Updated app to use the FancyButton class

```
// _MyHomePageState.build
  @override
  Widget build(BuildContext context) {
    final incrementButton = FancyButton(
      child: Text(
        "Increment",
        style: TextStyle(color: Colors.white),
      ),
      onPressed: _incrementCounter,
    );
```

Fancy button
representing the
Increment button

```
    final decrementButton = FancyButton(
      child: Text(
        "Decrement",
        style: TextStyle(color: Colors.white),
      ),
      onPressed: _decrementCounter,
    );
```

Fancy button
representing the
Decrement button

```
    List<Widget> _buttons = <Widget>[incrementButton, decrementButton];

    if (_reversed) {
      _buttons = _buttons.reversed.toList();
    }
  }
```

Creates a _buttons variable,
which will be passed into a
Row later, and displays
these widgets

If the _reversed member is true, reverses the
order of the buttons. Since this happens in the
build method, they're swapped whenever setState
is called and _reversed has been updated.

For both fancy buttons, the configuration resembles the configuration you'd need for a RaisedButton in Flutter.

I'll cover the rest of the build method (and in turn, using keys) next. First, I'd like you to press the Reset button and swap the buttons. The Reset button, when pressed, calls the method _resetCounter:

```
void _resetCounter() {
    setState(() => _counter = 0);        This method turns around and calls _swap,
    _swap();                             which will swap the buttons' locations.
}

  void _swap() {                         This method updates the _reversed Boolean
    setState(() {                        and calls setState, which triggers a rebuild!
      _reversed = !_reversed;
    });
}
```

You may notice that it isn't behaving the way we wanted. If your code is the same as mine, then when you press the Reset button, the buttons do indeed swap places, but the button background colors don't swap. That is, the button on the left has the same background color it did before the swap, even though the button itself is different. This is the result of elements, state objects, and widgets and how they all work together.

3.7.3 *The element tree and State objects*

A few things to keep in mind as I explain what's happening:

- State objects are actually managed by the element tree.
- State objects are long-lived. Unlike widgets, they aren't destroyed and rebuilt whenever widgets re-render.
- State objects can be reused.
- Elements have references to widgets.

The relationship between a single stateful widget, an element, and a state object is shown in figure 3.17.

It's helpful for me if I consider the element the brains of the operation. Elements are simple in that they only contain meta information and a reference to a widget, but they also know how to update their own reference to a different widget if the widget changes.

Anytime Flutter is rebuilding, the element's reference points to the *new widget in the exact location in the widget tree of the element's old reference.* When Flutter is deciding

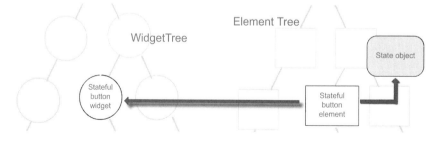

Figure 3.17   The relationship between an element and a widget

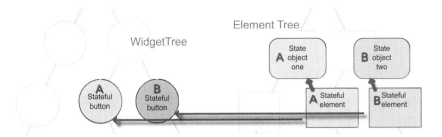

Figure 3.18   Each element points to a different widget and knows its type.

what to rebuild and re-render after `build` is called, an element is going to look at the widget in the exact same place as the previous widget it referenced (see figure 3.18). Then, it'll decide if the widget is the same (in which case it doesn't need to do anything), or if the widget has changed, or it's a different widget altogether (in which case it needs to re-render).

So, when you swap those two buttons, they replace each other in the widget tree, but the element's reference points to the same location. Each element is going to look at its widget and say, "Has this widget changed? Or is it a new widget altogether?" So, we'd expect the element to see that the widget's `color` property has changed, so it should in fact update its reference to the new widget.

The problem is what elements look at to decipher what's updated. They only look at a couple of properties on the widget:

- The exact type at runtime
- A widget's key (if there is one)

In this example, the colors of these widgets aren't in the widget configuration; they're in the state objects. The element is pointing to the updated widgets and displaying the new configuration, but still holding on to the original state object. So, the element is seeing the new widget that's been inserted into this place in the tree and thinking, "There's no key, and the runtime type is still `FancyButton`, so I don't need to update my reference. This is the correct widget to match my state object." (See figure 3.19).

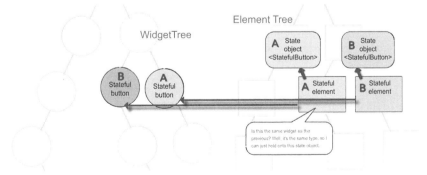

Figure 3.19   The elements think they're the same widgets because they're of the same type.

This issue presents another feature of Flutter: keys, which can be used by the framework to explicitly identify widgets.

> **An important note about elements**
>
> If you aren't convinced that you won't have to deal with elements directly, consider this anecdote: in my two years of developing production apps for Flutter, I've only written an element once. The problem I just discussed isn't fixed by diving into elements—it's solved using a common feature in Flutter, keys, which I'll discuss next.
>
> I can't stress enough that having a *basic* understanding of elements will arm you with a greater understanding of Flutter under the hood than almost everyone out there, but that's all you need: the basics.

3.7.4   *Widget keys*

Continuing with the problem of State and Element, let me present the easiest solution to the problem: keys. When working with widgets in collections, giving them keys helps Flutter know when two widgets of the same type are actually different. This is particularly useful for the children of multi-child widgets. Often, as in our example case, all the children in a row or column are of the same type, so it's ideal to give Flutter an extra piece of information to differentiate the children. In our app, let's solve the problem with a UniqueKey:

```
_buttons = <Widget>[
  FancyButton(                          Unique key that allows Flutter to identify this
    key: _buttonKeys.first,       ◁──── widget among widgets of the same type
    child: Text(
      "Decrement",
      style: TextStyle(color: Colors.white),
    ),
    onPressed: _decrementCounter,
  ),
  FancyButton(
    key: _buttonKeys.last,        ◁───  The first and last methods on Lists retrieve
    child: Text(                        the first and last elements, respectively.
      "Increment",
      style: TextStyle(color: Colors.white),
    ),
    onPressed: _incrementCounter,
  ),
];
```

There is quite a bit more to explore with keys, and they are extremely useful. Next, I'll talk about the different types.

KEY TYPES AND WHEN TO USE THEM

There are several types of keys: ValueKey, ObjectKey, UniqueKey, GlobalKey, and PageStorageKey. They're all related in a some way. PageStorageKey is a subclass of

ValueKey<T>, which is a subclass of LocalKey. And *that* is a subclass of Key. ObjectKey and UniqueKey also implement LocalKey. GlobalKey is a subclass of Key. They're all related, and they're all a Key type.

Those relationships may have been hard to follow. Luckily, there's no reason to memorize all of them—I'm just making a point, which is that the familial relationship of all the keys doesn't matter. They're all keys at the end of the day. The difference is that they're all used for specific cases. All that said, you can start organizing keys by putting them all into two camps: global and local.

> **NOTE** Using keys, especially global keys, generally is not necessary or recommended. Global keys can almost always be replaced with some sort of global state management. The exceptions to that rule are the issue we saw earlier, and using some specialized key like PageStorageKey.

GLOBAL KEYS

Global keys are used to manage state and move widgets around the widget tree. For example, you could have a GlobalKey in a single widget that displays a checkbox, and use the widget on multiple pages. This key tells the framework to use the same instance of that widget. So, when you navigate to different pages to see that checkbox, its checked state will remain the same. If you check it on page A, it'll be checked on page B.

It's important to note that using global keys to manage state is not advised (by me or by the Flutter team). You'll likely want a more robust way to manage state, which I'll discuss throughout this book. Global keys aren't used often, and they impact performance; using local keys is more common. Later in the book, I'll show you how to use a global key when the time is right.

LOCAL KEYS

Local keys are all similar in that they're scoped to the build context in which you created the key. Deciding which one to use comes down to the case:

- ValueKey<T>—Value keys are best when the object you're adding a key to has a constant, unique property of some sort. For example, in a todo list app, each widget that displays a todo probably has a Todo.text that's constant and unique.
- ObjectKey—Object keys are perfect when you have objects that are of the same type, but that differ in their property values. Consider an object called "Product" in an e-commerce app: two products could have the same title (two different sellers could sell Brussels sprouts). And one seller could have multiple products. What makes a product unique is the combination of the product name and the seller name. So, the key is a literal object passed into an ObjectKey:

```
Key key = ObjectKey({
    "seller": product.seller,
    "product": product.title
})
```

- UniqueKey—Unique keys can be used if you're adding keys to children of a collection and the children don't know their values until they're created. In the sample app, the product cards don't know their color until they're created, so a unique key is a good option.
- PageStorageKey—This is a specialized key used to store page information, such as scroll location.

3.8   A final note

If you're experimenting with Flutter for the first time, this chapter may have been a lot to take in. I just introduced many concepts that are practical, and that you will use day to day when writing Flutter apps, and concepts that are more conceptual, about how Flutter works.

I would encourage you not to get *too* bogged down in the details. From this point forward, the book is completely action-based. That is, you'll learn by writing code. With that in mind, I don't think it's necessary that you understand 100% of how constraints work, or the element tree, or most of the other concepts. I wrote this chapter to expose you to concepts that will come up over and over again, which means you'll understand them better the more you see them.

I think if you are comfortable with the basic syntax and anatomy of *writing* widgets, you're in a good spot. You'll see many more columns and flexible widgets. You'll have plenty of chances to create UIs. This chapter represents the foundation, so that when we dive into other topics, like routing, we can focus specifically on routing. But you'll have lots of opportunities to practice and revisit what was covered in this chapter.

Summary

- In Flutter, *everything* is a widget, and widgets are just Dart classes that know how to describe their view.
- A widget can define any aspect of an application's view. Some widgets, such as Row, define aspects of layout. Some are less abstract and define structural elements, like Button and TextField.
- Flutter favors composition over inheritance. Composition defines a "has a" relationship, and inheritance defines an "is a" relationship.
- Every widget must contain a build method, and that method must return a widget.
- Widgets should be *immutable* in Flutter, but state objects shouldn't.
- Widgets have const constructors in most cases. You can, and should, omit the new and const keywords when creating widgets in Flutter.
- A StatefulWidget tracks its own internal state, via an associated state object. A StatelessWidget is "dumb" and is destroyed entirely when Flutter removes it from the widget tree.
- setState is used to tell Flutter to update some state and then repaint. It should not be given any async work to do.

- `initState` and other lifecycle methods are powerful tools on the state object.
- `BuildContext` is a *reference* to a widget's location in the widget tree. In practice, this means your widget can gather information about its place in the tree.
- The element tree is the smart one. It manages widgets, which are just blueprints for elements that are actually in use.
- In Flutter, widgets are rendered by their associated `RenderBox` objects. These render boxes are responsible for the telling the widget its actual, physical size. These objects receive *constraints* from their parent, and then use those to determine their actual size.
- The `Container` widget is a "convenience" widget that provides a whole slew of properties that you would otherwise get from individual widgets.
- Flutter `Row` and `Column` widgets use the concept of flex layouts, much like Flex-Box in CSS.

Part 2

Flutter user interaction, styles, and animations

Flutter is, at its core, an SDK for writing the view layer of mobile (and soon, web) apps. It includes an engine and a lot that's going on under the hood, but in this part, we mostly care about writing the UI itself.

This part of the book uses a static weather app to demonstrate how the UI aspect of Flutter is done. First, I'll walk through some of the important base features and widgets that you'll use again and again in Flutter apps. The chapters in this section—chapters 4, 5, and 6—cover the bare minimum of what you need to start a Flutter project.

In the following chapters, I'll take deeper dives in two important UI-related subjects, forms and gestures, to handle user input and animations that make your app beautiful.

Flutter UI: Important widgets, themes, and layout

Flutter isn't just a framework. It's a complete SDK. And perhaps the most exciting piece of this SDK to me, as a web developer, is the massive library of built-in widgets that make building the frontend of your mobile app easy.

This chapter and the following two are all about the user interface (UI) and making an app beautiful. This chapter includes exploring some of the widgets built into Flutter, layout, styling, and more. In the following chapters, I'll go a bit further into the UI and talk about forms and user input, as well as animations. Figure 4.1 shows the app I'll use to explain the Flutter UI in the next few chapters.

Figure 4.1   Screenshots of the weather app

In this chapter, in particular, we'll look at these high-level categories:

- *Structural widgets* that outline the app.
- *Themes and styling*, which this app is heavy on. We'll set the custom color scheme and look at the MediaQuery class to help with styling.
- Widgets that help with *layout*. This broad category includes building-block widgets like Table, Stack, and BoxConstraint, as well as some fantastic convenience widgets like TabBar, which provide features for free.
- Additional layout widgets, specifically ListView. This widget can be *scrollable* and uses something called the *builder* pattern in Flutter.

Before we get started, there are a couple of caveats and disclaimers that I'd like to mention:

- There's no way a single book or app could (or should) cover all (or even most) of Flutter's built-in widgets (or features). The intention of this book is learning, and although you won't learn about every single widget, you will learn how to find and use what you're looking for when the time comes. Flutter's documentation is among the best I've ever seen, and all of the widget descriptions are robust. The Flutter team is hard at work adding more widgets and plugins every day. You can find all the widgets and their descriptions in the official Widget Catalog: https://flutter.dev/docs/development/ui/widgets.
- This is a book about Flutter, but a lot of the code in the example app doesn't have anything to do with Flutter. For example, models are just models, regardless of the language and framework you're using. I won't leave you wondering, though. I'll point out the relevant code when the time is right; I just won't walk through it line by line.

- This chapter is presented in the order in which you'll likely write actual Flutter code in the wild. The consequence is that some of the first widgets discussed, such as `MaterialApp` and `Scaffold`, are more involved than widgets discussed later. I encourage you to push through the chapter, because the ideas behind these complicated widgets will become clear as you get more comfortable with widgets in general.

4.1 Setting up and configuring a Flutter app

In the source code, there is a chapter_4_5_6 directory. That's where this chapter begins.

DOWNLOADING THE SOURCE CODE The repository code can be downloaded as part of the source code from the book's website: www.manning.com/books/flutter-in-action.

Listing 4.1 Weather app file structure

```
weather_app
├── README.md
├── lib
│   ├── controller
│   │   ├── forecast_controller.dart      ◁─────
│   ├── main.dart          ◁──────
│   ├── models
│   │   ├── // models...
│   ├── page
│   │   ├── // pages...
│   ├── styles.dart          ◁──────
│   ├── utils
│   │   ├── // many utils files...
│   ├── widget
│       ├── // all the custom widget's for this app
├── pubspec.lock
└── pubspec.yaml          ◁──────
```

Controller initializes data for the app from a repository. All the data in this app is fake: it's randomly generated in the /utils/generate_weather_data file.

Entry point for this app

This app uses many colors. I made an AppColors class so it's easy to reference the colors. It extends Color from dart:ui, the class Flutter uses to define Color. This file will be covered in this chapter.

Contains new Flutter-specific configuration that I haven't discussed

Let's begin in the pubspec.yaml file.

4.1.1 Configuration: pubspec.yaml and main.dart

All Dart applications require a pubspec.yaml file, which describes some configurations for the app. Dart has a build system that builds your app, and the first thing it does when you run your app is look for a pubspec.yaml file. When building a Flutter app, several specific configuration items need to exist in the pubspec.yaml in order for the app to run.

Listing 4.2 pubspec.yaml configuration for the weather app

```
// weather_app/pubspec.yaml
name: weather_app
description: Chapters 4-6, Flutter in Action by Eric Windmill
version: 1.0.0+1
```

100   CHAPTER 4   *Flutter UI: Important widgets, themes, and layout*

```
environment:
  sdk: ">=2.0.0-dev.68.0 <3.0.0"

dependencies:
  flutter:
    sdk: flutter

flutter:
  uses-material-design: true
  fonts:
  - family: Cabin
    fonts:
    - asset: assets/fonts/Cabin-Regular.otf
    - asset: assets/fonts/Cabin-Bold.otf
    // ...
```

This app uses Material Design, and this flag tells Flutter to include the material package.

When importing a font, give it a family that's used to reference the font throughout the app.

List all the font variations you want to use, much as you listed images in the previous chapter.

Along with declaring assets and importing libraries (as discussed in chapter 3), this is the only information you need for your Flutter pubspec.yaml file.

In addition to pubspec.yaml, your app must have an entry point: a file that includes a main function. In Flutter apps, the entry point is, by convention, a file called main.dart.

Check out weather_app/main.dart. The main() function runs the app, as in every Dart program, but it's also useful for setting up some configuration for the app before the app runs, as shown in the next listing.

Listing 4.3   The weather app main function

```
void main() {
  AppSettings settings = AppSettings();

  // Don't allow landscape mode
  SystemChrome.setPreferredOrientations(
        [DeviceOrientation.portraitUp, DeviceOrientation.portraitDown])
      .then((_) => runApp(
        MyApp(settings: settings),
      ));
}
```

Creates an instance of AppSettings: a class I made to fake persisting user settings. I'll explain this in depth throughout this chapter.

Talks to the SystemChrome class, which is the subject of the next section

You must include a call to runApp and pass it your root-level widget!

This app's main function doesn't have to do anything except call runApp. This app happens to have some configuration and setup that it needs to do, but it's added to make a point. Your main function must call runApp, but it can execute whatever code you'd like, as any Dart function can. The following is an example of the bare minimum runApp function for a Flutter app:

```
main() => runApp(MyApp());
```

4.1.2 *SystemChrome*

`SystemChrome` is a Flutter class that exposes some easy methods to control how your app displays on the native platform. This is one of the only classes you'll ever use to manipulate the device itself (unless you're writing plugins, which is outside the scope of this chapter).

In this app, I'm using `SystemChrome.setPreferredOrientations` to restrict the app to portrait mode, as shown in the next listing. It also exposes methods to control what the phone's overlays look like. For example, if you have a lightly colored app, you can ensure that the time and battery icon on your phone's status bar are dark (and vice versa).

> **Listing 4.4 `setPreferredOrientations` in the weather app**

```
void main() {
  AppSettings settings = AppSettings();

  // Don't allow landscape mode
  SystemChrome.setPreferredOrientations([
      DeviceOrientation.portraitUp,
      DeviceOrientation.portraitDown,
    ])
    .then((_) => runApp(
      MyApp(settings: settings),
    ));
}
```

Use then(callback) to asynchronously execute code when a Future completes. This is also the entry point of your app. Passing a widget into runApp is always the entry point.

The `SystemChrome` class is something you'll set once and then forget. I'm showing it to you up front so that you're aware of it, but there's no need to spend too much time on it. If you're curious, you can learn more here: https://api.flutter.dev/flutter/services/SystemChrome-class.html.

Before moving on, I need to address the `then` function used in listing 4.4. Asynchronous programming in Dart has its own chapter, but if you're unfamiliar with it, here's a quick introduction.

Just in time: Dart futures

The entirety of chapter 9 is devoted to async Dart, but you won't get very far into Dart without seeing some async methods here and there. A *future* is the foundational class of all async programming in Dart.

A future is a lot like getting a receipt at a burger quick-serve restaurant. You, the burger orderer, tell the employee that you want a burger. The server at the restaurant says, "Okay, here's a receipt. This receipt guarantees that sometime in the future, I will give you a burger as soon as it's ready."

So you wait until the employee calls your number, and then they deliver on the guarantee of a burger. The receipt is the future. It's a guarantee that a value *will* exist, but it isn't quite ready.

(continued)

Futures are *thenable* (that is, "then-able"), so when you call a future, you can always say

```
myFutureMethod().then((returnValue) => ... do some code ... );
```

`Future.then` takes a callback, which will be executed when the future value resolves. In the burger restaurant, the callback is what you decide to do with the burger when you get it (such as eat it). The value passed into the callback is the return value of the original future:

```
Future<Burger> orderBurgerFromServer() async {
    return await prepareBurger();
}
```
prepareBurger takes time (for the burger to cook). When it's done, return it.

```
orderBurgerFromServer()
    .then((Burger burger) => eatBurger(burger));
```
The callback—(Burger burger) => eatBurger(burger);—will be passed the return value of orderBurgerFromServer without the future, once the future is finished processing.

The `orderBurgerFromServer` method returns the type `Future`, with the subtype `Burger` (which, in a program, looks like `Future<Burger>`). So, `orderBurgerFromServer` will process, and *then* the callback will be called with the return value passed as an argument.

Asynchronous programming is a big topic. This is meant as an introduction; don't get too bogged down.

That's it for app configuration. I'll be talking about widgets for the rest of the chapter, starting with the top-level widget: `MyApp` in the weather_app/main.dart file.

4.2 Structural widgets and more configuration

There are a few convenience widgets that you'll likely use in every Flutter app you build. They provide configuration and structure to your app, with little work from you. In this section, I'll explain the `MaterialApp` widget, `Scaffold`, `AppBar`, and `Theme`.

4.2.1 MaterialApp widget

The `MaterialApp` widget provides a ton of benefits that effect its entire widget subtree. This section is the beginning of our discussion of many widgets that provide helpful functionality for free.

`MaterialApp` is an extension of the generic top-level widget provided by Flutter: `WidgetsApp`. `WidgetsApp` is a convenience widget that abstracts away a number of features required for most mobile apps, such as setting up a navigator and using an app-wide theme. `WidgetsApp` is completely customizable and makes no assumptions about default configuration, style, or how the UI of your app is structured. So, while it abstracts away some difficult pieces of functionality in your app, it requires more work to set up than `MaterialApp` or `CupertinoApp`. In this book, I won't worry about `WidgetsApp`, because it's a base class for the other two and rarely used directly by the developer.

`MaterialApp` is even more convenient than `WidgetsApp`. It adds Material Design-specific functionality and styling options to your app. It doesn't just *help* set up the `Navigator`, it does it for you. If you use the Material app widget, you don't have to worry about implementing the animations that happen when a user navigates between pages: the widget takes care of that for you. It also allows you to use widgets that are specifically in the Material widgets collection, and there are plenty of those.

It's called a *Material app* because it leans on Material style guidelines.[1] For example, page animations from one route to another are designed as you'd expect on an Android device. And all of the widgets in the Material widget library have that standard Google look and feel. This can be a concern if you have a specific design system that isn't similar to Material, but there is no drawback to using `MaterialApp`, even if you don't want to use Material Design guidelines. Your theme is still fully customizable. (In fact, the example app you'll build doesn't look very "Material" at all. That's on purpose, to drive this point home.) You can overwrite routing animations, and you don't have to use the widgets in the Material library. The `MaterialApp` widget provides quite a bit of convenience, but everything is reversible.

In the weather app, the `MaterialApp` widget is used in the `build` method of the `MyApp` widget. This is the convention used in every Flutter app. Here's the code in the main.dart file in the app, showing the `main` function again, as well as the root widget.

> ### Listing 4.5 The top-level widget in main.dart

```
// weather_app/lib/main.dart
void main() {                                    ⟵——— App entry point
  AppSettings settings = AppSettings();

  // Don't allow landscape mode
  SystemChrome.setPreferredOrientations(
        [DeviceOrientation.portraitUp, DeviceOrientation.portraitDown])
      .then((_) => runApp(            ⟵
        MyApp(settings: settings),         runApp is passed MyApp, the
      ));                                  root of your Flutter app.
}

class MyApp extends StatelessWidget {    ⟵
  final AppSettings settings;                MyApp is just a widget,
                                             like everything else.
  const MyApp({Key key, this.settings}) : super(key: key);

  @override
  Widget build(BuildContext context) {
    // ...                                    The build method of MyApp returns
    return MaterialApp(             ⟵——————— a MaterialApp as the top-level app.
      title: 'Weather App',
```

---

[1]Check out the Material Design specs at https://material.io/design.

```
      debugShowCheckedModeBanner: false,
      theme: theme,
      home: PageContainer(settings: settings),
    );
  }
}
```

Again, this is standard in Flutter apps. Your top-level widget is one that you write yourself; in this case, MyApp. That widget turns around and uses MaterialApp in its build method. This effectively becomes the root of your application. Looking at that build method again, let's talk about the arguments being passed to MaterialApp.

Listing 4.6   The `build` method of the `MyApp` widget

```
//
@override
  Widget build(BuildContext context) {
    // ...
    return MaterialApp(
      title: 'Weather App',

      debugShowCheckedModeBanner: false,

      theme: theme,

      home: PageContainer(settings: settings),
    );
  }
```

Returns a MaterialApp

MaterialApp takes care of the app-wide theme (covered shortly).

Flag that removes a banner that's shown when you're developing an app and running it locally. I turned it off so the book's screenshots are cleaner.

home represents the app's home page, which can be any widget. PageContainer is a widget written for the weather app (covered later).

4.2.2   *The Scaffold widget*

Like the MaterialApp widget, Scaffold is a convenience widget that's designed to make applications (that follow Material guidelines) as easy as possible to build. The MaterialApp widget provides configuration and functionality to your app. Scaffold is the widget that gives your app *structure*. You can think of MaterialApp as the plumbing and electricity of your app, while Scaffold is the foundation and walls.

Like MaterialApp, Scaffold (figure 4.2) provides functionality that you'd otherwise have to write yourself. Again, even if you have highly custom design style, and it's not Material at all, you'll want to use Scaffold. Per the Flutter docs, Scaffold defines the "basic Material Design visual layout," which means it can make your app look like this pretty easily.

It provides functionality to add a *drawer* (an element that animates in from one

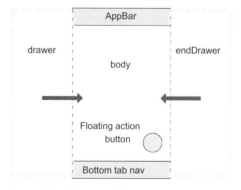

Figure 4.2   Diagram of the most important Scaffold widget properties

side and is commonly used for menus) and a *bottom sheet* (an element that animates into view from the bottom of the screen and is common in iOS-style apps). Unless you configure it otherwise, the AppBar in a scaffold is automatically set up to display a menu button in the top-left corner of your app, which will open the drawer; when you aren't on a screen that has a menu, the menu button changes to a back button. Those buttons are already wired up and work as expected.

Importantly, though, you can pick and choose which features you want and which you don't. If your app doesn't have a drawer-style menu, you can simply not pass it a drawer, and those automatic menu buttons will disappear.

The Scaffold widget provides many optional features, all of which you configure from the constructor. Here's the constructor method for the Scaffold class.

Listing 4.7 Scaffold full property list

```
// From Flutter source code. Scaffold constructor.
const Scaffold({
    Key key,
    this.appBar,
    this.body,
    this.floatingActionButton,
    this.floatingActionButtonLocation,
    this.floatingActionButtonAnimator,
    this.persistentFooterButtons,
    this.drawer,
    this.endDrawer,
    this.bottomNavigationBar,
    this.bottomSheet,
    this.backgroundColor,
    this.resizeToAvoidBottomPadding = true,
    this.primary = true,
  }) : assert(primary != null), super(key: key);
```

I wanted to show this so you can see that none of these properties are marked as @required. You can use an AppBar, but you don't have to. The same is true for drawers, navigation bars, and so on. For this app, I only used AppBar. The point is, again, that even if you're building an app that you don't want to look "Material," the Scaffold widget is valuable and I recommend using it.

In the weather app, you can see the scaffold in the ForecastPage widget.[2] It's common for each of the different screens in your application to have its own Scaffold widget.

The part I want to point out right now is at the very bottom of the file: the return statement of the ForecastPageState.build method. I only want to show you that Scaffold is just a widget, and like many widgets, most of the arguments are optional, making it highly customizable:

---

[2] ForecastPage is found in the directory at weather_app/lib/page/forecast_page.dart.

```
// weather_app/lib/page/forecast_page.dart
    return Scaffold(
        appBar: PreferredSize(...)        ◄─────

        body: GestureDetector(...)
```

> You can pass a widget to the appBar argument, and that widget will be placed at the top of the app screen. (AppBar and PreferredSize are covered in the next section.)

> body is a Scaffold argument that represents the main portion of the screen. If there is no app bar, body is essentially the entire screen.

Recall the `Scaffold` constructor method: it has over 10 named arguments. Here, I'm only using two. The point is that these widgets give you a lot but are highly customizable. In the next section, I'll show concrete examples of how a scaffold is used in the weather app.

4.2.3 *AppBar widget*

The `AppBar` widget is yet another convenience widget that gives you more features out of the box. `AppBar` is typically used in the `Scaffold.appBar` property, which fixes it to the top of the screen with a certain height.

The most notable feature of `AppBar` is that it provides navigation features for free. It automatically inserts a menu button if the app bar's parent is a scaffold and the `drawer` argument isn't `null`. And if the Navigator of your app detects that you're on a page that can navigate "back" (like a browser's back button), it automatically inserts a back button.

In the `AppBar` widget (figure 4.3), there are multiple parameters that expect widgets as arguments. These arguments correspond to specific positions within the app bar.

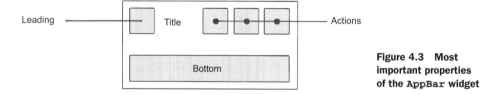

Figure 4.3   Most important properties of the `AppBar` widget

The property that handles these menu buttons and back buttons is called the *leading action,* and it can be configured with the `AppBar.leading` and `AppBar.automatically-ImplyLeading` properties. For example, maybe you don't want a menu button to appear. You can set `AppBar.automaticallyImplyLeading` to false and then pass the `leading` argument to whatever widget you wish. This will attempt to place that widget on the app bar's far-left side.

PREFERREDSIZE WIDGET

In Flutter, widget sizes are generally constrained by the parent. Once a widget knows its constraints, it chooses its own final size. I spoke about this quite a bit in chapter 3, but this concept's importance can't be overstated when it comes to the UI. The *constraints* passed to a widget by its parent tell the widget how big it *can* be, but they aren't concerned with its final size. The advantage of this system (as opposed to HTML, for example, where elements control their own constraints) is flexibility. It allows Flutter to make intelligent decisions about what your widgets should look like and removes some of that burden from the developer.

In some cases, flexibility isn't desirable, though. You may want to set explicit sizes for widgets. A good example is AppBar.

The AppBar class extends a widget called PreferredSize, which allows you to define an *explicit* height and width. Flutter will do its best to make sure the app bar is that size when the screen renders. This widget isn't commonly used in my experience, but it serves as an example for a valuable lesson.

The Scaffold.appBar property expects a widget that's specifically of the PreferredSize class, because it wants to know the size of the app bar before it sets constraints. In this app, I use a PreferredSize directly, rather than using an app bar in the Scaffold.appBar argument. The practical application is that you can wrap any widget in a PreferredSize and use it in place of the Material-specific AppBar widget. The lesson here is, again, that Flutter widgets are fleshed out by default while also being customizable. (There is a practical application, as well, which I'll cover in chapter 6.)

Listing 4.8 Using PreferredSize in a scaffold

Use PreferredSize to use any widget in the Scaffold.appBar
property. AppBar extends PreferredSize, and Scaffold.appBar
expects a PreferredSize, rather than an AppBar specifically.

```
// weather_app/lib/page/forecast_page.dart -- line ~217
return Scaffold(
    appBar: PreferredSize(

        preferredSize: Size.fromHeight(
            ui.appBarHeight(context),
        ),

        child: TransitionAppbar( ... )
    ),
);
```

PreferredSize's first argument: its preferredSize, which takes a Size class that defines a height and width

PreferredSize's second argument: its child. In this case, a widget called TransitionAppBar (see chapter 6), an AppBar that has custom animations written on it.

Now that I've talked about PreferredSize from a high level, let's look at the weather app for a concrete example. The point of using PreferredSize for this app is that the built-in AppBar widget doesn't provide a way to animate its colors by default. If you've poked around the app, you may have noticed that the colors change as the time of day changes. This required creating a custom widget, TransitionAppBar, that will be dissected in chapter 6; the important note here is that I've wrapped it in a PreferredSize, so the Scaffold accepts it in the appBar argument.

> **Named imports in Dart**
>
> You may have noticed in previous examples that I'm calling `ui.appBarHeight`, but `ui` doesn't seem to be a class. `ui` refers to the utils file with a name:
>
> ```
> import 'package:weather_app/utils/flutter_ui_utils.dart' as ui;
> ```
>
> This name requires you to prefix any class, method, or variable in that library with *ui*.

4.3   *Styling and themes in Flutter*

Styling your app in Flutter can be simpler than you'd expect. If you're diligent about setting up a theme when you start your Flutter app, you shouldn't have to do much work to keep the app looking consistent. The `Theme` widget allows you to set many default styles in your app, such as colors, font styles, button styles, and more. In this section, we'll look at how to use `Theme`, as well as other important pieces of styling in Flutter: media queries, fonts, animations, and Flutter's `Color` class.

4.3.1   *Theme widget*

The `Theme` widget lets you declare styles that will be, in some instances, automatically applied throughout your app. In instances where your styles are not applied or need to be overridden, the `Theme` widget is accessible anywhere in your widget tree.

To give you an idea of the many color-related styles that your theme can control, here are some (but not all) of the properties you can set on the widget that will permeate throughout the app. These properties affect all widgets in your app:

- `brightness` (which sets a dark or light theme)
- `primarySwatch`
- `primaryColor`
- `accentColor`

These are some properties that control specific features:

- `canvasColor`
- `scaffoldBackgroundColor`
- `dividerColor`
- `cardColor`
- `buttonColor`
- `errorColor`

That's only 6 of about 20 that are available just for colors. But there are almost 20 more arguments you can pass to `Theme` that set defaults for fonts, page animations, icon styles, and more. Some of those arguments expect classes themselves, which have their own properties, offering even more customizations for your app. The point is that the `Theme` widget is robust and can do a lot of the heavy lifting for you when it comes to styling.

While this level of theming is nice, it can be overwhelming to think about every last one of those properties. Flutter considered that, though. If you're using the `Material-App` widget at the root of your app, every property has a default value, and you can elect to only override the properties you care about. For example, `Theme.primaryColor` affects almost all widgets in your app: it changes the color of all widgets to your brand's color. In the app I'm building at my current job, we have an app that looks completely on brand (and not Material), and we only set eight properties on our theme.

In other words, you can be as granular or hands-off as you like. I've said it many times, but one of the aspects of Flutter that you should take advantage of is that it does so much for you *until* you decide you need more control. Let's look at how you can implement a theme in your Flutter app.

USING THEMES IN YOUR APP

The class you use to configure a theme is called `ThemeData`. To add a theme to your app, you pass a `ThemeData` object to the `MaterialApp.theme` property. You can also create your own `Theme` widget and pass it a `ThemeData` object. `Theme` is just a widget, which means you can use it anywhere you can use any widget!

The theme properties that any given widget uses are inherited from the *closest* `Theme` widget up the tree. In practice, this means you can create multiple `Theme` widgets throughout your app, which will override the top-level theme for everything in that subtree. Let's look at an example of using `ThemeData` in real life.

> **Listing 4.9 ThemeData in the weather app**

```
// weather_app/lib/main.dart
final theme = ThemeData(
  fontFamily: "Cabin",              ◁──  Tells Flutter to use the font that you
  primaryColor: AppColor.midnightSky,      told it about in the pubspec.yaml file
  accentColor: AppColor.midnightCloud,  ◁── AppColor is a class I created
  primaryTextTheme:                          because this app uses almost
      Theme.of(context).textTheme.apply(  ◁── all custom colors. You can find
        bodyColor: AppColor.textColorDark,   the class in styles.dart.
        displayColor: AppColor.textColorDark,
      ),                                   The apply method of theme classes
  textTheme: Theme.of(context).textTheme.apply(  copies the current theme but changes
      bodyColor: AppColor.textColorDark,         the properties you passed it.
      displayColor: AppColor.textColorDark,
    ),
);
```

The other case in which you'd use `ThemeData` is when you want to set a style property explicitly. For example, you may want to set a container's background to be the `accentColor` of the theme. Anywhere in your app, you can grab that theme data, thanks to `BuildContext`.

Earlier in the book, I mentioned that `BuildContext` provides information about a widget's place in the widget tree. This includes information about certain widgets that are higher in the tree, including `Theme`. If you want to know the `accentColor` of the theme for any given widget, you can say, "Hey, `BuildContext`, what's the accent color assigned to the `ThemeData` that's closest up the tree from this widget?" In the next section, I'll explain that sentence further and make it less abstract.

4.3.2   *MediaQuery and the of method*

If you came from web development, like I did, you may find writing styles in Flutter cumbersome at first—particularly spacing and layout. On the web, you use CSS; and in CSS, there are many different units of measurement that you can use anywhere sizing comes into play. In addition to the standard pixel, there are also units of measurement based on the percentage of space the element can take up, as well as a unit of measurement based on the size of the viewport.

In Flutter, there is only one unit of measurement: the logical pixel. As a consequence, most layout and sizing problems are solved with math, and much of this math is based on screen size. For example, you might want a widget to be one-third the width of the screen. Because there's no percentage unit of measurement, you have to grab the screen size programmatically by using the `MediaQuery` widget.

`MediaQuery` is a widget that's similar to `Theme` in that you can use `BuildContext` to access it anywhere in the app. This is done via a method of the `MediaQuery` class called `of`. The `of` method looks up the tree, finds the nearest `MediaQuery` class, and gives you a reference to that `MediaQuery` instance anywhere in your app. A few widgets built into Flutter provide an `of` method.

> **NOTE**   Later in the book, you'll see how you can create widgets that have their own `of` method, and how to access the state of those widgets anywhere in the tree. For now, all that matters is that certain built-in widgets can be accessed anywhere in your app.

As mentioned, the `MediaQuery` class is great for getting size information for the entire screen on which your app is rendered. You access that information by calling the static method `MediaQuery.of(context).size`, which returns a `Size` object with the device's width and height. Let me break that down a bit more.

Because it's a static method, you call `of` directly on the `MediaQuery` class, rather than on an instance of the class. Also, the `of` method can only provide the `MediaQuery` class if it knows the `BuildContext` in which `of` is called. That's why you pass it `context`. Finally, `size` is a getter of the `MediaQuery` class that represents the device's width and height.

Once you've grabbed the information, you can use it to determine the size of a widget, based on the screen size. For example, to get 80% of the width of the phone, you could write

```
final width = MediaQuery.of(context).size.width * 0.8;
```

Again, a widget's build context gives Flutter a reference to that widget's place in the tree. So, the `of` method—which always takes a context, regardless of which object it's defined on—basically says, "Hey, Flutter, give me a reference to the nearest widget of this type in the tree, above myself."

`MediaQuery` is the first place you should look if you're trying to get specific information about the physical device your app is running on, or if you want to manipulate the device. You can use it to

- Ask whether the phone is currently in portrait or landscape orientation
- Disable animations and invert colors for accessibility reasons
- Ask the phone whether the user has their text-size factor scaled up
- Set the padding for your entire app

In the weather app, I use `MediaQuery` to ensure that widgets are scaled to the proper size based on the size of the screen. Let's take a look at an example.

4.3.3   *ScreenAwareSize method*

Recall this code from the scaffold in the `ForecastPage`:

```
// weather_app/lib/page/forecast_page.dart -- line ~217
return Scaffold(
  appBar: PreferredSize(
    preferredSize: Size.fromHeight(ui.appBarHeight(context)),
    child: ...
    ),
  ),
```

The method `Size.fromHeight` is a constructor for the `Size` class that creates a `Size` object with the given height and an infinite width. That leaves the `ui.appBarHeight` method.

In the file at weather_app/lib/utils/flutter_ui_utils.dart, you'll find the code that defines the function `ui.appBarHeight(context)` from the previous code snippet, as shown in the following listing.

Listing 4.10   Screen-aware sizing methods

```
// weather_app/lib/utils/flutter_ui_utils.dart

final double kToolbarHeight = 56.0;
double appBarHeight(BuildContext context) {
  return screenAwareSize(kToolbarHeight, context);
}

const double kBaseHeight = 1200.0;
double screenAwareSize(double size, BuildContext context) {
  double drawingHeight = MediaQuery.of(context).size.height
      - MediaQuery.of(context).padding.top;
  return size * drawingHeight / kBaseHeight;
}
```

56.0 is the default height of the AppBar widget (copied from the Flutter source code).

Passes context into the method so I can use context to get MediaQuery information

The bulk of the functionality is in this line. I'm using the context to get information about the app and screen size.

`MediaQuery.of(context).size` returns a `size` that represents the screen size. `Media-Query.of(context).padding` returns a `Padding` that gives the padding details for the app itself; that is, the padding between the edge of the device screen and the top-level widget.

The purpose of these methods is to provide accurate sizing for the `PreferredSize` widget (and to see the `MediaQuery` class in action). These methods map the height of the app bar in the weather app to its appropriate size on *any given screen*. That is, if the "average" screen is 1,200 pixels tall, and on that screen the app bar is 56 pixels high, these functions give the equivalent height for the app bar on any given screen size.

> **NOTE**   The built-in `AppBar` widget is smart, but we need a custom widget because we'll eventually add custom style and animation to it.

Again, this function is used back in `ForecastPageState.Scaffold`:

```
// weather_app/lib/page/forecast_page.dart -- line ~217
return Scaffold(
  appBar: PreferredSize(
    preferredSize: Size.fromHeight(ui.appBarHeight(context)),
    child: ...
    ),
  ),
```

This bit of code tells the scaffold (the preferred size's parent) how big the app bar wants to be. Specifically, it tells Flutter to use a height to create a `Size` instance that's appropriate for any screen.

This example is specific, to be sure. The `appBarHeight` method is only useful for the app bar. The `screenAwareSize` method could be reused. In any case, the point is to show off the `MediaQuery` widget, which you'll likely use quite a bit when it comes to styling and layout.

For now, that's it for the `MediaQuery` class. We'll talk about `MediaQuery` more when we start using the `Canvas` widget, later in the book.

4.4   Common layout and UI widgets

This is the last big section in the entire book devoted to individual, basic layout widgets and widgets that represent physical UI elements. Of course, in Flutter, everything is a widget, so we'll never stop talking about widgets; but after this section, we'll be discussing complex widgets that *do stuff* rather than *show stuff*. In particular, in this section I cover `Stack`, `Table`, and `TabBar`: three built-in widgets used to define a layout.

4.4.1   Stack widget

`Stack` is what it sounds like. It's used to layer widgets (or stack them) on top of each other (figure 4.4). Its API can be used to tell Flutter exactly where to position widgets relative to the stack's border on the screen. (If you come from the web development world, this is much like `position: fixed` in CSS.) In this case, I'll use it to make a

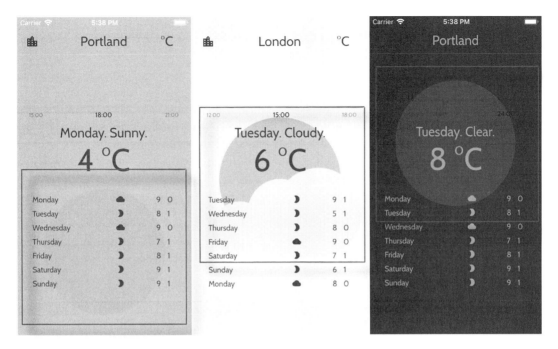

Figure 4.4   The background of the weather app

fancy background that reflects the time of day and current weather via images. The color of the sun will be animated to change as the time of day changes, and it'll also show clouds and weather conditions if the current weather reflects that.

The sun, the clouds, and the content are all different widgets stacked on top of each other. All the children of a stack are either *positioned* or (by default) *non-positioned*. Before I talk about the idea of positioning, it's important to understand the stack's default behavior.

The `Stack` widget treats non-positioned children in the same way a column or row treats its children. It aligns its children widgets by their top-left corners and lays them out, one after another, next to each other. You can tell a stack which direction to align in with its `alignment` property. For example, if you set the alignment to `horizontal`, then the stack will behave like a row. In other words, a stack can work *exactly* like a column, laying its children out vertically, unless you explicitly make a child positioned, in which case it's removed from the layout flow and placed where you tell it to be.

To make a widget *positioned*, you wrap it in a `Positioned` widget (figure 4.5). The positioned widget has these properties: `top`, `left`, `right`, `bottom`, `width`, and `height`. You don't have to set any of them, but you can set *at most* two horizontal properties (`left`, `right`, and `width`) and two vertical properties (`top`, `bottom`, and `height`). These properties tell Flutter where to paint the widget. The children are painted by the `RenderStack` algorithm:

1 It lays out all of its non-positioned children in the same way a row or column would. This tells the stack its final size. If there are no non-positioned children, then the stack tries to be as big as possible.

2 It lays out all of its positioned children relative to the stack's render box, using its properties: `top`, `left`, and so on. The positioned properties tell Flutter where to place the stack's children in relation to its parallel edge. For example, `top: 10.0` will place the positioned widget 10.0 pixels inset from the top edge of the stack's box.

3 Once everything is laid out, Flutter paints the widgets in order, with the first child being on the "bottom" of the stack.

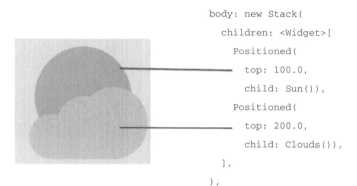

```
body: new Stack(
    children: <Widget>[
        Positioned(
            top: 100.0,
            child: Sun()),
        Positioned(
            top: 200.0,
            child: Clouds()),
    ],
),
```

Figure 4.5   An example of using `Positioned`

In the weather app, I use a stack in the `Forecast` page, in the `Scaffold.body` property. It has three children, which are basically all the content of the forecast page. It's important to note that the following code is *robust*. I encourage you to only pay attention to the lines that I've called out, and not spend too much time on the animation-related code.

Listing 4.11   `Stack` code in the forecast page

SlideTransition is covered in chapter 6. It represents the sun (or moon) painting in the background. Importantly, a SlideTransition contains a position property.

```
// weather_app/lib/page/forecast_page.dart -- line ~240
Stack(
    children: <Widget>[ ◁                    A Stack takes children, like a row or column.
        SlideTransition(
            position: _positionOffsetTween.animate( ◁    The position property is similar to the
                _animationController.drive(               Positioned.position property, because it
                    CurveTween(curve: Curves.bounceOut),  tells the widget explicitly where to be.
                ),                                        The difference is that the positioned
            ),                                            property on the SlideTransition class
            child: Sun(                                  takes a value that you can change.
                animation: _colorTween.animate(_animationController),
            ),
```

```
    ),
    SlideTransition(
      position: _cloudPositionOffsetTween.animate(
        _weatherConditionAnimationController.drive(
          CurveTween(curve: Curves.bounceOut),
        ),
      ),
      child: Clouds(
        isRaining: isRaining,
        animation: _cloudColorTween.animate(_animationController),
      ),
    ),
    Column(
      verticalDirection: VerticalDirection.up,
      children: <Widget>[
        forecastContent,
        mainContent,
        Flexible(child: timePickerRow),
      ],
    ),
  ],
),
```

The clouds are the second child in the stack, which overlaps the sun. ⟵ (points to `child: Clouds(`)

Represents all the content that's on the topmost layer of the stack ⟵ (points to `Column(`)

For the sake of example, this is what the app could look like if it wasn't animated. (This is the lesson for this portion of the chapter. I only showed you the previous code sample so you aren't confused when looking at the source code.)

Listing 4.12 Example of non-animated `Stack` code

```
Stack(
  children: <Widget>[
    Positioned(
        left: 100.0,
        top: 100.0,
      child: Sun(...),
    ),
    Positioned(
      left: 110.0,
      top: 110.0,
      child: Clouds(...),
    ),
    Column(
      children: <Widget>[
        forecastContent,
        mainContent,
        Flexible(child: timePickerRow),
      ]
    ),
  ],
),
```

`Stack` is your go-to widget if you want to place widgets either on top of each other or in an explicit way in relation to each other.

4.4.2   *Table widget*

The final static multi-child widget that I want to show you is `Table`, which uses a table layout algorithm to make a table of widgets (figure 4.6). Along with stacks, rows, and columns, tables are one of the core building blocks of layout (ignoring *scrollable* widgets for now). In the weather app, you'll use a table to lay out the weekly weather data on the lower half of the screen.

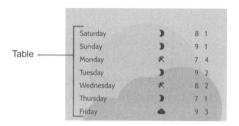

Figure 4.6   Screenshot showing the `Table` widget in the context of the weather app

`Table` is more strict than other layout widgets we've seen, because tables have (in theory) only one purpose: to display data in a readable manner. Tables line up widgets in columns and rows, and each cell in the table has the same height as every other cell in its row and the same width as every widget in its column. Flutter tables require explicit column widths, in advance, and no table cell can be empty. Given these rules, we implement a table in code similarly to other multi-child widgets. The simple version API looks like the next listing.

Listing 4.13   The API for the `Table` widget

Border for the entire table

```
Table(
    columnWidths: Map<int, TableColumnWidth>{},    ◁─┐  Map of the width of each column,
    border: Border(),                                  │  starting with the 0th row
    defaultColumnWidth: TableColumnWidth(),    ◁─┐
    defaultVerticalAlignment:                        │  Default column width, for column widths
        TableCellVerticalAlignment(),    ◁─┐          │  you don't want to explicitly set
    children: List<TableRow>[]                   │
);
```

List of the table rows. The table works by establishing rows, each of which has multiple children that represent the cells in the rows.

Optional argument that tells Flutter where to align the content of the cells within the cell itself

---

These are a few things worth mentioning when working with a table:

- You don't have to pass in `columnWidths`, but `defaultColumnWidth` cannot be `null`.
- `defaultColumnWidth` has a default argument, `FlexColumnWidth(1.0)`, so you don't have to pass in anything. But it can't be `null`. This effectively means you can't pass in `null` explicitly, or a variable that resolves to `null`. `defaulColumn-Width: null` would throw an error. However, because `defaultColumnWidth` has a default argument, you can ignore it if you want each column to be the same size, and you want the table to take up as much width as possible.
- You define column widths by passing a map to `columnWidths`. The map takes the index of the column (starting at 0) as the key and how much space you want the column to take up as the value. (More in a bit about `TableColumnWidth`.)

- The `children` argument expects `List<TableRow>`, so you can't just pass in any old widget willy nilly! This is a rare occurrence so far, but we'll see this happen more often as we get into more complex widgets throughout the book.
- `Border` is optional.
- `TableCellVerticalAlignment` only works if your row's children are `TableCells`, another widget we'll see in a bit.

With all that in mind, if you only pass in children (because the rest are optional), then all the columns will have the same width because they're all *flexed* (they size themselves in relation to each other). The elements in a row work together to take up the full width. I've configured the `Table` widget that displays on the forecast page to be spaced like figure 4.7. (The dotted lines are added for the example and are not actually in the code.)

Tuesday		)	9	1
Wednesday		)	5	1
Thursday		)	8	0
Friday		●	9	0
Saturday		)	7	1
Sunday		)	6	1
Monday		●	8	0

Figure 4.7   Table diagram with borders to show rows and columns

The following code defines the sizes of some rows. This is important: notice that there is no definition for the width of column 1!

Listing 4.14   Using `FixedColumnWidth` on rows 0, 2, and 3 makes row 1 flexed

```
// weather_app/lib/widget/forecast_table.dart -- line ~39
Table(
  columnWidths: {
    0: FixedColumnWidth(100.0),

    2: FixedColumnWidth(20.0),

    3: FixedColumnWidth(20.0),
  },
  defaultVerticalAlignment:
        TableCellVerticalAlignment.middle,

  children: <TableRow>[...],
);
```

Column I (0-based column count; second column visually) should take up as much space as possible, with the rest fixed. defaultColumnWidth defaults to being flexed, so you don't need to give it a width.

To reiterate, I skipped I in the map. This forces the table to be as big as possible and take up any leftover space after distributing the fixed widths to their columns.

Constant value on TableCellVerticalAlignment tells Flutter to lay out the content of the cells halfway between the cell top and cell bottom.

The remaining piece of the puzzle is `TableRow`. A table row is a bit simpler than a normal row. There are two important configurations to keep in mind, though:

- Every row in a table must have an equal number of children.
- You can, but don't have to, use `TableCell` in the children's sub-widget trees. `TableCell` doesn't have to be a direct child of `TableRow`, as long as somewhere above it in the widget tree it has a `TableRow` as an ancestor.

In this app, we're going to use `TableCell` because it makes alignment super easy. It knows how to control its children's alignment in the context of the table.

To complete this example, let's look at the code for the cells themselves. This table has four columns and seven rows. It would be cumbersome to write 28 widgets, so I'll generate each row. Later in this chapter, we'll explore what Flutter calls the *builder pattern*, which is important and used commonly in Flutter apps. The following lesson is a precursor to that.

Generating widgets from Dart's List.generate() constructor

Earlier in the book, I made it a point to tell you that *everything* in Flutter is Dart code. And what's more, Dart has features that make it specifically useful as a language to create a UI. Here, I want to show you a nifty example of how helpful it is that everything is in Dart code. Rather than pass a list to the `children` property of the table, we can use functions, constructors, and classes that return widgets.

Listing 4.15   Table code from the weather app

```
// weather_app/lib/widget/forecast_table.dart -- line ~39
Table(
  columnWidths: {
    0: FixedColumnWidth(100.0),
    2: FixedColumnWidth(20.0),
    3: FixedColumnWidth(20.0),
  },
  defaultVerticalAlignment: TableCellVerticalAlignment.middle,
  children: List.generate(7, (int index) {

    ForecastDay day = forecast.days[index];

    Weather dailyWeather =
        forecast.days[index].hourlyWeather[0];

    final weatherIcon =
        _getWeatherIcon(dailyWeather);

    return TableRow(
      children: [
        // ....
      ],
    ); // TableRow
  });
); // Table
```

Constructor for the Dart List class. It takes an int (the number of items the list will hold) and a callback to generate that many items in the list. The callback receives the current index as an argument and is called exactly as many times as the int it's passed; in this case, seven times.

Data our table cells will display. The interesting thing is that we're using the index to get different data for each iteration of a table row. For now, it's enough to know that forecast.days is a variable representing a list of daily weather descriptions.

More data we need. Not pertinent to Flutter, but provides hourly weather, which is used to display the current temperature.

Returns the correct icon to represent the weather based on the current weather

Returns whatever should be inserted into the generated list at the current index

This `List.generate` constructor function will execute at build time. If the concept seems confusing, it's fine to think of `List.generate` as a loop. It's functionally the same as writing something like this:

```
List<Widget> myList = [];
for (int i = 0; i < 7; i++) {
    myList.add(TableRow(...));
}
```

Just like that `for` loop, the `List.generate` constructor in the example code will run the code you give it seven times. (It's important to note that the index at each loop iteration will actually be 0-6, though.) At each iteration, you have an opportunity to do some logic—you have access to a different `index`. This means you can fetch the data for this widget without knowing what that data is.

`List.generate` is a Dart feature and not specific to Flutter. It's quite useful in Flutter, though, when you need to build several widgets for a row, column, table, or list. Specifically, `List.generate` is great when you know the number of items you want in the list, and they can be created programmatically. In this example, all the members of the list are the same widget type with the same configuration structure, but with different data.

Without using `List.generate`, we'd have to write more verbose code, which would look something like this:

```
Table (
  children: [
    TableRow(
        children: [
          TableCell(),
          TableCell(),
          TableCell(),
          TableCell(),
        ]
    ),
    TableRow(
      children: [
        TableCell(),
        TableCell(),
        TableCell(),
        TableCell(),
      ]
    ),
    //... etc., 5 more times
  ]
)
```

Ack! Even having stripped out all the actual content of each `TableCell`, you can see how that'd be cumbersome, especially because each group of rows and cells is the same as each other one. Using a function to programmatically build the rows is nice, and doing so is very common in Flutter.

WARNING One caveat in this example: this only works because the array of data is specifically ordered. If you can't guarantee the order of your list, and order matters, this may not be your best solution.

The important point is that this code is creating a list of widgets. And because the API for List.generate takes a callback as an argument, you can write the code to create each widget inline in your build method. It's not the most profound discovery, but it is an example of the advantage of writing purely Dart code, without a markup language.

The remaining code to implement is the table rows themselves, which only display basic widgets. TableCell, Text, Icon, and Padding are all used. For the sake of familiarizing yourself with Flutter code, here's a snippet of the rows.

Listing 4.16   Table cell examples from the weather app

This widget will be returned once
for each iteration of List.generate.

```
// weather_app/lib/widget/forecast_table.dart -- line ~52
children: List.generate(7, (int index) {
  ForecastDay day = forecast.days[index];
  Weather dailyWeather = forecast.days[index].hourlyWeather[0];
  final weatherIcon = _getWeatherIcon(dailyWeather);
  return TableRow(
    children: [
      TableCell(                          ⟵——— Displays the day of the week
        child: const Padding(
          padding: const EdgeInsets.all(4.0),
          child: ColorTransitionText(
            text: DateUtils.weekdays[dailyWeather.dateTime.weekday],
            style: textStyle,
            animation: textColorTween.animate(controller),
          ),
        ),
      ),
      TableCell(         ⟵——┐ Displays the icon that corresponds
        child: ColorTransitionIcon(   to current weather conditions
          icon: weatherIcon,
          animation: textColorTween.animate(controller),
          size: 16.0,
        ),
      ),
      TableCell(                          ⟵——— Displays the daily high temperature
        child: ColorTransitionText(
          text: _temperature(day.max).toString(),
          style: textStyle,
          animation: textColorTween.animate(controller),
        ),
      ),
      TableCell(                          ⟵——— Displays the daily low temperature
        child: ColorTransitionText(
          text: _temperature(day.min).toString(),
          style: textStyle,
          animation: textColorTween.animate(controller),
```

```
              ),
            ),
          ],
        );
      }),
      // ...
```

This is standard Flutter UI code. It's adding four table cells to each row with standard table cells and other widgets. Outside of the `List.generate` portion, there are no special tricks here.

Finally, let's look at the code that adds this `Table` widget to the tree. It's located in the `ForecastPageState.build` method.

Listing 4.17 A portion of the `ForecastPageState.build` method

```
// weather_app/lib/page/forecast_page.dart
return Scaffold(
      appBar: // ...
      body: Stack(          ← Houses all the content of the forecast page
        children: <Widget>[
          // ... sun and clouds positioned widgets
          // Important starts code here -- line ~264
          Column(          ← Reverses the direction of the column: the first child widget will be at the bottom.

            verticalDirection: VerticalDirection.up,
            children: <Widget>[

              forecastContent,          ← Variable that represents the Table widget

              mainContent,          ← More widgets in the weather app

              Flexible(child: timePickerRow),          ← Represents another widget we'll get to later
            ],
          ),
        ],
      ),
    );
```

Let's look at `VerticalDirection.up` before moving on. It's used to reverse the default flow of the column. I want the content of the column to be aligned at the bottom of the screen and laid out with the first child in the list at the bottom, the second "above" that, and so on. There are certainly other (more verbose) means of accomplishing this, but it's nice that you don't have to write your own layout code.

That was quite a bit about tables. Using them is generally not much different than using any other widgets, but the lessons in this section are valuable. Soon, you'll learn about the builder pattern, which is similar to the `List.generate` method.

4.4.3   *TabBar widget*

Tabs are a common UI element in mobile apps. The Flutter Material library provides built-in tab widgets that make it reasonably easy to work with tabs.

The built-in `TabBar` widget displays its children in a scrollable, horizontal view, and makes them "tappable." The widgets in the tab bar when tapped execute a callback that you can pass the tab bar widget. Tabs are most commonly used to switch between different pages or UI components without actually navigating. So, the callback passed to the tab bar's children widgets are most commonly used to swap out widgets on the page.

Figure 4.8 represents the basic idea behind tabs. When you click an element in the tab bar, the corresponding tab content changes. In the Flutter weather app, I use a tab bar to build the row of times that can be clicked to update the temperature for that time of day.

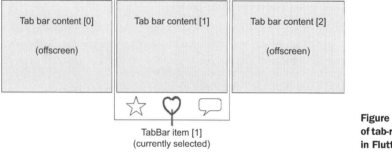

Figure 4.8   Diagram of tab-related widgets in Flutter

The `TabBar` widget (figure 4.9) has two important pieces: the children themselves (in this case, widgets that display the time of day the user wants to select) and the `TabController` (which handles the functionality).

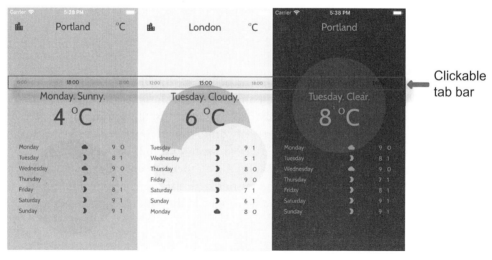

Figure 4.9   The outline shows the interactive tab bar.

TABCONTROLLER WIDGET

In Flutter, many widgets that involve interaction have corresponding controllers to manage events. For example, there's a `TextEditingController` that's used with widgets that allow users to type input. In this case, you're using a `TabController`. The controller is responsible for notifying the Flutter app when a new tab is selected so that your app can update the tab to display the desired content. The controller is created higher in the tree than the tab bar itself and then passed into the `TabBar` widget. This architecture is required because the parent of the tab bar is also the parent of the tab widgets. For a concrete example, the tab bar code in the weather app is in the weather_app/lib/widget/time_picker_row.dart file. Let's take a look.

In that file, you'll find the custom widget called `TimePickerRow`. It's a stateful widget whose main purpose is to display the tabs and also tell its parent when a tab change event happens, using `TabController`.

Listing 4.18 `TabController` and `TabBar` widget setup

Establishes properties that are passed into it. In this case, the widget expects a list of Strings, which are displayed as times of day ("12:00," "3:00," and so on).

```
// weather_app/lib/widget/time_picker_row.dart
class TimePickerRow extends StatefulWidget {
  final List<String> tabItems;

  final ForecastController forecastController;

  final void Function(int) onTabChange;

  final int startIndex;
// ...
}
```

Class that makes it easier to fetch forecast data. It's not important to Flutter, and I'll ignore it for now.

Callback the parent passes in. In this case, it's used to notify the parent when a new tab is selected.

Tells TabBar which tab is selected by default. In this case, the widget that represents the current time of day.

Those are the important properties passed into the widget itself, but the functionality all lives in the `State` object.

Listing 4.19 Implementing Flutter tabs in the weather app

```
// weather_app/lib/widget/time_picker_row.dart

// Full TimePickerRow widget
class TimePickerRow extends StatefulWidget {
  final List<String> tabItems;
  final ForecastController forecastController;
  final Function onTabChange;
  final int startIndex;

  const TimePickerRow({
    Key key,
    this.forecastController,
    this.tabItems,
```

```
      this.onTabChange,
      this.startIndex,
    }) : super(key: key);
```

A mixin that tells Flutter this widget has some properties that will animate. TabBars have built-in animations, so it's needed (discussed in chapter 6).

```
    @override
    _TimePickerRowState createState() => _TimePickerRowState();
  }


  class _TimePickerRowState extends State<TimePickerRow>
      with SingleTickerProviderStateMixin {
    TabController _tabController;
    int activeTabIndex;
```

Declares a tab controller to handle tab functionality. It's created in the constructor.

```
    @override
    void initState() {
      _tabController = TabController(
        length: utils.hours.length,
        vsync: this,
        initialIndex: widget.startIndex,
      );
```

Creates the controller. TabController must know how many tabs will exist.

I'm going to defer vsync to chapter 6 because it has to do with animations.

```
      _tabController.addListener(handleTabChange);
      super.initState();
    }
```

You can add a listener to your controller, to execute the callback whenever the tab changes.

```
    void handleTabChange() {
      if (_tabController.indexIsChanging) return;
      widget.onTabChange(_tabController.index);
      setState(() {
        activeTabIndex = _tabController.index;
      });
    }
```

Check that prevents a new event from starting in the middle of an animation

```
    // ...
  }
```

Just in time: listeners

This is the first time we've come across a *listener* in this book. Listeners aren't a specific object or type of object, but rather a naming convention that's used for different asynchronous functionality. There are many places in the Flutter library where you'll see the words *listener*, *change notifier*, and *stream*. They're all different flavors and pieces of the same kind of programming concept: observables.

Observables (known as *streams* in Dart) are covered thoroughly later in the book. Chapter 9 is devoted to async Dart. And before that, there's another brief explanation in chapter 7. In short, this topic is important and difficult to grok. For now, I'll focus on this specific example.

A listener is an aptly named piece of the "observable" ecosystem. It generally refers to a function that's called in response to some event that will happen at an unknown time. The function is just sitting around, *listening* for someone to say, "Okay, now's your time to execute."

The tab controller's `addListener` function is called when a user changes the tabs. This gives you a chance to update some values or state when a user changes tabs. So, for this specific example, the listener knows to execute the callback provided to it whenever a tab on the tab bar is tapped.

Along with listeners, `TabController` has getters that help you manage your tabs and corresponding content. Inside the _handleTabChange method, you could do something like this to make sure your app knows which is the "active" tab (the one that is currently displayed onscreen):

```
int activeTab;
void _handleTabChange() {
  setState(() =>
    this.activeTab = _tabController.index);       ←──  Returns the currently select tab
}                                                       index. In this example, I'm
                                                        assuming that some content relies
                                                        on our activeTab piece of state.
```

`setState` is also important here. In the weather app, when you tap a different time of day in the tab bar, the UI re-renders with the weather conditions for that time of day. This is possible because `setState` tells Flutter to re-render and to display the newly selected tab when it does. The `TabController.index` getter refers to the currently active tab.

The last note I'd like to make about `TabController` is that you don't ever have to change it directly. It's an object that's used to get information about the tabs and to update which tabs are active. But you only need to interact with it, not extend it into a custom class.

TABBAR WIDGET IN PRACTICE

Now that you've been exposed to the functionality of tabs and using the tab bar in Flutter, let's look at the example from the weather app in the next listing. While most of the tab bar functionality lives in the controller, we, the developers, care about the widget itself and passing it arguments. This is how the `TabBar` widget is used in the weather app.

Listing 4.20 TabBar widget in the build method

```
// weather_app/lib/widget/time_picker_row.dart          TabBar configuration
@override                                                options that define styles
Widget build(BuildContext context) {
  return TabBar(
    labelColor: Colors.black,                    ←──
    unselectedLabelColor: Colors.black38,             The TabController is passed into
    unselectedLabelStyle:                               the widget from the parent.
        Theme.of(context).textTheme.caption.copyWith(fontSize: 10.0),
    labelStyle:
        Theme.of(context).textTheme.caption.copyWith(fontSize: 12.0),
    indicatorColor: Colors.transparent,
    labelPadding: EdgeInsets.symmetric(horizontal: 48.0, vertical: 8.0),
    controller: _tabController,                                          ←──
```

```
    tabs: widget.tabItems.map((t) => Text(t)).toList(),

    isScrollable: true,
  );
}
```

By default, tabs aren't scrollable. This argument allows them to be scrollable.

tabItems are passed in from ForecastPage. I'm using Text, but it could be any widget. Icons are common. This is another instance of using Dart code to programmatically create widgets: it iterates through every String from tabItems and returns a Text widget for each one.

At this point, you've seen all the moving parts of `TabBar`. It's a lot of information, but the important take-aways are as follows:

- Using tabs requires a `TabController` and children widgets. The children are the widgets that are displayed and are tappable.
- The functionality to switch tabs when a widget in the tab bar is tapped is done via a callback. This callback should use the properties exposed by the `TabController` to tell Flutter when to render a new tab.

This is a common mental paradigm in Flutter, and you'll learn more about built-in controllers and updating Flutter to reflect interaction in chapter 5.

4.5   *ListView and builders*

`ListView` is arguably the most important widget thus far in the book. This is apparent from the sheer length of its documentation page on the Flutter website (https://api.flutter.dev/flutter/widgets/ListView-class.html). It's not only used frequently, but also introduces some patterns and ideas that are crucial in writing effective Flutter apps.

The `ListView` widget is like a column or row, in that it displays its children widgets in a line. Importantly, though, it is scrollable. It's used commonly when the number of children is unknown. For example, you could use a list view in a todo app to display all of your todos. There could be zero todos, or there could be many. The list view provides a way to say, "Hey, for each of these pieces of information, create a widget and add it to this list."

In the weather app, I'm using a `ListView` widget in the `SettingsPage` widget in lib/page/settings_page.dart (figure 4.10). It uses (fake-generated) data to build a scrollable list that lets you select which cities the user of the weather app cares about.

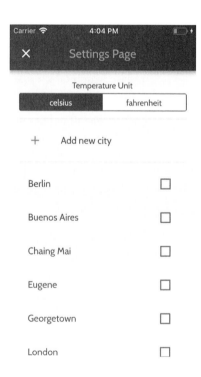

Figure 4.10   Weather app settings page

According to the docs, a list view is a "scrollable list of widgets arranged linearly." In human English, it's a scrollable row or column, depending on what axis you specify. The power of the list view is how flexible it is. It has a couple of different constructors that let you make choices based on the content of the list. If you have a static, small number of items to display, you can create a list view with the default constructor, and it will be created with code very similar to a row or column. This is the most performant option, but it may not be ideal if you have tens or hundreds of items to put in the list, or an unknown number of items.

What I want to focus on, though, is the builder pattern in Flutter. The *builder pattern* is found all over Flutter, and it essentially tells Flutter to create widgets as needed. In the default `ListView` constructor, Flutter builds all the children at once and then renders. The `ListView.builder` constructor takes a callback in the `itemBuilder` property, and that callback returns a widget. In our case, the callback will return a `ListTile` widget. This builder makes Flutter smarter about rendering items if you have a huge (or infinite) number of list items to display in your list. Flutter will only render the items that are visible on the screen.

Imagine a social media app like Twitter, which is essentially an infinite list of tweets. It wouldn't be possible to render all the tweets in that list every time some state changes, because there are an infinite number of tweets. So it renders them as needed, as the user scrolls the tweets into view. This is common in UI, and Flutter provides `ListView` as a built-in solution to this problem.

Let's look at an example in the weather app. `ListView` is used on the `SettingsPage`.

Listing 4.21 `ListView` builder code in the settings page

ListView expands on its main axis to be as big as possible. Because it's the child of a column in this app, it would expand infinitely if Expanded didn't constrain it.

Another way to protect against infinite size: tells ListView to try to be the size of its children

```
// weather_app/lib/page/settings_page.dart -- line ~83
Expanded(
    child: ListView.builder(
        shrinkWrap: true,
        itemCount: allAddedCities.length,
        itemBuilder: (BuildContext context, int index) {
            final City city = allAddedCities[index];
            return Dismissible(
                // ...
                child: CheckboxListTile(
                    value: city.active,
                    title: Text(city.name),
                    onChanged: (bool b) =>
                        _handleCityActiveChange(b, city),
                ),
            );
        },
    ),
);
```

A builder must know how many total items it will create.

Takes a callback that will be passed a build context and the index of the item in the list. This is the "builder" function: functions like it are used frequently in Flutter.

Convenience widget built into Flutter; displays a check box as children in ListView widgets

Controls the check box. The function you pass is called when the item is checked. I wrote the _handleCityActiveChange method to make sure the app knows which cities are active.

The list view probably seems more complicated than many of the previous widgets discussed in the book. The important piece of this example is the builder. The list view builder is a simple way to create a scrolling list with potentially infinite items. That's often what the builder pattern is used for in Flutter: to create widgets that display data when that data is unknown. It's worth noting that there are a couple other constructors for `ListView`:

- `ListView.separated` is similar to `ListView.builder` but takes two builder methods: one to create the list items and a second to create a separator that is placed between the list items.
- `ListView.custom` allows you to create a list view with custom children. This isn't quite as simple as updating the builder. Suppose you have a list view in which some list items should be a certain widget, and other list items are an entirely different widget. This is where the custom list view comes into play. It gives you fine-grained control over all aspects of how the list view renders its children. I'll talk more about creating customized list children later in this book.

`ListView` is one of the widgets that beautifully represents Flutter as a whole. It's clean and functional, but highly useful. The API is simple enough but doesn't pigeonhole you into a certain paradigm.

Summary

- Flutter includes a ton of convenient, structural widgets, like `MaterialApp`, `Scaffold`, and `AppBar`. These widgets give you an incredible amount for free: navigation, menu drawers, theming, and more.
- Use the `SystemChrome` class to manipulate features of the device itself, such as forcing the app to be in landscape or portrait mode.
- Use `MediaQuery` to get information about the screen size. This is useful if you want to size widgets in a way that ensures they scale by screen size.
- Use `Theme` to set style properties that will effect nearly every widget in your app.
- Use the stack widget to overlap widgets anywhere on the screen.
- Use the `Table` widget to lay out widgets in a table.
- The `ListView` and its builder constructor give you a fast, performant way to create lists with infinite items.

User interaction:
Forms and gestures

This chapter covers

- User interaction with gesture detectors
- Special interaction widgets like Dismissible
- Creating forms in Flutter
- Text input, drop-down lists, and more form elements
- Using keys to manage Flutter forms

This chapter is about letting users interact with your Flutter app. At the end of the day, all applications have one important job: to make it easy for a human to interact with data. And one side of that interaction is allowing users not only to look at data, but also to add to it and change it. This chapter is about that: letting users add and change data in your app. Specifically, this covers two different kinds of interactions: gestures and forms.

5.1 User interaction and gestures

Gestures are any kind of interaction event: taps, drags, pans, and more. First I'll cover how you detect and respond to these user gestures. To be honest, though, there isn't much involved here. Flutter has a convenience widget that allows you to add gesture detectors to any location of the widget tree that you'd like.

Without knowing it, perhaps, you've already used gestures. All the button widgets that have onPressed and onTap are just convenient wrappers around gesture detectors. Gesture detectors are used in a similar way.

5.1.1 The GestureDetector widget

The core user-interaction widget is called a GestureDetector. You can wrap this widget around any other widget and make that child widget listen for interaction from the user. The concept of *gesture detection* isn't complicated: you tell a widget to listen for interaction, and you give it a callback to execute when interaction is detected.

GestureDetector needs only two things passed to it: a widget (its child) and a callback to correspond to a gesture. Here's an example:

```
GestureDetector(
    onTap: () => print("tapped!"),
    child: Text("Tap Me"),
);
```

Although GestureDetector needs only one gesture callback, it can be passed many different callbacks and will respond differently based on the gesture it detects. These are some of the nearly 30 gestures it can work with:

- onTap
- onTapUp
- onTapDown
- onLongPress
- onDoubleTap
- onHorizontalDragStart
- onVerticalDragDown
- onPanDown
- onScaleStart

All of these arguments will call the callback you pass, and some will pass back "details." onTapUp, for example, passes back an instance of the TapUpDetails object, which exposes the globalPosition, or location on the screen that was tapped. Some of the more complicated gestures, like the drag-related ones, pass back more interesting properties. You can get details about the time a drag started, the position where it started, the position where it ended, and the velocity of the drag. This lets you manipulate drags based on direction, speed, and so on.

5.1.2 *GestureDetector in practice*

Let me show you how to use a gesture detector with a concrete example. In the weather app, I used a `GestureDetector` widget in the Forecast page (figure 5.1). If you double-tap anywhere on the screen, you should see the temperature switch between Fahrenheit and Celsius.

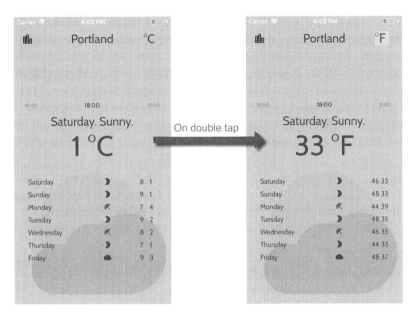

On double tap

Figure 5.1   Notice that the temperature changed from Celsius to Fahrenheit.

Implementing this should look familiar, because you've seen button widgets that use gesture callbacks. For this example, I wrapped the entire body of the `Scaffold` with a gesture detector in the `ForecastPageState` widget, as shown in the next listing.

Listing 5.1   Using the drag gesture

GestureDetector is the base widget that listens for interaction from a user.

```
// weather_app/lib/page/forecast_page.dart -- line ~ 246
body: GestureDetector(
    onDoubleTap: () {              ⟵─── One of many gestures defined by Flutter
      setState(() {
        widget.settings.selectedTemperature =
            widget.settings.selectedTemperature == TemperatureUnit.celsius
            ? TemperatureUnit.celsius
            : TemperatureUnit.fahrenheit;
      });
    },
    onVerticalDragUpdate: (DragUpdateDetails v)
            => _handleDragEnd(v, context),     ⟵─
    child: ColorTransitionBox(
    ...
```

GestureDetector takes any widget as a child. This child now responds to the gestures.

Another gesture that is more complicated, because it provides gesture details. Many gestures pass details about the gesture to their corresponding callbacks on the gesture detector.

The most complicated piece of this example is the `GestureDetector.onVertical-DragUpdate` argument. The callback passed as an argument to `GestureDetector.onVerticalDragUpdate` is called repeatedly as you drag your finger up or down on the screen. When called, it's passed information about the drag as an argument, as an instance of the `DragUpdateDetails` class. This class gives several details, but in this case, we only care about `DragUpdateDetails.globalPosition`. Anytime `onVerticalDragUpdate` is called, you have the opportunity to find out exactly where on the screen the user is dragging, and you can perform an action based on the location of the drag.

For example, you can see this in practice in the `ForecastPageState._handleDragEnd` method that's called when `onVerticalDragUpdate` is called. From a high level, this function does the same thing as choosing a tab in the `TimePickerRow` widget. That is, while dragging up and down, you're selecting a new time of day to display.

I made this happen by conceptually separating the screen into eight rows (because there are eight times of day to choose from in the tab bar). Basically, the top eighth of the screen represents 3:00 (the earliest time) in the `TimePickerRow`. The second eighth represents 6:00, and so on.

If you're dragging your finger vertically on the screen and enter the top 8th segment, then the app will update to display the forecast for that time of today (3:00 am). This is the code in the app.

Listing 5.2   Handling the end of a drag gesture

Uses MediaQuery to get the screen height, which will be used
to calculate the eight conceptual segments of the screen

```
// weather_app/lib/page/forecast_page.dart -- line ~90
void _handleDragEnd(DragUpdateDetails d, BuildContext context) {
    double screenHeight =
        MediaQuery.of(context).size.height;

    double dragEnd = d.globalPosition.dy;

    double percentage =
        (dragEnd / screenHeight) * 100.0;

    int scaleToTimesOfDay =
        (percentage ~/ 12).toInt();
    if (scaleToTimesOfDay > 7) scaleToTimesOfDay = 7;

    _handleStateChange(scaleToTimesOfDay);
}
```

globalPosition.dy is the position on the screen's y-axis where the pointer was located when onVerticalDragUpdate was called.

Uses the previous two numbers to convert the position to a number between 0 and 100 (representing 100% of the screen height)

Converts that number to a scale of 0-7 because we're working with a
0-based list to choose the time of day, and there are eight options

Generating mocked data for the weather app

If you're wondering where the numbers come from for the time-of-day numbers, they're generated in the `WeatherDataRepository` class, which creates fake data for the app. In a method called `dailyForecastGenerator`, I'm generating eight forecasts per day. In the UI, this is where the `TimerPickerRow` choices come from (3:00, 6:00, 9:00, and so on).

This function is quite long and entirely unimportant for learning Flutter; I'm only pointing it out for the sake of transparency. The important lines are annotated:

```
// weather_app/lib/utils/generate_weather_data.dart -- line ~51
ForecastDay dailyForecastGenerator(City city, int low, int high) {
    List<Weather> forecasts = [];
    int runningMin = 555;
    int runningMax = -555;

    for (int i = 0; i < 8; i++) {
      startDateTime =
        startDateTime.add(Duration(hours: 3));
      int temp = _random.nextInt(high);
      final tempBuilder = Temperature(
        current: temp,
        temperatureUnit: TemperatureUnit.celsius,
      );
      forecasts.add(
        Weather(
          city: city,
          dateTime: startDateTime,
          description: randomDescription,
          cloudCoveragePercentage:
              generateCloudCoverageNum(randomDescription),
          temperature: tempBuilder,
        ),
      );
      runningMin = math.min(runningMin, temp);
      runningMax = math.max(runningMax, temp);
    }
    final forecastDay = ForecastDay(
      hourlyWeather: forecasts,
      min: runningMin,
      max: runningMax,
      date: dailyDate,
    );
    dailyDate.add(Duration(days: 1));
    return forecastDay;}
```

> **Each day has eight forecasts, one for every three hours, starting with 3:00 am. This list will hold those weather conditions.**

> **Loops from 0–7**

> **startDateTime is 0:00 (midnight). Each loop iteration adds three hours.**

> **Shoves a new Weather instance into the list, generated randomly in this app**

With the generic gesture detector explanation under your belt, I'll now cover a built-in gesture-detecting widget that's very common in modern mobile apps: the `Dismissible` widget.

5.1.3   *The Dismissible widget*

The `Dismissible` widget is worth highlighting because it's trickier than some of the other gesture widgets. First, let's look at how it's used in the weather app. If you aren't sure what a dismissible is, you will recognize it in figure 5.2.

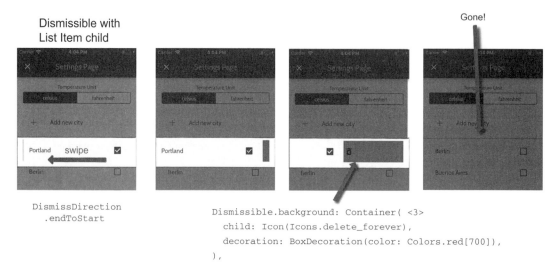

Figure 5.2   Example of a `Dismissible` widget

On the settings page, you can remove cities from your list of cities by swiping the list item from right to left. This is implemented in Flutter by using the built-in `Dismissible` widget, which requires more setup than most widgets. The easiest way to explain it is with an example, so take a look at the following listing.

Listing 5.3   Using `Dismissible` in a collection

Built-in widget that responds to specific user gestures

```
// weather_app/lib/page/settings_page.dart -- line ~81
child: ListView.builder(
    shrinkWrap: true,
    itemCount: allAddedCities.length,
    itemBuilder: (BuildContext context, int index) {
        final city = allAddedCities[index];
        return Dismissible(
            onDismissed: (DismissDirection dir)
                => _handleDismiss(dir, city),
            background: Container(
                child: Icon(Icons.delete_forever),
                decoration: BoxDecoration(color: Colors.red[700]),
            ),
            key: ValueKey(city),
            child: CheckboxListTile(
                value: city.active,
```

onDismissed is the dismissible's equivalent of a button's onTap. This is the widget's main action. The callback is passed an enum value of type DismissDirection, which you can use to take actions based on the direction the user swipes.

Widget that's shown as feedback behind the list item as it's dismissed.

You can pass it any widget as a child.

If the dismissible is a list item, as it is here, it must have a unique key. Dismissibles are almost always list items.

```
          title: Text(city.name),
          onChanged: (bool b) => _handleCityActiveChange(b, city),
        ),
      );
    }
  ),
),
```

Along with being another great example of what you get out of the box with Flutter, `Dismissible` is an important example because it's one of the only widgets that requires you to pass in a `Key`. This is also a great example of why keys are important. What would happen if you didn't give a dismissible in a list a key? Imagine this interaction in which there is a list with five dismissible items, and you dismiss the second item in the list:

1 Dismissible 2 is swiped and thus removed from the widget tree.
2 Flutter knows it's time to rebuild, because `setState` is called when the widget is dismissed.
3 At this point, the widget tree has changed, because there is one less `Dismissible` widget. All the elements in the element tree start looking at their associated widgets, as they always do when Flutter rebuilds. Because there are no keys, the elements compare the widgets in their location with the widgets that were previously in that location in the tree, before the re-render.
4 One element says, "Hey, my widget is gone! There's nothing in its location in the tree anymore. Maybe it's one of these others of the same type in this collection."
5 Now there's an issue, because there are five elements trying to claim only four widgets. All the other dismissibles already have elements pointing at them. This element thinks there is an error, because it should have a widget to point at.

It's an error in Flutter if there are elements that have no widget to point to. Using keys solves this, because an element knows by looking at the other dismissible widgets that they all have different keys, so the element knows it's no longer needed.

Other than that, `Dismissible` isn't that different relative to other user-interaction widgets. This is, in fact, the point. There are several widgets with built-in interactions, and you'll likely create some of your own. They all follow the same basic rules:

- They generally wrap widgets that aren't interactive, adding gesture-detecting functionality.
- They provide callbacks that pass details of the interaction event, which gives you a chance to handle the data however you'd like.

The `Dismissible` widget, to be sure, is a bit more involved than these basic rules. For example, it's an error in Flutter if there is no background widget to be displayed as the dismissible is moving across the screen. The background widget is easiest explained with figure 5.3, which you saw earlier.

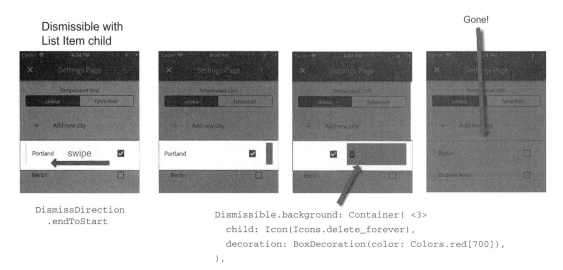

DismissDirection
.endToStart

Dismissible.background: Container(<3>
    child: Icon(Icons.delete_forever),
    decoration: BoxDecoration(color: Colors.red[700]),
),

Figure 5.3   Example of a dismissible widget

The takeaway I'd like you to get from this section is that all gesture-detecting widgets are implemented with similar APIs, although many have specific aspects that must be handled, such as the background of dismissibles. As a bonus takeaway, be aware that there are many built-in gesture-detecting and interaction widgets, which removes a lot of UI code that you'd otherwise have to write yourself. (You can find all the interaction widgets in this portion of the official widget catalog: https://flutter.dev/docs/development/ui/widgets/interaction.)

Some interactive widgets differ from what we've seen so far: widgets that take input, such as a text input field. They're similar, but a bit more involved. Those are covered in the remainder of this chapter, where we'll look at forms.

5.2   Flutter forms

On any platform, handling forms and user input can be tricky. There are often many moving parts: you have local state to deal with, events to listen to, and input values that must be massaged into something useful for your database. For the rest of this chapter, I'm going to spend a lot of time in one file, add_city_page.dart, and explain how forms work in Flutter.

In particular, there's a form on the add_city_page.dart page that allows the user to add new cities to the list of cities for which they want to see the weather. Let's talk about the requirements to make that happen:

- Create the UI for the form, including form fields for users to add the relevant data.
- Implement a way to grab all the data when the user submits the form. Ideally, this will all happen at once, rather than field by field. (Hint: keys are helpful!)

- Validate the data to ensure that it's usable. This functionality might actually be more useful on a field-by-field basis, which adds a new layer of complexity.
- Pass the data to the business logic, which will know how to submit the data to a database.

NOTE We aren't concerned with business logic or databases in this chapter, but we will cover talking to outside services later in the book.

For the next few pages, I will cover how Flutter forms work in general, and then show you the implementation in the weather app.

5.2.1 The Form widget

The Form widget is a wrapper of sorts that provides some handy methods and integrates with all the form field widgets in its subtree. The long and short of it is that the form manages the state of *all* the fields in the form, removing the need to handle state for each field individually. Before we dive too deep into the specifics, take a look at the high-level example from the weather app in figure 5.4. All the nitty-gritty details of each individual field have been removed, so you can see some key features: Form, FormState keys, and form fields. In the weather app, this form is created in weather_app/lib/page/add_city_page.dart.

```
Form(

    key: GlobalKey<FormState>,

    child: Column(

        children: [

                TextFormField(),

                TextFormField(),

                DropdownButtonFormField(),

                FormField(child: Checkbox()),

                // ...

                Button(

            child: Text("Submit"),

            onPressed: FormState.save()

        // ...
```

Figure 5.4   A form example

The built-in Flutter way to interact with Form is by passing it a key of type FormState. The widget associates that global key with this particular form's state object, giving you access to the state object anywhere. This is the only situation in which I recommend using global keys.

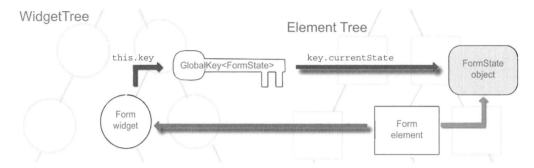

Figure 5.5 The form state is saved in the element tree.

Like all widgets, `Form` is managed by an associated `Element` (figure 5.5). That element has a reference to a `FormState` object, which is created internally in Flutter. This state object is an instance of the `State` class created for any `StatefulWidget`, but it's extended with more functionality. The difference is that this state object is created internally, when you create the global key. In practice, this means you can access it throughout your form with this key reference.

If this seems like a lot, that's okay. I'll talk about the `FormState` object more throughout this chapter.

5.2.2 *GlobalKey<FormState>*

Using a form key (which is actually a global key of subtype `FormState`) is *a lot* like using a controller on many other widgets. For example, in the previous chapter, we looked at `TabController`. `FormState` is a built-in class that provides a number of handy methods to maintain form logic. We'll see concrete examples in the next few pages, but some of the `FormState` methods you'll want to use are `FormState.save`, `FormState.reset`, and `FormState.validate`.

When working with forms, it's common to use keys, which can provide reference to the `FormState` object. All the logic and properties that live on the `FormState` object are accessible via this key that you'll make, which means you can interact with it in all the widgets that live in your form, including the children.

> **NOTE** This is one of very few places where using global keys is acceptable, and the only place in this book that I'll use global keys.

5.2.3 *The structure of the AddCityPage form*

The add_city_page.dart form is ~200 lines of code, and it does a lot. So, before I dive into explaining individual pieces, I want you to see the code as a whole (condensed for legibility). Listing 5.4 is meant to show you the overall API and moving parts involved in this feature, and in no way should you understand this code entirely at this moment. It's meant to be a reference that illustrates how everything fits together. The remainder of the code samples are going to be pieces of code extracted from this file; I encourage you to return to this sample as needed.

Listing 5.4   add_city_page.dart outline

```
import ...

class AddNewCityPage extends StatefulWidget {
  final AppSettings settings;
  const AddNewCityPage({Key key, this.settings}) : super(key: key);

  @override
  _AddNewCityPageState createState() => _AddNewCityPageState();
}

class _AddNewCityPageState extends State<AddNewCityPage> {
  City _newCity = City.fromUserInput();          ◁──── The value that will eventually
  bool _formChanged = false;            ◁──┐             be submitted to the repository
  bool _isDefaultFlag = false;             │
  FocusNode focusNode;                     └──── Used to manage the UI state of the form

  final GlobalKey<FormState> _formKey =
    GlobalKey<FormState>();              ◁──┐ Used to manage the
                                            └─ form's current state
  @override
  void initState() {...}

  @override
  void dispose() {...}

  bool validateTextFields() {...}

  @override
  Widget build(BuildContext context) {
    return Scaffold(
      appBar: AppBar(...),
      body: Padding(              The root of the Form. All form
        padding: ...             fields will be descendants of
        child: Form(       ◁──┘  this widget.
          key: _formKey,
          onChanged: _onFormChange,
          onWillPop: _onWillPop,
          child: Column(
            children: <Widget>[
              Padding(           ◁──── The City form field
                padding: ...
                child: TextFormField(...),
              ),
              Padding(           ◁──── The State or Territory form field
                padding: ...
                child: TextFormField(...),
              ),
              CountryDropdownField(...),   ◁──┘ The drop-down field in the form
              FormField(...),        ◁──── The check box for default city
```

```
                    Divider(...),
The bottom  ┌──▷ Row(
section of the │        mainAxisAlignment: MainAxisAlignment.end,
form, where  │        children: <Widget>[
the user     │          Padding(
cancels or   │            padding: ...
submits their│            child: FlatButton(...),   ◁─── The Cancel button
input        │          ),
                        Padding(
                          padding: ...
                          child: RaisedButton(       ◁─── The Submit button
                            color: Colors.blue[400],
                            child: Text("Submit"),
                            onPressed: _formChanged
                                ? () {
                                    if (_formKey.currentState.validate()) {
                                      _formKey.currentState.save();
                                      _handleAddNewCity();
                                      Navigator.pop(context);
                                    } else {
                                      FocusScope.of(context)
                                          .requestFocus(focusNode);
                                    }
                                  }
                                : null,
                          ),
                        )
            // ... many more closing brackets
        );
    }
    void _onFormChange() {...}
    void _handleAddNewCity() {...}
    Future<bool> _onWillPop() {
      if (!_formChanged) return Future<bool>.value(true);
      return showDialog<bool>(
        context: context,
        builder: (BuildContext context) {
          // the dialog shown when leaving the page with un-submitted data
          return AlertDialog(...);
      }
    }
}
```

5.2.4 *Implementing the form in the weather app*

Let's make this more concrete with the example from the weather app. The form is created in the weather_app/lib/page/add_city_page.dart file. In the following listing, I've omitted several lines that aren't important; we'll take a look at the complete example in a bit.

> **Listing 5.5 Initial form setup in the weather app**

```
// weather_app/lib/page/add_city_page.dart -- line ~ 9
class AddNewCityPage extends StatefulWidget {
  final AppSettings settings;
```

```
  const AddNewCityPage({Key key, this.settings}) : super(key: key);
  @override
  _AddNewCityPageState createState() => _AddNewCityPageState();
}

class _AddNewCityPageState extends State<AddNewCityPage> {
  // ...
  final GlobalKey<FormState> _formKey =
    GlobalKey<FormState>();                    ◀──────  This key now has a subtype of FormState, a
                                                        built-in Flutter state object. Flutter knows to
                                                        create a FormState object that's accessible
  @override                                             like a key.
  Widget build(BuildContext context) {
    return Scaffold(
      // ... appbar
      body: Padding(
        padding: EdgeInsets.symmetric(horizontal: 8.0),
        child: Form(                           ◀──────
          key: _formKey,          ◀──────               Creates a new Form widget. This is a stateful
          // ...                                         widget, and its state object is associated with
                                                         the key passed to its key object.
        The state of this form can be accessed
     anywhere in the widget subtree via the key.
```

In this code, I've created a form and given it a key. This is the important detail to remember in creating a form. Now I have a reference to the form's state object via that key.

> **NOTE** It's worth mentioning that you don't have to use the `Form` widget in Flutter in order for a user to enter text input. You can use the `TextInput` widget into your app and manage its input individually.

5.3 FormField widgets

Forms come in handy because of the functionality that `FormState` gives you when you're working with multiple input fields that are related to each other. In order for the form to manage these inputs, they must be `FormField` widgets. Any input widget can be wrapped in a form field, not just text input widgets. For example, you can use a `Checkbox` in your form, but it should be wrapped in a form field:

```
return FormField(
    child: Checkbox(
        //...
```

There are three `FormField` widgets:

- `FormField`—The standard field, which can turn any input widget into a form field
- `TextFormField`—A specialized form field that wraps a text field
- `DropdownButtonFormField`—A convenience widget that wraps a `DropdownButton` in a form field

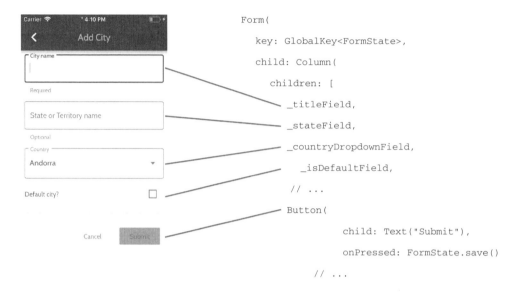

```
Form(
    key: GlobalKey<FormState>,
    child: Column(
        children: [
            _titleField,
            _stateField,
            _countryDropdownField,
             _isDefaultField,
            // ...
            Button(
                child: Text("Submit"),
                onPressed: FormState.save()
            // ...
```

Figure 5.6   Form field types

In the weather app, on the Add City page, there are four form fields (figure 5.6). I will use them to explain the different form field types and how to use form fields in general.

5.3.1   *The TextFormField widget*

In this section, we'll examine each of the three types found in the add_city_page.dart file. To start, let's look at TextFormField: I've created a variable for it called _titleField.

Listing 5.6   `TextFormField` example

A TextFormField is a combination of TextField and FormField, and takes many of the same arguments.

```
// weather_app/lib/page/add_city_page.dart -- line ~77
Padding(
    padding: const EdgeInsets.symetric(verical: 8.0),
    child: TextFormField(

        onSaved: (String val) => _newCity.name = val,

        decoration: InputDecoration(
            border: OutlineInputBorder(),
            helperText: "Required",
            labelText: "City name",
        ),
        autofocus: true,

        autoValidate: true,
```

A special FormField method: calls this method on all the child form fields

InputDecoration is a property of TextField, but not other form elements.

Also a property of TextField, used to ensure that this is the first thing highlighted when you navigate to this page

Indicates whether this field should validate after every interaction. In a bit, you'll see how to work with validators.

```
    validator: (String val) {                          ◁───   A special FormField
      if (val.isEmpty) return "Field cannot be left blank";    method: takes a
      return null;                                             callback that's used
    },                                                         to validate user input
  ),
```

The three properties of `TextFormField` that we're interested in right now are the `validator` callback, the `autoValidate` flag, and the `onSaved` callback:

- `validator` is an argument on all form fields that expects a callback. In the case of the text form field, the callback is passed the input of this field as a `String`. Whatever is returned from this callback is added as error text to the field. If it returns nothing or `null`, then the form field doesn't show any error text.

  The `validator` function is the first of a few that are handled by the `Form-State` on all the form fields in its subtree. You validate the user's input in form fields by calling `FormState.validate()`, which turns around and calls all of the form field's `validator` callbacks. Or you can `autoValidate` a widget.

- `autoValidate` is a Boolean flag on form fields. When set to `true`, it calls the `validator` callback straight away when the form field changes. This is my preferred method, simply because it gives the user instant feedback.

- `onSaved` works the same as `validator`. It's an argument that you pass a callback to. That callback is executed when `FormState.save()` is called.

The text field example in the weather app, again, is shown next.

Listing 5.7 `TextFormField` example

```
// weather_app/lib/page/add_city_page.dart -- line ~112
Widget get _titleField {
    // ...
    child: TextFormField(
      onSaved: (String val) => _newCity.name = val,     ◁──┐  This field will be validated
      decoration: InputDecoration(                          │  as soon as it gains focus,
      // ...                                                 │  and with every change.
      autofocus: true,
      autoValidate: true,                        ◁──┐  The only validation I'm checking
      validator: (String val) {                     │  for is that it's not blank.
        if (val.isEmpty)
            return "Field cannot be left blank";   ◁──┐  When FormState.onSave is
        return null;                                  │  called, I want to update the
      },                                              │  new instance of city with this
    ),                                                │  new name.
  ),
}
```

5.3.2 *The DropdownFormButton widget*

`DropdownFormButton` is another extension of the `FormField` widget. It works in much the same way `TextFormField` does, other than the data that it displays and how the user makes a selection. In the weather app, figure 5.7 shows what the `DropdownButton-FormField` looks like.

```
DropDownExpanded<Country>(
    decoration: InputDecoration(
        border: OutlineInputBorder(),
        labelText: "Country",
    ),
    value: _newCity.country ?? Country.AD,
    onChanged: (Country newSelection) {v
        setState(() =>
            _newCity.country = newSelection);
    },
    items: Country.ALL.map((Country country) {
        return DropdownMenuItem(
            value: country,
            child: Text(country.name));
//...
```

When element is tapped,
items are displayed.

Figure 5.7   Drop-down form field example

Flutter had a bug!

In this example, I'm using a class called `DropDownExpanded`, which I wrote myself. It's a replica of the `DropdownButtonFormField` widget in every way, except for the fact that it can optionally pass a Boolean flag called `isExpanded`. If `isExpanded` is true, my version of the drop-down widget will pass that information to its child, which is a `DropdownButton`; and if the built-in `DropDownButton` has `isExpanded` set to `true`, it wraps its children in an `Expanded` widget.

The bug is that the built-in `DropdownButtonFormField` doesn't accept an argument for `isExpanded`, so we can never access that property of its child (a `DropDownButton`) if we're using the form field version of that drop-down button.

This code inside `DropdownButton` creates the widget that displays the value of the button:

```
Widget result = DefaultTextStyle(
    style: _textStyle,
    child: Container(
    // ...
        child: Row(
            mainAxisAlignment: MainAxisAlignment.spaceBetween,
            mainAxisSize: MainAxisSize.min,
            children: <Widget>[
                widget.isExpanded
                    ? Expanded(child: innerItemsWidget)
                    : innerItemsWidget,
                // ...
```

This is where passing isExpanded makes a difference. Wrapping the children in Expanded matters if the phone's width is too small, because without it the widget tries to be as big as it wants, rather than being constrained.

Again, because the `isExpanded` property isn't exposed on the *form field* wrapper over the drop-down, `widget.isExpanded` will always be `false`.

By the time you're reading this, the bug might be fixed. But this is a cool lesson: if you want to tweak something in Flutter to work for you, it's pretty easy to do in a variety of ways. Everything is available to you as the developer in the API, and it's open-sourced.

Back in the weather app, take a look at how the drop-down form field is used. It's implemented similarly to `TextFormField`, with the notable difference that you pass it items to display when the button is tapped.

For this form field, I added a smaller, separate widget to make the code a bit more readable. It's called `CountryDropdownField`, and you can find it at weather_app/lib/widget/country_dropdown_field.dart.

Listing 5.8 `DropdownButtonFormField` example

```
// weather_app/lib/widget/country_dropdown_field.dart
class CountryDropdownField extends StatelessWidget {
  final Function onChanged;
  final Country country;

  const CountryDropdownField({
    Key key,
    this.onChanged,
    this.country,
  }) : super(key: key);

  @override
  Widget build(BuildContext context) {
    return Padding(
      padding: const EdgeInsets.symmetric(vertical: 8.0),
      child: DropDownExpanded<Country>(
        isExpanded: true,
        decoration: InputDecoration(
          border: OutlineInputBorder(),
          labelText: "Country",
        ),
        value: country ?? Country.AD,        ◁──

        onChanged: (Country newSelection)
              => onChanged(newSelection),     ◁──

        items: Country.ALL.map((Country country) {    ◁──
          return DropdownMenuItem(
            value: country,
            child: Text(country.name),
          );
        }).toList(),
      ),
    );
  }
}
```

value is the selected value that should be displayed when the dropdown is closed.

onChanged is called whenever a new selection is made. In Flutter's drop-down field widgets, the new selection is passed to the callback of onChanged.

items expects a list of a specific widget: DropdownMenuItem<T>. I decided to write a function that returns a List<DropdownMenuItem<Country>>, but you could also use a list literal.

I've only pointed out the different properties on this method. It also accepts an onSaved callback and a validator callback, as you'd expect on a form field.

This widget is built in the app from add_city_page.dart. The code is shown in the following listing.

Listing 5.9   Creating CountryDropdownField in the AddNewCity widget

```
// weather_app/lib/page/add_city_page.dart -- line ~93
CountryDropdownField(
  country: _newCity.country,
  onChanged: (newSelection) {
    setState(() => _newCity.country = newSelection);
  },
),
```

5.3.3   *Generic form fields*

If you want to use any other input type, such as a check box, date picker, or slider, you can wrap any widget in a FormField widget. This widget exposes the same functionality as the previous two form fields I've talked about, extending the functionality of all the other user input widgets.

In the weather app, I used a FormField to wrap the check box shown in figure 5.8. It's implemented much the same way as the previous form fields.

```
return FormField(
  onSaved: (val) => _newCity.active = _isDefaultFlag,
  enabled: _enabled,
  builder: (context) {
    return Row(
      mainAxisAlignment: MainAxisAlignment.spaceBetween,
      children: <Widget>[
        Text("Default city?"),
        Checkbox(
          value: _isDefaultFlag,
          onChanged: (val) {
            setState(() => _isDefaultFlag = val);
        // ...
```

Figure 5.8   A check box as a form field

Listing 5.10   Implementing the check box form field

```
class _AddNewCityPageState extends State<AddNewCityPage> {
  City _newCity = City.fromUserInput();
  bool _formChanged = false;
  bool _isDefaultFlag = false;                    ◁──  Boolean flag used to manage
  final GlobalKey<FormState> _formKey = GlobalKey<FormState>();    the check box's state.
  FocusNode focusNode;
```

```
// ... other class members
  Widget build(BuildContext context) {
  return Scaffold(
    // ... parent widgets
    // ... begin check box region -- line ~ 99
    FormField(

      onSaved: (val) => _newCity.active =
        _isDefaultFlag,

      builder: (context) {
        return Row(
          mainAxisAlignment: MainAxisAlignment.spaceBetween,
          children: <Widget>[
            Text("Default city?"),
            Checkbox(
              value: _isDefaultFlag,
              onChanged: (val) {
                setState(
                  () => _isDefaultFlag = val
                );
              },
            ),
          ],
        );
      },
    ),
  }
```

The onSaved callback is slightly different, because the form field doesn't know what type of data this field is working with. That's why I've used val as an argument, with no type declaration.

Many of the properties, such as onSaved, are the same as the previous widgets.

FormField takes a builder rather than a child. You can return whatever widget you'd like. Any widget can be a form field, technically.

You should call setState when updating the Boolean flag, so Flutter knows to re-render with the new check box state.

This check box behaves just as any check box outside of the form. You give it a Boolean so it knows whether it's checked.

That's really everything there is to know about form fields' functionality. Like all things in Flutter, the learning curve comes from knowing what you can do. When you figure out what that is, you'll realize that most of the UI work is taken care of by the framework. Now that you know how to create form fields, let's bring it all together with styling, UI, and using that FormState key to finish the functionality.

5.4 Form UI and working with focus nodes

I want to briefly explain styling forms. All in all, it follows the same pattern as styling any other widget in Flutter: you wrap fields in Padding, Center, and other layout widgets to work with the position, and style the widgets individually using whichever properties they expose. In addition to styling, I also want to discuss the FocusNode class, which is used to manage which fields gain focus programmatically.

5.4.1 InputDecoration

All input and form fields take an argument called decoration, which you pass an InputDecoration. This is a common pattern in Flutter. For example, the Container widget has a decoration argument, which you pass a BoxDecoration.

The InputDecoration class accepts many arguments that you can use to style your form field. You can set the background color, change the colors based on whether the field has focus, change the shape of the field, style all the text—in both the input and the helper labels—and more.

In the weather app, I opted for the outlined look shown in figure 5.9. And when you focus into the input, the label text animates to the top. It's pretty slick.

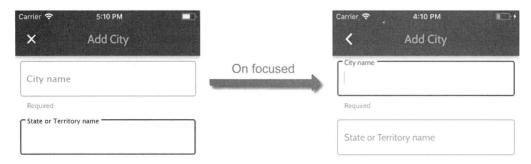

Figure 5.9   Adding smooth UI animations to form fields

This was all done via the `decoration` property and required no additional work on my part. I used another class, provided by the framework, to make all that happen. Here's the code in the second text field.

Listing 5.11   `InputDecoration` example

```
// weather_app/lib/page/add_city_page.dart -- line ~75
  Padding(
    padding: const EdgeInsets.symmetric(vertical: 8.0),
    child: TextFormField(
      focusNode: focusNode,
      onSaved: (String val) => print(val),
      decoration: InputDecoration(
        border: OutlineInputBorder(),

        helperText: "Optional",

        labelText: "State or Territory name",
      ),
      validator: (String val) {
        if (val.isEmpty) {
          return "Field cannot be left blank";
        }
        return null;
      },
    ),
  ),
```

> This OutlineInputBorder, provided by Flutter, does all the heavy lifting.

> The helper text is always displayed, unless there is a validation error. The error replaces the helper text in that case.

> The label text is always displayed.

> This validator is very similar to previous validator methods.

The point is this: that's some top-notch UI, but there's no need to pull in an external library, and there isn't much code to write. It's in the widget library that already exists in the framework by default.

5.4.2   *Improving the UI with FocusNodes*

Recall the `TextFormField` widget you saw earlier. The widget takes a named argument called `autoFocus`. Here's a refresher:

```
// weather_app/lib/page/add_city_page.dart -- line ~112
TextFormField(
  onSaved: (String val) => _newCity.name = val,
  decoration: InputDecoration(
    border: OutlineInputBorder(),
    helperText: "Required",
    labelText: "City name",
  ),
  autofocus: true,              <──┐ Ensures that this form field has
  autovalidate: _formChanged,        focus as soon as the page renders
  validator: (String val) {
    if (val.isEmpty) return "Field cannot be left blank";
    return null;
  },
),
```

This kind of experience is expected by users today. Reducing the number of taps or interactions required will go a long way toward making your app a joy to use.

Along with `autofocus`, you can also programmatically move focus in a form with an object called `FocusNode`. In your app, you might want to change focus based on an external event or a validation error. For example, a user might be signing up for your app and accidentally leave a required field blank on the sign-up form. A good user experience would give that blank field focus automatically.

In the weather app, the form is set up in such a way that it won't let the user submit the form if the two text fields are blank. Specifically, if the user presses Submit and the `State` field is blank, then the validation error is shown and the focus is given to that text field. This is done with just a few lines of code.

To start, you have to create a focus node. There's nothing special happening here; we're just defining and creating a `FocusNode` object. Since focus nodes are long-lived objects, you manage their lifecycle using a `State` object. We'll look at lifecycle in depth later, but the lifecycle of widgets gives you the ability to create and destroy long-lived objects in unison with the widget itself. Create a `FocusNode` instance inside the `initState()` method, as shown here:

```
// weather_app/lib/page/add_city_page.dart -- line ~17
class _AddNewCityPageState extends State<AddNewCityPage> {
  City _newCity = City.fromUserInput();
  bool _formChanged = false;
  bool _isDefaultFlag = false;
  final GlobalKey<FormState> _formKey = GlobalKey<FormState>();
  FocusNode focusNode;              <──┐ Defines the focus node

  @override
  void initState() {
```

```
    super.initState();
    focusNode = FocusNode();            ◁——   To manage the lifecycle, create the focus node in
}                                              the initState method so it can be disposed later.
```

A focus node is passed to a text field. Let's pass it to the second TextFormField in the form, which is assigned to the _stateName variable:

```
// weather_app/lib/page/add_city_page.dart -- line ~75
  Padding(
    padding: const EdgeInsets.symmetric(vertical: 8.0),
    child: TextFormField(
      focusNode: focusNode,
      onSaved: (String val) => print(val),        ◁——   Text form fields have a named
      decoration: InputDecoration(                       argument called focusNode that
        border: OutlineInputBorder(),                    expects a focus node. This associates
        helperText: "Optional",                          that focus node with this widget.
        labelText: "State or Territory name",
      ),
      validator: (String val) {              ◁——   We'll look at FormState.validate method
        if (val.isEmpty) {                           soon. For now, it's enough to know that
          return "Field cannot be left blank";       this validator is called before the form
        }                                            submits and will throw a validation
        return null;                                 error if the value is empty.
      },
    ),
  ),
```

That's all there is to associating a focus node with a widget. Now we have to wire up the logic. Remember, the goal is to give that second widget focus whenever the user tries to submit the form when the text fields are empty. This logic lives in the callback passed to the Submit button's onPressed argument:

```
// weather_app/lib/page/add_city_page.dart -- line ~80
RaisedButton(
  color: Colors.blue[400],                  Form state methods are
  child: Text("Submit"),                    discussed in the next section.
  onPressed: _formChanged                    _formKey.currentState.validate ()
      ? () {                                 returns false if the validator
          if (_formKey.currentState.validate()) {  ◁——  callbacks fail.
            _formKey.currentState.save();
            _handleAddNewCity();
            Navigator.pop(context);
          } else {
            FocusScope.of(context)
                .requestFocus(focusNode);   ◁——   FocusScope is the widget that
          }                                        manages passing focus to the
        }                                          appropriate nodes.
      : null,
),
```

The line of code that actually requests focus for a node should look somewhat familiar. It's using that old of method again to grab a reference to a widget somewhere else in the tree. In this case, it's grabbing the `FocusScope` widget. This class has a method called `requestFocus` that will attempt to give focus to the text field associated with the focus node passed in. In our case, that's the `_stateName` text field.

That's the bulk of using focus nodes. It can get more complicated, but the foundation remains the same. If you want to programmatically give focus to any text field, you have to use a `FocusNode` widget and request focus for it.

5.5 *Managing form state with form methods*

At this point, I've talked about nearly all the pieces of the puzzle needed to use forms in Flutter. Let's tie it all together and learn how to use the form state itself. In particular, we care about how to respond to changes in the form, and what the app should do when the user is finished with the form. These things are achieved with a couple of methods of the `Form` widget and `FormState`.

In the weather app, the best place to start is the top of the form's build method again. Earlier in this chapter, I briefly showed the beginning of the build method, but I omitted some important lines.

Listing 5.12   Form methods

A blank City object that's submitted to the database when the form is submitted

```
// weather_app/lib/page/add_city_page.dart -- line ~17
class _AddNewCityPageState extends State<AddNewCityPage> {
  City _newCity = City.fromUserInput();
  bool _formChanged = false;
  bool _isDefaultFlag = false;
  final GlobalKey<FormState> _formKey = GlobalKey<FormState>();
  FocusNode focusNode;

  @override
  Widget build(BuildContext context) {
    return Scaffold(
      appBar: AppBar(
        //...
      body: Padding(
        padding: const EdgeInsets.symmetric(horizontal: 8.0),
        child: Form(
          key: _formKey,
          onChanged: _onFormChange,
          onWillPop: _onWillPop,
          child: Column(
          // ... form fields
        ),
      ),
    ),
  );
```

This flag is switched to true as soon as the form is updated the first time. We can use it to handle how the form behaves based on whether the user is actually trying to use the form.

Called when any form field is changed

Called when the user is going to leave the page. This method is extremely useful, as I'll show you in a bit.

5.5.1 Form.onChange

onChanged and onWillPop are the only two methods the form itself expects. First, take a look at how onChanged is used in the weather app:

```
// weather_app/lib/page/add_city_page.dart -- line ~160
void _onFormChange() {
  if (_formChanged) return;          ◁──┐  If _formChanged is already true,
  setState(() {                         │  prevents Flutter from re-rendering by
    _formChanged = true;   ◁──┐         │  preventing setState from being called
  });                         │
}
```

Sets the _formChanged flag to true and calls setState so that Flutter knows to re-render widgets that rely on this flag for configuration

The neat part is that Flutter knows to re-render widgets that rely on this flag for configuration. I use that flag for two things. First, it tells Flutter to not worry about auto-validating if the form is still blank. If autoValidate is on, the callback you give to autoValidate is called as soon as the widget renders, which means every field would fail validation and show an error before the user even has a chance to type anything in.

Listing 5.13 Conditional auto-validation

```
// weather_app/lib/page/add_city_page.dart -- line ~112
TextFormField(
  onSaved: (String val) => _newCity.name = val,
  decoration: InputDecoration(
    border: OutlineInputBorder(),
    helperText: "Required",
    labelText: "City name",
  ),
  autofocus: true,                        Doesn't auto-validate until the
  autovalidate: _formChanged,   ◁──┘      user has interacted with the form
  validator: (String val) {
    if (val.isEmpty) return "Field cannot be left blank";
    return null;
  },
),
```

The second use is more interesting to me: buttons are disabled if their onPressed callback is null (figure 5.10). There's no reason the user should be able to submit something if they haven't changed the form, so we can programmatically make the button disabled to start out:

```
// weather_app/lib/page/add_city_page.dart -- line ~80
RaisedButton(
  color: Colors.blue[400],
  child: Text("Submit"),          If formChanged is false, the callback
  onPressed: _formChanged   ◁──┘  should be null, disabling the button.
```

```
      ? () {
        if (_formKey.currentState.validate()) {
          _formKey.currentState.save();
          _handleAddNewCity();
          Navigator.pop(context);
        } else {
          FocusScope.of(context).requestFocus(focusNode);
        }
      }
    : null,
),
```

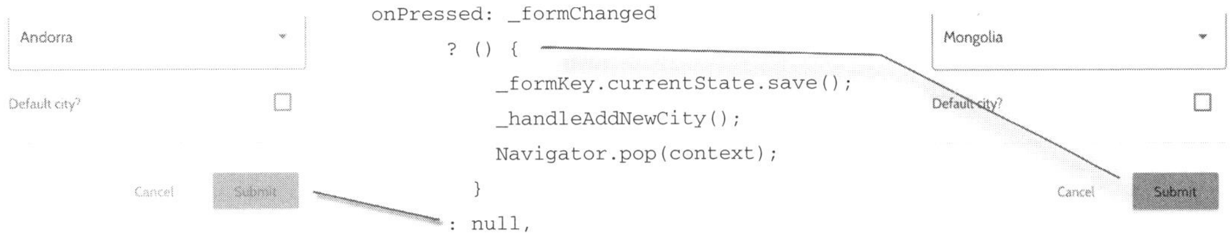

Figure 5.10 Buttons are disabled if the callback is `null`.

5.5.2 FormState.save

The most important part of forms, of course, is submitting the data. The `Form` widget wraps up this process with the `FormState.save` method. In the previous code snippet, I removed the code block that's executed when the Submit button is pressed. The following listing shows the full example.

Listing 5.14 Saving the form state from a button

```
// weather_app/lib/page/add_city_page.dart -- line ~80
RaisedButton(
  color: Colors.blue[400],
  child: Text("Submit"),
  onPressed: _formChanged
      ? () {
          if (_formKey.currentState.validate()) {
            _formKey.currentState.save();

            _handleAddNewCity();

            Navigator.pop(context);
          } else {
            FocusScope.of(context).requestFocus(focusNode);
          }
        }
      : null,
),
```

Constructs a new city object from the various form values and adds it to the database

Method that calls FormState.save. Keys are just references to widgets. If the widget is stateful, you can access its state via the Key.currentState getter. In this case, this is a reference to the FormState.

When the form is submitted, the user probably doesn't care about being on this page anymore, so navigates back.

The magic is really in the _formKey.currentState.save() method. I mentioned it earlier, but this method tells the form to find all the form fields in this portion of the app's widget tree and call onSaved. In the weather app, particularly, that means three methods are called, as shown in the following listing.

Listing 5.15   Methods called when the form is saved

```
// weather_app/lib/page/add_city_page.dart -- line ~42
  @override
  Widget build(BuildContext context) {
    return Scaffold(
      appBar: AppBar(...),
      body: Padding(
        padding: const EdgeInsets.symmetric(horizontal: 8.0),
        child: Form(
          key: _formKey,
          onChanged: _onFormChange,
          onWillPop: _onWillPop,
          child: ListView(
            shrinkWrap: true,
            children: <Widget>[
              Padding(
                padding: const EdgeInsets.symmetric(vertical: 8.0),
                // Form field -- line ~42
                child: TextFormField(
                  onSaved: (String val) =>
                    _newCity.name = val,            ◁──┐  Sets the city name on the new
                  // ...                                │  City object to the value of the
                                                        │  first text field
              Padding(
                padding: const EdgeInsets.symmetric(vertical: 8.0),
                // Form field -- line ~77
                child: TextFormField(
                  focusNode: focusNode,                   I'm printing out here, because I don't
                  onSaved: (String val) =>                actually care about the state. I only
                    print(val),            ◁──────────── included it for an extra example.
                  // ...

              // Begin check box Form Field -- line 99
              FormField(
                onSaved: (val) =>
                  _newCity.active = _isDefaultFlag,  ◁─┐ Again, sets the proper value
                builder: (context) {                   │ on the new city object when
                                                       │ the form is submitted
      // ... remainder of class
```

That's the core value of the Form widget in a nutshell: the onSaved methods make it easy to work with forms that could, in theory, be way more complex.

The _handleAddNewCity() method isn't Flutter specific, but in the interest of showing the full functionality, here it is:

```
// weather_app/lib/page/add_city_page.dart -- line ~167
  void _handleAddNewCity() {
    final city = City(
      name: _newCity.name,
      country: _newCity.country,
      active: true,
    );

    allAddedCities.add(city);
  }
```

Creates a new city instance to add to
the list of cities for which the user
wants to see weather information

Adds the new city to
the user's list of cities

The final neat trick with forms lets you be clever with the way the app behaves when the user wants to leave the form.

5.5.3 *Form.onWillPop*

You've likely filled out long, complicated forms. Particularly in a mobile app, nothing is worse than having to re-fill the form because you needed to navigate away for some reason.

Flutter has a built-in way to handle such situations via the Form.onWillPop method. This method gives you the chance to execute a function when the user is about to leave a form page for any reason. In the weather app, I decided to make the user confirm that they want to leave the page if they start filling out the app and then try to press the Back button (figure 5.11). Another good option would be to save the form information in some way, so that you could populate the form with that information if the user came back to the page.

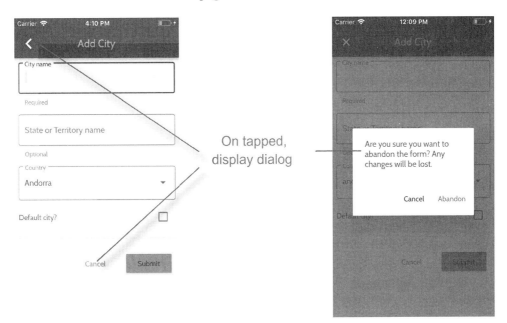

Figure 5.11 Displaying an alert dialog

The code for the app is all handled in the _onWillPop method. It's called from the form here:

```
// weather_app/lib/page/add_city_page.dart -- line ~50
body: Padding(
  padding: const EdgeInsets.symmetric(horizontal: 8.0),
  child: Form(
    key: _formKey,
    onChanged: _onFormChange,
    onWillPop: _onWillPop,          ⟵── Called when the user is
    child: Column(...)                   navigating away from the form
  ),
);
```

And this listing shows the part we care about.

Listing 5.16   Using `onWillPop` on a form page

The callback passed to Form.onWillPop
must return a Future<bool>.
```
     // weather_app/lib/page/add_city_page.dart -- line ~176
└──▷ Future<bool> _onWillPop() {

       if (!_formChanged)                           If the user hasn't changed the form,
           return Future<bool>.value(true);   ⟵──  there's no reason to concern ourselves
                                                    about routing away, because there's
                                                    no information to be lost.
    ▷  return showDialog<bool>(
         context: context,
         builder: (BuildContext context) {          A dialog that expects a message, as
           return AlertDialog(            ⟵──       well as actions for the user to take,
             content: Text(                          such as Cancel and Save
Shows a dialog that    "Are you sure you want to abandon
asks the user if they   the form? Any changes will be lost."
want to navigate away.  ),
(showDialog is a built-  actions: <Widget>[
in Flutter method; see     FlatButton(
chapter 7.)                  child: Text("Cancel"),
                             onPressed: () =>
                                 Navigator.pop(context, false),  ⟵──  If the user decides they
                             textColor: Colors.black,                 don't want to navigate away,
                           ),                                         returns call Navigator.pop,
                           FlatButton(                                which removes the modal
                             child: Text("Abandon"),                  and passes a value of false
                             textColor: Colors.red,                   back to the method
                             onPressed: () =>
                                 Navigator.pop(context, true),   ⟵──  If they do want to navigate
                           ),                                         away, does the same action
                         ],                                           but passes true back from
                       );                                             the dialog
                     });
     }
```

There's a bit in this section about routing and Navigator, which will be covered in depth in the future. For now, just know a couple of things:

- A dialog is a route as far as the navigator is concerned.
- Any route can pass a value back to the previous route via the pop method.

So, the showDialog method is technically routing to a new route (showing the dialog). Then, when the user taps the Cancel or Abandon button, the modal (which is a route) passes back false or true to the outer function, _onWillPop. This function returns a Future<bool>, so it's just waiting for the return value from showDialog, which it returns to the Form.onWillPop method.

Routing is a big subject, and I don't expect you to get it from one paragraph. The point is that when the Form.onWillPop method is called by the form, it expects to eventually receive a boolean. If it receives false, then it won't let the navigator return the previous page. If it receives true, it will.

Summary

- User interaction in flutter is handled via two kinds of widgets: inputs and gesture detectors.
- Flutter handles gestures and user interaction events via GestureDetector widgets.
- If you want to programmatically give focus to any text field, you have to use a FocusNode widget and request focus for it.
- A gesture detector can listen for many gestures via its various callbacks. These are only 5 of about 30:
  - onTap
  - onLongPress
  - onDoubleTap
  - onVerticalDragDown
  - onPanDown
- Built-in widgets listen for these gestures as well: Dismissible, Button, Form-Field, and many more.
- Flutter forms are convenient wrappers around several input widgets that make managing complex forms easier.
- A form's state can be managed with a GlobalKey<FormState>, which is a reference to a FormState object.
- Forms are aware of widgets below them in the widget tree that are wrapped in FormField widgets, and can take advantage of this relationship.
- Form fields provide several methods: onChange, onSave, and validator. These methods are used to respond to user actions and wire up to the FormState.
- Forms have two valuable methods: onChange and onWillPop.

Pushing pixels: Flutter animations and using the canvas

6

This chapter covers

- Using AnimatedWidget
- Using the canvas and the CustomPaint class
- The Paint class
- Animation controllers, tweens, and tickers
- SlideTransition, TweenSequence, and other convenience widgets

The built-in widgets you've seen so far are all about building a structural interface with Flutter. In this chapter, we'll explore a couple of new widgets to create custom animations, as well as look at the Canvas widget. These widgets are used to tell Flutter *exactly* what we want it to paint on the screen. In particular, we'll look at two things:

- *Animations*—In the weather app, almost every display widget on the screen will animate in some way. All the text will change color, all the background objects will change color and move around the screen, and the icons will change shape and color. The most interesting note here is that the app will still be buttery smooth, despite changing entirely with almost every interaction from a user.

  The bulk of the logic needed to build these animations is in the `forecast_ page` and a couple of methods are in the `forecast_controller`. We'll cover most of that in the next section, which covers animating the `Sun` class from start to finish.

- *The canvas*—We're going to make the cloud shape in the background from scratch, using the `Canvas` widget. The canvas allows you to tell Flutter what to draw, pixel by pixel. It requires math, and it's fun.

But before we jump in, this topic requires some conceptual explanations of animations in applications.

6.1 Introducing Flutter animations

Using animations is perhaps the best thing you can do to make an app feel polished, slick, and intuitive. Animations are often an afterthought, because they can require a fair amount of work. Luckily, many built-in widgets in Flutter, especially Material Design widgets, have motion animations out of the box. And custom animations aren't much harder to create, either.

In general, there are two main types of animations in Flutter: tween animations and physics-based animations. *Tween animations*, which we're looking at in this chapter, are animations that have a defined start and finish. For example, in the weather app, when you choose a different time and the sun and cloud background animate to a new location on the screen, they know that end position before the animation starts running.

A *physics-based animation*, on the other hand, relies on user interaction. A good example is a *fling*, which you've probably seen in many apps. The harder you swipe your finger up on a long list that is scrollable, the faster and longer the scroll will take place. Physics-based animations are out of the scope of this chapter, but they're similar enough, and the foundation is the same. From here on out, I will be referring specifically to tween animations when I say *animations*.

> **NOTE** If you're interested in physics animations, this video by Tensor Programming is the best resource I've found: www.youtube.com/watch?v= LHZ0KSvTTqQ.

An animation in Flutter is built by combining four pieces that you have to implement for each animation. The rest of this section is devoted to explaining these pieces:

- A tween
- A curve
- An animation controller
- A ticker (via a `TickerProvider`)

6.1.1   *Tweens*

A *tween* is an object that's given a start value and an end value for whichever property you're animating (such as color, opacity, or position on the screen). Tweens tell Flutter how to transition between the start value and the end value. Tween is an apt name: it's short for "in-betweening."

For example, a tween that changes color might have a start value of `yellow` and an end value of `red`. The animation library will do the heavy lifting of determining the values in between yellow and red at every stage in the animation.

> **NOTE**   The concept of tweens is not specific to Flutter. Writing animations on many different platforms involves tweens. Refer to this Wikipedia article if you'd like to learn about tweens in general: https://en.wikipedia.org/wiki/ Inbetweening.

Tweens map the value at any given moment in an animation to a number between 0.0 and 1.0. If you wanted to animate a color from yellow to red, it may look something like figure 6.1 (but with many more steps than I can diagram).

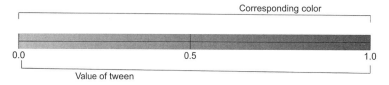

Figure 6.1   Example of tween values

> **NOTE**   In reality, there is a tween value (between 0.0 and 1.0) for each frame. This means that if your app is performing at its best possible frame rate, there will be 60 tween values per second in the animation.

Again, it's important to understand that Flutter is determining those tween values for you. Tweens are declarative: you only have to tell Flutter the start and end values, and it handles calculating the values in between the start and finish.

In the weather app, the position of the sun animates depending on the time of the day selected in the tab bar. Rather than using a color-based tween, like the previous example, with start and end values that are colors, animating a widget's position is done by changing its offset on each (figure 6.2). An *offset* describes the location of a widget relative to its own original position.

Remember, we'll see concrete examples of tweens throughout this chapter. At this point, I only want you to understand what a tween is, not how to implement it.

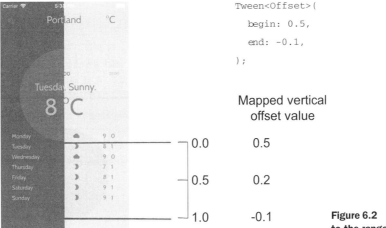

```
Tween<Offset>(
  begin: 0.5,
  end: -0.1,
);
```

Mapped vertical
offset value

0.0	0.5
0.5	0.2
1.0	-0.1

Figure 6.2   Tweens map a value to the range of 0.0 to 1.0.

6.1.2   *Animation curves*

A *curve* is used to adjust the *rate of change* of an animation over time, allowing the animation to speed up or slow down at specific points, rather than move at a constant speed. Flutter comes with a set of common, predefined curves in the Curves class. The default curve is called *linear*, because it moves at a constant speed.

Understanding curves is best done by comparing a linear curve, which is the default, to another common curve, called an *ease in* (figure 6.3). The ease-in curve tells the animation to start slowly and then increase its speed as it animates.

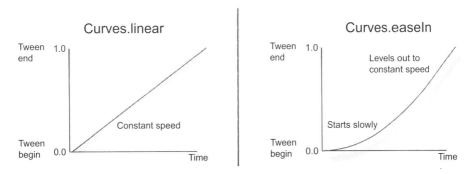

Figure 6.3   Ease-in curve compared to a default linear curve

To be clear, I'll say again that this section is just about concepts. Code examples are coming.[1]

---

[1]This page provides a look at many common curves: https://easings.net/en. They aren't specific to Flutter.

6.1.3   *Ticker providers*

Tickers are special in that they are specific to Flutter. Animations on all platforms work similarly, but they might not call this piece of functionality a ticker.

A ticker houses the logic that lives under the hood and gives the whole animation life. Tickers can be used by any object that wants to be notified every time a frame change triggers. Any time the screen changes in Flutter—or on any digital device, for that matter—there's actually a series of tiny, subsecond re-renders that make the change look natural.

> **NOTE**   Flutter re-renders at 60 frames per second. Animations are, in reality, Flutter re-rendering quite quickly, all the while painting animated objects at a small, increasing interval between the object's start value and its final value. It happens so fast that it looks smooth to our naked, human eyeballs.

Tickers may seem complicated, but they're aptly named and easy to understand if you consider each frame in a re-render as a "tick," like the tick of a clock's second hand. In practice, tickers are easy to use. You may never even have to deal with a ticker directly because Flutter provides a class called `TickerProvider` that does just what its name suggests: it provides a ticker for your widget.

The most common way to use this is to extend a `State` class from a `StatefulWidget` with a `TickerProviderStateMixin`. This gives your stateful widget all the internal functionality it needs to be notified about frame changes:

```
class _MyAnimationState extends State<MyAnimation>
        with TickerProviderStateMixin {}
```

I'm required to say, again, that this discussion is about concepts—we aren't writing code yet. However, the difference with tickers is that adding `with TickerProvider-StateMixin` to your class is all the code you'll need to write to use them. That class extends your widget with special methods needed to handle animations, but they're mostly used internally by Flutter.

6.1.4   *AnimationController*

Finally, animations are orchestrated by an object called `AnimationController`. The `AnimationController` object does what its name implies: controls animations. It's aware of the `Ticker` object, which gives it life and tells the controller each time there's a new frame, or tick. The animation controller then knows how to look at the widgets you'd like to animate, and calculate their updated value on each tick, based on the widget's tweens and curves.

The `AnimationController` class contains methods that start and stop animations, reset an animation, play an animation in reverse, and repeat it indefinitely. The class also has getters that give you information about the animation as it's happening. The only required arguments to create an `AnimationController` are a ticker and a time duration (how long the animation should last from start to finish). Because your `State` object extends `TickerProviderStateMixin`, the widget itself is the ticker.

In listing 6.1, you can see how to create an animation controller. This is a barebones example of making an animation controller that animates the color of a widget. It's meant to show the controller, not the tweens and curves. Also, this is a generic example, and it isn't from the weather app. Because there are so many moving parts, it's valuable to look at a simple example before diving into the implemented code.

Listing 6.1 Animation controller example

Extending the TickerProviderStateMixin class makes this (the State object) a ticker.

```
class _AnimatedContainerState extends State<AnimatedContainer>
      with TickerProviderStateMixin {
  AnimationController _controller;

  @override
  void initState() {
    super.initState();
    _controller = AnimationController(
      vsync: this,
      duration: new Duration(milliseconds: 1000),
    );

    startAnimation();
  }

  Future<void> startAnimation() async {
    await _controller.forward();
  }
  @override
  Widget build(BuildContext context) {
    return Container(
      color: _colorTween.animate(_controller).value;
      child: //...
    );
  }
}
```

You must pass a ticker into the vsync property on all animation controllers. In this case (and most cases), the ticker will be the State object itself (this).

The length of time the animation lasts from start to finish, using the Duration class from Dart

AnimationController.forward tells the controller to start the animation.

You animate a value by calling animate on a tween and passing it an AnimationController. This returns an Animation, from which you can pull out the value property. The value property is what you really want out of this whole process.

That's the core of what you need for every animation you'll ever make in Flutter: a controller to ... er ... control everything, a ticker to give it life, and a tween to map the value of that ticker to a value you can use. Curves, as you'll see, are optional because all tweens have a default curve value.

6.1.5 *AnimatedWidget*

The last thing an animation needs, because otherwise it would be useless, is the widget that you actually want to animate. The widget you want to animate isn't the same widget that extends `TickerStateProviderMixin`, but rather is the child (or children) of that widget. The concepts discussed previously in this chapter are all about setting up an animation. In short, they all work together to get a new *value* from a tween at every frame change. That value needs to be given to a widget, though. For example, if you're animating an object's color from yellow to red, the concepts discussed so far are about calculating the updated color value at every frame change. Now you need to give that color value to a widget. This can be done most simply with `AnimatedWidget`, a built-in object in the Flutter SDK.

`AnimatedWidget` is a class that extends `StatefulWidget` and has a bit more functionality. I encourage you to look at the source code for the `AnimatedWidget` class on GitHub (http://mng.bz/6w4G); you may be surprised how simple it is.

> **WARNING**   In animations, there are a lot of moving parts. This is a prime example of a concept that is difficult to grok at first, but that will "click" more easily once you've seen the bigger picture. With that in mind, don't get too caught up on any single paragraph. Continue moving forward, even if you're not quite sure about something. Examples will make the concepts more concrete.

The internal logic of an animated widget is fairly simple. It's a stateful widget that knows to rebuild when the value of its property *listenable* changes. It's your job to pass a `Listenable` object into the animated widget. `Listenable` is a class that emits new values asynchronously to any object that wants to listen to it. In the context of animations, `AnimatedWidget` is a class that "listens" for new values being emitted from a tween as an animation is happening.

To be more concrete, `Animation` is a subclass of `Listenable`, and therefore an animated widget can respond to new values from an animation and rebuild when necessary. You can create and return an animation from a method on `Tween` objects, aptly named `Tween.animate(AnimationController)`. So, you can pass the return value of calling `Tween.animate` to an `AnimatedWidget`, which will then know to rebuild each time that value updates.

Let me break that down a bit more with an example, because there are a lot of moving parts. Let's look at the `Sun` widget from the weather app, which represents the background of the app. Although the sun's position seems to animate, as well as its color, the color animation is the focus for now. We'll start by looking at the `Sun` widget itself, *not* the parent widget, which creates the `AnimationController`.

The animation is created in the parent on a tween. Later, I'll show you how to wire it all up, but for now, it's important to understand that an `Animation` object is being passed into the widget, so you don't need to define a tween or animation controller in this widget itself. That's managed by the parent, which I'll cover in a bit.

`Sun` is an animated widget that requires a `Listenable` as an argument, which needs to be passed straight through to its superclass. With that listenable being passed through to the superclass, we can make the animation valid by using it in the `Sun.build` method.

Listing 6.2 The complete animated Sun widget

To use animated widgets, extend AnimatedWidget.

```
// weather_app/lib/widget/sun_background.dart
class Sun extends AnimatedWidget {
  Sun({Key key, Animation<Color> animation})
      : super(key: key, listenable: animation);
```
AnimatedWidget instances must be passed a listenable.

```

  @override
  Widget build(BuildContext context) {
    final Animation<Color> animation = listenable;
    double maxWidth = MediaQuery.of(context).size.width;
    double margin = (maxWidth * .3) / 2;
```
Type casts the Listenable object to an Animation type, which is a subclass of Listenable

```

    return AspectRatio(
      aspectRatio: 1.0,
      child:  Container(
        margin: EdgeInsets.symmetric(horizontal: margin),
        constraints: BoxConstraints(
          maxWidth: maxWidth,
        ),
        decoration:  BoxDecoration(
          shape: BoxShape.circle,
          color: animation.value,
        ),
      ),
    );
  }
}
```
Where the animation value is used

Now, in that same `build` method, you can pass the current value of an animation to the `color` argument of its `BoxDecoration`:

```
decoration: BoxDecoration(
  shape: BoxShape.circle,
  color: animation.value,
),
```
Gives the color argument the value of the animation, which is, in any given single frame, a color

Now this animated widget will be the color of the *value* of the animation on any given frame. The animated widget rebuilds as that value changes, so we don't have to handle that functionality ourselves.

That's all it takes to make a widget an `AnimatedWidget`. Most of the animation work is done above the widget in the tree and passed into it. Here's the final code for the `Sun` class, for reference. (It's the same as the previous code sample.)

```
// weather_app/lib/widget/sun_background.dart
class Sun extends AnimatedWidget {
  Sun({Key key, Animation<Color> animation})
      : super(key: key, listenable: animation);
```
Passes in an animation, straight through to the AnimatedWidget superclass

```

  @override
```

```
Widget build(BuildContext context) {
  final Animation<Color> animation = listenable;          ◁─┐  Grabs a reference to
  double maxWidth = MediaQuery.of(context).size.width;        the animation with the
  double margin = (maxWidth * .3) / 2;                         correct type in the
                                                               build method

  return AspectRatio(
    aspectRatio: 1.0,
    child: Container(
      margin: EdgeInsets.symmetric(horizontal: margin),
      constraints: BoxConstraints(
        maxWidth: maxWidth,
      ),
      decoration: BoxDecoration(          ┌ Extracts the value
        shape: BoxShape.circle,           │ from the animation
        color: animation.value,      ◁────┘
      ),
    ),
  );
}
```

6.1.6 Implementing the animation controller and tween for the background

In order to make the color of the Sun widget animate, you need to build the actual Animation object that will be passed into the Sun.animation argument. To start, check out this code that creates an instance of the Sun widget. It's a single line, but it contains quite a bit of functionality. I will break it down piece by piece in the following pages.

Listing 6.3 Passing an animation into an animated widget

An animated widget (in this case, Sun) should be passed an animation. An animation is created by calling animate on a tween object and passing it an AnimationController object.

```
//weather_app/lib/page/forecast_page.dart -- line ~257
Sun(
  animation: _colorTween.animate(_animationController),
),
```

At this point, assuming that the _colorTween and _animationController variables exist and are valid, you've seen a majority of the functionality required to animate the sun background color. All that's left is to create those variables.

The _colorTween object is a Tween object, and _animationController is an AnimationController that will "manage" the _colorTween. Let's look at how those are made. They both live in the _ForecastPageState class. This chapter actually uses multiple tweens and two animation controllers. The following code example shows all the class members, and I've annotated the two members we care about right now:

```
class _ForecastPageState extends State<ForecastPage>
    with TickerProviderStateMixin {
  int activeTabIndex = 0;
  ForecastController _forecastController;              ┌ The animation controller
  AnimationController _animationController;       ◁────┘ we care about for now
```

```
AnimationController _weatherConditionAnimationController;
ColorTween _colorTween;
ColorTween _backgroundColorTween;
ColorTween _textColorTween;
ColorTween _cloudColorTween;
Tween<Offset> _positionOffsetTween;
TweenSequence<Offset> _cloudPositionOffsetTween;
ForecastAnimationState currentAnimationState;
ForecastAnimationState nextAnimationState;
Offset verticalDragStart;


  // ... rest of class definition
}
```

The only tween we care about for now

Now it's a matter of assigning these two variables to instances of `Tween` and `Animation-Controller`. For this app, we're going to fire off animations pretty often. Every time the state changes, in fact, an animation is executed. That includes when the selected city changes and when the time of day selected in the tab bar changes. In other words, the animation values need to be ready to animate every time the state changes.

To wire this up correctly, we should create an `AnimationController` to assign to the `_animationController` variable as soon as the widget is made. This can be done in the `initState` method on the `State` object.

> **NOTE** If you look at the code for the `ForecastPage.initState` method, it's just calling `_render()`. The `_render()` method is doing the heavy lifting. I've set it up this way because we're going to want to repeat this logic not only when the page builds for the first time, but also when the configuration for `ForecastPage` updates. This is handled via a *lifecycle* method in Flutter. We'll go over this in depth later in this book. For now, it's okay to just think of `_render` as the logic in `initState`.

`ForecastPageState._render` calls a method called `ForecastPage._handleState-Change`. In that method, you'll find the beginning of the logic for these animations. But it also calls more methods: `ForecastPage._buildAnimationController`, `ForecastPage._buildTweens`, and `initAnimation`. The goal for the moment is to only animate the color of the sun, so I'll cover the logic that specifically makes that happen. First, the following listing represents the general `State` object setup.

Listing 6.4 Setting up the `State` object for animation use

```
class _ForecastPageState extends State<ForecastPage>
    with TickerProviderStateMixin {
  // ... class members
  ForecastController _forecastController;
  AnimationController _animationController;
  ColorTween _colorTween;

  @override
  void initState() {
```

```
    super.initState();
    _forecastController = ForecastController(widget.settings.activeCity);
    _render();
}


@override
void didUpdateWidget(ForecastPage oldWidget) {
    super.didUpdateWidget(oldWidget);
    _render();
}

@override
void dispose() {
    _animationController?.dispose();
    _weatherConditionAnimationController?.dispose();
    super.dispose();
}

// ... rest of class
}
```

> **Ensures that the animations are fired when this widget's configuration changes** — `void didUpdateWidget(ForecastPage oldWidget) {`

> **It's important to dispose of animation controllers when you're done with them.** — `void dispose() {`

Again, this is just some basic class setup code. These methods are important to the functionality, but we don't have to interact with them directly in the rest of the code.

Now let's move on to domain-specific logic. There are several methods, all of which are somewhat complicated. I will walk through each one in the following listings. It's important that you don't get too bogged down. The _render method, for example, is important because it is involved in setting up the *initial* animation data in the app, but it's doing just that setup. The Flutter animation functionality, specifically for the Sun widget, lives beyond the _render method. I'm just showing you for the sake of completeness.

> **Listing 6.5　`_ForecastPageState._render` method**

```
class _ForecastPageState extends State<ForecastPage>
    with TickerProviderStateMixin {
  // ... class members
  void initState() {...}
  void didUpdateWidget(ForecastPage oldWidget) {...}
  void dispose() {...}

  void _render() {
    _forecastController.city =
        widget.settings.activeCity;
    intstartTime =
        _forecastController.selectedHourlyTemperature.dateTime.hour;
    currentAnimationState =
        AnimationUtil.getDataForNextAnimationState(
      selectedDay: _forecastController.selectedDay,
      currentlySelectedTimeOfDay: startTime,
    );
```

> **This method is mostly used to set up configuration needed when the page is rendered. Importantly, we'll need to ensure that the _forecastController is in sync with the current app state and displays the correct city.** — `widget.settings.activeCity;`

> **The most important piece. We'll look deeper into this method soon. For now, know that it tells this entire object what its current animation state is; that is, all the values it needs for the beginning of an animation.** — `AnimationUtil.getDataForNextAnimationState(`

```
    final activeTabIndex =
        AnimationUtil.hours.indexOf(startTime)
    _handleStateChange(activeTabIndex);      ⟵
  }
```

> **Passes information to the _handleStateChange method, where much more of the functionality happens**

As it pertains to this chapter, the _render method essentially deciphers the starting tab index and weather data based on the current time. For example, when you launch the app, if it's 8:46 AM, then the _render method is responsible for deciding that the starting tab selection should be the one labeled "9:00" and determining the weather data based on that.

After the app is launched, though, there is already state in the application. This state is what the _handleStateChange method relies on to properly execute animation and data changes. So, the _handleStateChange method is also called in response to certain user interactions. Specifically, it's called when the user selects a new tab from the TimePickerRow widget.

Listing 6.6 Creating the `TimePickerRow` widget

```
// weather_app/lib/page/forecast_page.dart -- line ~227
final timePickerRow = TimePickerRow(
  tabItems: Humanize.allHours(),
  forecastController: _forecastController,
  onTabChange: (int selectedTabIndex) =>
    _handleStateChange(selectedTabIndex),   ⟵
  startIndex: activeTabIndex,
);
```

> **When the tab is changed, based on a user tapping a new tab, this widget executes its callback. Its callback passes the new selected tab index into _handleStateChange, which kicks off the animation process.**

The two previous sections are, again, not necessary for animations themselves, but they're logic specific to this app that prepares the state that the animations need to execute. I've shown you these methods in order to paint a full picture in your mind of how the animation works from start to finish. The Flutter-specific animation code starts next in the _handleStateChange method.

Before I move on to _handleStateChange, let's recall what the goal is for this section. At the highest level, it's animating the color of the sun—nothing more. I'm showing you more code than necessary so the pieces all snap together more easily. But remember, we only care about creating the _colorTween and _animationController right now. We'll get there shortly.

Also, importantly, the _render method is only one of three places that call _handleStateChange. That's because the state technically changes any time the widget's configuration changes (via initState or didUpdateWidget), and also when certain user interactions take place; namely, when the user selects a new time from the TimePickerRow.

Listing 6.7 The `_ForecastPageState._handleStateChange` method

_handleStateChange, the tweens, and controllers need to be rebuilt
because the tweens have several different start and end values based
on the current selected time of day in the TimePickerRow.

```
class _ForecastPageState extends State<ForecastPage>
    with TickerProviderStateMixin {
  // ... class members
  void initState() {...}
  void didUpdateWidget(ForecastPage oldWidget) {...}
  void dispose() {...}
  void _render() {...}


  void _handleStateChange(int activeIndex) {
    if (activeIndex == activeTabIndex) return;

    nextAnimationState =
        AnimationUtil.getDataForNextAnimationState(

      selectedDay: _forecastController.selectedDay,
      currentlySelectedTimeOfDay:
        _forecastController.selectedHourlyTemperature.dateTime.hour,
    );
    _buildAnimationController();
    _buildTweens();
    _initAnimation();
    setState(() => activeTabIndex = activeIndex);

    intnextSelectedHour =
        AnimationUtil.getSelectedHourFromTabIndex(
      activeIndex,
      _forecastController.selectedDay,
    );

    _forecastController.selectedHourlyTemperature
        = ForecastDay.getWeatherForHour(
          _forecastController.selectedDay,
          nextSelectedHour,
        );
    currentAnimationState = nextAnimationState;
  }
```

If the same tab is chosen,
there's nothing to animate.

The next animation state
represents the end values
for the next animation that
fires. (It will also become
the starting values for the
next animation cycle.)

These methods build all the relevant objects
and call AnimationController.forward().

Gets the
hour
associated
with the
selected
tab index

At this point, multiple values on
this object have been updated.
Even though only activeTabIndex
is set within the callback of
setState, all of the changed
values on this object will be
built appropriately.

Sets the
selectedHourlyTemperature
on the controller with the
data from the new values.
This way, the data for the
next animation cycle is
already loaded in.

Earlier in the chapter, you saw how the _colorTween is animated and passed into the
Sun widget. As a reminder, here's that code:

```
//weather_app/lib/page/forecast_page.dart -- line ~257
Sun(animation: _colorTween.animate(_animationController)),
```

So far, we haven't gotten to the bottom of building that _colorTween or _animation-
Controller. Those are built, believe or not, in the class members _buildAnimation-
Controller and _buildTween, which you saw in listing 6.6 in the _handleStateChange
method. Let's look at those and finish up this process.

Listing 6.8 `_ForecastPageState` animation helper methods

The _initAnimation method turns around and calls
AnimationController.forward; forward is the method
that tells the animation to begin.

```
// weather_app/page/forecast_page.dart
  void _initAnimation() {
    _animationController.forward();
    // ... other animationControllers
  }

  void _buildAnimationController() {
    _animationController?.dispose();

    _animationController = AnimationController(
        duration: Duration(milliseconds: 500),
        vsync: this,
    );
  }

  void _buildTweens() {
    _colorTween = ColorTween(
      begin: currentAnimationState.sunColor,
      end: nextAnimationState.sunColor,
    );
    // ... a bunch more tweens
  }
```

dispose is an **AnimationControllers** method
that tells it to stop listening and stop using
any resources to calculate or execute
animations. Calling this directly before
building a new animation controller
ensures that resources are being cleaned
up properly and animations are being
stopped at the right time.

Instantiates a new animation
controller every time the state
changes. This is a precautionary
move, because once an
animation controller is disposed
of, it cannot be restarted.

This ColorTween is concerned with
the color when the animation starts,
which is the current color of the sun.
And it's concerned with the color
when the animation ends, which is
the next color of the sun.

TIP You will see `dispose` in many classes in Dart that perform some sort of passive action. These include classes that provide asynchronous activity, Widget `State` objects, animation controllers, and more. The `dispose` method is always used for the same general function: to tell an object to stop using resources.

This has been a lot, but it explains everything needed to animate *only* the color of the sun. There are many more `Tween` objects, animated widgets, and an additional `AnimationController` to discuss in order to execute the entire animation for this app.

Before I move on to those animation pieces, though, another task needs to be finished. The `Cloud` widget needs to be created. I encourage you to move on and give your brain a break from animations. Later in the chapter, when we revisit the animations, you'll be primed and ready to absorb more of the concept.

NOTE "The Flutter Boring Development Show," a video series by the Flutter team, takes deep dives into specific topics. This video will show you how to implement animations in a super-simple example: https://www.youtube.com/watch?v=dNSteCm-cEY.

6.2   *CustomPainter and the canvas*

The Clouds widget is a bit more involved than the sun. It animates in two ways: it changes color and positions itself on and off the screen when necessary. Also, importantly, it's not made up of only widgets. The Clouds class itself is a widget; and its child, CustomPainter, is also a widget. But the painter's child isn't (see figure 6.4): it's a custom painter.

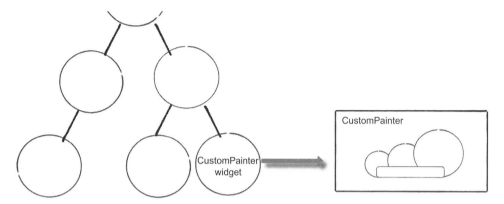

Figure 6.4   Canvas in a widget tree

A *custom painter* is a special object that lets you draw directly on the screen. You can literally control every single pixel by drawing shapes, lines, and dots of any color you want. The object that you paint on in a custom painter is called the *canvas*.

In the weather app, I've used a custom painter to create the clouds. In this section, I'll explain how the canvas and painters work. In general, creating a painter requires implementing the following objects and methods:

- The canvas
- The Paint class
- A Size parameter, which defines the size of the canvas
- The shouldRepaint method

The canvas is the widget you're painting on. It's blank when it's defined. It represents a portion of the device's screen in which you want to paint. Size is an object that you use to define the width and height of the canvas (figure 6.5).

Then, the Paint class is used to define a "brush" of sorts, with which you "paint" onto the canvas. This class has an API to define the color you want to use, the strokeWidth you

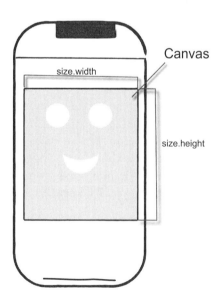

Figure 6.5   A canvas is placed on the screen, and its size is given by the widget that creates it.

want to paint with (in pixels), and other properties such as strokeCap, which defines the shape of the end of the line.

The methods of the Canvas object are what you use to tell Flutter *what* to draw with this painter. It has methods like drawRect and drawLine. These methods require a Paint object, which dictates the style in which shapes are drawn. You'll see concrete examples of this soon.

Finally, the shouldRepaint method is a lifecycle method called whenever the configuration of this painter changes. It must be defined and return a Boolean, and it's used to Flutter to repaint the canvas (or when *not* to repaint, because the configuration is the same). It's expensive to repaint all the time, and this method gives you control over the repaint process.

6.2.1 *The shapes used to make up the clouds*

Before we dive into the code, take a look at figure 6.6, which outlines the different shapes that are created using the canvas and paint objects. In reality, the cloud painting is a collection of a few different shapes painted to the screen. Don't dwell on this figure, because I'm going to break it down in a bit.

```
void CustomPainter.paint(Canvas canvas, Size size) {

  var paint = new Paint()..color = Colors.white;

  canvas.drawCircle(Offset center, double radius, Paint paint);

  canvas.drawCircle(Offset center, double radius, Paint paint);

  canvas.drawCircle(Offset center, double radius, Paint paint);

  canvas.drawRRect(Rect rect, Paint paint);

}
```

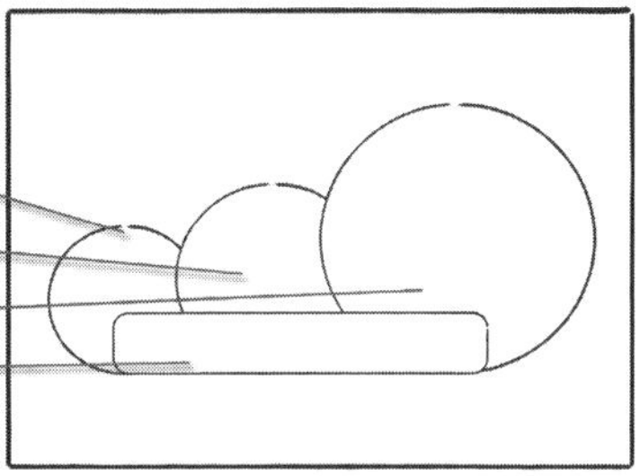

Figure 6.6 Canvas draw method examples

6.2.2 *Defining the CustomPainter and the Paint object*

Let's walk through the Clouds class in the weather app to make all these concepts less abstract. First, in the following listing, the Clouds class defines what's needed for the CustomPainter.

Listing 6.9 The Clouds class

```
// weather_app/lib/widget/clouds_background.dart
class Clouds extends AnimatedWidget {
  final bool isRaining;

  Clouds({
    Key key,
    Animation<Color> animation,
    this.isRaining = false,
  }) : super(key: key, listenable: animation);
```

```
Widget build(BuildContext context) {
  final Animation<Color> animation = listenable;

  Size screenSize = MediaQuery.of(context).size;
  Paint _paintBrush = Paint()
    ..color = animation.value
    ..strokeWidth = 3.0
    ..strokeCap = StrokeCap.round;

  return Container(
    height: 300.0,
    child: CustomPaint(
      size: screenSize,
      painter: CloudPainter(
        cloudPaint: _paintBrush,
        isRaining: isRaining,
      ),
    ),
  );
}
}
```

Because the clouds move all around the background, the size of the canvas is the full screen size.

A Paint class takes no arguments, but it does have setters that you can use to define qualities. As you'll see, you're likely to want to update properties of the Paint class, which I imagine is why it was written with setters rather than parameters.

The screen size we grabbed a few lines earlier

When using a canvas to draw, you wrap it in CustomPaint, which is a widget. You must pass it a size and a painter.

I've defined a class that extends CustomPainter. isRaining is a property we'll look at later.

In short, this class defines some objects and properties we need for the painter, such as the height and the `Paint` object.

Next, take a look at the `CloudPainter` class, which is where we draw on the canvas. This shows the minimum you need for every custom painter object: a `paint` method and a `shouldRepaint` method.

Listing 6.10 The bare minimum for a custom painter

The constructor arguments are specific to this app, but you don't have to pass in a Paint. You could, and often will, create the Paint in the CustomPainter, rather than pass it in. In this app, we'll need it to be there when we add animations.

```
// weather_app/lib/widget/clouds_background.dart -- line ~34
class CloudPainter extends CustomPainter {
  final bool isRaining;
  final Paint cloudPaint;
  CloudPainter({this.isRaining, this.cloudPaint});

  @override
  void paint(Canvas canvas, Size size) {
    // paint on the canvas
  }

  @override
  bool shouldRepaint(CustomPainter oldDelegate) {
    return false;
  }
}
```

A CustomPainter must have a paint method. This is similar to the build class in widgets. It's what the Flutter framework fires to kick off the painting. The method is passed a Canvas and a Size, which it knows about because we told the CustomPaint widget the size of the screen.

This method is required as well, because CustomPainter is an abstract class. It's called when a new instance of this class delegate is provided to its corresponding render object. If the new instance represents different information than the old instance, then the method should return true; otherwise, it should return false.

At this point, I've only shown you how to set up a custom painter. Next, we'll actually paint to the screen in the `CustomPainter.paint` method.

6.2.3 The CustomPainter paint method

The logic in this class lives in the `paint` method. The simplest explanation for painting on the canvas is that it requires you to give *exact* instructions of where to paint what. If you were instructing a friend what to paint on a literal canvas, you might say, "Draw a red line from the top-left corner to the center." Then, you could follow that up with another command: "Draw a small blue circle in the center."

There are two things to note. First, order matters. In the human example, the blue circle would overlap the red line because it was drawn after the line. Second, I'd like to remind you that computers can't decipher vague commands. Because computers are dumb, we have to give them precise locations in our commands. Unlike our smart friend, a computer doesn't know what the "top-left corner" is. Precision is key in `paint` methods.

Before we look at the code, think about what we're trying to achieve: the cloud shown in figure 6.7. These are some of the ideas we need to think about:

- It's centered.
- The canvas is the entire screen, but the drawing doesn't take up the whole screen.
- The cloud is made up of four shapes: three circles and one rectangle with rounded corners.
- Phone screens are all different sizes, so we have to make the measurements malleable.

Figure 6.7 A screenshot of the cloud that's created via the Canvas API

With all this in mind, we know that we need to give location-based commands that rely on the exact size of the device the app is running on. We can use the painter's `Size` property and math to get these specific locations, and then tell the painter to draw four shapes to the screen. The following listing shows what this ends up looking like.

Listing 6.11 Half of the `CloudPainter.paint` method

Uses rectTop to place the rounded rectangle. This
is somewhat arbitrary, but aesthetically correct.

```
// weather_app/lib/widget/clouds_background.dart -- line ~41
@override
void paint(Canvas canvas, Size size) {
    double rectTop = 110.0;
    double rectBottom = rectTop + 40.0;

    double figureLeftEdge = size.width / 4;
    double figureRightEdge = size.width - 90.0;
    double figureCenter = size.width / 2;
```

Again, arbitrary but purposeful.
Forty pixels just looks right, but
it isn't based on any logic.

Variables that place the cloud along
the horizontal axis of the screen

```
Rect cloudBaseRect = Rect.fromPoints(
  Offset(figureLeftEdge, rectTop),
  Offset(figureRightEdge, rectBottom),
);
RRect cloudBase = RRect.fromRectAndRadius(
  cloudBaseRect,
  Radius.circular(10.0),
);
canvas.drawCircle(
  Offset(figureLeftEdge + 5, 100.0),
  50.0, cloudPaint,
);
canvas.drawCircle(
  Offset(figureCenter, 70.0),
  60.0,
  cloudPaint,
);
canvas.drawCircle(
  Offset(figureRightEdge, 70.0),
  80.0,
  cloudPaint,
);
cloudPaint.strokeWidth = 3.0;
canvas.drawRRect(cloudBase, cloudPaint);
// ...
```

◁— **Rect.fromPoints creates a rectangle from the top-left and bottom-right corner offsets.**

◁— **RRect is a rectangle with rounded corners.**

◁— **Canvas.drawCircle tells the canvas to actually execute the painting.**

◁— **Canvas.drawRRect paints the RRect.**

I use three general steps to frame the logic of my `paint` methods:

1. Define the spatial and location variables (such as `rectTop`)
2. Create the figure instances, like `Rect`
3. Paint the figures to the canvas with `Canvas.draw` methods

The first step makes the code easier to understand and reason about. In this example, `size.width / 4` will return exactly one-fourth of the canvas's width, which I've added as padding to the left. `size.width - 90.0` is somewhat arbitrary but will give exactly 90 pixels of padding to the right. I decided on 90 pixels because the clouds look best slightly offset from center (That's my opinion, but I'm not a visual artist, so take it with a grain of salt).

The second step is the preparation. The canvas has built-in methods to draw common shapes: `drawRect` draws a rectangle, `drawLine` draws a line, and so on. To draw a rectangle, you need to create a rectangle object to give to the `drawRect` method. The `Rect` class, `Line` class, `Circle` class, and all the other shapes have constructors that use different measurements to define the shape. For example, I used `Rect.fromPoints`, which takes two offsets and draws the smallest rectangle that encloses both points. There's also `Rect.fromLTWH`, which means "from left, top, width, height." I encourage you to explore all the options for creating shapes when you next use a custom painter; you can find them in the documentation at http://mng.bz/omZN.

In this example, I chose to use the `Rect.fromPoints` constructor because it takes two `Offset` objects as parameters. Offsets are used quite a bit in UI development, and it's comfortable for me to work with them. That's the only reason.

> **NOTE** None of the constructors are necessarily better than any of the others. Rather, they're different means to the same end.

Offsets represent points from the *origin of the vector*, which is the top-left corner of the canvas (the top-left corner of the screen in our case, because the canvas is the entire background of the screen). To create the rect that represents the base of the clouds, provide the `Rect.fromPoints` constructor with the top-left point of the rectangle and the bottom-right point.

It's important to note that thus far we haven't drawn anything on the canvas. We've just declared an instance of the `Rect` class.

The rectangle we're building for the cloud base needs to have rounded corners. Luckily, Flutter gives us a class called RRect. You can pass the previously built rectangle to `RRect.fromRectAndRadius`, which will build a rounded rectangle, known in the Canvas API as an RRect.

As we move down the `paint` method, you can see that we begin to draw the circles that make up the rest of the cloud painting. Importantly, at this point, the RRect has *not* been painted to the canvas, only defined. The circles are defined and drawn onto the canvas in single lines of code. As a reminder, this is the `paint` method.

Listing 6.12 The `CloudPainter.paint` method

```
// weather_app/lib/widget/clouds_background.dart -- line ~38
@override
void paint(Canvas canvas, Size size) {
  double rectTop = 110.0;
  double rectBottom = rectTop + 40.0;

  double figureLeftEdge = size.width / 4;
  double figureRightEdge = size.width - 90.0;
  double figureCenter = size.width / 2;
  Rect cloudBaseRect = Rect.fromPoints(
    Offset(figureLeftEdge, rectTop),
    Offset(figureRightEdge, rectBottom),
  );
  RRect cloudBase = RRect.fromRectAndRadius(
    cloudBaseRect,
    Radius.circular(10.0),
  );
  canvas.drawCircle(
    Offset(figureLeftEdge + 5, 100.0),
    50.0, cloudPaint,
  );
  canvas.drawCircle(
    Offset(figureCenter, 70.0),
    60.0,
```

Where the circles begin to be painted. Notice that the process for drawing these circles is different than the process for drawing the rectangle, because we don't define the circle shape in advance.

```
      cloudPaint,
    );
  canvas.drawCircle(
    Offset(figureRightEdge, 70.0),
    80.0,
    cloudPaint,
  );
  cloudPaint.strokeWidth = 3.0;
  canvas.drawRRect(cloudBase, cloudPaint);
  // ...
```

drawCircle is different than drawing a rectangle, because you don't have to create a circle object in advance. This makes sense, to me, because a circle isn't based on multiple points. It only needs an Offset that represents the center of the circle, and a double that represents the radius of the circle. And to paint a circle to the canvas, you'll need a Paint object. That's why each of these three circles is created on the spot, rather than predefined.

It might help to look at the diagram of the clouds one more time before we finish up this painting. You can see it in figure 6.8 As we move down the Cloud-Painter.paint method, we're at the point where we've defined the rounded rectangle and actually painted the three circles to the screen. Now we only need to paint the base of the clouds that give them a flat bottom. We already did the hard part of creating the RRect; we just need to call canvas.drawRRect, and we're good to go. This method is called in the paint method, and it looks like this:

```
canvas.drawRRect(cloudBase, cloudPaint);
```

This method requires a shape, represented by the cloudBase variable, and a Paint object, which we assigned to the cloudPaint method (see figure 6.8).

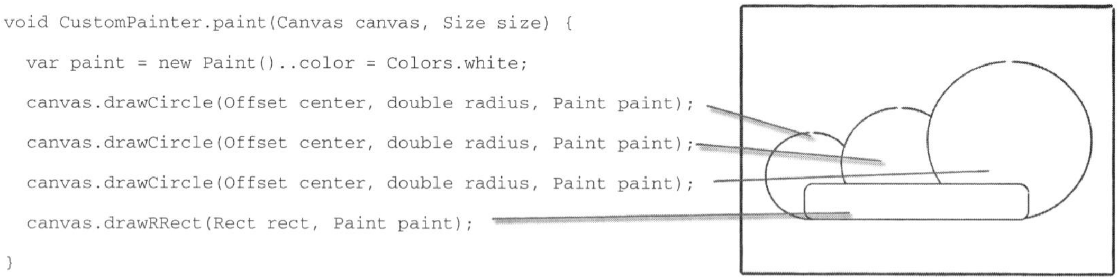

```
void CustomPainter.paint(Canvas canvas, Size size) {
  var paint = new Paint()..color = Colors.white;
  canvas.drawCircle(Offset center, double radius, Paint paint);
  canvas.drawCircle(Offset center, double radius, Paint paint);
  canvas.drawCircle(Offset center, double radius, Paint paint);
  canvas.drawRRect(Rect rect, Paint paint);
}
```

Figure 6.8   Canvas draw method examples

That's the entirety of the cloud portion of the drawing. A whole second part of the paint method draws the raindrops (when appropriate). It's a lot more of the same: math and drawing lines. It's already written in the project repository, and I encourage you look at it. (You can find the source code at https://www.manning.com/books/flutter-in-action. The code you're looking for is in the weather app project in the file located at lib/widget/clouds_background.dart.)

At this point you should see the cloud on your screen. It's nice, but we need to animate it—both the color and the position. In the next section, we're going to do some more complicated animations.

6.3 Staggered animations, TweenSequence, and built-in animations

Now that we've painted the clouds, we can animate them. So, we'll return to animations and see some more examples, and build on the foundation from earlier in this chapter.

This section is all about coordinating multiple animations from the `Forecast-PageState` class. The background in this app contains complex animations that have to be executed in a specific order and with specific timing. We'll take multiple individual animations and orchestrate them with only two animation controllers.

Quite a few widgets are animated in some way in this app. In total, there are seven tweens animating more than 10 properties across many widgets. Importantly, these animations are all related. They all need to happen at the same time. Consider when you select a new time of day in the tab bar. Doing so changes the position and color of the sun and moon background. It also changes the color of the background of the entire app. Therefore, the text color across this page must be changed too, so that it's readable on the newly updated background color. To explain how to orchestrate this, I'm going to talk about a few built-in `AnimatedWidgets`, like `SlideTransition`, using a custom class to manage the state of the animation, and my favorite animation-related convenience feature: `TweenSequence`.

It's important to note that, as I mentioned, coordinating all these animations requires building the seven tweens, each of which has its own start and end values. Some of the tweens are used to animate color, and some are used to animate position. The point, though, is that we'll be working with multiple tweens.

6.3.1 Creating a custom animation state class

The nature of this app requires that the sun and moon graphics in the background at any given time reflect a weather pattern, which couldn't possibly be known in advance. And what's more, the color of the text and the background of this page are animated as well. This means many properties of these widgets need to be calculated whenever the state changes. Specifically, each time the user selects a new time of day, the app needs to build tweens based on the weather data for that time and then kick off the animations immediately. The rest of this chapter is devoted to examining my solution to this problem.

First, let's think through the logical steps to implement all the different animations that happen on each state change. What do we know so far, and what do we want to do here?

- We know that every tween in an animation needs a beginning and an end.
- We know that, in our case, we need to get those values every time the state is updated, which happens when the user taps a new time in the tab bar.

- We know that the values are based on the time that's selected and the weather forecast at that time. For example, the color values and sun's position are based on the time of day, and the visibility of the clouds and rain is based on the type of weather.

With this in mind, what do we need to accomplish?

- On tap, we need to gather all the time and weather data for the time selected. (We also need to know what the *current* weather data is, for the start values of the tweens.)
- With that data, we need to decide what the end value is for each tween.
- We need to build the tweens, pass them into the widgets, and call forward on the animation controller.

In the app, this involves a few different moving parts:

- ForecastAnimationState—A helper class I added to make this easier to reason about. All it does in reality is hold a reference to all the different values this animation needs at any given begin or end state. It also has a factory constructor that picks all the correct values based on the weather and time data. It's basically a giant, hard-coded switch statement.
- AnimationUtil.getDataForNextAnimationState—Coordinates the logic needed to create a ForecastAnimationState. It says, "Oh, you chose that tab index? Well, let me grab the associated time and weather data and then build a new Forecast-AnimationState." In the app, the code looks like this:

```
// weather_app/lib/utils/forecase_animation_utils.dart
class AnimationUtil {
  static ForecastAnimationState getDataForNextAnimationState({
    ForecastDay selectedDay,
    int currentlySelectedTimeOfDay,      ◁─── Refers to the currently selected hour in the
  }) {                                        tab bar. It can be 3, 6, 9, 12, 15, 18, 21, or 24.
    final newSelection =
        ForecastDay.getHourSelection(    ◁─── The newSelection variable will be a Weather
      selectedDay,                            object associated with the given time of day.
      currentlySelectedTimeOfDay,
    );
    final endAnimationState =
      ForecastAnimationState.stateForNextSelection(   ◁─── Creates an animation
        newSelection.dateTime.hour,                        state based on the
        newSelection.description,                          weather information
      );

    return endAnimationState;
  }
```

To continue with the moving parts in a custom animation state class for the weather app:

- `ForecastPageState.currentAnimationState` and `ForecastPageState.next-AnimationState`–Used to set values of all the tweens needed in the `Forecast-PageState._buildTweens` method.

  Whenever a state change happens and the animation kicks off, we'll grab the values we need to animate *to*, build the tweens, and then set the `current-AnimationState` to the end values of the just-fired animation, because that's where we want the next animation to begin. This happens in the `Forecast-PageState.handleStateChange` method. We saw that method when animating the sun, but let's revisit it because it's one of the more complicated methods in this app.

- Values from the `ForecastAnimationState` objects—Update the tweens, which makes the animations we've written thus far work as expected.

These parts are shown in the following two listings (6.13 and 6.14).

Listing 6.13 `ForecastPageState.handleStateChange` method

```
// weather_app/lib/page/forecast_page.dart -- line ~78
  void _handleStateChange(int activeIndex) {
    if (activeIndex == activeTabIndex) return;

    nextAnimationState =
        AnimationUtil.getDataForNextAnimationState(     ⟵   Grabs the next
          selectedDay: _forecastController.selectedDay,     animation state based
          currentlySelectedTimeOfDay:                       on the new tab selection
            _forecastController.selectedHourlyTemperature.dateTime.hour,
        );
                                        Builds the animation
    _buildAnimationController();   ⟵   controllers and tweens
    _buildTweens();
    _initAnimation();                             Calls setState so Flutter knows
                                                  to rebuild. The animations are
    setState(() => activeTabIndex = activeIndex);  ⟵   already being executed, but
                                                  Flutter still needs to know to
                                                  change the selected tab and
    intnextSelectedHour                           the relevant weather data.
        = AnimationUtil.getSelectedHourFromTabIndex(
          activeIndex,
          _forecastController.selectedDay,
        );                                        Fetches the weather data
                                                  associated with the current
    _forecastController.selectedHourlyTemperature  ⟵   hour selection and assigns it
        = ForecastDay.getWeatherForHour(          to the controller's
          _forecastController.selectedDay,        selectedHourlyTemperature
          nextSelectedHour,                       variable
        );
    currentAnimationState = nextAnimationState;   ⟵
  }
```

Grabs the hour associated with the new tab index

After the animation fires, sets ForecastPageState.currentAnimationState to the value of ForecastPageState.nextAnimationState so it's ready for the next state change

Listing 6.14 `ForecastPageState._buildTweens` method

```
// weather_app/lib/page/forecast_page.dart -- line ~147
void _buildTweens() {
  _colorTween = ColorTween(
    begin: currentAnimationState.sunColor,        ◁─┐   Uses the values from our
    end: nextAnimationState.sunColor,               │   animation state rather than
  );                                                 │   static colors
  _cloudColorTween = ColorTween(
    begin: currentAnimationState.cloudColor,
    end: nextAnimationState.cloudColor,
  );
  // ...
}
```

That's the complete process required for specifically animating the colors of the sun and cloud widgets. Now that there are tweens, animation controllers, and widgets to animate, the animations will work. Further, let me remind you where all this work is being used: it's passed into the sun and cloud widgets.

Listing 6.15 Passing animation values into widgets

```
// weather_app/lib/page/forecast_page.dart -- line ~263
child: Stack(
  children: <Widget>[
    SlideTransition(            ◁────── SlideTransition will be covered shortly.
      // ...
      child: Sun(
        animation:
          _colorTween.animate(       ◁─┐   Remember, AnimatedWidgets need to be
            _animationController          │   passed an animation. You can create an
          ),                             │   Animation object by calling Tween.animate.
      ),
    ),
    SlideTransition(
      // ...
      child: Clouds(
        isRaining: isRaining,
        animation:
          _cloudColorTween.animate(   ◁─┐   Again, passes the animation into the widget,
            _animationController,          │   but this time the tween is specifically the one
          ),                             │   that tracks the cloud color.
      ),
    ),
  ],
),
```

6.3.2 *Built-in animation widgets: SlideTransition*

The cloud and sun background pieces also animate their positions. Flutter gives us a nice widget for just that use case, because it's so good to us. There's a widget called `SlideTransition` that slides its child widget across the screen using offset coordinates.

Flutter also comes with `ScaleTransition`, `SizeTransition`, and `FadeTransition`, among many others.

These widgets all extend `AnimatedWidget`, so we can use them exactly as we use the sun and cloud animations. We only need to pass an animation to the `position` property and a `child` widget. Since we're already using a `Stack`, all we need to do is replace the `Positioned` widgets with `SlideTransition` widgets, passing the same widgets to the `child` property.

Now we need to build the tweens. We need two different `Tween<Offset>` objects: one for the sun and one for the clouds. The sun is controlled by the `Tween<Offset>` `_positionOffsetTween` variable. It's exactly like the tweens we've used thus far. You can see it in `ForecastPageState._buildTweens`:

```
// weather_app/lib/page/forecast_page.dart -- line ~113
void _buildTweens() {
    // ...
    _positionOffsetTween = Tween<Offset>(
      begin: currentAnimationState.sunOffsetPosition,
      end: nextAnimationState.sunOffsetPosition,
    );
    // ...
```

Now the sun background widget needs to know about that tween. That's set up in the `build` method of this same widget:

A built-in animated widget that animates the position property. It's generally used in place of a Positioned widget and as a child of a Stack. It animates the position of its child.

This tween is used the same as a ColorTween, such as the ones we've seen already. It just tracks a different type of data: an offset rather than a color.

```
// weather_app/lib/page/forecast_page.dart -- line ~263
child: Stack(
  children: <Widget>[
    SlideTransition(
      position: _positionOffsetTween.animate(
      _animationController.drive(
        CurveTween(curve: Curves.bounceOut),
        ),
      ),
      child: Sun(
        animation: _colorTween.animate(_animationController),
      ),
    ),
    SlideTransition(
      position: _cloudPositionOffsetTween.animate(
        _weatherConditionAnimationController.drive(
          CurveTween(curve: Curves.bounceOut),
        ),
      ),
      child: Clouds(
        isRaining: isRaining,
        animation: _cloudColorTween.animate(_animationController),
      ),
    ),
  ],
),
```

I'm showing the Clouds slide transition as another, similar example.

You can call the drive method on an animation controller for more control over the animation. It allows you to change the animation's default behavior. In this case, I'm using drive to pass in Curve so the trajectory of the animation will be different.

6.3.3 Building animations for the Clouds widget

This should seem fairly similar to color animations. The next part is more interesting, in my opinion: animating the clouds.

The first time I wrote this animation, I used the same animation controller to move the clouds onscreen and offscreen, which had unwanted results. The clouds were animating directly (diagonally) to their place offscreen. Because the cloud and sun figures also animate up and down based on the time of day, figure 6.9 shows what was happening. This isn't wrong, but it doesn't look great.

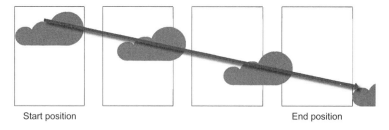

Start position   End position

Figure 6.9   Single position slide animation

This positioning animation should be two steps. It needs to animate up or down, and then horizontally on or off the screen as shown in figure 6.10.

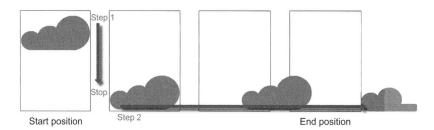

Start position   Step 2   End position

Figure 6.10   Staggered position slide animation

These are two steps to make this happen:

1. Use a second `AnimationController` that has a longer duration. The clouds should animate vertically at the same rate as the sun, and then the extra time is used to slide on or off the screen.
2. Use a `TweenSequence`. This class takes a list of tweens, each of which it will execute in the order you've listed them, distributed over the duration of the animation.

The first step, making a new `AnimationController`, is nothing new. It's absolutely reasonable to add multiple `AnimationController` classes to a single widget. In fact, Flutter has a different ticker mixin for this exact case: `TickerProviderStateMixin` (rather than `SingleTickerProviderStateMixin`).

I've declared the variable in the `ForecastPageState` class: `AnimationController _weatherConditionAnimationController`. To use it, you should assign that variable a new `AnimationController` object in `ForecastPageState._buildAnimationController`, and then initialize the animation in `ForecastPageState._initAnimation`. This is more of the same, so I won't cover it, but you can see all the code in the relevant methods mentioned in this paragraph. (These are all found in the weather app in the lib/page/forecast_page.dart file in the source code.)

6.3.4   *TweenSequence*

`TweenSequence`, however, is new, so let's talk about it. A `TweenSequence` can be used anywhere a `Tween` can be, because it's just a complicated tween under the hood, with a nice API for the developer.

   Its constructor takes a list of `TweenSequenceItems`. Each `TweenSequenceItem` requires two parameters: a tween and this item's *weight*. An item's weight is relative to all the other items, so the number assigned to any given weight is arbitrary. Flutter adds up the total weights and divides the total by the number of items.

> **TIP**   I like my math to be easy to reason about, so I like to use weights that add up to 100. You don't have to do this. The only requirement is that the total weight of all the items is greater than 0.0.

This code belongs in the `ForecastPageState._buildTweens` method.

Listing 6.16   The `ForecastPageState._buildTweens` method

```
// weather_app/lib/page/forecast_page.dart --- line ~169
void buildTweens() {
  // ...
  // line ~135
  OffsetSequence cloudOffsetSequence =
    OffsetSequence.fromBeginAndEndPositions(          ← OffsetSequence is a helper class
        currentAnimationState.cloudOffsetPosition,      I wrote to make this easier to
        nextAnimationState.cloudOffsetPosition,         reason about (see listing 6.17).
  );
  _cloudPositionOffsetTween =                         Builds a new
    TweenSequence<Offset>(         ←                  TweenSequence<Offset>, which
      <TweenSequenceItem<Offset>>[                     takes a list of TweenSequenceItems
        TweenSequenceItem<Offset>(
          weight: 50.0,             ←——— Gives the item an arbitrary weight
          tween: Tween<Offset>(
            begin: cloudOffsetSequence.positionA,
            end: cloudOffsetSequence.positionB,
          ),
        ),
        TweenSequenceItem<Offset>(
          weight: 50.0,
          tween: Tween<Offset>(
            begin: cloudOffsetSequence.positionB,
            end: cloudOffsetSequence.positionC,
```

Passes in a tween → (points to `tween: Tween<Offset>(`)

```
      ),
    ),
  ],
);
```

`OffsetSequence` only makes it easier to read the code within the `TweenSequence`. Because I know 100% of the time that I want three offsets for the clouds, and I know that the animation will always move vertically and then horizontally, I can determine the second position based on the start and end positions.

Listing 6.17   The `OffsetSequence` class

```
class OffsetSequence {
  final Offset positionA;
  final Offset positionB;
  final Offset positionC;

  OffsetSequence({this.positionA, this.positionB, this.positionC});

  factory OffsetSequence.fromBeginAndEndPositions(
    Offset offsetBegin,
    Offset offsetEnd,
  ) {
    return OffsetSequence(
      positionA: offsetBegin,          ◁

      positionB: Offset(               ◁
        offsetBegin.dx, offsetEnd.dy,
      ),

      positionC: offsetEnd,            ◁
    );
  }
}
```

This offset is the starting position of the clouds (in this example).

Because I know that the animation will always move vertically and then horizontally, I can determine the second position based on the start and end positions.

This offset represents the final position of the clouds.

Again, I'm showing you this tangential code for the sake of completeness, but the focus is on `TweenSequence`. This class is extremely useful for staggering animations. I spent hours writing really ugly code to get the same effect before I knew this class existed. Anytime you want to animate the same property on the same item multiple times in a single animation, this is what you should reach for.

The last step of this animation, again, is to wrap the `Cloud` widget with a `Slide-Transition` in the `build` method. We saw this code earlier, but it's worth revisiting:

```
// weather_app/lib/page/forecast_page.dart -- line ~277
    SlideTransition(
      position: _cloudPositionOffsetTween.animate(
        _weatherConditionAnimationController.drive(
          CurveTween(curve: Curves.bounceOut),
        ),
      ),
      child: Clouds(
```

Animates the position of the clouds

```
    isRaining: isRaining,
    animation:
      _cloudColorTween.animate(    ◁──── Animates the color
        _animationController,              of the clouds
      ),
  ),
),
```

With that, you've seen the most complicated animation in the app. Clearly many more animations are happening, though. In particular, there are many widgets whose colors are animating when the state changes. Next, I'd like to show you a recipe for how all those widgets animate.

6.4 *Reusable custom color transition widgets*

In the lib/widget/ directory, you'll notice four similar classes:

- `ColorTransitionText`
- `ColorTransitionIcon`
- `ColorTransitionBox`
- `TransitionAppbar`

These four classes are used throughout the app to transition all the colors. `Color-TransitionBox` animates the background, and `TransitionAppbar` animates the color of the app bar. The other two do just what they say they do. Because the background color of the app changes drastically, the app's text and icons must change to be readable.

From here, I'll quickly walk through `ColorTransitionBox`, and then leave the rest up to you to explore on your own if you'd like:

```
// weather_app/lib/widget/color_transition_box.dart
class ColorTransitionBox extends AnimatedWidget {    ◁──┐ All four of the color
  final Widget child;                                    │ transition classes are simple
                                                         │ AnimatedWidget objects.
  ColorTransitionBox({
    this.child,
    Key key,
    Animation<Color> animation,    ◁──┐ Don't forget to pass
    }) : super(key: key, listenable: animation);    │ in an animation.

  @override                                              ┌ Grabs a new reference
  Widget build(BuildContext context) {                   │ to that animation on
    final Animation<Color> animation = listenable;    ◁──┘ every build
    return DecoratedBox(
      decoration: BoxDecoration(
        color: animation.value,    ◁──┐ Gives the color property
      ),                              │ an animation value
      child: child,
    );
  }
}
```

The steps to implementing this animation are similar to the steps covered several times in this chapter:

- Build a new tween (variables have already been declared)
- Replace the necessary widgets with their animated counterparts (for example, replace `Text` widgets with `TransitionText`)
- Pass in an animation via the `Tween.animate(AnimationController)` method

If you take one thing away from this chapter, I hope it's this: Flutter provides an API for animating your app, and it's simpler than many animation libraries on other platforms. Animations in your app should seldom be more complicated than what's shown in this chapter. You can dive deep and make things complicated. But why should you? Flutter's built-in animation library covers every use case I've ever had. I've never had to write custom `lerp` methods or go much deeper than `AnimatedWidget`. Flutter did a good job of solving this problem for us, and we should take advantage of that. This is especially handy because animations are often "nice to haves," but when they're more approachable, there's no reason *not* to polish up the UI with them.

Summary

- Many Material Design widgets have built-in animations. If you're using the Material library, you'll want to make sure the widgets you're using aren't already animated. You can override any built-in widgets, but doing so may be a waste of time if the animations are built-in.
- Animations require the developer to implement three pieces at a minimum: a controller, a tween, and a ticker. Flutter will take care of the curve for you, if you don't want to customize it.
- Tweens map values of an animatable property to a number scale.
- Tickers are what give life to animations, calling their callback on every frame change.
- Classes that have `AnimationController` objects as properties should extend `SingleTickerProviderStateMixin` or `TickerProviderStateMixin`.
- All widgets that extend `AnimatedWidget` require an animation as a parameter, which provides the value of whichever property you're animating.
- You can paint exactly what you want, pixel by pixel, using the `CustomPaint` widget.
- The `CustomPaint` widget takes a child that extends `CustomPainter` and has a `paint` method.
- Painting to the canvas generally consists of drawing a series of shapes and lines using the `Canvas` class.
- The `TweenSequence` class is extremely useful for making staggered animations.

Part 3

State management and asynchronous Dart

This part is going to be different, but just a bit. So far in this book, you've learned how to build beautiful, functional apps with Flutter. But that's only part of the battle. In this part, I'm going to continue to explain core aspects of the Flutter SDK, like routing, but I'm also going to start covering some subjects that aren't Flutter-specific. Namely: state management.

Flutter isn't opinionated about state management. It's up to you to weigh the pros and cons of different state management patterns. That said, I've decided to make a choice and teach the bloc pattern. After the routing chapter, I'll explain what the bloc pattern is, as well as cover Flutter-specific tools that help with implementing this pattern. Finally, using the bloc pattern, we'll look at a Dart-specific feature, streams, and how they're used in concert with Flutter to make asynchronous programming easier.

Flutter routing in depth

7

This chapter covers

- Setting up named routes
- Building routes on the fly
- Using the Navigator
- Custom page transition animations

When I was planning this chapter, I was trying to answer these questions: "Why?" or "Who cares?" These are standard questions that Manning encourages their authors to think about before writing a chapter. And, well, this time, these were pretty easy to answer: everyone who doesn't want to make an app with a single page. Thus, a chapter on routing.

Routing can be a real pain on many platforms (but it shouldn't have to be!). This point is all too clear in the web world. There are countless libraries that solely implement routing for different frameworks. And, speaking of the web world, I think the folks behind React Router nailed the solution. It's easy to use, and it's flexible. It matches the reactive and composable UI style of React.

According to their docs, they're in the business of "dynamic routing," rather than static. Historically, most routing was declarative, and routes were configured before the app rendered. The creators of React Router (https://reacttraining.com/react-router/) explained it well in their docs:

> *"When we say dynamic routing, we mean routing that takes place as your app is rendering. Not in a configuration or convention outside of a running app."*

I'm talking about React Router right now, because the mental-model needed for routing in Flutter is the same. And, to be candid, I didn't know how to approach this topic, so I looked to people who are much smarter than me. (Thanks, React Router team).

7.1 Routing in Flutter

The advantage to dynamic routing is that it's flexible. You can have a super complicated app without ever declaring a route, because you can create new pages on the fly. The Flutter Navigator also gives you the option of declaring routes and pages, if you want to take the static approach. And you can (and probably will) mix and match static routes and "on-the-fly" routes.

> **NOTE**   Routing in Flutter is never *really* static, but you can declare all your routes up front, so the mental model is the same.

In Flutter, pages are just widgets that we assign to routes. And routes are managed by the Navigator, which is (you guessed it) just a widget! A `Navigator` widget is an abstraction over a widget that lays its children out in a stack nature. Because they're widgets, you can nest Navigators up and down your app, willy-nilly. (Routers in routers in routers ….) But before we get into the how-tos, let's take a look at the app that I'm using as reference for the next couple of chapters.

7.1.1 The Farmers Market app

I live in Portland, Oregon, where people love Farmers Markets. I mean deeply *love* them. In an unnatural way. So, I thought I'd get rich by breaking into that market. Figure 7.1 shows the app I made for people to buy veggies and other treats from farmers.

Figure 7.1   Screenshots of the Farmers Market app

The routing structure of the app isn't too complicated. It's only four pages. Our job in this chapter is to wire up the menu with some routes and create a few on-the-fly routes. Then, we're going to make it fancy with some page transition animations.

The interesting thing about the routes in this app, in my very biased opinion, is that all the pages share the same structural elements. The app bar, the cart icon, the menu, and some of the functionality and the scaffold are all written once, and I pass in the configuration based on the route. This is possible for two reasons: the way you compose an UI in Flutter and the fact that the Navigator is a widget that doesn't have to be top-level.

7.1.2　The app source code

In the Git repository, you'll find the relevant files for this book and, in particular, this app. The following listing shows these files.

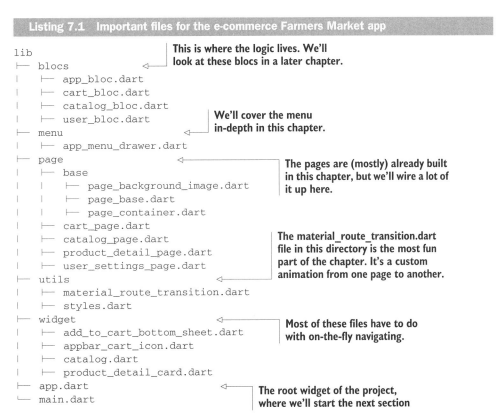

Listing 7.1　Important files for the e-commerce Farmers Market app

```
lib
├── blocs            ◁──── This is where the logic lives. We'll
│    ├── app_bloc.dart      look at these blocs in a later chapter.
│    ├── cart_bloc.dart
│    ├── catalog_bloc.dart
│    ├── user_bloc.dart
├── menu             ◁──── We'll cover the menu
│    ├── app_menu_drawer.dart    in-depth in this chapter.
├── page             ◁
│    ├── base              The pages are (mostly) already built
│    │    ├── page_background_image.dart   in this chapter, but we'll wire a lot of
│    │    ├── page_base.dart      it up here.
│    │    ├── page_container.dart
│    ├── cart_page.dart
│    ├── catalog_page.dart       The material_route_transition.dart
│    ├── product_detail_page.dart   file in this directory is the most fun
│    ├── user_settings_page.dart    part of the chapter. It's a custom
├── utils            ◁──── animation from one page to another.
│    ├── material_route_transition.dart
│    ├── styles.dart
├── widget           ◁
│    ├── add_to_cart_bottom_sheet.dart   Most of these files have to do
│    ├── appbar_cart_icon.dart     with on-the-fly navigating.
│    ├── catalog.dart
│    ├── product_detail_card.dart
├── app.dart         ◁────┐ The root widget of the project,
└── main.dart              │ where we'll start the next section
```

7.2　Declarative routing and named routes

If you've built web apps or mobile apps on nearly any other platform, you've likely dealt with declarative routing. On the other application platforms that I've used (such as Ruby on Rails, Django, and front-end libraries of the not-very-distant past), routes are defined in their own "routes" file, and what you declare is what you get. In Angu-larDart, your routes page might look like the next listing.

Listing 7.2   AngularDart Router route definitions

```
static final routes = [                    The name of the route
    new RouteDefinition(
        routePath: new RoutePath(path: '/user/1');   ◁──┐  The component to
        component: main.AppMainComponentNgFactory),   ◁──┘  render at that route
    new RouteDefinition(
        routePath:  new RoutePath(path: '/404');
        component: page_not_found.PageNotFoundComponentNgFactory)
    //... etc.
  ];
```

Understanding Angular code isn't important. This is an example of up-front route declarations written in Dart. The point is that you tell your app explicitly which routes you want to exist and which views they should route to. Each `RouteDefinition` has a path and a component (which is probably a page). This is generally done at the top level of an app. Pretty standard stuff here.

Flutter supports this. Although the routes and pages are still built while the app is running, the mental model that you can approach this with is that these are *static*. Mobile apps often support tens of pages, and it's perhaps easier to reason about if you define them once and then reference them by name, rather than creating unnamed routes all over the app.

Flutter routes follow the path conventions of all programming, such as /users/1/ inbox or /login. And as you'd expect, the route of the home page of your app is / (a single forward slash).

7.2.1   Declaring routes

There are two parts to using named routes. The first is defining the routes. In the e-commerce app you're building in this chapter, the named routes are set up in the lib/app.dart file. If you navigate to that file, you'll see a `MaterialApp` widget with the routes established, and in the utils/e_commerce_routes.dart file, you'll see the static variables with the actual route names. (This is just so I can safely use routes without fearing typos in the strings.)

Listing 7.3   Define routes in the `MaterialApp` widget

```
// e_commerce/lib/app.dart -- line ~ 51
// ...
return MaterialApp(
  debugShowCheckedModeBanner: false,
  theme: _theme,
  routes: {                                    ◁──┐
    ECommerceRoutes.catalogPage: (context) =>
        PageContainer(pageType: PageType.Catalog),
```

Define the rest of your named routes here. Named routes are defined in a Map, where the key is the name of the route (/), and the value is a function which returns a widget.

```
    ECommerceRoutes.cartPage: (context) =>
        PageContainer(pageType: PageType.Cart),
    ECommerceRoutes.userSettingsPage: (context) =>
        PageContainer(pageType: PageType.Settings),
    ECommerceRoutes.addProductFormPage: (context) =>
        PageContainer(pageType: PageType.AddProductForm),
  },
  navigatorObservers: [routeObserver],
);
```

> **We'll cover routeObserver soon. Don't worry about it for now.**

```
// e_commerce/lib/utils/e_commerce_routes.dart
class ECommerceRoutes {
  static final catalogPage = '/';
  static final cartPage = '/cart';
  static final userSettingsPage = '/settings';
  static final cartItemDetailPage = '/itemDetail';
  static final addProductFormPage = '/addProduct';
}
```

> **The ECommerceRoutes class maps to these routes for constant variable safety.**

7.2.2 Navigating to named routes

Navigating to named routes is as easy as using the `Navigator.pushNamed` method. The `pushNamed` method requires a `BuildContext` and a route name, so you can use it anywhere that you have access to your `BuildContext`. It looks like this:

```
final value = await Navigator.pushNamed(context, "/cart");
```

Pushing and popping routes is the bread and butter of routing in Flutter. Recall that the Navigator (figure 7.2) lays its children (the pages) out in a "stack" nature. The stack operates on a "last in, first out" principle, as stacks do in computer science. If you're looking at the home page of your app, and you navigate to a new page, you "push" that new page on top of the stack (and on top of the home page). The top item on the stack is what you see on the screen. If you pushed another route, we'll call it page three, and wanted to get back to the home page, you'd have to "pop" twice.

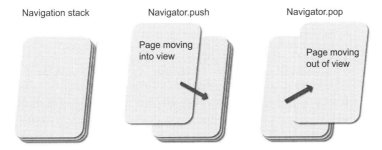

Figure 7.2 Flutter's Navigator is a stack-like structure.

The `Navigator` class has a bunch of helpful methods to manage the stack. I find myself using only a handful of the methods:

- pop
- popUntil
- canPop
- push
- pushNamed
- popAndPushNamed
- replace
- pushAndRemoveUntil

One important note about pushing named routes is that they return a Future. If you're not familiar with the await keyword, it's used to mark expressions that return an asynchronous value. We're not going to get into async Dart quite yet. But the quick version is that when you call Navigator.pushNamed, it immediately returns a Future object, which says, "Hey, I don't have a value you for you *yet*, but I will as soon as this process finishes." In the specific context of routing, this means: "As soon as they navigate back to here from the page they're on now, I'll give you whatever value they pass back from that page." Later in this chapter, we'll explore passing values between routes more in-depth.

In the e-commerce project repository, you can find an example of using Navigator .pushNamed in the AppBarCartIcon widget found in the lib/widget/appbar_cart_icon .dart file. Figure 7.3 shows the widget.

Figure 7.3   Highlighting the `AppBarCartIcon` widget

This icon has a little bubble on it that keeps track of how many items are in the user's cart. And the widget is actually an IconButton widget. It's wired up to navigate to the cart page when it's tapped and the onPressed callback is called:

```
onPressed: () {
    return Navigator.of(context).pushNamed("/cartPage");
},
```

That's all there is to it. For another example of using named routes, you can find a tutorial in the official docs at https://flutter.dev/docs/cookbook/navigation/named-routes.

> **NOTE** You might notice that Navigator.of(context).pushNamed(String routeName) function signature isn't the same as the previously mentioned Navigator.pushNamed(BuildContext context, String routeName) signature. These are interchangeable.

7.2.3 *MaterialDrawer widget and the full menu*

If you've seen a Material Design app, you're probably familiar with the type of app drawer shown in figure 7.4.

Because this chapter is about routing, I think now's a good time to explore how to build that menu. First, let's think about what we actually want it to do:

1 The menu should display when a user taps a menu button.

2 There should be a menu item for each page, which navigates to a route on tap.

3 There should be an About menu item, which shows a modal with app information.

4 There should be a menu header, which displays user information. When you tap on the user settings, it should route to the user settings page.

5 The menu should highlight which route is currently active.

6 The menu should close when a menu item is selected or when a user taps the menu overlay to the right of the menu.

7 When the menu is opened or closed, it should animate nicely in and out.

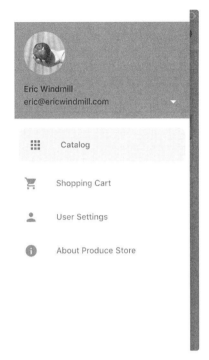

Figure 7.4   Screenshot of the menu drawer in the Farmers Market app

This particular menu drawer is a combination of only five required widgets, all of which are built into Flutter:

- Drawer
- ListView
- UserAccountsDrawerHeader
- ListTile
- AboutListTile

The Drawer is the widget that houses this menu. It takes a single widget in its child argument. You can pass it whatever you want (because everything is a widget). A Drawer will most likely be passed to a Scaffold in its drawer argument.

If you also have an AppBar in a scaffold with a drawer, then Flutter automatically sets the right-side icon on the app bar to a menu button, which opens the menu on tap. The menu will animate out nicely, and close when you swipe it left or tap the overlay to the right.

> **NOTE** You can override the automatic menu button by setting Scaffold .automaticallyImplyLeading to false.

7.2.4 *Menu items and the appropriate widgets: ListView and ListItems*

Next, the `ListView`. A *list view* is a layout widget that arranges widgets in a scrollable container. It arranges its children vertically by default, but it's quite customizable. We'll talk about scrolling and scrollable widgets in-depth in the next chapter. For now though, you can use this widget just like you'd use a `Column`. You only need to pass it some children, which are all widgets.

A `ListTile` is a widget that has two special characteristics: they're fixed-height, making them ideal for menus, and they're opinionated. Unlike other generalized widgets, which expect an argument called `child`, the `ListTile` has properties like `title`, `subtitle`, and `leading` (figure 7.5). It also comes equipped with an `onTap` property.

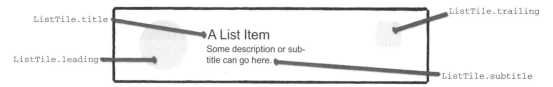

Figure 7.5 Annotated Material `ListTile` widget

There are some other special Flutter widgets that are used specifically to enhance a `ListView` into a more "material-esque" menu drawer. Before looking at those directly, look at the structure of the menu in the code. (This code has some details removed as it's meant to be a high-level overview of the `Drawer`'s widgets.)

Listing 7.4 AppMenu widget's `build` method, condensed to widgets only

```
@override
  Widget build(BuildContext context) {
    _activeRoute ??= "/";
    return Drawer(
      child: ListView(
        children: <Widget>[
          StreamBuilder(
            // ...
            builder: (
              BuildContext context,
              AsyncSnapshot<ECommerceUser>
            ) => UserAccountsDrawerHeader(),
          ), // StreamBuilder
          ListTile(
            leading: Icon(Icons.apps),
            title: Text("Catalog"),
            selected: _activeRoute == ECommerceRoutes.catalogPage,
            onTap: () => _navigate(ECommerceRoutes.catalogPage),
          ),
          ListTile(...),
          ListTile(...),
          AboutListTile(...),
```

> StreamBuilder will be discussed in-depth in chapter 9. For now, keep in mind that it follows the builder pattern, rather than expecting a child.

> AsyncSnapshot is a "jargon-y" name, which will also be discussed later.

> UserAccountsDrawerHeader is a special widget that's discussed in the next section.

> ListTile is an opinionated widget, used to make all the children in a ListView uniform.

> In this menu, there's a ListTile for each menu item.

> This is another special widget, also discussed soon.

```
      ],
    ),
  );
}
```

First, I'd like to discuss these various widgets within the drawer from a high level, starting with the two special widgets, as their use cases are specific. Then, I'll move into `List-Tile`, which is more generic. In a couple pages, we'll look at the nitty-gritty code details.

The `UserAccountsDrawerHeader` is a Material widget that's used to display crucial user information. Imagine a Google app like GMail, which lets you switch between user accounts with the tap of the button. That GMail-like UI is built into Flutter, using the `UserAccountsDrawerHeader`. We don't need this for this app. There's no lesson here. It's just a great example of how much Flutter gives you for free.

Finally, the `AboutListTile`. This widget can be passed into the `ListView.children` list, and configured in just a few lines of code, as the following listing shows.

> **Listing 7.5 Flutter's `AboutListTile` Material widget**

```
// e_commerce/lib/menu/app_menu_drawer.dart -- line ~81
AboutListTile(
  icon: Icon(Icons.info),
  applicationName: "Produce Store",
  aboutBoxChildren: <Widget>[
    Text("Thanks for reading Flutter in Action!"),
  ],
),
```

With that small amount of Flutter code, you get a fully functional menu button that displays a modal on tap, complete with a button to close the modal. Figure 7.6 shows what it looks like.

With all that in mind, I think this brings our requirements list to this:

- The menu should display when a user taps a menu button.
- There should be a menu item for each page, which navigates to a route on tap.
- There should be an About menu item, which shows a modal with app information.
- There should be a menu header, which displays user information. When you tap on the user settings, it should route to the user settings page.
- The menu should highlight which route is currently active.

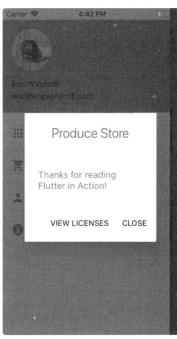

Figure 7.6 Screenshot of the About app dialog

- The menu should close when a menu item is selected, or when a user taps the menu overlay to the right of the menu.
- When the menu is opened or closed, it should animate nicely in and out.

This is *slightly* over-exaggerated. Of course, you have to actually write those five lines of code for the `AboutListTile`. But that's a heck of a lot easier than writing the logic to show a modal and then writing the layout for the modal itself.

IMPLEMENTING THE MENU DRAWER

With all this widget knowledge in mind, most of the work is done for you. The bulk of implementing this menu is in the routing. This works well, because this is a chapter about routing. Most of this work is done in the lib/menu/app_menu_drawer.dart file.

For starters, menu items, when tapped, should route to a new page. In the `build` method, there is a `ListTile` for each of these menu items. One `ListTile` looks like the next listing.

Listing 7.6   Menu drawer item in a `ListTile` widget

If selected is true, ListTile configures its children's colors to reflect the active route. I'll talk about this more in the next section.

```
// e_commerce/lib/menu/app_menu_drawer.dart -- line ~63
ListTile(
    leading: Icon(Icons.apps),
    title: Text("Catalog"),
    selected:
        _activeRoute == ECommerceRoutes.catalogPage,

    onTap: () =>
        _navigate(ECommerceRoutes.catalogPage),
),
```

ListTile.onTap is the perfect place to call a method which navigates to a new route.

Tapping that list item calls `AppMenu._navigate`, which looks like the following code.

Listing 7.7   Navigating from the `AppMenu` widget

```
void _navigate(String route) {
    Navigator.popAndPushNamed(context, route);


}
```

Navigator.popAndPushNamed is another method to manage the route stack, like push and pushNamed. This method pops the current page off though, to ensure that there isn't a giant stack of pages.

You can see another example of adding a page to the stack in the `UserAccountsDrawer-Header` widget in this same build method.

Listing 7.8   `UserAccountsDrawerHeader` usage in `AppMenu` widget

```
UserAccountsDrawerHeader(
  currentAccountPicture: CircleAvatar(
    backgroundImage:
```

Takes a CircleAvatar as a child, which crops any image into a circle

```
        AssetImage("assets/images/apple-in-hand.jpg"),
    ),
    accountEmail: Text(s.data.contact),
    accountName: Text(s.data.name),

    onDetailsPressed: () {
      Navigator.pushReplacementNamed(
          context, ECommerceRoutes.userSettingsPage);
    },
  ),
),
```

> Accepts some crucial details of user, such as contact information and name

> Passes in user information from the aforementioned AsyncSnapshot, which is one way to get data asynchronously. (More on this soon).

Navigator.pushReplacementNamed ensures that the route stack won't just keep adding new pages. It'll remove the route you're navigating from when the new route is finished animating in.

7.2.5 *NavigatorObserver: Highlighting the active route with RouteAware*

Another interesting aspect of the Flutter router is *observers*. You won't get far into Dart programming without using observers and streams and emitting events. There's an entire chapter devoted to that later in this book, but for now, I'm going to focus specifically on a `NavigatorObserver`. A navigator observer (figure 7.7) is an object that tells any widget that's listening, "Hey, the Navigator is performing some event, if you're interested." That's really its only job—but it's an important one.

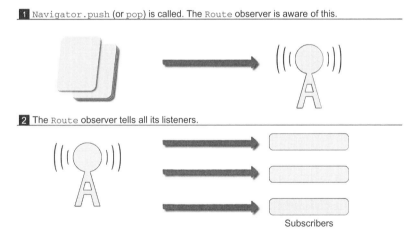

Figure 7.7 Route observer process diagram

A subclass of `NavigatorObserver`, and the one we're interested in here, is `Route-Observer`. This observer specifically notifies all its listeners if the current active route of specific type changes (for instance, `PageRoute`).

This `RouteObserver` is how you're going to keep track of which page is active, and use it to highlight the correct menu item in the menu. For many cases, you'll only need one `RouteObserver` per `Navigator`. Which means there'll likely be only one in your app. In this app, the route observer is built in the app file.

```
final RouteObserver<Route> routeObserver =
    RouteObserver<Route>();

class ECommerceApp extends StatefulWidget {
  @override
  _ECommerceAppState createState() => _ECommerceAppState();
}

// ... rest of file
```

> By giving it a type of **<Route>**, the observer will notify listeners of any route change. Alternatively, **<PageRoute>** would only notify page routes.

I created the observer in the *global scope*, not protected by the safety of any class, because I needed it to be visible through out the whole app. Also, if it was added to a class, it would be the singular member on that class, which is unnecessary. This is common for `RouteObserver` objects. After this, you need to tell your `MaterialApp` about it, in the same file, as shown in this listing.

Listing 7.9   Pass route observers into the `MaterialApp` widget

```
// e_commerce/lib/app.dart -- line ~51
return MaterialApp(
    debugShowCheckedModeBanner: false,
    theme: _theme,
    home: PageContainer(pageType: PageType.Catalog,),
    routes: { ... }
    navigatorObservers: [routeObserver],
);
```

> Tell MaterialApp about the **routeObserver** that it needs to notify when a routing event takes place.

That's all the set up; now you can listen to that observer on any `State` object. It has to be `stateful` though, because you'll need to use some state lifecycle method. For our purposes, this is going to happen back in the `AppMenu` widget you've been working with in this section. First, the state object needs to be extended with the mixin `Route-Aware`, as shown here:

```
// e-commerce/lib/menu/app_menu_drawer.dart -- line ~14
class AppMenu extends StatefulWidget {
  @override
  AppMenuState createState() => AppMenuState();
}

class AppMenuState extends State<AppMenu>
    with RouteAware { ... }
```

> **with** is the Dart keyword needed to use mixins.

This `RouteAware` mixin is an abstract class that provides an interface to interact with a route observer. Now, your state object has access to the methods `didPop`, `didPush`, and a few others.

In order to update the menu with the correct active route, we need to be notified when there's a new page on the stack. There are two steps to that: first, listen to the changes from the route observer, and second, listen to the observer to be notified when the route changes.

Listing 7.10 Listen to the route observer

**The class variable I use to track
the currently active route**

```
// e_commerce/lib/menu/app_menu_drawer.dart -- line ~19
class AppMenuState extends State<AppMenu> with RouteAware {
  String _activeRoute;
  UserBloc _bloc;

  @override
  void didChangeDependencies() {
    super.didChangeDependencies();
    routeObserver.subscribe(
      this,
      ModalRoute.of(context),
    );

    _bloc = AppStateContainer.of(context)
      .blocProvider.userBloc;
  }
// ... rest of class
}
```

**This is a widget lifecycle method,
and the correct place to listen to
new streams and observers. We'll
cover this in the next chapter.**

**Accesses the created global
routeObserver variable; subscribe is
a method that listens to the observer.
This method expects a RouteAware
object (which this state object is,
because it extends the RouteAware
class), and the route in which you're
interested—in this case, the route
you're on now.[1]**

**The UserBloc lines can be ignored for now. I'm
showing these for the sake of completeness.**

Now that this widget is aware of route changes, it needs to update its active route variable when any Navigator activity happens. This is done in the didPush method that it inherited from RouteAware:

**Called when a route is pushed onto the stack. This happens as the
menu itself is transitioning off screen. So, the next time you build the
drawer (by opening the menu), the build method is called again.
Thus, it's redundant to call setState.**

```
// e_commerce/lib/menu/app_menu_drawer.dart -- line ~30
@override
void didPush() {

  _activeRoute =
    ModalRoute.of(context).settings.name;

}
```

**This line gets the name of
the current route. Using
context to grab route
settings is similar to using
a theme (discussed in
chapter 4), but that
paradigm will be
explained in-depth in
the next chapter.**

Using the navigation observer and route aware is, in my opinion, the most complicated topic in this chapter. This list of resources might help if you want to read through more examples:

- https://api.flutter.dev/flutter/widgets/RouteObserver-class.html
- https://stackoverflow.com/questions/46165705/
  flutter-how-the-navigatorobserver-class-works

---

[1] A ModalRoute is a route that covers the screen, even if it isn't opaque on the whole screen. In other words, any route that disables interaction with any route underneath it. Examples would be pages, popups, and drawers.

7.3   *Routing on the fly*

Routing on the fly is the idea that you can route to a page that doesn't exist until it's generated in response to an event. For example, you may want to navigate to a new page when the user taps a list item. You don't have to establish this route ahead of time, because routes are just widgets. Here's some example code.

Listing 7.11   Example code showing routing on the fly

Recall that named routes are navigated to via Navigator.pushNamed.
Navigator.push requires a widget instead of a route.

```
void _showListItemDetailPage() async {
    await Navigator.push(
        context,
        MaterialPageRoute(
            builder: (context) => SettingsPage(
                settings: settings,
                ),
            fullscreenDialog: true,
        ),
    );
}
```

This is just a built-in widget made to display like a page …

… if you want it to! This tells Flutter to make it fullscreen.

In Flutter, everything that seems like a new widget on the route stack is a route. Modals, bottom sheets, snack bars, and dialogs are all routes, and these are perfect candidates for routing on the fly.

7.3.1   *MaterialRouteBuilder*

The first important place that we route on the fly in this app is when we tap a product in the catalog page and navigate to a product detail page.

> **NOTE**   On this page, there are a lot of widgets and concepts not yet covered in this book, like Stream-Builder and Slivers and all kinds of goodies. We will cover those later in the book.

Around line 93 in the lib/widget/catalog.dart file, I build the ProductDetailCard (figure 7.8), which is listening for a tap to navigate to another page.
   The code for the product detail page looks like this:

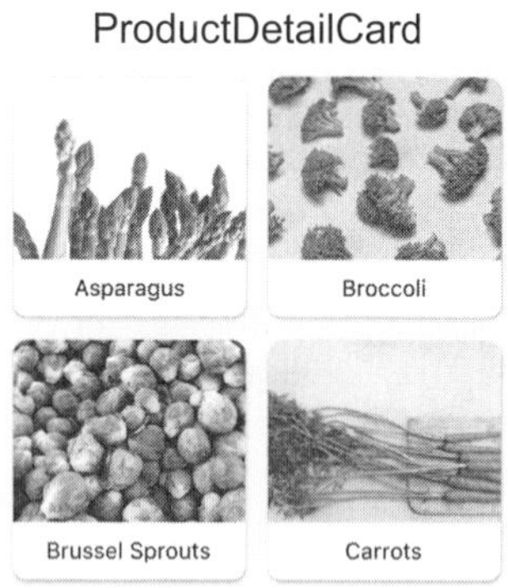

ProductDetailCard

Figure 7.8   Screenshot of product detail cards

```
// e_commerce/lib/widget/catalog.dart -- line ~93
return ProductDetailCard(
    key: ValueKey(_product.imageTitle.toString()),
    onTap: () => _toProductDetailPage(_product),
    onLongPress: () => _showQuickAddToCart(context, _product),
    product: _product,
);
```

This onTap responds to a gesture and calls the important method to us, _toProductDetailPage.

When that item is tapped, the next listing shows the method that will execute.

Listing 7.12 Navigate to a new route on the fly

Like the previous routing, you can use
Navigator.push to add a new page to the stack.

```
// e_commerce/lib/widget/catalog.dart -- line ~37
Future _toProductDetailPage(Product product) async {
    await Navigator.push(
        context,
        MaterialPageRoute(
            builder: (context) =>
            ProductDetailPageContainer(
                product: product,
            ),
        ),
    );
}\
```

MaterialPageRoute is a subclass of
PageRoute, and it provides all the
Material widget functionality in the
new place in the widget tree.

Route objects like MaterialPageRoute
require a builder argument, which
takes a callback and returns a widget.

That's it for navigating to new pages that aren't established. Routes that don't cover the whole screen are similar. This includes modals, dialogs, bottom sheets, and more.[2]

7.3.2 showSnackBar, showBottomSheet, and the like

Flutter has widgets and logic to make it super easy to use routes that aren't pages, like modals and snackbars. These are technically routes, but under the hood, they just don't render like a whole page would. They're still widgets that get added on the stack of the Navigator, rather than being attached to a page (figure 7.9).

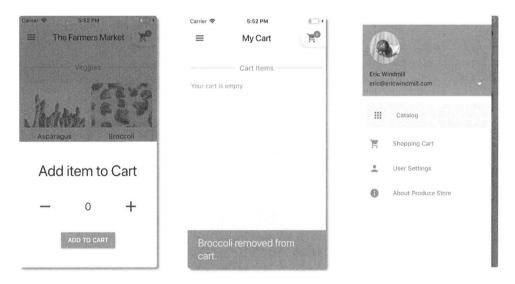

Figure 7.9 Some routes don't cover the entire screen.

---

[2]For a super simple second example of routing without named routes, check out this page in the official documentation: https://flutter.dev/docs/cookbook/navigation/navigation-basics.

In this app, we make use of the bottom sheet (which is common in iOS apps) and a snackbar. These are similar in the fact that they appear from the bottom of the screen and only cover a portion on the screen. They're different, though, because a bottom sheet is a `ModalRoute`. Meaning that when it's in view, you cannot interact with the page beneath it. A snack bar doesn't obstruct the app, so you can still interact while it's in view.

The bottom sheet is implemented in the same `Catalog` widget, and kicked off by pressing and holding a `ProductDetailCard` via the `ProductDetailCard.onLongPress` method:

```
// e_commerce/lib/widget/catalog.dart -- line ~93
return ProductDetailCard(
    key: ValueKey(_product.imageTitle.toString()),
    onTap: () => _toProductDetailPage(_product),
    onLongPress: () =>                              On a long press,
        _showQuickAddToCart(_product),    <------  show a bottom sheet.
    product: _product,
);
```

This method, `_showQuickAddToCart`, is in the business of showing the `BottomSheet` (figure 7.10), waiting for the user to interact with it, and listening to the data that the bottom sheet passes back.

1 Product detail card is tapped, calling `showBottomSheet`.

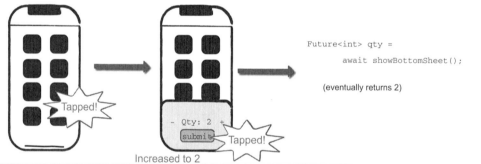

2 When Submit is tapped, `showBottomSheet` completes the `Future` value.

Figure 7.10   Bottom sheet widget example

The `_showQuickAddToCart` method looks like this:

```
// e_commerce/lib/widget/catalog.dart -- line ~48
void _showQuickAddToCart(BuildContext context, Product product) async {
  CartBloc _cartBloc = AppState.of(context).blocProvider.cartBloc;

  int qty = await showModalBottomSheet<int>(              <-----
```

There's a lot going on in this line alone. For starters, showModalBottomSheet is a global method, provided by Flutter, which takes care of the routing for you. The type declaration (<int>) tells us what type of data we can expect to be passed back from the bottom sheet. This line is also assigning a value to the return value of showModalBottomSheet. You have to use the await keyword, because the method returns a Future. This Future basically says, "Hey, I'm going to give you the proper value as soon as the user dismisses the bottom sheet and I get the correct value."

```
    context: context,
                                            ◄─────
    builder: (BuildContext context) {  ◄─────
        return AddToCartBottomSheet(
            key: Key(product.id),
        );
    });
    _addToCart(product, qty, _cartBloc);
}
```

All routes need a BuildContext so Flutter knows where to insert them into the tree.

All route change methods expect a callback that returns a widget.

To complete this implementation, we need to look at the `AddToCartBottomSheet` code. Within that widget, there's a `RaisedButton`, which corresponds to this button on the screen (figure 7.11).

This `AddToCartBottomSheet` method is nearly 100 lines of code, but much of it is basic Flutter widget building. I would like to point out some pieces to complete this specific lesson. (Hint: the most important part for this lesson is the `RaisedButton` near the bottom of the code sample.)

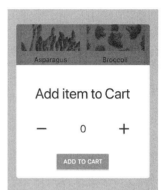

Figure 7.11
Bottom sheet screenshot from Farmers Market app

Listing 7.13 Choice code from the `AddToCartBottomSheet` widget

I'm highlighting this first line just to show that this special kind of partial route, a bottom sheet, is just a widget. There is nothing special about it at all.

```
// e_commerce/lib/widget/add_to_cart_bottom_sheet.dart
class AddToCartBottomSheet extends StatefulWidget {
  const AddToCartBottomSheet({Key key}) : super(key: key);

  @override
  _AddToCartBottomSheetState createState() => _AddToCartBottomSheetState();
}

class _AddToCartBottomSheetState extends State<AddToCartBottomSheet> {
  int _quantity = 0;
  // ...

  @override
  Widget build(BuildContext context) {
    return ConstrainedBox(    ◄─────
      constraints: BoxConstraints(
        minWidth: MediaQuery.of(context).size.width,
        minHeight: MediaQuery.of(context).size.height / 2,
      ),
      child: Column(
        children: <Widget>[
          Padding(
            // ...
            child: Text("Add item to Cart"),
          ),
          Padding(
```

This is a good example of using box constraints, which is limiting the size of the bottom sheet.

```
      // ...
      child: Row(                          ┌── This row is where the user adjust the
        children: <Widget>[          ◄──┤   quantity they would like to add to the cart.
          IconButton(...) // decrease qty button
          Text(...) // current quanity
          IconButton(...) // increase qty button
        ],
      ),
    ),
    RaisedButton(                          ┌── This RaisedButton is where the most
      color: AppColors.primary[500],  ◄──┤   important pieces of this lesson lie.
      textColor: Colors.white,
      child: Text(
        "Add To Cart".toUpperCase(),
      ),
      onPressed: () =>                     ┌── This single line is what we care
        Navigator.of(context).pop(_quantity),  ◄──┤   about specifically for routing.
    )
  ],
  ),
);
}
```

This is a pretty run-of-the-mill button. The part we're interested in is its `onPressed`
callback. When the button is pressed, it pops the top route off the Navigator (which
is the bottom sheet itself), and then passes that variable (`_quantity`), back to code
that added this route onto the stack. Recall that this route was added to the stack by
the `Catalog._showQuickAddToCart` method. Let's revisit that code as shown in the
next listing.

Listing 7.14   `_showQuickAddToCart` method revisited

```
// e_commerce/lib/widget/catalog.dart -- line ~48
void _showQuickAddToCart(BuildContext context, Product product) async {
CartBloc _cartBloc = AppState.of(context).blocProvider.cartBloc;

  int qty = await showModalBottomSheet<int>(   ◄── This method pushes a bottom sheet
    context: context,                              on the Navigator stack. And it's
    builder: (BuildContext context) {             awaiting a response, which can be
      return AddToCartBottomSheet(   ◄──┐          saved as a variable.
        key: Key(product.id),
      );
  });                                   └── This is where we're building the
                                            AddToCartBottomSheet widget.

  _addToCart(product, qty, _cartBloc);   ◄──┐ Here, the point of this whole exercise. We're
}                                            passing the value returned from the bottom
                                             sheet into a different method.
```

The point of this whole section is that bottom sheets and the like behave exactly like
routes. And when you pop these routes off the Navigator, you can pass data back to
the previous screen, as we're doing with the qty variable.

Other pop-up style widgets work just as easily. For example, to show a snackbar, you can call showSnackbar, which lives on a scaffold: Scaffold.of(context).showSnackBar (Widget content);.

7.4 *Routing animations*

The final piece of the routing puzzle is making it pretty, which is my favorite part about writing apps. Believe it or not, though, there's almost no work involved in adding custom route transitions. The real work, actually, is in writing the animation, if you want to do it super fancy. But as you saw in the previous app, Flutter gives you quite a few animations out of the box.

Before we dive in, consider how page transitions work in Flutter, by default. The following facts are important:

- Pages are just widgets, so they can be animated like any other widget.
- Pages have default transitions, which differ by platform: iOS style or Material style.
- All transitions involve two pages, one of which is coming into view, and one that is leaving view.

With that in mind, lets dive in. Transitions are handled by PageRoute, or in our case, MaterialPageRoute, which extends PageRoute, which extends ModalRoute, which extends TransitionRoute. Somewhere in this mess, there's a method called buildTransitions, which, among other things, takes two animations as arguments. One is for itself as it exits, and the second to coordinate with the route that's replacing it. MaterialPageRoute already implements transitions, which means you can override MaterialPageRoute.buildTransitions.

All this method has to do is return a widget. And by overriding it, you don't have to worry about writing the AnimationController or Tween—that's all taken care of in the superclass. Which means you can simply return a page that's wrapped in an animated widget, and it will animate accordingly. Take a look at the code to make that less abstract. This can be found in lib/util/material_route_transition.dart.

> ### Listing 7.15 Writing a custom page transition

To write this transition, we're going to lean heavily on what Flutter gives us out of the box. Extend the MaterialPageRoute, and pass this class's properties to the superclass by calling super.

```
// e_commerce/lib/util/material_route_transition.dart
class FadeInSlideOutRoute<T> extends
    MaterialPageRoute<T> {
  FadeInSlideOutRoute({WidgetBuilder builder, RouteSettings settings})
      : super(builder: builder, settings: settings);

  @override
  Widget buildTransitions(
    BuildContext context,
    Animation<double> animation,
```

This overridden method is called internally, so we don't have to mess with building the animation itself, but you could if you wanted!

```
    Animation<double> secondaryAnimation,
    Widget child,
  ) {
    if (settings.isInitialRoute) return child;
    if (animation.status == AnimationStatus.reverse) {
      return super.buildTransitions(
        context,
        animation,
        secondaryAnimation,
        child,
      );
    }
    return FadeTransition(
        opacity: animation,
        child: child,
    );
  }
}
```

Return a built-in Flutter FadeTransition, and pass it in the animation built by the superclass. Now anytime you push a FadeInSlideOutRoute onto the stack, it'll use these animations.

There's a bit of abstraction in that example, to be sure. But the most important line, by far, is the return statement. This buildTransitions method overrides the same method on the superclass, MaterialPageRoute, and does all the hard work of calculating how to animate between pages and implementing those transitions.

FadeTransition tells buildTransitions specifically to build a transition that fades the new page in. And buildTransitions is called internally. We never explicitly call it in the code. If you wanted to create something highly customized, you would need to call buildTransitions on your own, and you would likely be using WidgetsApp rather than a MaterialApp at the root of your application.

With all that in mind, FadeTransition is what we, the developers, really care about. You could also use one of the many other transitions that Flutter's material library provides:

- SlideTransition
- SizeTransition
- RotationTransition
- AlignTransition
- and more

These are all provided by the framework, and implementing them is just as straight forward.

To use this, all you need to do is go to Catalog._toProductDetailPage and replace MaterialPageRoute with FadeInSlideOutRoute. Now when you tap a product detail card, the routes will fade. I guess it's worth saying that you could get as fancy and wild with this as you wanted. You're limited only by the animation you write. Finally, if you'd like to read another explanation, this article written by Divyanshu Bhargava on Medium is quite good: https://medium.com/flutter-community/everything-you-need-to-know-about-flutter-page-route-transition-9ef5c1b32823.

Summary

- Flutter uses dynamic routing, which makes routing much more flexible and fluid.
- Flutter's Navigator allows you to create routes "on the fly" in your code, just as some user interaction takes place or the app receives new data.
- Flutter supports (practically) static routing using named routes. (Although these routes are still technically created as the app is running.)
- Define your named routes in your `MaterialApp` widget or whichever top-level `App` widget you're using.
- The Navigator manages all the routes in a stack manner.
- Navigating to routes is done by calling variations of `Navigator.push` and `Navigator.pop`.
- `Navigator.push` calls return a `Future` that awaits a value which is to be passed back by the new route.
- Creating a full Material-style menu drawer in Flutter involves several incredibly generous widgets: `Drawer`, `ListView`, `ListTile`, `AboutListTile`, and `Drawer-Header`.
- You can anticipate changes in routing by setting up a `RouteObserver` and subscribing to it on any widget's state object.
- Several UI elements are managed with the Navigator and are technically routes, though they aren't pages, such as snackbars, bottom sheets, drawers, and menus.
- You can listen for user interactions using the `GestureDetector` widget.
- Implementing custom page transitions is done by extending `Route` classes.

Flutter state management 8

This chapter covers

- `StatefulWidget` and the state object
- Widget tree vs. element tree
- State object lifecycle
- InheritedWidget and blocs for state management
- Introduction to streams and async Dart

This chapter is going to be my favorite for two reasons: first, there isn't one approach to state management (in Flutter or elsewhere). There are many different state management patterns, and all developers have opinions about each of them. And second, developers (including myself) are … passionate … about their opinions.

With that in mind, I won't be able to do a deep dive on every state management pattern that's popular right now. I thought a lot about which patterns I *should* cover, and I came up with this two-pronged litmus test to decide:

1 Will it help you expand your Flutter and Dart skills?
2 Is it unopinionated enough that its concepts can be applied elsewhere?

This is what I came up with for this chapter in general:

- Deep dive into the `StatefulWidget`. This is information you need regardless of your state management approach.
- The `InheritedWidget`. The inherited widget is the "third" widget (along with stateless and stateful). It's enough to handle state in a smaller app on it's own, and all heftier libraries likely use this under the hood. It's likely that any Flutter app you use will use inherited widgets, even when you're also using a fancy library.
- Google's BLoC pattern for app state management. I basically decided that this was the best pattern to spend time on because it's not verbose and it doesn't require an outside library. Patterns like Redux have significant boilerplate code. You have to pull in an outside library, and those are extremely opinionated.

NOTE There are some open-sourced libraries that abstract away the bloc pattern implementation. Some of these are fantastic and widely used. That said, the concept of blocs does not rely on any specific implementation.

The next section is all about stateful widgets and state objects. It's mostly conceptual. The code writing begins in the following section.

8.1   Deep dive into StatefulWidgets

Here's a small review. A `StatefulWidget` has two jobs: it holds on to immutable variables, just like a `StatelessWidget`, and no property on the `StatefulWidget` can be updated. Its second job is to create an associated `State` object.

Listing 8.1　`StatefulWidget` example

```
class ItemCounter extends StatefulWidget {
    final String name;                        ◁───  This property is immutable.
                                                    It's marked final.
    ItemCounter({this.name});

    @override
    _ItemCounterState createState() =>        ◁───────  Creates an associated state object
        _ItemCounterState();
}
```

The `State` object has many jobs. Its basic jobs are keeping track of an internal (mutable) state and building child widgets with `State.build`. But the state objects in Flutter can get a bit trickier than that. It's worth knowing how they're treated differently in the widget tree, as well as how to deal with its lifecycle.

8.1.1   The widget tree and the element tree

Flutter knows how to render widgets to the screen by building the *element tree*. The widget tree isn't directly rendered, because widgets are "blueprints" for renderable elements. We, the developers, build a widget tree of blueprints, which Flutter internally maps to an element tree.

It's worth reviewing how different types of widgets interact with the element tree. A *stateless* widget gets mapped, one to one, to an element. As the app is rendering and Flutter is crawling the widget tree, it'll say, "Hey element tree, can you make an element that corresponds to this widget?" And the element tree does.

The element tree (figure 8.1) doesn't handle *stateful* widgets the same way. When Flutter asks the element tree to make a stateful widget, the element tree says, "Sure. Hey, new stateful widget, can you create a state object for me?" And so it does.

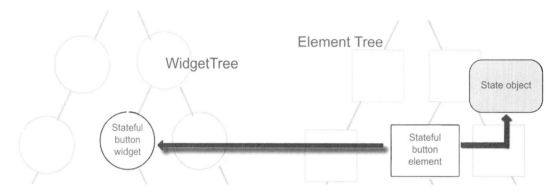

Figure 8.1   Elements have a reference to widgets and their state objects.

If this is handled internally, why do we care? It's useful to understand because state objects and elements are *long-lived*. If the StatefulWidget is replaced in the tree, and a new widget is of the same type (and has the same key), the corresponding element keeps pointing to the same spot in the tree and references the new stateful widget, but the associated State object stays right where it is and is reused.

Flutter provides methods on the state object that allow you to respond to changes in the element tree. These methods are called in a specific sequence. This sequence is generally referred to as the widget's *lifecycle*.

8.1.2   *The StatefulWidget lifecycle and when to do what*

I like to think of the lifecycle in two pieces: the first part, the main thread, is a sequence of methods that will be called in order and at least once in the state object's lifecycle, no matter what. The second part is three methods that can be called depending on different events. They all trigger rebuilds.

> **NOTE**   After this section, we'll start writing code. In the code, you'll see these lifecycle methods used, and I'll explain what's happening with them. Before that, it'll be helpful to give you a quick overview of the whole process. Don't get bogged down in the details quite yet.

Figure 8.2 shows the lifecycle, in order.

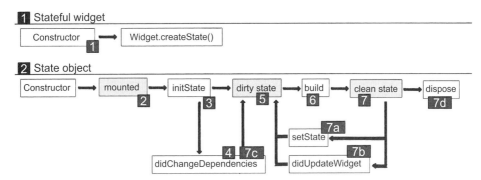

Figure 8.2 State object lifecycle

In the figure

1 The state class constructor is called (as it is for every class in Dart). The widget isn't in the tree yet, so most state-specific initialization shouldn't be done here.

2 The state object is associated with a `BuildContext`, or location, in the tree. The widget is now considered "mounted." You can check if a widget is mounted with `Widget.mounted`.

3 `State.initState` is called. This method is called exactly once. This method should be used to initialize properties on the `State` object that depend on its associated stateful widget or build context.

4 `State.didChangeDependencies` is called. This method is special because it's called once immediately after `initState`, but can also be called later in the life-cycle (which I'll cover in a minute). This method is where you should do initialization that involves an `InheritedWidget`.

5 At this point, the state is considered "dirty," which is how Flutter tracks which widgets need to be rebuilt. Any time a state object needs to be built, including the first time, it marks itself as dirty.

6 The state object is fully initialized, and the `State.build` method is called.

7 After a new build, the state is marked "clean." Up to this point, the lifecycle has been on a single track. When the state is clean, nothing is happening. The state object is displayed as it's intended, and it's waiting for the framework to give it further directions. Several things can happen now:

   a `state.setState` is called from your code, which always marks the state as dirty.

   b An ancestor widget can request that this location in the tree be rebuilt. If the location is to be rebuilt with the same widget type and key, then the framework will call `didUpdateWidget` with the previous widget as an argument. This also marks the state as dirty, and thus rebuilds the state.

   c If your widget depends on an `InheritedWidget`, and that inherited widget changes, then the framework calls `didChangeDependencies`. At this point, the widget will be rebuilt.

d   Finally, there's one action that's guaranteed to occur. The state object is going to be removed from the tree so `State.disposed` is called. This method is where you should clean up any resources used by the widget, such as stopping active animations or closing streams. Once `disposed` is called, the widget can never build again. It is an error to call `setState` at this point.

That list is a primer for the rest of this chapter. Again, no need to get too bogged down yet.

Next, you're going to see different *state management* patterns. State management is a combination of passing data around the app, but also re-rendering pieces of your app at the right time. All the re-rendering in Flutter is dependent on the `State` object and its lifecycle.

8.2   Pure Flutter state management: The InheritedWidget

The most basic state management in Flutter is just passing state around the tree from widget to widget. This can get cumbersome, and I can't recommend you do that. You might try instead a slightly better version known as *lifting state up*.

Lifting state up (figure 8.3) is a pattern in which mutable state lives high in the widget tree and is managed by passing properties way down the tree, as well as passing

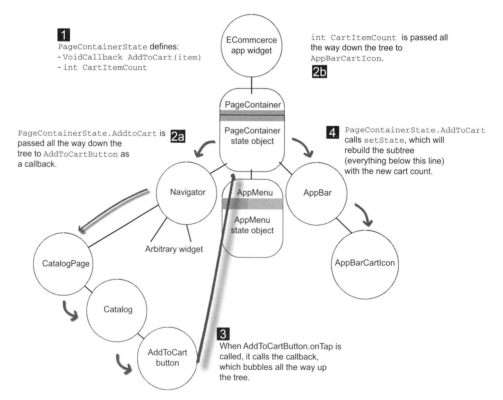

Figure 8.3   This widget tree passes state all the way down the tree, making code verbose and state hard to reason about.

methods that call `setState` way down the tree. This can make your state hard to reason about, and it requires a lot of extra code to pass a property down from widget to widget.

More importantly, it makes development more painful than it needs to be. If you had a tree that looked like figure 8.3, and you decided you'd rather the `AppBarCart-Icon` be a child of the `CartPage`, you'll have to remove all the code that passes properties down to the icon, and then add all the code to pass that information down through the Navigator and to the cart page (figure 8.4).

Luckily, Flutter gives us a better way: the `InheritedWidget`. You've likely seen inherited widgets before: `Theme`, `MediaQuery`, and `Scaffold` are all inherited. These widgets are special, because any widget in the inherited widget's subtree can access the inherited widget. You don't have to pass properties from widget to widget, because you can just grab the properties directly from the `InheritedWidget`. Then, if you want to move widgets around the tree in development, you don't have to change the code of any other widgets. You can just move it.

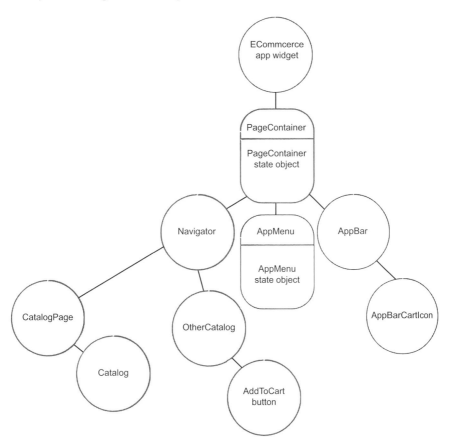

Figure 8.4   When state is managed naively, moving a widget in your source code requires you to edit many widgets.

8.2.1   *Creating a Central Store wth an InheritedWidget/StatefulWidget team*

The boiler plate for an inherited widget as a state management device can be verbose. If you look at the documentation of the `InheritedWidget` class, you'll see that it's a third type of widget, and importantly, not an extension of the stateful widget class. According to the documentation, this widget is a "base class for widgets that efficiently propagate information down the tree."[1]

The point is that inherited widgets are meant to send information, not to be sent information. This means you have to combine a stateful widget with an inherited widget to make it work as a central storage. In the code, start by looking in lib/main.dart file, where `runApp` is being called:

```
// e_commerce/lib/main.dart -- line ~36
runApp(
    AppStateContainer(                        ◄──────   This class, AppStateContainer, is
        blocProvider: blocProvider,                     a StatefulWidget. Its State.build
        child: ECommerceApp(),                          method returns an InheritedWidget.
    ),
);
```

If you're confused by that code sample and the corresponding explanation, you aren't alone. It's a bit tricky. But the trick of the whole thing is in the `AppState` class. A big chunk of the extra required code lives in the `AppStateContainer.of` method, which provides the rest of your app with a way to interact with the `AppState` class.

8.2.2   *The inheritFromWidgetOfExactType and of methods*

If you want to get information from an inherited widget down your widget tree, you'll likely provide a reference to that inherited widget with a method called `of`. This method looks up the tree and finds the closest parent inherited widget of that type. For example, when you call `Theme.of(BuildContext).primaryColor`, Flutter is looking up the tree for the nearest `Theme` widget, as in figure 8.5, and grabbing the `primaryColor` property from it.

The `of` method is a Flutter convention, not something you get out of the box. Most `of` methods are defined on the inherited widgets themselves, and they usually turn around and call `BuildContext.inheritFromWidgetOfExactType` with the `Build-Context` you provide. `inheritFromWidgetOfExactType` is the actual method that looks up the tree, and it relies on the `BuildContext` to access the tree and look at its ancestors.

---

[1]Documentation can be found at https://docs.flutter.dev/flutter/widgets/InheritedWidget-class.html.

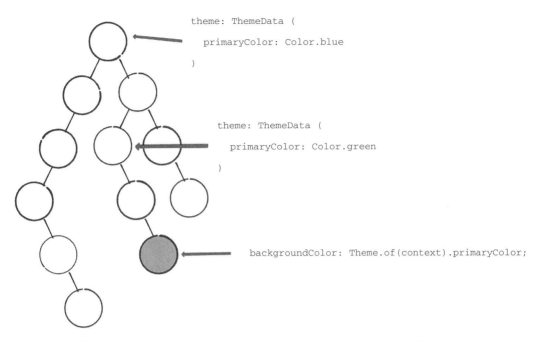

```
theme: ThemeData (

    primaryColor: Color.blue

)




theme: ThemeData (

    primaryColor: Color.green

)




backgroundColor: Theme.of(context).primaryColor;
```

Figure 8.5 Using an `InheritedWidget`, you can grab references to widgets higher in the tree with the `of` method.

Because this method is static, it can be called from anywhere, without any reference to an instance of the class. The `of` method is really the secret to the inherited widget.

Listing 8.2 Custom `of` method

```
// e_commerce/lib/blocs/app_state.dart -- line ~13
class AppStateContainer extends StatefulWidget {
  final Widget child;
  final BlocProvider blocProvider;
  const AppStateContainer({
    Key key,
    @required this.child,                        The of method must be passed a
    @required this.blocProvider,           BuildContext object. It's the only object
  }) : super(key: key);                      that can freely examine the widget tree.

  @override
  State<StatefulWidget> createState() => AppState();

  static AppState of(BuildContext context) {
    return (context.inheritFromWidgetOfExactType(_AppStoreContainer)
        as _AppStoreContainer).appData;
  }
}
```

Grab a reference to the InheritedWidget you want
with the inheritFromWidgetOfExactType method,
and return the appData property on that widget
(which, as you'll see, is a StatefulWidget)

There are four important pieces to that method:

- AppState—The widget that you want to access. In this case, it's a state object.
- BuildContext—You don't want a new instance of AppState. You specifically want the one that's been created, is already managing state, and lives above any given location in the widget tree. In other words, the one that's associated with the current build context.
- inheritedWidgetOfExactType—A method on instances of BuildContext that can find an ancestor inherited widget of the type passed in.
- as statement—The type casting that inherited the widget into its subclass, so you can access members of the returned inherited widget. In this case, we want to return appData. Importantly, appData is a property that I've defined, which you'll see soon. It's not something that lives on all InheritedWidget implementations.

With all that in mind, we can look at the _AppStoreContainer widget, which is the inherited widget retrieved by AppStateContainer.of.

Listing 8.3   Handle a state object with the inherited widget

**The appData property is the AppState
(state object) created by AppState.**

```
// e_commerce/lib/blocs/app_state.dart -- line ~52
class _AppStoreContainer extends InheritedWidget {
  final AppState appData;
  final BlocProvider blocProvider;

  _AppStoreContainer({                        This inherited widget
    Key key,                                  expects an AppState object.
    @required this.appData,       
    @required child,                   The widget also expects a child widget.
    @required this.blocProvider,
  }) : super(key: key, child: child);
                                   The child can be passed through to the superclass.
  @override                        It doesn't need to be touched in this app itself.
  bool updateShouldNotify(_AppStoreContainer oldWidget)
      => oldWidget.appData != this.appData;
}                                   The only other method required
                                    when creating an inherited widget.
                                    I will talk about this in a bit.
```

So now, we have a method called of that gives us a reference to the InheritedWidget.appData property anywhere in the widget subtree. And the InheritedWidget.appData is just a state object! This means you can access the same state object anywhere in your app. If that doesn't excite you, then I don't know what will. This is one of my favorite built-in Flutter features.

Finally, I just want to take a look at the AppState.build method.

Listing 8.4 `AppState.build` method

```
// e_commerce/lib/blocs/app_state.dart -- line ~36
class AppState extends State<AppStateContainer> {
  BlocProvider get blocProvider => widget.blocProvider;

  @override
    Widget build(BuildContext context) {
      return _AppStoreContainer(
        appData: this,
        blocProvider: widget.blocProvider,
        child: widget.child,
      );
    }
}
```

Returns an instance of the _AppStoreContainer inherited widget

Passes itself in as the appData property

Passes the associated StatefulWidget child straight through to the inherited widget. Remember that this child is passed in from the runApp method, and it represents the rest of the widget tree.

The third annotation in the previous code sample leads to an interesting point. The child widget is passed into the `AppStateContainer` stateful widget, then passed to the `AppState` state object via `widget.child`, and then passed in via the `build` method to `_AppStoreContainer`, which itself passes this child widget straight to its superclass. (This is demonstrated in figure 8.6.) This means we never have to touch the child widget in this entire state management implementation. (You can, of course. It's completely valid to make the `build` method of the `AppState` class more robust, as you would with any old state object.)

The `updateShouldNotify` method

As a quick aside, I need to talk about the single required method on the Inherited-Widget class: updateShouldNotify. When an inherited widget rebuilds, it may need to tell all the widgets that depend on its data to rebuild as well. This method is called after rebuilds and always passes in the old widget as an argument. This gives you a chance to check if Flutter should rebuild or not. For example, if your new widget is rebuilt with the same data, then there's no need to make Flutter do the expensive work. Here's an example:

```
// e_commerce/lib/blocs/app_state.dart -- line ~64
bool updateShouldNotify(_AppStoreContainer oldWidget) =>
    oldWidget.appData != this.appData;
```

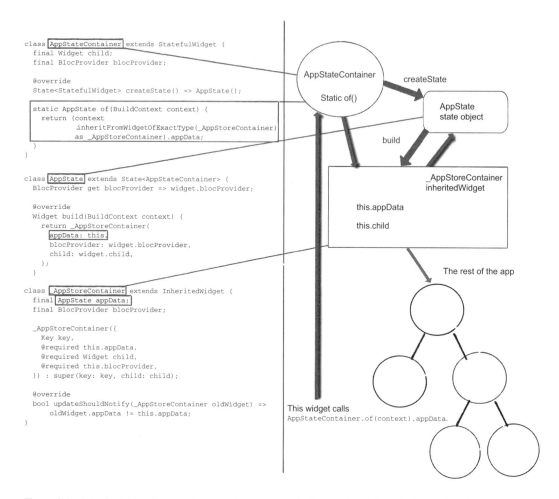

Figure 8.6 **Inherited widgets give you a way to access an instance of a state object anywhere in the tree.**

8.2.3   *Use the of method to lift up state*

Using an inherited widget at the top of the tree is a cleaner style of lifting state up, in a way. Your state still lives in a widget at the top of the tree, but it's easier to manage and reason about. Using this method, all of your `setState` methods can live in the `AppState` state object, and you can call them using `AppState.of(context).callMyMethod()`.

When any given method is called that changes the state of an inherited widget, it needs to know whether the change should trigger rebuilds in widgets down the tree. Let's walk through an example, starting in the `AppState` class, where the state is actually changed. In that class, find the comment that says "lifting state up region." In listing 8.5, you'll find a couple of class members that use the lifting-state-up method. Anywhere in the app, you could call `AppState.of(context).updateCartCount`, and it would call the `updateCartCount` method in the `AppState` class.

Listing 8.5   Functionality to control quantity with `InheritedWidget`

```
// e_commerce/lib/blocs/app_state.dart -- line ~49
class AppState extends State<AppStateContainer> {
  BlocProvider get blocProvider => widget.blocProvider;

  // ... build method and other class members

  // 'LIFTING STATE UP' REGION:
  int cartCount = 0;
  void updateCartCount(int count) {
    setState(() => cartCount += count);       ◁──┐
  }
}
```

> Calling setState is important because it causes relevant widgets to be rebuilt.

When `AppState.setState` is called, it rebuilds itself. This causes its inherited child widget to rebuild, and then it calls `updateShouldNotify` internally. If that returns true, then `didChangeDependencies` is called on stateful widgets that depend on this inherited widget, and then they'll get rebuilt as well.

I use that `updateCartCount` method in the `AddToCartBottomSheet`. Notice that this class has overridden `didChangeDependencies`, as shown in the next listing. This is important if you're using inherited widgets, because if the widgets that `AddToCart-BottomSheet` depends on change for any reason, the widgets will need to reassign their reference to the updated inherited widget.

Listing 8.6   Override the `didChangeDependencies` method

Define a class-level member
reference to AppStateContainer.

```
// e_commerce/lib/widget/add_to_cart_bottom_sheet.dart -- line ~49
class _AddToCartBottomSheetState extends State<AddToCartBottomSheet> {
  int _quantity;
  AppState state;          ◁┈┈┈

  @override
  void didChangeDependencies() {
    super.didChangeDependencies();     ◁──
    state = AppStateManager.of(context);   ◁──┐
  }

  @override
  Widget build(BuildContext context) {
    return ConstrainedBox(...),
      child: Column(
        children: <Widget>[
          // ...
          RaisedButton(
            color: AppColors.primary[500],
            textColor: Colors.white,
            child: Text(
              "Add To Cart".toUpperCase(),
            ),
```

> This override should always call super.

> Reference the AppStateContainer class the first time it's safe to do so. Remember that the of method returns a reference to the AppStateContainer.appData, which is the state object, rather than the inherited widget itself.

```
            onPressed: () =>
                state.updateCartTotal(_quantity)
        )
    ],
  ),
);
}
```

◁─── **The call to the inherited widget itself. More on this in a bit.**

For the sake of simplifying this code example, here's the `RaisedButton` tweezed out of the above example, which is making the call to the state management widget itself.

Listing 8.7   Call method from the inherited widget from the bottom sheet

```
// e_commerce/lib/blocs/add_to_cart_bottom_sheet.dart -- line ~75
//...
RaisedButton(
  color: AppColors.primary[500],
  textColor: Colors.white,
  child: Text(
    "Add To Cart".toUpperCase(),
  ),
  onPressed: () => state.updateCartTotal(_quantity) ◁──┐

//     onPressed: () =>
//         Navigator.of(context).pop(_quantity),                ◁─────┐

)
```

Because your widget's state property is a specific instance of the AppState class, you can call updateCartTotal; be sure that you're updating the right state.

Make sure this line is commented out! This app switches between two state management architectures in this chapter, and some methods will need to be commented or uncommented.

That's the entire lifting-state-up pattern. If you're using the inherited widget as your store, then all changes to app-wide state should be done in that `AppState` class. This makes it less likely you'll get into sticky situations with state management (compared to just passing state around willy-nilly).

8.2.4   *State management patterns beyond Flutter*

In the beginning of this chapter, I expressed anxiety around the options and opinions of state management. To touch on that a bit more, I want to talk about all the options in Flutter.

It's important to note that Flutter is just the rendering layer of your app. (I mean, it's so much more, and it gives us so much, but as far as writing code goes, it's a UI library.) With that in mind, you can use whatever state management patterns you want. Flutter doesn't care about how it gets data, it only cares about painting that data on the screen.

There are fantastic libraries made by the community (for example, Redux, MobX, and ScopedMode).[2] Of course, no one option is better than another. And everyone has opinions. But don't listen to those opinions—use the patterns that work for you.

---

[2]You can see excellent code examples of different state management and architecture styles at http://flutter samples.com/, a helpful site by community leader Brian Egan. Find Brian here: https://github.com/brianegan.

Just this morning on Twitter, I saw a big name from the JavaScript world tweet something about how awful event emitters are. This guy is undoubtedly brilliant, but I love event-based architecture. We have different opinions, and that's great.

That being said, I can't cover everything, so I'm going to cover what I like the most. But more importantly, I'm going to cover what I believe is the most useful in learning generic concepts for writing Flutter applications: the B.L.o.C. pattern. Other libraries, like Redux, are great because they abstract away so much logic. As long as you follow the pattern, it's likely going to work. But I don't want to abstract that much away for the sake of teaching.

Under the hood, Redux uses inherited widgets and event emitters. The BLoC pattern deals with these directly. It's hard to get very far in Dart programming or Flutter without streams and the `InheritedWidget`, so I'd like you to learn how those fit into the whole situation. Then, when you want to switch to Redux, the whole thing will make more sense because you'll have a nice foundation.

8.3   *Blocs: Business Logic Components*

B.L.o.C. stands for Business Logic Components (or simply *blocs* from here on out). This pattern was first revealed at Dart Conference (aka DartConf) 2018, and its purpose is to make UI business logic highly reusable. Specifically at DartConf, it was presented as a nice way to share all UI logic between Flutter and AngularDart.

The bloc pattern's mantra is that widgets should be as dumb as possible, and the business logic should live in separate components. This in itself isn't unique, compared to other approaches, of course, but the devil is in the details. In general, blocs are what they are for two main reasons:

- Their public API consists of simple inputs and outputs only.
- Blocs should be *injectable*, which means platform-agnostic. This means you can use the same blocs for Flutter and the web.

Those are broad ideas, of course, but they're made clearer by the following *non-negotiable* rules. These rules were described in the original talk at DartConf 2018 and live in two categories: application design and UI rules.

For application design:

1. Inputs and outputs are sinks and streams only! No functions, no constants, no variables! If you aren't familiar with streams, put a pin in your questions for a couple more paragraphs.
2. Dependencies must be injectable. If you're importing any Flutter libraries into the bloc, then that's UI work, not business logic, and those should be moved into the UI.
3. Platform-branching is not allowed. If you find yourself in a bloc writing `if (device == browser)`…, then you need to reconsider.
4. Do whatever else you want, so long as you follow these rules.

For UI functionality:

1 In general, blocs and top-level Flutter pages have a one-to-one (1:1) relation-ship. In reality, the point is that each logical state subject has its own bloc. For example, in the Farmers Market app, I have a `CartBloc` and a `Catalog` bloc.

2 Components should send inputs as is, because there shouldn't be business logic in the widget! If you need to format text or serialize a model, it should be done in the bloc.

3 Outputs should be passed to widgets ready to use. For example, if you have a number that needs to be converted into displayable currency, that should be done in the bloc.

4 Any branching should be based on simple bloc Boolean logic. You should limit yourself to a single Boolean stream in the bloc. For example, in Flutter, it's acceptable to write `color: bloc.isDestructive ? Colors.red : Colors.blue`. It is considered wrong if you have to use complex Boolean clauses like `if (bloc.buttonIsDestructive && bloc.buttonIsEnabled && bloc.userIsAdmin) { ....` If you find yourself doing this, you can probably move this logic to the bloc.

Of course, who am I (or the speaker at DartConf) to attach hard rules to how you design your app? The rules are intended to ensure that your Flutter app is as simple and dumb as possible, but they're merely suggestions. With all that information, figure 8.7 shows what the basic view layer architecture of a Flutter app that uses blocs looks like.

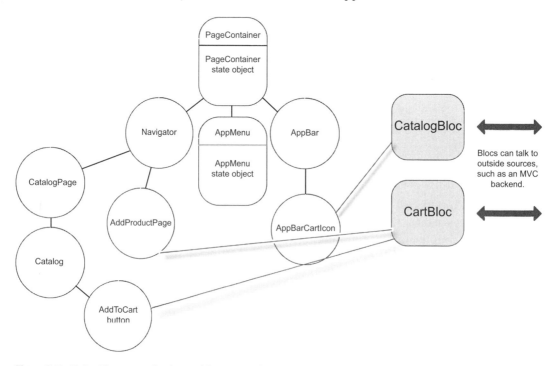

Figure 8.7   Using blocs, your view layer widgets can refer to the same few stateful classes throughout the widget tree.

NOTE The chart in figure 8.7 doesn't represent how data flows from widgets to blocs. It shows that multiple widgets communicate with the same, few blocs that represent a logical piece of state; in this case, the cart bloc and catalog bloc.

These blocs are the middleman between services, backends, and even between two widgets. If you're using blocs, there aren't many cases when you should be using a `StatefulWidget`. (The general exception being widgets that are in forms and have state that hasn't been submitted yet.)

Wherever possible, your widgets should be dumb, stateless widgets whose only jobs are rebuilding when they're told to. Flutter provides a built-in solution to avoiding `StatefulWidgets` with blocs, which we'll cover in a future chapter on async Flutter.

8.3.1 *How do blocs work?*

In general, blocs have two jobs. They should expose streams that allow widgets to update state (data flows in), and they should tell widgets when there's new information and they need to re-render.

Figure 8.8 shows how a user might check out in an e-commerce app. It also shows how an outside source might give the bloc new information, and the bloc would know how to update the relevant widgets. Importantly, though, that is two different processes. Perhaps one of the processes is the result of the first, but they're still separate. In this diagram, let's start at the top-left corner and talk about steps 1-3:

1. A user might tap a Submit button, which calls `CartBloc.checkOut`.
2. The method handles whatever business logic it needs to, like serializing some models into JSON perhaps, and then calls out to a service.
3. The service calls `hypotheticalBackend.submitPayment`.

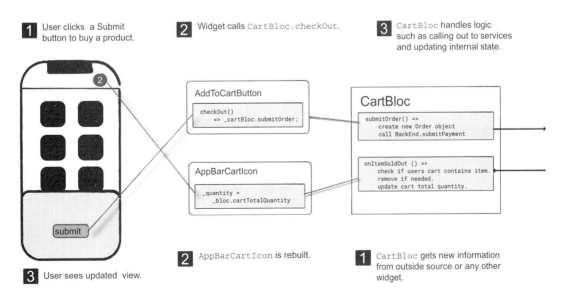

Figure 8.8 How two widgets can interact with the same bloc to manage state

That's the end of that process. The process that starts in the bottom-right corner is triggered not by the previous process, but by the backend replying with new information, which this bloc is listening for:

1 Perhaps the information that comes back for this item is that this transaction was successful. When the bloc gets that information from a backend, it now says, "Great, I'll update some internal state for the user."

2 Because the app is made of dumb widgets that just do what they're told, they're waiting to be told to rebuild when said internal state updates.

3 The widgets rebuild to show the new information.

Those processes, again, are related, because one relied on the first, but they're also independent, and one could happen without the other. That's the basic tenant of blocs. They take in information or data, manipulate it, and pass it back to the appropriate party.

8.3.2 *Implementing the bloc architecture*

The architecture of the bloc pattern isn't much different than the `InheritedWidget` example (such as in listing 8.3). The only difference is that the `AppState` passed around via the inherited widget is going to expose the blocs to the rest of your widgets. Let's talk about what needs to happen for this to work:

- Revert or update some of the code changed for the `InheritedWidget`.
- Feed the blocs to an inherited widget.
- Connect the blocs to whatever external APIs they need.

We'll talk about what goes inside the blocs in the next section, but first, let's wire it all up.

APPSTATEMANAGER AND BLOCPROVIDER

The first thing you *have* to do to make this work is uncomment some code! In order to stop using the lifting-state-up methods from the previous section, you should go to the `AppBarCartIcon` widget and comment out the `Text` at line ~43, and uncomment the `StreamBuilder` below that. After you're done, it should look like this.

Listing 8.8   Blocs work with stream builders (their outputs are all streams)

```
// ecommerce/lib/widget/appbar_cart_icon -- line ~41
//child: Text(
//    AppStateContainer.of(context).cartCount.toString(),
//    style: TextStyle(fontSize: 8.0, color: Colors.white),
//    textAlign: TextAlign.center,
//),
  child: StreamBuilder(              ⟵——— Don't worry about what
    initialData: 0,                        this means right now!
    stream: _bloc.cartItemCount,
    builder: (BuildContext context, AsyncSnapshot snapshot) => Text(
        snapshot.data.toString(),
```

```
          style: TextStyle(fontSize: 8.0, color: Colors.white),
          textAlign: TextAlign.center,
        ),
    ),
```

And also, switch out the onPressed callbacks in RaisedButton in the AddToCart-BottomSheet:

```
// ecommerce/lib/widget/add_to_cart_bottomsheet.dart -- line ~75
RaisedButton(
  color: AppColors.primary[500],
  textColor: Colors.white,
  child: Text(
    "Add To Cart".toUpperCase(),
  ),
//  onPressed: () => state.updateCartTotal(_quantity)
  onPressed: () => Navigator.of(context).pop(_quantity),
```

With those two tasks done, we can talk more about how blocs work.

The solution I've chosen to work with for the blocs involves the InheritedWidget class you've already written, but it's worth noting that blocs and inherited widgets don't care about each other. You could also use blocs by passing them down the widget tree. (That said, though, it's likely—but not desirable—to pass blocs around the tree. It's easiest to combine them with InheritedWidgets that act as *providers*.)

To start, navigate to lib/bloc/app_state.dart file. The following pieces of code in this file matter to us right now.

Listing 8.9   The BlocProvider class (for cleaner code)

```
class BlocProvider
 {
  CartBloc cartBloc;
  CatalogBloc catalogBloc;

  BlocProvider({@required this.cartBloc, @required this.catalogBloc});
}
```

This class is used solely to make it easier and cleaner to pass the blocs around. This is defined at the bottom of the file, but it's used at the top, where I want to start explaining the functionality. Recall that this is the same class that defined the of method.

Listing 8.10   AppStateContainer stateful widget

```
class AppStateContainer extends StatefulWidget {
  final Widget child;
  final BlocProvider blocProvider;        ⟵——  This widget takes a bloc
  const AppStateContainer({                     provider as an argument
    Key key,                                     to its constructor.
    @required this.child,
```

```
        @required this.blocProvider,
    }) : super(key: key);                       ◁─────┐  I've dedicated this argument
    //...                                                 @required, because the app won't
                                                          work without any business logic.
```

Next, the associated state class, `AppState`, has two relevant pieces of code: a simple
getter and the `build` method.

Listing 8.11   Relevant pieces of the `AppState` class

```
class AppState
 extends State<AppStateManager> {           ┌─  This getter references the bloc
  BlocProvider get blocProvider =>    ◁──────┘   provider for outside classes.
    widget.blocProvider;

//...

@override
  Widget build(BuildContext context) {          Recall that the this keyword is a variable
    return AppStateContainer(                    that refers to this specific widget.
      appData: this,                  ◁──────────
      blocProvider: widget.blocProvider,   ◁───┐
      child: widget.child,                         Pass the blocs through
    );                                             to the inherited widget.
  }
}
```

That's all it takes. Now those blocs will be exposed to the entire app.

REFERENCING THE BLOCS IN WIDGETS

Referencing the blocs in the widgets is the same as referencing other `InheritedWidget`
properties from earlier in this chapter. I'll show you an example from the lib/widget/
appbar_cart_icon.dart file. First, at the top of the `AppBarCartIcon.build` method, I'm
grabbing a reference to the `CartBloc`:

```
// ecommerce/lib/widget/appbar_cart_icon.dart -- line ~14
CartBloc _bloc = AppStateContainer.of(context).blocProvider.cartBloc;
```

Then, in the same file, head down to line ~49, the `StreamBuilder`.

> **WARNING** Don't get bogged down in this snippet. There's an entire chapter
> coming up on async Flutter, including `StreamBuilders`. I've annotated the
> important part.

Listing 8.12   The Flutter stream builder example

```
                                          The stream property refers to the information
child: StreamBuilder(                     source. In this case, it lives on our bloc, and it
  initialData: 0,                         sends down integers.
  stream: _bloc.cartItemCount,    ◁──────
  builder: (BuildContext context, AsyncSnapshot snapshot) => Text(
    snapshot.data.toString(),
```

```
      style: TextStyle(fontSize: 8.0, color: Colors.white),
      textAlign: TextAlign.center,
    ),
  ),
```

At this point, the blocs are wired up and working with `InheritedWidgets`, which expose the blocs to the rest of the app. Now, we can implement the bloc itself, but only after we touch on streams in Dart.

8.3.3 *Intro to streams and async Dart*

Streams are a big part of Dart programming. A *stream* is an object in Dart, but it's also an asynchronous programming concept. In many languages, streams are called *observables*. From a high level, streams just provide a way to emit events and to have other classes listen for and respond to these events.

> **NOTE** `Stream` is actually a specific class, and only one piece of the observable pattern. In general, though, *stream* is the word used to describe the concept as a whole.

The word *stream* is apt for this class, because a stream emits new values repeatedly, as often and for as long as it needs to. Information is emitted by a `StreamController` and then flows "down the stream." Elsewhere, objects can "listen" to the stream and grab the values that are flowing down the stream. It might be helpful to think about streams as a collection of three pieces, all of which have specific jobs:

- The `StreamController` is the object that you pass new values to, and it turns around and emits the event.

> **NOTE** A `Sink` is a specific subtype of stream controller—the standard type. When discussing the concept, *sink* refers to a stream controller.

- The stream itself, which is all the new events emitted from the controller.
- The listener, which is the object that is notified when new information is emitted down the stream.

For a less abstract example, consider our Farmers Market app. Each time an item is added to a users cart, the cart icon should update with the new quantity of items. You could achieve this with a stream.

When an item is added to the cart, your code would also give the updated quantity to the stream controller. The controller "adds this number to a stream," which effectively means that it sends a message to everyone who's listening to the stream. Each time a listener is notified, it will call a callback that you provide. For example, the cart icon calls a function that changes the quantity and then calls set state, triggering a re-render. I don't want to belabor this concept, but I'm going to give one more example, because it's super important for the rest of this chapter, but it isn't easy.

Imagine a stream as an actual stream of water. The `StreamController`, when handed a new value, would toss the new value into the stream. The value would flow down the stream, and any listener of that stream would see the new value and then perform whichever action you'd like it to with the new information.

You've actually already worked with streams once in this book. RouteObservers in Flutter function the same way as streams. When a route changes, the Navigator sends a message to all route observers and says, "Hey, just to let you know, the route changed." The route observer then takes the appropriate action.

The most important single idea to grasp with streams is that you don't know when or if you're going to get new information. Rather than manually determining when to update code in response to an event, stream listeners just sit there, waiting patiently for new information.

8.3.4   *Implementing streams in the CartBloc*

That's how streams work conceptually, but implementing them is different, of course. As I'm writing this, I'm realizing that blocs are the perfect example to teach streams, because all the stream logic lives side by side in one class. For the rest of this chapter, you'll implement the CartBloc class and I'll show the code for streams along the way.

The base of all blocs is inputs and outputs. Like I mentioned earlier, blocs are all about taking in some data, handling or manipulating the data in the bloc itself, and then outputting data, if necessary. Inputs are basically whatever we want to "tell" the bloc, and outputs are basically whatever we want to "ask" the bloc.

The input/output API for CartBloc will be simple. It will look like this:

- Inputs
  - Add an item to the cart
  - Remove an item from the cart
- Outputs
  - Get all items in cart
  - Get number of items in the cart

ADD AN ITEM TO THE CART

To add an item to the cart from widgets in the app, it's best if you can make it as simple and dumb as possible, from the widgets point of view. Ideally, you could add an item from the cart by calling

```
CartBloc.addProductSink.add(Product item, int qty)
```

Following that model (which I am), these are the steps you need to take to implement this bloc:

1 Implement CartBloc.addProductSink. A *sink* is a type of StreamController. Calling add on a sink will cause it to stream whatever data is added to it.
2 Listen to the stream from the addProductSink.
3 When the stream is notified, call the service that adds an item to the user cart in the database.

That's the whole input process. Remember, inputs and outputs are separate. Perhaps the service call will update an output, but the input doesn't concern itself with that. Implementing the input is done in the lib/blocs/cart_bloc.dart file, following these three steps:

1 Define a `StreamController`:

To define a stream controller, be sure to give it a subtype (**StreamController<AddToCartEvent>**). Also, this is an input, so it should be publicly exposed.

```
// ecommerce/lib/blocs/cart_bloc.dart
class CartBloc {
//...
StreamController<AddToCartEvent> addProductSink =
    StreamController<AddToCartEvent>();
```

2 Listen to the stream:

```
CartBloc(this._service) {
    addProductSink.stream.listen(
        (_handleAddItemsToCart)
    );
}
```

StreamController.stream is a stream object, which is the object that is listenable by other objects. The listen method on the stream takes a callback, and it will be called when a new value is passed to the stream controller.

3 Write `_handleAddItemsToCart`:

```
void _handleAddItemsToCart(AddToCartEvent e) {
  _service.addToCart(e.product, e.qty);
}
```

For our purposes, there isn't really any business logic, but if there was, this is where it could be done. For example, if you wanted to serialize an object to JSON.

Finally, to actually add a product to that stream, look in the lib/widget/catalog.dart file, at the method called _addToCart:

```
// ecommerce/lib/widget/catalog.dart -- line ~43
void _addToCart(Product product, int quantity, CartBloc _bloc) {
  _bloc.addProductSink.add(
    AddToCartEvent(product, quantity),
  );
}
```

AddToCartEvent is a class I made to give the sinks type-safety and to simplify the code.

StreamController.add is the method you use to add a new event to a stream, which in turn will emit that new value from the stream to its listeners.

That's the whole process. In general, that's how all streams work in Dart (with some variations that we'll cover in the async Flutter chapter).

I want to stop here and say that observables and streams are hard to wrap your head around if you aren't used to them. If you don't understand them the first time, don't get upset. Go take a nap, eat some pizza, then come back and try again.

REMOVE AN ITEM FROM THE CART

The other side of blocs is the *outputs*. Outputs are streams, so the setup is similar. One of the outputs in the Farmers Market app is the cart item quantity. I'll use that as an example.

Output events are generally kicked off from an external source, like an API. The output we're working on depends on an in-app event (a user adding or removing an item from their cart), but that data is coming from our backend. (I made a mock backend that imitates Firebase's Firestore. Firestore is real-time and reactive, so you can tell it to notify you anytime a value you're interested in updates.) In the Farmers Market app, I've asked the mock-Firestore to notify me when the number of items in the cart changes. The output event is a result of that notification, not directly kicked off in the client-side code.

With that explanation out the way, I'll show you how to implement an output. All of this code is in the lib/bloc/cart_bloc.dart file.

1 Instantiate the objects you need:

BehaviorSubject is a fancier StreamController, which gives you extra functionality: importantly, a seed value. As soon as the app fires up, if there isn't any data in the Firestore yet, or if it just hasn't loaded, it sends the seed value out immediately.

```
// e_commerce/lib/bloc/cart_bloc.dart -- line 26
StreamController _cartItemCountStreamController =
    BehaviorSubject<int>(seedValue: 0);

Stream<int> get cartItemCount =>
    _cartItemCountStreamController.stream;
```

This stream is the public-facing stream that your UI will get its information from.

2 Add data to the stream controller from an external source. I set this up in the constructor of the `CartBloc` class:

```
// e_commerce/lib/bloc/cart_bloc.dart -- line 30
CartBloc(this._service) {
//...
    _service
        .streamCartCount()
        .listen((int count) =>
            _cartItemCountStreamController.add(count));
```

Anytime you get a new value from the real-time database, add that value to the stream controller.

NOTE `_service.streamCartCount` is a method on an external service. It's also implemented with streams, but it has nothing to do with the bloc, so don't get confused by it. The Flutter Firestore implementation uses streams because it's real-time. It could just as easily be a method that's called whenever you get a success response from hitting a REST API.

COMPLETE THE BLOCS

That's technically a small part of the bloc functionality in this app, but all the rest of the functionality would be repeating these steps. Setting up blocs could be simplified to three aspects: the architecture, implementing inputs, and implementing outputs.

With that in mind, I encourage you to try to understand the other bloc functionality in this app for extra practice. This is the functionality that wasn't covered in this chapter (but using the same concepts):

- Cart bloc
  - Remove from cart input
  - Cart items output

- Catalog bloc
  - Add new product input
  - Update existing product input
  - All products output
  - Products by category output

The catalog bloc is interesting at this point. The products by category output is tricky because it's actually a list of streams. If this is your first time using streams, it may be tough, but I'll cover it in more detail in the async chapter (the next one).

Summary

- A stateful widget lifecycle gives fine-grain control over rebuilding widgets in Flutter using the methods:
  - `initState`
  - `didChangeDependencies`
  - `build`
  - `widgetDidUpdate`
  - `setState`
  - `dispose`
- State objects are long-lived and can even be reused.
- Using only stateful widgets, you can implement a management pattern called "lifting state up."
- `InheritedWidgets` are special widgets optimized to pass data down the tree. Access `InheritedWidgets` anywhere in its subtree with an `of` method that calls `inheritFromWidgetOfExactType`.
- Combining an `InheritedWidget` and a `StatefulWidget` gives you a cleaner way to lift state up.
- The bloc pattern is a state management pattern that encourages a simple API and reusable business logic components.
- Blocs inputs and outputs should only be sinks and streams, respectively.
- Streams, also know as *observables*, are first-class citizens in Dart and are used for reactive, asynchronous programming.
- Streams emit events to listeners, which are always waiting patiently for an update from streams.

Async Dart and Flutter and infinite scrolling

This chapter covers

- Futures in Dart
- Streams and sinks in Dart
- Async builder in Flutter
- Slivers and scrollable widgets
- Scroll physics

This chapter could contain the most difficult concepts to wrap your head around, unless you're familiar with async UI programming. The beginning of this chapter is only about asynchronous concepts and implementing them in Dart. After that, I examine how those concepts are useful in Flutter.

> **NOTE** If you're okay with the following code listing, then you should skip to section 9.2, where we begin the Flutter portion.

Listing 9.1 Example Dart code using streams and sinks

```
// Streams and Sinks
StreamController<bool> _controller = StreamController<bool>();
Stream get onEvent => _controller.stream;

void handleEvent() {
    onEvent.listen((val) => print(val));
}

// async / await
void getRequest() async {
    var response = await http.get(url);
    return response;
}
```

If you aren't comfortable with this listing, then strap in. Async programming is mandatory in modern UIs, but it can be difficult to grok at first.

Dart programming makes heavy use of a specific async pattern, which is known in many languages as *observables*. (Observables are also the foundational concept of Rx libraries.) In Dart, observables are called *streams*. You won't get very far into any Dart code before you have to start dealing with streams. And, in fact, I'd claim they're necessary for effective Flutter programming.

Streams aren't the only async feature in Dart, though. Futures, completers, streams, sinks, the `async` and `await` keywords, and the `listen` keyword are classes or features of Dart that you'll see often, and they all provide asynchronous functionality. Streams are probably the hardest to grok, though, so we'll start with the basics and build up to streams.

9.1 Async Dart

In this section, I'll start with the `Future` class briefly, and then focus on streams in depth. I'll also explain some convenience features like `async`/`await`. Starting in the next section, I'll shift back to Flutter and show how all this ties in with the Farmers Market app.

9.1.1 Future recap

`Future` is the foundational class of all async programming in Dart. In chapter 4, there was a brief section on the `Future` class, but here I'd like to give some concrete examples in addition to the explanation.

Imagine you're visiting a hamburger restaurant. In the restaurant, you order your burger at the counter and get a receipt. Futures are a lot like that receipt. You, the burger order-er, tell the server that you'd like to buy a burger. The server gives you a receipt, which guarantees that you'll get a burger as soon as one is ready.

So, you wait until the server calls your number and then delivers on the guarantee of a receipt, much like the caller in figure 9.1. In this scenario, the receipt represents the future. The receipt is your proof of purchase, a symbol that proves you are waiting

Figure 9.1   A Dart future cartoon

for a burger. It's a guarantee that a value *will* exist, but it isn't quite ready. The burger is the value, not the future.

In code, a *future* is a placeholder for a value that will exist. A common scenario for using futures is fetching values over the network. In a UI, specifically, you could pass a Future<List<String>> into a list of items to display to the user. But you might need to go fetch that list from outside the API, over HTTP. So you say, "Hey, UI, show a loading sign until this future completes, but know that a list of strings for you to display is coming eventually."

Futures are *thenable* (that is, then-able). When you call a future, you can always say

```
myFutureMethod().then((returnValue) => ... do some code ... );
```

Future.then takes a callback, which will be executed when the future value resolves. In the burger restaurant, the callback is what you decide to do with the burger when you get it. The value passed into the callback is whatever the return value of the original future is. In pseudo-code, using then would look like this: orderBurger().then (eatBurger());.

Let's look at a concrete example of futures in listing 9.2. This code block shows that futures work *asynchronously*. The order that the code is written in doesn't reflect the order in which the operations are executed: a Future doesn't block code that comes after it.

Listing 9.2   A Future example

```
void main() {
  print("A");
  futurePrint(Duration(milliseconds: 1), "B")
        .then((status) => print(status));      ◁─────  Duration is a Dart class that
    print("C");                                        defines a period of time. In
    futurePrint(Duration(milliseconds: 2), "D")        this case, it represents I ms.
        .then((status) => print(status));
  print("E");
}


Future<String> futurePrint(Duration dur, String msg) {
  return Future.delayed(dur)
        .then((onValue) => msg);    ◁──────  All futures are used by calling the callback that you
  }                                          give to them when the callback passed into the
                                             future completes. Here, Future.delayed is a special
// prints                                    constructor that starts a timer (you tell it how long),
A                                            and when that timer finishes, it calls its callback.
C
E
B
D
```

Although simple, this example shows what the `then` function does. It says, "Once the first function is done, execute the callback. But you must wait until it's finished to execute." In other words, the example is calling `futurePrint`, which knows not to print until the specified time duration has passed. While the `futurePrint` is waiting for the duration to pass, the remainder of the code keeps processing. This is what makes it *asynchronous*. (Because computers are so fast, waiting only one millisecond ensures that the process is executed after the print statements that aren't delayed.)

In many languages, including Dart, there are special keywords that make writing async code more concise and readable. We'll explore those next.

9.1.2   The async/await keywords

The keywords `async` and `await` are the easiest ways to wrap your head around async programming (in my opinion). In a nutshell, you can mark any function as `async` and then tell that function to `await` any async processes to finish before moving on. It's basically like saying, "Hey, function, if you see the word *await* anywhere, just pause right there and wait for it to finish before moving to the next line." In a way, these keywords turn async code into (conceptually) synchronous code.

There are some async processes that must complete in order for the following processes to run properly. For example, if you have a process that requires data provided from an external API to run, the process of fetching that data will completely finish first. Look at what happens in the next listing when we reuse the preceding example, but add a couple `await` keywords in the mix; `await` will tell the code to pause until that line completes.

Listing 9.3 `async` and `await` example

```
void main() async {
    print("A");
    await futurePrint(Duration(milliseconds: 1), "B")
        .then((status) => print(status));
    print("C");
    await futurePrint(Duration(milliseconds: 2), "D")
        .then((status) => print(status));
        print("E"); }

Future<String> futurePrint(Duration dur, String msg) {
    return Future.delayed(dur).then((onValue) => msg);
}

// prints
A
B
C
D
E
```

Mark the function as asynchronous with the async keyword.

Mark the line (which should be a future) you want to pause on with await.

Mark the line (which should be a future) you want to pause on with await.

Now the letters print in alphabetical order!

The point here is that you can make asynchronous code synchronous. That sounds strange, to be sure, but it's often handy. This example is contrived, because you could get the same effect by simply writing

```
void main() {
    print("A");
    print("B");
    print("C");
    print("D");
    print("E");
  }
```

This only works because, in our example, we know exactly what the async code will do: print letters. In real life, you likely are waiting for some information from an HTTP call, and you want to "pause" the code until that HTTP call completes. This listing shows the pseudo-code for getting data asynchronously.

Listing 9.4 Get data asynchronously

```
void main() async {
    var user = await http.get("http://my-database.com/user/1");
    print(user);
  }
```

You want the code to pause until the HTTP call finishes, or there will be no data in the user variable.

9.1.3 *Catching errors with futures*

Catching errors in async code is important. Consider this: you have an async function that calls out to an API, but that API's server is down. You don't want your app to crash because it's relying on specific data—you want to fail gracefully. You can catch errors with async code in two ways, so you can handle errors or failed network calls without disrupting the user experience.

The first way to catch errors is used with plain ol' future types. There's a method called catchError for this, as shown in the following listing.

Listing 9.5 The `catchError` method

```
Future futrePrint(Duration dur, String msg) async {
    return Future.delayed(dur).then((onValue) => msg);
 }

main() {
    futrePrint(Duration(milliseconds: 2), "D")
        .then((status) => print(status))
        .catchError((err) => print(err));
 }
```

> If there's an error in this code, the error will print rather than crashing your app.

Just like async and await make writing async code clearer than Future objects, there's also a nicer way to catch errors: the try/catch block, which is common across many languages. Let's look at that next.

9.1.4 *Catching errors with try and catch*

try/catch blocks are especially useful with async/await operations. In the following example, the code in the try block will run no matter what. If it completes successfully (that is, without any errors), the compiler will skip the catch block and just keep going with the other code as expected. The catch block is a fail-safe that will be executed if there is an error in the try block.

Listing 9.6 `try/catch` with async calls

```
void main() async {
    try {
      print("A");
      await futrePrint(Duration(milliseconds: 1), "B")
        .then((status) => print(status));
      print("C");
      await futrePrint(Duration(milliseconds: 2), "D")
        .then((status) => print(status)).catchError((err) => print);
      print("E");
    } catch(err) {
      print("Err!! -- $err");
    }
}
```

> If anything fails in the entire try block ({...}), then the catch block will run.

> The catch block won't run if there are no errors. This is extremely useful in async programming, and we'll use it later in this chapter.

Thus far, everything I've covered in this chapter is primer. The real meat of what's important is working with streams. In general, you should remember a few concepts:

- Futures are the base of asynchronous programming in Dart.

- You can use `Future.then` or `async`/`await` to control whether the code should pause to wait for async code, or it should simply keep going and worry about the future when it's done.
- `onError` and `try`/`catch` are both used to handle errors in async Dart.

9.2   *Sinks and streams (and StreamControllers)*

One of the biggest concerns in building UIs, it seems, is how to handle data asynchronously, such as rendering a list of information even though you need to fetch the information with an HTTP request first. Streams are the way the Flutter team has decided to handle rendering data from the internet. Streams are a big part of Dart programming. You won't get far in Dart without running into streams, because they're first-class citizens in Dart.

Streams are an asynchronous programming pattern, often called observables in other languages. From a high level, streams provide a way for classes or objects to be *reactive*. It allows them to wait passively, only executing code when they're notified of an event happening. If this seems abstract or hard to grok, keep reading for now. Examples will help solidify this.

> **NOTE**   `Stream` is actually a specific class in Dart and only one piece of the observable pattern. In general, though, *stream* is the word used to describe the concept as a whole.

The stream (or observer) pattern reflects real life more than other architecture patterns, in my opinion. Throughout the day, how often are you given updates by email, from apps, or from real-life conversations, and react to those? Perhaps you get an email asking you to complete a task. You couldn't have possibly known that you needed to complete this task until that email told you to do so. So you react to getting an email. (This is a hint as to why it's called *reactive* programming.)

In real-life examples, you aren't being proactive. Using the email example again, one often sends an email as a response to an email they've received. You're *reacting* to an email. This means that you don't have to worry about constantly asking all your colleagues, "Hey, should I send you an email?" Rather, you don't even think about it until it's brought to your attention.

In code, the *observer pattern* is just that. There'll be one object that's passively waiting to be notified by another object. Whenever it's updated, it takes appropriate action.

To expand on the burger future example, a subscriber might be the cook that's actually making the burgers. That cook's job is completely reactive. The cook knows how to make a burger when one is ordered, but doesn't actively seek out burger-eaters to make burgers for them. The cook just sits by the grill, waiting to be told what to cook.

The active part of this relationship is handled by the server behind the register. This server is given orders from customers, and then turns around and passes that order (via an *event*) to the cook. An event is a concept. In general, it's anything that happens in the code that kicks off the process of a stream notifying a subscriber. Figure 9.2 depicts this relationship.

1 The caller orders a burger, and it's added to the sink.

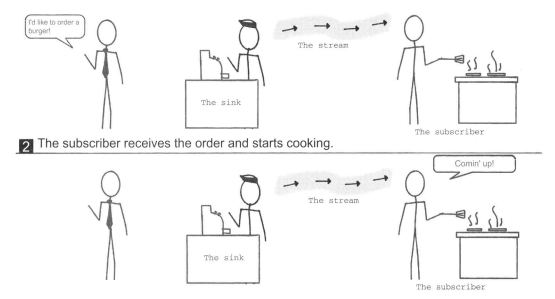

2 The subscriber receives the order and starts cooking.

Figure 9.2 Dart streams depicted by a hamburger observation

9.2.1 *Anatomy of the observer pattern with Dart streams*

There are three pieces of the observer pattern:

- *Sinks are the first stop for events in the observer pattern.* A sink is the piece of the puzzle that you feed data into. It's kind of the *central source* for the whole process. In Dart, a Sink is an abstract class that's implemented by more specific types of sinks. The most common of these is the StreamController.
- *Streams are properties on the* Sink. When the sink needs to notify listeners of new events, it does so via streams.
- *Subscribers are the external classes or objects that are waiting to be notified.* This is done by listening to streams.

9.2.2 *Implementing streams*

Listing 9.7 is basically the boilerplate you need for any stream. Using the burger example, it handles notifying the cook when a new order comes in. You can see the complete source code in the repository in the chapter_9/streams_part_one/main.dart file.

Listing 9.7 Stream using the hamburger restaurant example

```
import 'dart:async';

class BurgerStand {
  StreamController _controller = StreamController();
```

> A stream controller is an implementation of a sink with extra functionality. It has a stream property.

```
Stream get onNewOrder => _controller.stream;
Cook cook = Cook();

void deliverOrderToCook() {
  onNewOrder.listen((newOrder) {
    cook.prepareOrder(newOrder);
  });
}

void newOrder(String order) {
  _controller.add(order);
}
}

class Cook {
  void prepareOrder(newOrder) {
    print("preparing $newOrder");
  }
}

main() {
  var burgerStand = BurgerStand();
  burgerStand.deliverOrderToCook();

  burgerStand.newOrder("Burger");
  burgerStand.newOrder("Fries");
  burgerStand.newOrder("Fries, Animal Style");
  burgerStand.newOrder("Chicken nugs");
}
```

This getter exposes the stream, which other functions can listen to.

This Cook class is just to make the example clearer. (A burger stand would have Cooks in OOP.)

This method needs to be called once, which opens up the conversation between the stream and the cook.

The simplest method to listen to streams is listen. When there's a new value added to the sink, this callback will be called.

StreamController.add(value) (or Sink) is the method used to tell the controller about a new event or data. It starts the process of delivering new information to a subscriber (aka a listener).

Figure 9.3 shows the same example, but with more annotations.

1 Set up the stream by "listening" for a new order.

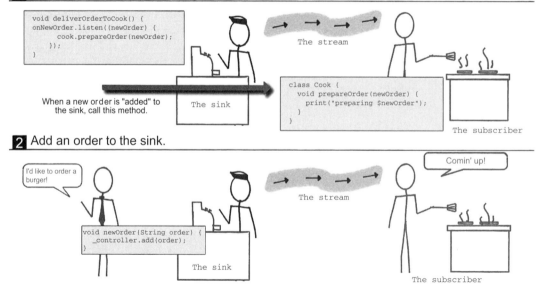

2 Add an order to the sink.

Figure 9.3   This is the same example as in figure 9.2, but with more in-depth annotations.

9.2.3 Broadcasting streams

In our burger code, the cook is probably getting pretty flustered. He's working the burger station, the fries station, and the chicken nugget stand. That's too many jobs. This burger place probably needs to a hire a second cook and split the responsibility.

In the code, that means there will be two cooks listening to the server and reacting based on the information. But sinks, by default, can only be listened to once. This is where the *broadcast streams* come in. `StreamController.broadcast()` is a constructor that returns a controller that can be listened to by multiple subscribers. This is shown in figure 9.4.

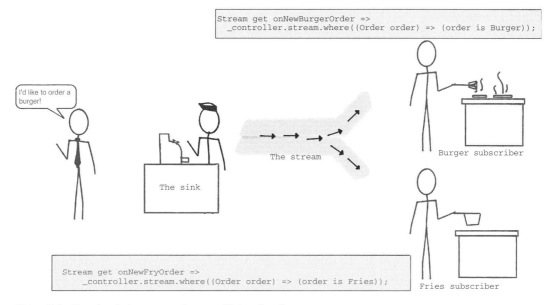

Figure 9.4 Broadcast streams can have multiple subscribers.

I updated the burger example a bit to showcase this. The changes have been annotated. You can find this code in the repository at chapter_9/broadcast_streams/main.dart.

Listing 9.8 Broadcast stream controller example

```dart
import 'dart:async';

class Cook {
  void prepareOrder(newOrder) {
    print("preparing $newOrder");
  }
}

class Order {}
class Burger extends Order {}
class Fries extends Order {}
```

I made three classes to be sure the right type of data is being passed into the controller, but also to determine what subtype of Order it is.

```
class BurgerStand {
  StreamController<Order> _controller = StreamController.broadcast();
  Cook grillCook = Cook();
  Cook fryCook = Cook();

  Stream get onNewBurgerOrder =>
    _controller.stream.where((Order order) => (order is Burger));
  Stream get onNewFryOrder =>
    _controller.stream.where((Order order) => (order is Fries));

  void deliverOrderToCook() {
    onNewBurgerOrder.listen((newOrder) {
      grillCook.prepareOrder(newOrder);
    });

    onNewFryOrder.listen((newOrder) {
      fryCook.prepareOrder(newOrder);
    });
  }

  void newOrder(Order order) {
    _controller.add(order);
  }
}

main() {
  var burgerStand = BurgerStand();
  burgerStand.deliverOrderToCook();

  burgerStand.newOrder(Burger());
  burgerStand.newOrder(Fries());
}
```

This is where the interesting part starts. Both of these getters are listening to the same stream, but only emitting the events that receive the correct types. It's explained in more detail later.

Now there are two cooks, one for each cooking device.

In this method, there are now *two* listeners on the same stream, but it only passes the event to the correct cook.

The newOrder method expects an Order type (or subtype).

The important part of all this is that both of the getters are referring to the same stream. So, when the two listeners are created in the deliverOrderToCook method, they're being called on two different references to the stream (onNewBurgerOrder and onNewFryOrder), but they're listening to the same stream (as in figure 9.5). This wouldn't be possible on a standard stream, only broadcast streams.

Also, it's worth noting that where is one of many methods on lists that perform some action on each element in the list. More common methods of the same type are forEach and map. List.where basically filters out any element in the list if the callback argument doesn't return true.

In this case, onNewBurgerOrder is saying, "I only care about the elements of this stream where the type of the element is Burger." It works because both Burger and Fries subclass Order.

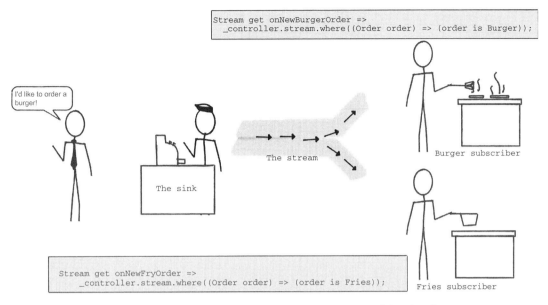

```
Stream get onNewBurgerOrder =>
    _controller.stream.where((Order order) => (order is Burger));
```

I'd like to order a burger!

The sink

The stream

Burger subscriber

```
Stream get onNewFryOrder =>
    _controller.stream.where((Order order) => (order is Fries));
```

Fries subscriber

Figure 9.5 **Broadcast streams are just like normal streams, but can have multiple subscribers.**

9.2.4 *Higher-order streams*

Because streams are so common in Dart and Flutter, it won't be long until you'll want to get a stream of data and perform an action on every new piece of data emitted from the stream. A stream that returns a stream is called a *higher-order stream*. (Similarly, higher-order functions are functions that return new functions. That's where the name comes from.)

Consider the hamburger shop again. Everything is ordered via meal numbers, like this:

1:	Burger, Drink
2:	Cheeseburger, Drink
3:	and so on...

But this hypothetical hamburger shop serves roughly 10,000 different food items. Oh, and the cooks are actually robots that only understand binary. This means the human server needs to emit information in a stream, but that stream needs to be fed into a translator, which will manipulate the data and then output a new stream with the same information in binary. This is pictured in figure 9.6.

1 The caller orders a burger, and it's added to the sink, but there's a problem.

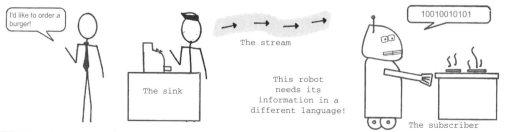

2 The stream transformer translates the values into something the robot can use.

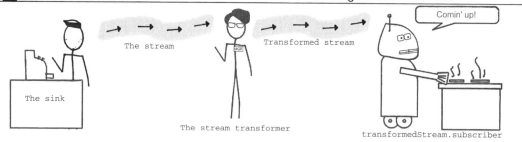

Figure 9.6   Stream transformers are used to manipulate the values from a stream and output them as a new stream.

You can find this code in the repository at chapter_9/stream_translator/. There are two files: main.dart houses all the code that's simply been updated for this example, such as the BurgerStand and Cook classes, and translator.dart holds the new class that translates streams.

Listing 9.9   `GoodBurgerRestaurant` class

```
class GoodBurgerRestaurant {
  Cook cook = Cook();
  StreamController _controller = StreamController.broadcast();
  Stream get onNewBurgerOrder => _controller.stream;

  void turnOnTranslator() {
    onNewBurgerOrder
      .transform(BeepBoopTranslator())      ⊲─────
      .listen((data) => cook.prepareOrder(data));  ⊲──

  }

  void newOrder(int orderNum) {
    _controller.add(orderNum);    ⊲───
  }
}
```

The Stream.transform method accepts a StreamTransformer, which changes data based on logic you provide.

Stream.transform itself emits a stream and can be listened to.

Add data to the _controller as in the last example. It still has the same entry point.

And the `StreamTransformer` looks like the following listing.

Listing 9.10 Custom stream transformer class

Extend StreamTransformerBase, which wraps a transformer and its functionality.

```
class BeepBoopTranslator<S, T>
    extends StreamTransformerBase<S, T> {
  final StreamTransformer<S, T> transformer;

  BeepBoopTranslator() : transformer =
    createTranslator();

  @override
  Stream<T> bind(Stream<S> stream) =>
    transformer.bind(stream);
  // continued in next code block
```

This class should have a StreamTransformer.

Initialize the transformer with this static method on create.

This is a required override because StreamTransformer will call it internally. I only need to call its own transformer's bind.

Listing 9.11 Custom stream transformer class, *continued*

This method is where the goods are.

A new StreamTransformer takes a callback, which it automatically passes its inputStream (the base stream being transformed) and that stream's cancelOnError property.

```
  static StreamTransformer<S, T>
                    createTranslator<S, T>() =>
    StreamTransformer<S, T>(
      (Stream inputStream, bool cancelOnError) {
        StreamController controller;
        StreamSubscription subscription;

        controller = StreamController<T>(
          onListen: () {
            subscription = inputStream.listen(
              (data) => controller.add(binaryNum(data)),
              onDone: controller.close,
              onError: controller.addError,
              cancelOnError: cancelOnError);
          },
          onPause: ([Future<dynamic> resumeSignal]) =>
              subscription.pause(resumeSignal),
          onResume: () => subscription.resume(),
          onCancel: () => subscription.cancel(),
        );

        return controller.stream.listen(null);
      },
    );

  static int binaryNum(int tenBased) {
    // convert num into binary
  }
}
```

Within this callback, you create a new, inner StreamController. This controller's stream is returned *after* the data is transformed.

On listen, you can take the base inputStream, listen to that, and use its callback to manipulate data and then emit it to the new controller. That's complicated, but in the plainest language, the stream controller (when listened to) is turning around, listening to the original stream, using its callback to transform data, and then emitting that new data.

Returns the listen function on the new stream

I realize that code may have made it harder, but passing around and manipulating streams is *hard*. If you fully understand everything up to higher-order streams, but don't understand these yet, I suggest you move on and not worry about the higher-order streams until you have to. Streams are something that you just have to get used to by seeing them repeatedly.

9.3   *Using streams in blocs*

For a less abstract example, consider our Farmers Market app. Each time an item is added to a users cart, the cart icon should update with the new quantity of items. The logic to accomplish this is done in the `CatalogBloc` via streams.

When an item is added to the cart, your code will add the additional quantity to the stream controller. The controller will then send a message to every object that's subscribed to the stream. Each time a listener is notified, it will call the callback function that you provide. For example, the cart icon can call a function that changes the quantity it displays, and then call set state, triggering a re-render. The functionality that involves the UI specifically is discussed in the previous chapter, so I'll focus on the bloc code now.

9.3.1   *Blocs use inputs and outputs*

There are three different stream setups in the following bloc. The first streams all the products in the catalog. So when a new one is added, it will push out an updated list of products. It's an *output* of the bloc. This stream has a pretty standard setup:

```
// e_commerce/lib/blocs/catalog_bloc.dart
class CatalogBloc {
  StreamController _productStreamController =
    StreamController<List<Product>>();
  Stream<List<Product>> get allProducts =>
      _productStreamController.stream;
  // ...


  final _productInputController =
    StreamController<ProductEvent>.broadcast();
  // ...

  CatalogBloc(this._service) {
    _productInputController.stream
        .where((ProductEvent event) => event is UpdateProductEvent)
        .listen(_handleProductUpdate);
    _productInputController.stream
        .where((ProductEvent event) => event is AddProductEvent)
        .listen(_handleAddProduct);
  }
}
```

Elsewhere in the app, widgets can subscribe to allProducts.

The _productStreamController is the subject listened to here. When values are added to this controller, the allProducts stream emits a notification to its listeners. These bloc inputs are covered in depth in a few paragraphs.

The second example is another output, and it allows widgets to listen to different product categories. It's how I've been able to split up the catalog page by category. Specifically, I'm referring to the fact that each category has its own header, as shown in figure 9.7.

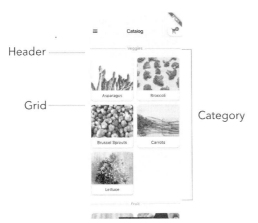

Header

Grid

Category

Figure 9.7 **The catalog page from the Farmers Market app; each page has its own header.**

This output is more involved. It basically uses the same pattern, but I've created a new stream controller for each `ProductCategory` programmatically.

Listing 9.12 Multiple streams for each category

```
// e_commerce/lib/blocs/catalog_bloc.dart
class CatalogBloc {
  StreamController _productStreamController =
      BehaviorSubject<List<Product>>(
        seedValue: populateCatalog().availableProducts,
      );
  Stream<List<Product>> get allProducts => _productStreamController.stream;

    // This is the new stream controller
  List<StreamController> _controllersByCategory = [];
  List<Stream<List<Product>>> productStreamsByCategory = [];

  CatalogBloc(this._service) {
    _productInputController.stream
        .where((ProductEvent event) => event is UpdateProductEvent)
        .listen(_handleProductUpdate);
    _productInputController.stream
        .where((ProductEvent event) => event is AddProductEvent)
        .listen(_handleAddProduct);

      // This is the new code
    ProductCategory.values.forEach(
      (ProductCategory category) {
        var _controller =
            StreamController<List<Product>>();
      _service.streamProductCategory(category)
        .listen((List<Product> data) {
          return _controller.add(data);
      });
```

Lists of streams and stream controllers. These will effectively be the same as creating a new stream and stream controller for each product category.

In the constructor, loop through each ProductCategory.

For each category, create a new stream controller.

You should not pay too much attention to this. I created a fake service that mimics subscribing to a real-time database like Firestore.

When the service pushes the new data, this callback returns and executes the method _controller.add(data), adding data to the correct category's stream controller.

```
    return _controllersByCategory.add(        ◁──┐  Add the new stream controller
      _controller                                │  to the list of stream controllers.
    );
  });
  _controllersByCategory.forEach(                ◁──┐  Create a reference to each
    (StreamController<List<Product>> controller,    │  controller's stream and put
  ) {                                               │  them in a new list.
    productStreamsByCategory.add(controller.stream);
  });
}
```

If you aren't familiar with streams, this may seem pretty complicated and confusing. That's okay; you shouldn't beat yourself up. This is probably the most complicated piece of code in the entire book. The code certainly is confusing, but it's easier to think of a simpler version of that code. I could've written something like this instead.

Listing 9.13 A longer way to create a list of controllers

```
StreamController _veggieStreamController =
    StreamController<List<Product>>();
Stream<List<Product>> get veggieProducts =>
    _productStreamController.stream;


StreamController _fruitStreamController =
    StreamController<List<Product>>();
Stream<List<Product>> get fruitProducts =>
    _productStreamController.stream;


StreamController _proteinStreamController =
    StreamController<List<Product>>();
Stream<List<Product>> get proteanProducts =>
    _productStreamController.stream;


// etc.
```

This code, at the end of the day, is just creating a list of controllers and a list of streams for each controller. Then, in the UI in the `Catalog` widget, I'm iterating through the `CatalogBlog.productStreamsByCategory` and creating widgets based on each stream. I'll cover that in the next few pages.

The more important point, for our purposes, is that the same pattern is repeated here. The concept of streams might be intuitive to you, or it might be insane. The implementation of streams might be easy to remember, or it might not be. Either way, though, the pattern of implementing streams doesn't change. You need three pieces:

- A `StreamController` (or `Sink`)
- A `Stream`
- A subscriber (also called an observer or listener)

9.3.2 Implementing a bloc input

The other use of streams in the `CatalogBloc` is the bloc's *inputs*. Recall from the previous chapter that inputs in the blocs are always sinks. In this bloc, there are sinks to add new products to the catalog or update existing ones. I'll walk through creating a new product.

You saw the following code in previous code samples, but now I'll be more thorough on their use, specific to blocs. The bloc in the next listing uses streams as inputs to work with state outside the widget.

Listing 9.14 Stream as input to work with state outside the widget

```
// lib/e_commerce/blocs/catalog_bloc.dart -- line ~28
// ...
final _productInputController =                          Create broadcast stream
    StreamController<ProductEvent>.broadcast();   ←───
Sink<ProductEvent> get addNewProduct =>
    _productInputController.sink;                    In the constructor, listen to the controller
                                                     and call the _handleAddProduct callback
                                                     anytime a new event comes in that's of type
CatalogBloc(this._service) {        ←────────────    AddProductEvents.
    _productInputController.stream
        .where((ProductEvent event) => event is AddProductEvent)
        .listen(_handleAddProduct);
}

// ...
// line ~67                                          Call the faked service, and add a
_handleAddProduct(ProductEvent event) {              new product to it. In real life, this
    var product = Product(                           would probably add a product to
        category: event.product.category,                         a database.
        title: event.product.title,
        cost: event.product.cost,
        imageTitle: ImageTitle.SlicedOranges); // This is faked.
    _service.addNewProduct(product);        ←────────
}
```

Reference the sink of that stream controller.

Again, this is a lot. But all ~20 lines of code in this example accomplish a single goal. This code basically says, "Hey, app, I'm exposing this sink called `addNewProduct`. You can add some data to this stream, `addNewProduct`, and I'll add that data to the database via the `_productInputController.stream` in the constructor."

In the UI, this is all handled in the `AddProductForm` widget. There's a method that's called when the form that talks to the bloc is submitted. The relevant line is annotated here:

```
// e_commerce/lib/page/add_product_form.dart -- line ~272
void _submitForm() {
    _formKey.currentState.save();
    _bloc.addNewProduct.add(         ←──── Call CatalogBloc.addNewProduct.add and pass in
        AddProductEvent(_newProduct),       a new event of type AddProductEvent, bringing
    );                                       this example full circle. It'll kick off the process
    _userBloc.addNewProductToUserProductsSink.add(   of adding a product to the database.
```

```
        NewUserProductEvent(_newProduct),
      );
    Navigator.of(context).pop();
  }
```

With all that knowledge of streams, we can now talk about my favorite part of Flutter. StreamBuilder is a feature of Flutter that consumes streams of data and turns them into widgets, with no work on our part. It's pretty incredible.

9.4   *Async Flutter: StreamBuilder*

StreamBuilder is a class that generates widgets, but does so with async data. If you wanted to display a list of, for example, products in an e-commerce app, but you knew the list of available products was always changing, you'd want to use a stream builder. This class automatically listens to a stream you pass it, and updates and re-renders the widget it produces when the stream gets new information. You could, of course, write a widget or widget builder that does this. But the beautiful thing about Flutter is that you don't have to. It does this for you, so you can focus on the more interesting problems of writing an app.

The stream builder is used all over this app, but I'll once again use the Catalog widget as the main example. That widget is comprised of a single CustomScrollView widget, which calls a method I wrote, _buildSlivers, and passes the return value of that method into the custom scroll view. This creates the list items for the scroll view. The code that matters right now is in the _buildSlivers method.

> **NOTE**   The word *slivers* refers to a specific widget type. Don't worry about it in this code example. I talk about slivers in depth at the end of this chapter.

Listing 9.15   StreamBuilder displays data that constantly changes

The StreamBuilder class has an ancestor of StatefulWidget, so it can be used anywhere you'd use a widget. This builder displays the category title.

```
// e_commerce/lib/widget/catalog.dart -- line ~66
List<Widget> _buildSlivers(BuildContext context) {
    if (slivers.isNotEmpty && slivers != null) {
      return slivers;
    }
  _bloc.productStreamsByCategory.forEach(
      (Stream<List<Product>> dataStream) {
    slivers.add(StreamBuilder(
        stream: dataStream,
        builder: (context, AsyncSnapshot snapshot) {
        return CustomSliverHeader(
          headerText:
            Humanize.productCategoryFromEnum(
              snapshot?.data?.first?.category,
            ) ?? "header",
        );
      })));
```

The builder also needs a builder argument, which will always be passed the current BuildContext and a snapshot of the stream you told the builder about. A snapshot is the data in the stream at this moment.

StreamBuilders always need to be told what their stream is. In this case, it's an instance of a stream from the list of streams in the catalog bloc that represent each category.

You can use the snapshot to extract pieces of data from the bloc.

This stream builder cares about the same information.

Another stream builder for the products themselves

```
            slivers.add(StreamBuilder(
              stream: dataStream,
              builder: (context, AsyncSnapshot<List<Product>> snapshot) {
                return SliverGrid(
                  gridDelegate: SliverGridDelegateWithFixedCrossAxisCount(
                    crossAxisCount: 2,
                    mainAxisSpacing: 8.0,
                    crossAxisSpacing: 8.0,
                  ),
                  delegate: SliverChildBuilderDelegate(
                    (BuildContext context, int index) {
                      var _product =
                          snapshot.data[index];
                      return ProductDetailCard(
                        key: ValueKey(_product.imageTitle.toString()),
                        onTap: () => _toProductDetailPage(_product),
                        onLongPress: () => _showQuickAddToCart(context, _product),
                        product: _product,
                      );
                    },
                    childCount: snapshot.data?.length ?? 0,
                  ),
                );
              }));
          });
          return slivers;
        }
```

Delegates are very specific to custom scroll views (covered in depth later in this chapter). For now, just know that this delegate is being used for each Product in the snapshot, which is a list of products.

Get the product information from the snapshot by using the index, which is always available in snapshots

Again, I know that was a lot. Unfortunately, we've come to a place in the book where features all rely on each other to explain, in a circular manner. With that in mind, this section is about `StreamBuilder` widgets. The takeaway here is that Flutter has *built-in* widgets that handle streams of data. If you have a list of widgets that could change anytime the app becomes aware of new data, Flutter has you covered.

This has finally brought us the final major chunk of Flutter functionality that you'll probably need for every app: first-class scroll behavior.

9.5   *Infinite and custom scrollable widgets*

The catalog in the Farmers Market widget is special because, in theory, it could be infinitely long. It's as long as the data in the database tells it to be. There are 20 products or so, so it's that long, but it could be 5,000 products long.

This is pretty standard functionality in a modern UI. Instagram, Facebook, and Twitter all use infinite scrolling in their core features. Those services probably use different techniques to handle rendering a list with an unknown, potentially infinite number of items, but it's undoubtedly a common feature to have to handle.

This is a book about creating UIs, so I'm going to focus on the UI aspects of scrolling. In real life, it's likely that you'd want to fetch items incrementally from a service, but this isn't real life. This is about assuming that you have an unknown number of list items, and probably more than can fit on a single screen.

9.5.1   *CustomScrollView and slivers*

The base class for infinite scrolling widgets in Flutter is the CustomScrollView. On top of this widget, the ListView is built. The list view is the most commonly used scrollable widget, as it just arranges widgets linearly (like a column or row), but it can scroll. A list view's children are all passed to its children property, just like a row or column.

CustomScrollView is slightly different; it works directly with *slivers*. Slivers are just portions of scrollable views. In fact, they're basically just widgets, but they lazily build when they scoll into view, so they're performant. If you want to build a scrollable list that combines grids and columns, using slivers is a better option. You could achieve a complicated scroll view with the ListView, but it would likely be janky if the list was customized in any way.

In the Catalog widget, I used the CustomScrollView because I have a custom header for each category, and the headers "pin" to the top. In general, this non-standard behavior is smoother in custom scroll views.

> **NOTE**   All scrollables work similarly. In fact, they aren't much different than working with any other multi-child widgets, like rows and columns. Plus, this is a good opportunity to talk about slivers because people seem to be intimidated by them. I used to be afraid of slivers, until I realized they're basically just lower-level widgets.

The official definition of slivers from the docs makes it easy to digest: "A sliver is a portion of a scrollable area. You can use slivers to achieve custom scrolling effects." I want to say more about them, but there really isn't much more to say. These are widgets that exist specifically in custom scroll views.

9.5.2   *Catalog widget scroll view*

In the app, I implement the custom scroll view in the Catalog widget, using two methods—CatalogState.build and CatalogState._buildSlivers—and a handful of widgets. First, look at the build method:

```
// e_commerce/lib/widget/catalog.dart -- line ~107
@override
Widget build(BuildContext context) {          A CustomScrollView
  return CustomScrollView(                     expects a list of slivers.
    slivers: _buildSlivers(context),    ⟵─┘
    physics: BouncingScrollPhysics(),   ⟵─
  );                                           physics lets you change the way the
}                                              scrollable behaves. I'll cover this shortly.
```

This is a pretty standard implementation for this scroll view. But it's worth noting that this custom scroll view has quite a few configuration options that give you more control. You can make it horizontal rather than vertical. You can use scroll controllers to manage saving and detecting scroll position. The name of the game with this widget is *custom* (and its second name would be *performant*). The real action takes place in the _buildSlivers method.

Listing 9.16 `StreamBuilder` widget

```
// e_commerce/lib/widget/catalog.dart -- line ~67
List<Widget> _buildSlivers(BuildContext context) {
  _bloc.productStreamsByCategory.forEach((
      Stream<List<Product>> dataStream
  ) {
    slivers.add(StreamBuilder(
      stream: dataStream,
      builder: (context, AsyncSnapshot<List<Product>> snapshot) {
        return CustomSliverHeader(
          headerText:
            snapshot?.data?.first?.category.toString() ?? "header",
        );
    }));
    slivers.add(StreamBuilder(
      stream: dataStream,
      builder: (context, AsyncSnapshot<List<Product>> snapshot) {
        return SliverGrid(
          gridDelegate:
            SliverGridDelegateWithFixedCrossAxisCount(
              crossAxisCount: 2,
              mainAxisSpacing: 8.0,
              crossAxisSpacing: 8.0,
            ),
          delegate: SliverChildBuilderDelegate(
            (BuildContext context, int index) {
              var _product = snapshot.data[index];
              return ProductDetailCard(
                key: ValueKey(_product.imageTitle.toString()),
                onTap: () => _toProductDetailPage(_product),
                onLongPress: () => _showQuickAddToCart(context, _product),
                product: _product,
              );
            },
            childCount: snapshot.data?.length ?? 0,
          ),
        );
    }));
  });
  return slivers;
}
```

_bloc.productStreamsByCategory is a list of streams.

For each one of those streams, we want to create a new stream builder for the category title and then add it to the slivers list.

The stream builder needs to return a sliver because this is a custom scroll view.

Now, still inside the same iteration of that loop over the list of streams, create the actual grid of products under that category.

SliverGrid is a sliver builder provided by Flutter, which lays out in a grid view.

Multi-child sliver builders use delegates to create new slivers. They're similar to widget builders, and I'll explain them soon.

The SliverGrid has two delegates: one for the grid layout and one for the grid cells. This is also explained later.

This is probably the most complicated widget building I've done in this app, so let me walk through it from a high level, before I jump into the details of sliver grids and delegates. First, recall the list of streams from the `CatalogBloc`, which delivers a list of streams separated by category, as shown in the next listing.

Listing 9.17 Catalog bloc output for products, by category

```
// e_commerce/lib/blocs/catalog_bloc.dart
List<StreamController<List<Product>>> _controllersByCategory = [];
List<Stream<List<Product>>> productStreamsByCategory = [];
```

```
// ...
ProductCategory.values.forEach((ProductCategory category) {
  var _controller = BehaviorSubject<List<Product>>();
  _service.streamProductCategory(category).listen((List<Product> data) {
    return _controller.add(data);
  });
  return _controllersByCategory.add(_controller);
});
_controllersByCategory
    .forEach((StreamController<List<Product>> controller) {
  productStreamsByCategory.add(controller.stream);
});
```

We make use of this output in the CatalogState._buildSlivers method. We're grabbing that list of streams via the _bloc.productStreamsByCategory output, and looping through it to create a heading and grid for each category as shown in figure 9.8.

Header

Grid

Category

Figure 9.8   The catalog page is broken into categories.

In that loop, there are two steps, really. First, create the header with this loop and add it to the slivers list that will be returned by this method, as shown next.

Listing 9.18   A header sliver for the current category

```
// e_commerce/lib/widget/catalog.dart -- line ~67
List<Widget> _buildSlivers(BuildContext context) {
    if (slivers.isNotEmpty && slivers != null) {
      return slivers;
    }
    _bloc.productStreamsByCategory.forEach(
      (Stream<List<Product>> dataStream
      ) {
        slivers.add(StreamBuilder(
          stream: dataStream,
          builder: (context, AsyncSnapshot<List<Product>> snapshot) {
            return CustomSliverHeader(
              onTap: (String text) => print(text),
              headerText:
```

```
                    Humanize.productCategoryFromEnum(
                        snapshot?.data?.first?.category
                    ) ?? "header",
                );
            }));
        slivers.add(StreamBuilder(...);
    });
    return slivers;
}
```

Then, add the body of this section, which is the product cards for that same category. This code block handles displaying the products for a category, as the following listing shows. The product data itself comes from another stream, so we can use a Stream-Builder here again.

Listing 9.19 Display the products for a category

```
List<Widget> _buildSlivers(BuildContext context) {
    if (slivers.isNotEmpty && slivers != null) {
      return slivers;
    }
    _bloc.productStreamsByCategory.forEach(
      (Stream<List<Product>> dataStream) {
        slivers.add(StreamBuilder(...);

        // important code for this sample:
        slivers.add(StreamBuilder(
          stream: dataStream,
          builder: (context, AsyncSnapshot<List<Product>> snapshot) {
            return SliverGrid(
              gridDelegate: SliverGridDelegateWithFixedCrossAxisCount(
                // ...
              ),
              delegate: SliverChildBuilderDelegate(
                (BuildContext context, int index) {
                  var _product = snapshot.data[index];
                  return ProductDetailCard(
                    key: ValueKey(_product.imageTitle.toString()),
                    // ...
                    product: _product,
                  );
                },
                // ...
              ),
            );
          }));
      });
      return slivers;
    }
```

Here, the stream builder is taking that dataStream (a single category stream) and turning it into a snapshot in the builder function. The delegate can then grab the specific product by indexing into the snapshot.data. The rest of this chapter is about new Flutter terms and widgets, like SliverGrid and delegates.

9.5.3 *The SliverGrid widget*

The `SliverGrid` widget places its widgets in a two-dimensional arrangement. You tell the sliver grid how many columns there are, and it'll lay them out in their order, from left to right first. When that row is full, it'll begin on the left side of the next row. The `SliverGrid` itself is a pretty simple widget, accepting only two properties: `SliverGrid.gridDeletate` and `SliverGrid.delegate`.

9.5.4 *Delegates*

A `delegate` is a class that provides children for slivers. Some delegates, as you'll see in a bit, are wrappers around builder functions, while some provide layout information. They're specifically for slivers, which usually construct their children *lazily*.

At any given time, a delegate only creates widgets that are visible through the viewport. This purpose of this is performance. You don't want Flutter to have to render 500 list items every time a user scrolls, and slivers handle that problem for you. Not only do they lazily build the children, but they also efficiently destroy the elements and states when they're scrolled out of view, and replace those with a new sliver in the same position. Delegates all have a bit in common, so I'll cover two that'll give a good idea of how they work.

SLIVERCHILDBUILDERDELEGATE: THE BASIC BUILDER DELEGATE

The `SliverChildBuilderDelegate`, shown in listing 9.20, is a class that wraps a builder's functions and exposes some semantic scrolling behavior. What we care about is the builder. This builder's function looks exactly like builders we've seen elsewhere. In fact, this class basically is just a builder function that lazily builds its children for the sliver.

> **Listing 9.20 `SliverChildBuilderDelegate` usage**

Pass the SliverChildBuilderDelegate to the SliverGrid.delegate argument (in this example).

```
// e_commerce/lib/widget/catalog.dart -- line ~90
delegate: SliverChildBuilderDelegate(          // The builder function passed in
  (BuildContext context, int index) {
    var _product = snapshot.data[index];       // The builder function should
    return ProductDetailCard(                  // return a widget, as usual.
      key: ValueKey(_product.imageTitle.toString()),
      onTap: () => _toProductDetailPage(_product),
      onLongPress: () => _showQuickAddToCart(context, _product),
      product: _product,
    );
  },
  childCount: snapshot.data?.length ?? 0,       // The child count is required as
),                                             // Flutter uses it to be more efficient.
```

That's all that you need to create children for slivers. Under the hood, slivers might seem complicated, but just think of them as widgets and they're nothing new.

SLIVERGRIDDELEGATEWITHFIXEDCROSSAXISCOUNT: A DELEGATE WITH A LONG NAME, AND THERE-FORE INTIMIDATING, BUT ACTUALLY SIMPLE

As I mentioned, there are also delegates that define layout and structure. This widget with a very long name, `SliverGridDelegateWithFixedCrossAxisCount`, is one of those. (There's also `SliverGridDelegateWithMaxCrossAxisExtent`.) This delegate is basically responsible for defining the number of columns in the grid in the catalog.

```
// e_commerce/lib/widget/catalog.dart -- line ~83
 return SliverGrid(
    gridDelegate:
      SliverGridDelegateWithFixedCrossAxisCount(
        crossAxisCount: 2,
        mainAxisSpacing: 8.0,
        crossAxisSpacing: 8.0,
    ),
      delegate: SliverChildBuilderDelegate(...),
  );
```

Use this delegate by passing it to the SliverGrid.gridDelegate property.

crossAxisCount is required; in this example, it defines the number of columns.

The other two properties define the space between the grid cells.

There isn't a whole lot to this delegate (or other layout delegates). They're required, but straightforward.

9.5.5 *Custom slivers*

The final piece of slivers worth discussing is that you can (like everything else in Flutter) create your own sliver classes. I've done this in the catalog by creating the custom sliver that acts as each category header. On line ~74 in the catalog, this is being returned from the first `StreamBuilder`:

```
slivers.add(StreamBuilder(
  stream: dataStream,
  builder: (context, AsyncSnapshot<List<Product>> snapshot) {
    return CustomSliverHeader(
      onTap: (String text) => print(text),
      headerText:
          Humanize.productCategoryFromEnum(
            snapshot?.data?.first?.category
          ) ?? "header",
    );
  }));
```

That class, `CustomSliverHeader`, is a custom widget. This code is all in the sliver_header .dart file.

All that's really going on in that file is that I'm creating a widget, `CustomSliver-Header`, which returns Flutter's built-in `SliverPersistentHeader`, which itself returns a custom sliver delegate. That sounded confusing just typing it out, so as you're looking at the code, this is the point: slivers are more or less just widgets for potentially infinite scrollables, and the advantage to using them is that Flutter is smarter about rendering them.

Catalog page slivers with pinned titles

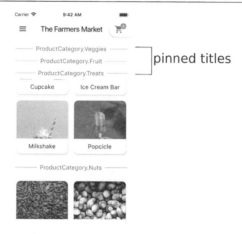

Figure 9.9   Each category has a title, which is a sliver.

First, the widget class, `CustomSliverHeader`, which is highlighted in figure 9.9.

Listing 9.21   The setup for the custom header

```
// e_commerce/lib/widget/scrollables/sliver_header.dart
class CustomSliverHeader extends StatelessWidget {      ◁——— This is just a standard
  final String headerText;                                    stateless widget.
  final GestureTapCallback onTap;

  const  CustomSliverHeader(
      {Key key, this.scrollPosition, this.headerText, this.onTap})
      : super(key: key);

  @override                                             The built-in sliver widget,
  Widget build(BuildContext context) {                  SliverPersistentHeader, is
    return SliverPersistentHeader(         ◁——————————   used for headers.
      pinned: true,
      delegate: SliverAppBarDelegate(       ◁——— This is a custom sliver class
        minHeight: Spacing.matGridUnit(scale: 4),    as well (discussed next).
        maxHeight: Spacing.matGridUnit(scale: 8),
        child: Container(
          color: Theme.of(context).backgroundColor,
          child: GestureDetector(
            onTap: () => onTap(this.headerText),
            child: Stack(
              children: <Widget>[
                Center(
                  child:
                    Container(decoration: BoxDecoration(
                      color: AppColors.textColor),
                      height: .5,
                    ),
```

The pinned property,
when true, gives the
headings the effect of
not scrolling off screen,
but stacking at the top.

```
              ),
              Center(
                child: Container(
                  padding: EdgeInsets.symmetric(
                    horizontal: Spacing.matGridUnit(),
                  ),
                  decoration: BoxDecoration(
                    color: Theme.of(context).backgroundColor,
                  ),
                  child: Text(
                    headerText,
                    style: Theme.of(context).textTheme.subhead,
                  ),
                ),
              ),
            ],
          ),
        ),
      ),
    ),
  );
  }
}
```

The big difference in widgets and sliver widgets is that sliver widgets have a should-Rebuild method, which you can see in this snippet for the SliverAppBarDelegate. You create custom slivers by extending a built-in Flutter class that implements Sliver.

Listing 9.22   Custom slivers

**To create a sliver, extend a sliver
class as you would create a widget.**

```
// e_commerce/lib/widget/scrollables/sliver_header.dart -- line ~58
class SliverAppBarDelegate
    extends SliverPersistentHeaderDelegate {
  final double minHeight;
  final double maxHeight;
  final Widget child;
  SliverAppBarDelegate({
    @required this.minHeight,
    @required this.maxHeight,
    @required this.child,
  });

  @override
  double get minExtent => minHeight;
  @override
  double get maxExtent => math.max(maxHeight, minHeight);
  @override
  Widget build(
      BuildContext context, double shrinkOffset, bool overlapsContent) {
    return SizedBox.expand(child: child);
  }
```

**These values aren't different than creating
a widget; they're class members used to
configure the sliver. Of course, these
specific properties are specific to this sliver.**

**Pass in min and max heights because this is
in a vertically laid-out scrollable. It's labeled
minExtent because it could also be horizontal.**

**The build methods for
slivers are slightly
different. Namely, you're
passed two pieces of
information: shrinkOffset
and overlapsContent.**

```
  @override
  shouldRebuild(SliverAppBarDelegate oldDelegate) {
    return maxHeight != oldDelegate.maxHeight ||
        minHeight != oldDelegate.minHeight ||
        child != oldDelegate.child;
  }
}
```

> **shouldRebuild is what makes slivers special. It's used to decide if a sliver should rebuild.**

The shouldRebuild method is the new method here (but doesn't it kind of explain itself?). This is what matters to us, as developers, that makes slivers efficient. Basically what you want to say is, "If this is the same widget and of the same size, don't rebuild it as you scroll."

The min and max extents are important, because slivers can change if they're configured, based on the other slivers in the viewport. Our sliver is always the same size though.

Summary

- Asynchronous programming is difficult, but hugely important in UI development.
- Futures provide values that don't yet exist, but will soon.
- async and await make async programming easier because they're more readable than using futures. Functionally, they accomplish the same task.
- StreamController objects are used to define streams and sinks.
- A Sink is the entry point of data for a stream.
- A Stream is what other pieces of code listen to in order to get data from streams as it becomes available. Streams can be transformed, and functions that take in streams and output a stream of transformed data are called *higher-order streams*.
- A bloc is a business logic component that relies on streams to build inputs and outputs your widgets can interact with as the state management logic in your widget.
- Flutter provides async widgets via the StreamBuilder class, which make an async UI much cleaner.
- Stream builders are often, but not necessarily, used to build infinite and dynamic scroll views. These are usually built with CustomScrollView widgets.
- A Sliver is a special widget that's smart about rebuilding, making scrollables more efficient.
- A Sliver builds its children with functions called *delegates*.

Part 4

Beyond foundations

The title of this part, in my mind, is debatable. In it, I talk about two main topics: interacting with outside data and testing. I'm not sure that these topics really are beyond the foundation. But neither are requirements for making an app.

Chapter 10, which is on working with data, isn't a requirement because it makes assumptions: it covers using an HTTP library, working with JSON, and touches on Firebase a bit. These are extremely popular choices for tooling, but they aren't the only ones. In that sense, they're optional.

Testing is, of course, optional. It shouldn't be, but it is. If you're learning Flutter for the first time, you may not be concerned with testing. After all, you probably need to know what you're testing first. That said, Flutter does make testing pretty easy, and it's a valuable skill. It's also the most exciting topic, so I've saved the best for last.

Working with data: HTTP, Firestore, and JSON

At this point in the book, if you've been following along in order, you're ready to build a full, production-ready frontend in Flutter. Truly, you're finished! If you work at a company that's considering building a Flutter app, you have all the information you need to start that project or to convince your manager it's worth it.

But there are an infinite number of topics that, although similar in Flutter to various other SDKs, are pertinent in writing applications. For the rest of the book, I'm going to depart from a Flutter focus on topics you need to leverage in any mobile app. Particularly in the app we're going to build in this chapter, you probably want to know how to work with a backend or data store. And to talk to almost any backend, you'll probably want to turn Dart objects into some universal data format, like JSON. That's what this chapter is about: talking to backends.

With that in mind, the UI work for the remainder of the book is light. In fact, the app that I'm going to make in this chapter looks like the one shown in figure 10.1.

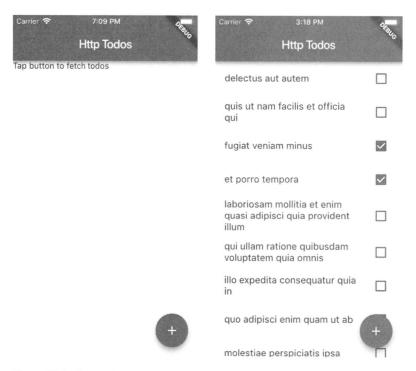

Figure 10.1   Screenshot of the todo app built in this chapter

It's very plain. That's on purpose. For this chapter, there's no reason to get bogged down in how an app looks, but rather in how it *interacts* with other pieces of software.

10.1   *HTTP and Flutter*

While writing this book and thinking about which apps to build as examples, I've tried my hardest to leave as much "setup" out of the apps as possible. I didn't want to include sections on, for example, retrieving weather data from a specific public API. That information would only help if you happened to be writing a weather app.

That idea continues in this chapter and the following (to an extent). In the first half of this chapter, I want to discuss communication over HTTP, but I don't want to focus on the backend itself. Thus, I'm using a free service from Typicode called JSON-Placeholder, which is used to mock arbitrary API calls over the network.[1] The point is

---

[1] The Typicode JSONPlaceholder service can be found at https://jsonplaceholder.typicode.com/.

that there's no backend code to write or databases to set up. You can make HTTP calls to the Typicode service, and it will return pre-determined JSON objects.

The goal for this first part of the chapter is to make HTTP GET and POST requests in order to simulate using a "real" backend. Using Typicode, I'm going to fetch a list of todos, turn it into Dart objects we can use, and then render them to the screen. I'll also write a POST request, which will update the todos when marked complete. In general, this requires four steps:

1 Adding the Flutter `http` package to your project
2 Getting the todos with the `http` package from Typicode
3 Converting the JSON response into Dart objects
4 Displaying the data using a `ListView`

10.1.1 *HTTP package*

With Flutter, the `http` package makes it easy to communicate with other APIs via HTTP. To start, the package must be added to the pubspec.yaml file as shown in the following listing.

Listing 10.1 Adding the HTTP dependency to your Flutter app

```
// backend/pubspec.yaml -- line ~19
dependencies:
  http: ^0.12.0+2
```

This is the latest version of the package as of this writing. I highly suggest you use this version while following along with this book. I can't guarantee that newer versions will work with the code in this book.

Once a dependency is added, you must run `flutter packages get` in your terminal from the project root, which downloads the package and makes its code available in your Flutter project. From here we can move on to using the package in a project.

10.1.2 *GET requests*

Now that the `http` package is installed, you can see how it's used in the services directory of the app. I suggest that you read this code *and* the remarks about it that follow before getting caught up in confusion. After I show you the example, I will be able to explain the concepts in depth, but the context will help you understand it.

Listing 10.2 An HTTP GET request

HttpServices is a custom class, not one provided by the package. It houses all calls over HTTP. More on this shortly!

```
// data_backend/lib/firestore/services.dart -- line ~13
class HttpServices implements Services {

    Client client = Client();

    Future<List<Todo>> getTodos() async {
```

Client is a class included in the http package, which exposes methods to make HTTP requests.

getTodos is the function that I wrote to make the GET request. It provides a list of Todo objects for Flutter to display.

```
final response =
    await client.get(
      'https://jsonplaceholder.typicode.com/todos',
    );

if (response.statusCode == 200) {
  var all =
    AllTodos.fromJson(
      json.decode(response.body),
    );
  return all.todos;
} else {
  throw Exception('Failed to load todos ');
}
}
}
}
```

This line actually makes the HTTP request. You must await it, because network calls have to be asynchronous to work.

This line ensures that the request was successful. If it was successful, then we have the data we need to proceed.

Returns the Todo objects in a list

Else the call failed and should throw an error.

This line turns data from the HTTP request into data we can use by de-serializing the body of the respond. JSON serialization is covered in a few pages, but this basically says, "Turn this String of JSON into a Dart object we can use in the app."

This might seem simple—and it is. There isn't much to making HTTP requests. (Of course, this JSON server doesn't require headers or authentication, so this is a basic example.)[2] The point is that making HTTP requests in Flutter (and Dart server-side apps) is fairly straight-forward.[3]

To be fair, though, there is an essential piece of code that was the most glossed over in the example: using JSON serialization to turn the information gathered over the wire into Dart objects we can use. This part is actually more involved than the HTTP request itself, and I'll cover that next.

10.2 JSON serialization

First, what do we mean by *serialization*? In the context of making network calls, it's a term that means something like "converting objects in a programming language to a lightweight, standard data format that can be sent over the network." De-serialization is the opposite. It's the act of converting that lightweight, standardized data into code, specific to the programming language you're using. Usually, that standard data format is JSON, which I'll focus on in this book.

THERE ARE OTHER OPTIONS   There are, of course, other standardized data formats that can be sent over HTTP requests, such as XML. The fundamentals remain the same regardless of the format. In this book, I'm specifically talking about turning JSON into Dart objects and Dart objects back into JSON.

---

[2]If you aren't familiar with HTTP requests and need more information about headers, you can look to this general article about HTTP: https://developer.mozilla.org/en-US/docs/Web/HTTP/Headers.

[3]You can also look at this repository for more examples of the `http` package: https://github.com/dart-lang/http.

In Flutter apps, you have two options when it comes to serialization:

- Manual serialization
- Auto-generated serialization using a package

I want to talk about both. Manual serialization is worth doing in small apps with classes that aren't too robust. And if you aren't familiar with serialization, seeing it implemented manually helps clarify the concept. That said, auto-generating classes with serialization is *far* easier when writing Dart code, and you'll almost always want to do that in the real world. If you're a veteran app developer, you can probably skip to the section about auto-generation, because I'll discuss the Dart (and Flutter) package that provides this functionality for you.

10.2.1 *Manual serialization*

So far, I've only shown you one code listing in this chapter: making an HTTP GET request. That GET request returns a JSON object. That JSON object is actually just a string with specific formatting and placement of braces and semicolons. It looks like the following listing when we get it from the GET request.

> **Listing 10.3   JSON object from `getPosts` call**

```
// JSON
'[
  {
    "userId": 1,
    "id": 1,
    "title": "delectus aut autem",
    "completed": false
  },
  {
    "userId": 1,
    "id": 2,
    "title": "quis ut nam facilis et officia qui",
    "completed": false
  },
  {
    "userId": 1,
    "id": 3,
    "title": "fugiat veniam minus",
    "completed": false
  },
  // ... more todos
]
```

Notice the quotes on the very outside of this object. It is important to understand that this "map" is truly just a string, but the string happens to have very specific formatting. If you disregard the fact that this is actually a string, you'll see that this data is a list of maps. (Importantly, it could be a Map at the highest level. This example just happens to be a List, but JSON, in general, provides a way to organize data using only maps, lists, numbers, booleans, and strings.)

Now, in order to use that data in a Flutter app, we can convert the JSON string into Dart objects. Once those todos are usable objects that our Dart code understands, we can use them to configure widgets in the UI.

First, let me show you how you might use these objects in widgets. Then, I'll work backwards and show you how to turn the JSON into Dart objects.

REVISITING THE ListView The following example uses the ListView widget, which was discussed way back in chapter 3. Using this widget isn't the focus right now, but if you don't remember the API for that widget, it might be helpful to revisit it. That said, the new, more important parts all live in the if/else block.

Listing 10.4   Using todos in the UI

todos is a List<Todo> type at runtime, so it should have a length, even if it's 0. We provide a backup value of 1 because itemCount cannot be null in the ListView widget.

```
// Imagine todos is a variable that's a list of Todo objects
 that have been
// converted from JSON. A pseudo-code example would be:
// List<Todo> todos = TodoController.getTodosAsObjects();
ListView.builder(
  itemCount: todos != null ? todos.length : 1,

    itemBuilder: (ctx, idx) {
      if (todos != null) {
        return CheckboxListTile(
          onChanged:(bool val) => updateTodo(todos[idx], val),
          value: todos[idx].completed,
          title: Text(todos[idx].title),
        );
      } else {
        return Text("Tap button to fetch todos");
      }
    });
```

In the builder method, the value and title of the CheckboxListTile corresponds to a single todo. If the todos have been fetched and converted into Dart objects, they can be used to configure the children of the ListView. Otherwise, we still need to fetch them, so display a button.

Recall that the ListView.builder callback exposes the index of the todo in the list that we're using to configure the children of ListView.

This code example is just showing how you'd configure your UI (read: widgets) from Dart objects. The point is to demonstrate that you'd likely use something like a List-View because you don't know the length of the list of data before runtime.

Before you can use those objects in your UI, though, you have to fetch the data and then massage it into Dart objects. That's the meat of what this section will be about. In general, that's done in three steps:

1   Fetch the data over HTTP, which returns a JSON blob.
2   Parse the JSON into a generic Dart object (like a Map).
3   Turn that object into a specific type (Todo).

ABOUT STEP 2 Step 2 is a necessary interim step because Dart provides ways to turn a JSON string into a Map. Otherwise, you'd have to turn a string of JSON into a object (like a `Todo`) directly, and that would require a pretty gnarly algorithm.

Finally, as a side note, this app has an extra step because the JSON is actually a `List` of `Map` types. Dart's JsonSerialization library (and most libraries for other languages) are specifically designed to process JSON that represents an object, as opposed to JSON that's a list at the top level. (This makes sense if you consider an object-oriented language like Dart. Serialization is all about turning raw data into the building blocks of the language: *objects*. This will become more clear by the end of this section.) For now, though, let's just look at turning a single todo from the JSON into a `Todo`. The JSON in this example will look like the next listing.

> **Listing 10.5 Example of a todo from the Typicode JSONPlaceholder service**

```
{
    "userId": 1,
    "id": 1,
    "title": "delectus aut autem",
    "completed": false
}
```

As you can see, it's just a map. It's a collection of keys and values. Perhaps those keys and values can be turned into the properties on an object. To start, the `Todo` class looks like the following code.

> **Listing 10.6 Todo class**

```
// shared/lib/src/todo_model.dart
class Todo {
  final int  userId;
  final int id;
  final String title;
  bool completed;

  Todo(
    this.userId,        ◁────┐  Notice that each property
    this.id,                 │  reflects a key in the JSON map.
    this.title,
    this.completed,
  );

// ...
```

This may be obvious at this point, but I'd like to walk you through an example of converting that map into a `Todo` anyway. The first step is actually to write the method that will turn a Dart `Map` into the `Todo`. (We'll worry about converting the string from the HTTP response into a `Map` next.)

In order to convert that `Map`, it's convention to write a `factory` method for the class called `fromJson()`. This method will take in a `Map` as an argument and then create a new `Todo` from that `Map`. The `Todo.fromJson` looks like the next listing.

Listing 10.7   `fromJson` factory methods

```
class Todo {
  final int  userId;
  final int id;
  final String title;
  bool completed;

  Todo(this.userId, this.id, this.title, this.completed);

  factory Todo.fromJson(
    Map<String, dynamic> json,        ◁──── The argument name json is actually kind of
  ) {                                        misleading because, by this time, it's already
    return Todo(                             a Map. But that's convention.
        json['userId'] as int,        ◁────
        json['id'] as int,                   For each property in the Todo class, pull the same
        json['title'] as String,             property out of the JSON because, in this case, the
        json['completed'] as bool            property names are all the same.
    );
  }
}
```

This instance of a `fromJson` method is fairly simple. You're literally just extracting properties from the map using square bracket notation. Using the `as` keyword ensures that the properties are the correct type, or it throws an error if they can't be parsed into the right type.

That's most of what's required (by the developer) to convert JSON into an object. You can probably guess that a robust, complicated class would be much less fun to deserialize manually. (For example, imagine a class whose properties contain `List` objects and other custom objects. Imagine that instead of `userId`, there's a property on the `Todo` that specifies a `User` object. You'd need to call `User.fromJson` *within* the `Todo.fromJson` method. I'll show you a way to do that with ease in a bit.)

There's one more step, though, and it happens in the GET request we looked at earlier, as shown in the next listing.

Listing 10.8   Parsing data out of an HTTP response

```
// backend/lib/services/todos.dart -- line 18
  Future<List<Todo>> getTodos() async {
    final response =
      await client.get('https://jsonplaceholder.typicode.com/todos');

    if (response.statusCode == 200) {
      // If the call to the server was successful, parse the JSON
      var all =
```

```
AllTodos.fromJson(
    json.decode(response.body),
  );
// ...
```

> The important piece from this line is the json.decode method.

Recall that the `Todo.fromJson` factory method requires a `Map<String, dynamic>` type as an argument, but the data we get from the response is really a `String`. Part of the Dart standard library contains a nice JSON converter. Simply calling `json.decode (String)` will turn that into a `Map` for you. You technically could decode the JSON blob yourself, but there's never any circumstance in Dart where you'd need to write that code. Therefore, in this situation, I won't spend time showing you how to do that conversion manually.

10.2.2 *Auto-generated JSON serialization*

There are multiple packages that will generate Dart classes for you. The simplest, and the one I like to use, is called `json_serializable`. When using this package, you write classes as you always have, and you also write a `fromJson` and `toJson` method on those classes. These two methods, `fromJson` and `toJson`, are just stubs that call out methods that this package generates for you. In short, you don't have to write the cumbersome code of extracting every key-value pair yourself. This package is pretty slick.

To use `json_serializable`, you actually need to add three dependencies to your project:

```
// backend/package.yaml -- line ~9
dependencies:
  flutter:
    sdk: flutter
  http: ^0.12.0
  json_annotation: ^2.0.0

dev_dependencies:
  flutter_test:
    sdk: flutter
  build_runner: ^1.0.0
  json_serializable: ^2.0.0
```

> json_annotation provides a simple way to tell the project to generate the JSON serializing methods for this class.

> build_runner is the package you use to run the json_serializable package. It includes running Dart web apps in development mode.

> json_serializable is the package that actually knows how to generate the code.

Once those are installed and `flutter packages get` has been run, you can start writing the code needed to generate the `fromJson` and `toJson` methods. To show this, start by updating the `Todo` class.

10.2.3 *Updating the Todo class*

The `Todo` class in the project, which uses `json_serializable`, actually looks like the following listing, which has *everything* you need to generate some code that will serialize and deserialize JSON.

Listing 10.9   Creating a serializable model

```
import
  'package:json_annotation/json_annotation.dart';          ◁──────  Import the json_annotation
                                                                    package.
part 'todo.g.dart';     ◁─────

                                Allows the Todo class to access private members in the generated
@JsonSerializable()    ◁─────   file. Any file that ends in *.g.dart is a generated file.
class Todo {
  final int  userId;
  final int id;
  final String title;          Tells the code generator that this
  bool completed;              class needs the logic to be generated

  Todo(this.userId, this.id, this.title, this.completed);

  factory Todo.fromJson(Map<String, dynamic> json) =>
    _$TodoFromJson(json);
                                                          ◁──────    This factory method will
  Map<String, dynamic> toJson() =>                                   call a generated method,
    _$TodoToJson(this);     ◁─────                                   _$TodoFromJson(json).
}                           Creating JSON from a class also
                            calls a generated method.
```

If this was a new project, and the generated code didn't exist yet, you'd have errors in that file because `todo.g.dart` doesn't exist yet, nor do the methods that are being called from that file. (In fact, if you're following along with the source code, you can delete the `todo.g.dart` file from the repo to watch the magic happen.) To generate that file, you need to go to your terminal and run

```
flutter packages pub run build_runner build
```

By running this command in the root of your project directory, `build_runner` finds all the classes that need code generated and generates it. (As a reminder, these classes are those that are annotated with `@JsonSerializable()`). The package creates (or overwrites) the `todo.g.dart` file, which has this logic in it.

Listing 10.10   Code generated by the `json_serialization` package

```
// backend/lib/model/todo.g.dart
// GENERATED CODE - DO NOT MODIFY BY HAND

part of 'todo.dart';

// ******************************************************************
// JsonSerializableGenerator
// ******************************************************************

Todo _$TodoFromJson(Map<String, dynamic> json) {     ◁──────   The generated code includes
  return Todo(                                                 this method that turns JSON
    json['userId'] as int,                                     into a Todo ...
```

```
      json['id'] as int,
      json['title'] as String,
      json['completed'] as bool,
    );
}

Map<String, dynamic> _$TodoToJson(Todo instance) =>
    <String, dynamic>{
      'userId': instance.userId,
      'id': instance.id,
      'title': instance.title,
      'completed': instance.completed
    };
```

◁── ... and this, which
does the opposite.

That's all there is to taking advantages of packages that generate serialization functionality for you. If you have a big app with robust classes, it's much quicker to run a command in the terminal than to write the code that will parse the maps on your own.

10.2.4 *Bringing it all together in the UI*

Now that you know the app can grab data over the network, and you know that the data can be serialized into proper Dart classes, it's time to bring it all together for its original purpose: to display that information in the UI. For the sake of focusing on the task at hand, I chose to use, basically, no state management pattern. The information is fetched from a controller right from the widgets. There are three pieces of code involved here:

- Todo controller
- Updates to `main.dart`
- The widgets in `todo_page.dart`

TODO CONTROLLER

This is a class that basically acts as a messenger between the HTTP services and the widgets. It's responsible for telling the UI what the todos are, and what to render. That's a bit abstract, so let's look at the code in the next listing.

Listing 10.11 Todo controller

The services are passed into the class.

```
// backend/lib/controllers/todo.dart
class TodoController {
  final Services services;
  List<Todo> todos;

  StreamController<bool> onSyncController =
    StreamController();
  Stream<bool> get onSync => onSyncController.stream;

  TodoController(this.services);

  Future<List<Todo>> fetchTodos() async {
```

These todos are
what will eventually
be rendered.

This stream tells the UI if
the todos are currently
loading. If they are, then
the UI should show some
sort of loading widget.

This is the method that
will talk to the services.

```
    onSyncController.add(true);
    todos = await services.getTodos();
    onSyncController.add(false);
    return todos;
  }
}
```

> Tells the app that the list is loading, so it knows not to try to display the list

> Now we have the todos, so the app can go ahead and render them where appropriate.

> Makes the call to get the todos. This is an await call, so the function will pause until that's finished.

This controller method, in human English, is saying, "Oh, UI, you want some data to render? Okay, then set your status to loading while I grab that data from the services." Some time passes. Then it says, "Okay, I got your data, you aren't loading anymore, you can render this."

The point of this controller is basically to keep the UI as dumb as possible. The UI knows about this controller because it's passed in from `main.dart`.

CREATE THE CONTROLLER IN THE MAIN FUNCTION

The `main` function can be used for any setup that needs to be done before the app renders. In this case, we need to create the controllers and services that the app will use.

Listing 10.12   The root of the Flutter app

> Create an instance of the class that makes the actual HTTP calls.

```
void main() async {
  var services = HttpServices();
  var controller = TodoController(services);

  runApp(TodoApp(controller: controller));
}

class TodoApp extends StatelessWidget {
  final TodoController controller;

  TodoApp({this.controller});

  @override
  Widget build(BuildContext context) {
    return MaterialApp(
      home: TodoPage(controller: controller),
    );
  }
}
```

> Create an instance of the controller that calls those services.

> Pass the controller into the app.

> Pass the controller further down in to the widget that needs it.

There isn't much to this. I just wanted to show you this so that when I show you the widget, you know where it got its reference to the `controller`.

TODO PAGE UI

The Todo page, shown in listing 10.13, is a `StatefulWidget` that just grabs the todos and displays them in a list (figure 10.2).

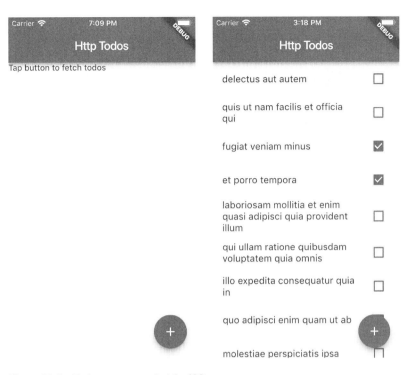

Figure 10.2 Todo app screenshot for iOS app

The state object of this widget has three aspects:

1 It displays a `ListView` of todos.
2 It displays a `CircularProgressIndicator` instead, if the todos are loading.
3 It fetches the todos when a button is tapped.

Listing 10.13 The Todo list page

```
// backend/lib/todo_page.dart -- line ~14
class _TodoPageState extends State<TodoPage> {
  List<Todo> todos;
  bool isLoading = false;          ◁——  By default, the todos
                                         aren't loading.
  void initState() {
    super.initState();
    widget.controller.onSync.listen(
      (bool syncState) => setState(() {   ◁——  When this widget renders, tells the
          isLoading = syncState;                controller that it needs to know when
        }));                                    the todos are loading
  }
```

```
void _getTodos() async {
  var newTodos =
      await widget.controller.fetchTodos();
  setState(() => todos = newTodos);
}
// ...
```

This method makes a
call to the controller.

Use setState so that Flutter knows to re-
render when you've grabbed the todos.

That's the first half of the _TodoPageState object. That's the functionality so you have
context for the widgets in the build method, shown in the following listing.

Listing 10.14 The `_TodoPageState` build method

The body of this widget will change depending on isLoading,
which changes in response to the controller.onSync stream.

```
// backend/lib/todo_page.dart -- line ~37
Widget get body => isLoading
    ? CircularProgressIndicator()
    : ListView.builder(
        itemCount:
          todos != null ? todos.length : 1,
        itemBuilder: (ctx, idx) {
          if (todos != null) {
            return CheckboxListTile(
              onChanged:(bool val) => updateTodo(todos[idx], val),
              value: todos[idx].completed,
              title: Text(todos[idx].title),
            );
          } else {
            return Text("Tap button to fetch todos");
          }
        });

@override
Widget build(BuildContext context) {
  return Scaffold(
    appBar: AppBar(
      title: Text("Http Todos"),
    ),
    body: Center(child: body),
    floatingActionButton: FloatingActionButton(
      onPressed: () => _getTodos(),
      child: Icon(Icons.add),
    ),
  );
}
```

CircularProgressIndicator is a built-in
Material widget that shows a spinner
(seen later).

The todos are
rendered with
our old pal, the
ListView.builder.

If there are no todos, I'd
like to display a different
widget than if there are.

The
CheckboxListTile
is used to display
individual todos.

Display the value of the body
widget (annotation I in this list).

This app doesn't fetch todos
automatically; you have tell
it to by tapping a button.

This screen really has three states: Loading; Not loading, but there's no data; and Not
loading, and there is data. Figure 10.3 shows examples of these states.

This chapter, so far, might be fairly straightforward if you're both comfortable with
Flutter and a veteran app builder. Fetching JSON over HTTP and deserializing that
JSON isn't specific to Flutter. And what's more, Flutter and Dart provide straightforward
APIs to do so.

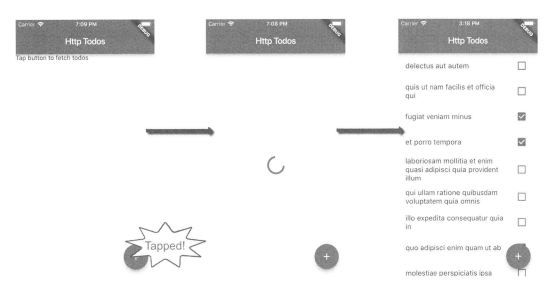

Figure 10.3   Todo app progression

But this isn't (necessarily) the "Flutter" way. The Flutter team seems to be all about using Firebase as a backend. (To be clear and not misrepresent anyone, they didn't say that. I'm inferring that because such a large majority of official Google tutorials and docs use Firebase.) Because of that, the rest of this chapter will be devoted to using Firebase, rather than the HTTP package. Think of it as a different method of accomplishing the same thing: talking to external backends.

10.3   Working with Firebase in Flutter

Firebase is a cloud platform by Google that provides a ton of features. In the simplest terms, it's a backend-as-a-service. It can handle auth, it has a database, it can be used to store files like images, and it does more. It's a pretty incredible product, really, because of how all-encompassing it is. In this book, though, I want to focus on a database service that's part of Firebase, called Firestore.

> **THE TRUE POTENTIAL OF FIRESTORE**   Firestore is not, technically, only a database. It also handles the communication between your app and the data in Firestore, and does so in an opinionated way. It's fair to think of it more as a complete solution to storing data and working with the data in your app.

Again, Firestore isn't just a NoSql database. It also provides a way to *reactively* interact with its data. Specifically, you can subscribe to the data.

When code subscribes to data in Firestore, that code knows when the specified data changes, and your app can respond accordingly. We aren't going to be concerned with that in this simple app, but it's helpful to keep in mind that Firestore excels in reactive programming. (This is likely why the Flutter team uses Firestore in examples so often. They go together like peanut butter and jelly.)

NoSQL in two paragraphs

Firestore is a NoSQL database, like Mongo (but it's also much more). First, I have to make clear that NoSQL (and SQL) are outside of the scope of this book.

The short explanation of NoSQL databases is this: NoSQL databases store your data as nested objects, like a giant JSON blob. The data isn't structured in a specific way, and there aren't tables. There aren't relationships, and you cannot join data tables like you can in SQL. Instead, there are collections and documents. Collections represent a List of documents, and documents are basically Map objects that represent records of data. Documents can have collections as properties. In a robust app, your data basically ends up as one giant key-value map.

This is how Firestore stores data. It provides a JSON-like blob of unstructured data. In fact, every document in a collection can have *different* properties than its siblings. This wouldn't be ideal, but it is possible.

10.3.1 *Installing Firestore*

Unfortunately, I have to break the one rule I've tried to stick to throughout this book: avoid setup. Firebase can't be used without doing some configuration in the android and iOS folders of the Flutter lib. This is the first (and only) time in this book that you'll need to interact with platform-specific code. So please bear with me while I give you step-by-step instructions to do this monotonous task.

The good news is that it's as easy as copying and pasting, because there's no logic involved. If there are no issues, you can be set up in a couple of minutes. The other good news is you don't have to write any Objective-C or Java; you only have to update the configuration.

In general, you need to follow these steps (the sections following this outline this process):

1 Sign up for a (free) Firebase account.
2 Start a new Firebase project.
3 Add Firestore database to your project.
4 Register your Android or iOS app with Firestore.
5 Tinker with the native folders.
6 Add Firebase and Firestore to your pubspec.yaml file.
7 Use them.

A DISCLAIMER ABOUT INSTALLING FIRESTORE   A giant disclaimer here is that this is (for some readers) a book. And a book doesn't have WiFi or a data plan, so you can't click links. That said, I'm going to tell you exactly which websites you need to go to for an in-depth guide to installing Firestore. And it's all well documented. These steps should be sufficient if you don't run into any issues. If you do run into a problem and my explanation isn't getting you anywhere, Google has provided this thorough guide: https://codelabs.developers.google .com/codelabs/flutter-firebase/.

10.3.2 Create a Firestore project

First, you have to go to firebase.google.com and set up an account. It's a standard, quick process. Then, create a project. In Firebase, you'll basically have a new project for every app you build. Here are some instructions directly from the Firebase docs:[4]

1 In the Firebase console, click Add Project; then select or enter a project name.
2 (Optional) Edit the project ID. Firebase automatically assigns a unique ID to your Firebase project. After Firebase provisions resources for your Firebase project, you cannot change your project ID. To use a specific identifier, you must edit your project ID during this setup step.
3 Follow the remaining setup steps in the Firebase console, and then click Create Project.
4 Firebase automatically provisions resources for your Firebase project. When the process completes, you'll be taken to the overview page for your Firebase project in the Firebase console.

10.3.3 Configure your app

Now comes the fun part. Before we can use the Firebase packages in Flutter, we need to tell the native app platforms (iOS and Android) that we're using those. The process is different for the two platforms, so you should follow the one that you use when developing. For example, I do all my testing for Flutter in iOS, so I wouldn't bother adding Firebase to the Android app unless I plan on releasing the app to production.

CONFIGURE IOS

1 In the Firebase console, select Project Overview in the left navigation pane. Then click the iOS button under Get started by adding Firebase to your app. You'll see the dialog shown in the following modal (figure 10.4).

Figure 10.4 A screenshot from the web GUI for Firebase

---

[4]These steps come from https://firebase.google.com/docs/flutter/setup.

2   The important value to provide is the iOS bundle ID, which you'll obtain using the following three steps.

3   In the command-line tool, go to the top-level directory of your Flutter app.

4   Run the command `open ios/Runner.xcworkspace` to open Xcode.

5   In Xcode, click the top-level Runner in the left pane to show the General tab in the right pane as shown in figure 10.5. Copy the Bundle Identifier value.

Figure 10.5   A screenshot from Xcode, showing where to configure your Firestore database

6   Back in the Firebase dialog, paste the copied Bundle Identifier into the iOS bundle ID field, then click App.

7   Continuing in Firebase, follow the instructions to download the GoogleService-Info.plist config file.

8   Go back to Xcode. Notice that Runner has a subfolder also called Runner (as shown in figure 10.5).

9   Drag the GoogleService-Info.plist file (that you just downloaded) into that Runner subfolder.

10 In the dialog that appears in Xcode, click Finish.

11 Go back to the Firebase console. In the setup step, click Next, then skip the remaining steps and go back to the main page of the Firebase console.

CONFIGURE ANDROID

I think Android is less cumbersome to set up because you don't have to deal with any third-party application like Xcode:

1   In the Firebase Console, select Project Overview in the left nav, then click the Android button under Get started by adding Firebase to your app. You'll see the dialog shown in figure 10.6.

2   The important value to provide is the Android package name, which you'll obtain using the following two steps.

3   In your Flutter app directory, open the file android/app/src/main/AndroidManifest.xml.

4   In the manifest element, find the string value of the package attribute. This value is the Android package name (something like `com.yourcompany.yourproject`). Copy this value.

**Figure 10.6   A screenshot
from the web GUI for Firebase**

5 In the Firebase dialog, paste the copied package name into the Android package name field.

6 Click App.

7 Continuing in Firebase, follow the instructions to download the google-services .json config file.

8 Go to your Flutter app directory; then move the google-services.json file (that you just downloaded) into the android/app directory.

9 Back in the Firebase console, skip the remaining steps and go back to the main page of the Firebase console.

10 Finally, you need the Google Services Gradle plugin to read the google-services .json file that was generated by Firebase. In your IDE or editor, open android/ app/build.gradle and add the following line as the last line in the file:

```
apply plugin: 'com.google.gms.google-services'
```

11 Open android/build.gradle. Then, inside the `buildscript` tag, add a new dependency:

```
buildscript {
    repositories {
        // ...
    }
    dependencies {
        // ...
        classpath 'com.google.gms:google-services:3.2.1'   // new
    }
}
```

And you're done!

10.3.4 Add Firebase to your pubspec

I'm sorry if that was painful. Configuration and setup is my least favorite part of making software. But now we can get back to Flutter. The last setup step is adding the right packages to your pubspec.yaml file. The next listing shows the finished `dependencies` list for this example app.

Listing 10.15 The finished pubspec file

```
// backend/pubspec.yaml
dependencies:
  flutter:
    sdk: flutter
  http: ^0.12.0
  json_annotation: ^2.0.0
  firebase_core: ^0.3.4       ◄─┐
  cloud_firestore: ^0.9.1     ◄─┘
```

Firebase core is needed for all Firebase features.

Cloud Firestore is the package specific to the database, which we'll use.

10.3.5 Using Firestore

From a high level, there are two steps to using Firebase now. First, write the services that talk to Firestore. Then, call the services in the app. (Of course, this is an oversimplified explanation.)

First, let's just talk about the services in the next listing. This is all found in the lib/services/todo.dart file.

Listing 10.16 Implement Firebase services

```
import
  'package:cloud_firestore/cloud_firestore.dart';   ◄──
```
Import the Firestore package so we can use the API.

```
class FirebaseServices implements Services {   ◄──
    // ...
```
This class implements the same interface as the http package so we can use dependency injection. If that seems like nonsense, put a pin in your questions for a couple of pages. This chapter closes with a section on dependency injection.

```
  @override
  Future<List<Todo>> getTodos() async {
    QuerySnapshot snapshot =        ◄──
        await Firestore
          .instance
          .collection("todos")
          .getDocuments();
    AllTodos todos =
        AllTodos.fromSnapshot(snapshot);
    return todos.todos;
  }
}
```

Firebase uses objects called snapshots, which represent the database records in a single moment. I will cover this in depth later.

AllTodos.fromSnapshot is a method I wrote, which I'll cover later.

The important part of that code, for this section, is the line that deals with the object QuerySnapshot. There's a lot going on there. Let me talk about it piece by piece.

QuerySnapshot is a class that represents some data from the database at any given moment. The term *snapshot* is used because Firestore is a real-time database, so the data is theoretically changing all the time. A snapshot says, "This is the data you wanted in the moment that you asked for it." It's a common term in NoSQL databases.

On the other side of the equals sign, the first important chunk is Firestore .instance. instance is a static getter on the Firestore package that represents the database itself. All calls to Firestore in your app will start by grabbing Firestore. instance.

Next, collection is a method that retrieves a *collection* from your database. There are two types of objects in Firestore: documents and collections (which are a Map of documents). The collection expects a path that corresponds to the data in your database. In this case, todos is a top-level collection in the database. If you were looking for sub-todos of a todo, the path might be todos/$id/subtodos, where id represents a specific todo, and subtodos is a collection on that document. (This app doesn't deal with nested data, so that's just an example.) And finally, getDocuments grabs all the documents from that collection and returns them as a QuerySnapshot.

So, from a high level, this function is basically saying, "Hey, Firestore, give me all the documents you have nested under the key todos at this exact moment." Then the function passes that QuerySnapshot to AllTodos.fromSnapshot, which turns that snapshot into some Dart classes we care about. The AllTodos.fromSnapshot method looks like the following listing.

Listing 10.17 Convert a Firestore QuerySnapshot into a Dart object

```
factory AllTodos.fromSnapshot(QuerySnapshot s) {
   List<Todo> todos = s.documents.map<Todo>(
      (DocumentSnapshot ds) {                    <─── Iterate over all the individual
         return Todo.fromJson(ds.data);   <───┐        documents (that are of the
      }).toList();                                      type DocumentSnapshot) ...
   return AllTodos(todos);
 }
```

Iterate over all the individual documents (that are of the type DocumentSnapshot) ...

... and turn them into Todo objects, which our UI knows how to render

That's a simple example, and maybe it seems like there's a lot more that I haven't covered yet, but that's what using Firestore is about. If you have a good understanding of streams, which you hopefully do from the previous chapter, and can work with Query-Snapshots and the Firestore.instance, that's 99% of what you need to know to work with Firestore. Basically, using Firestore is all about making queries and then deserializing data into Dart objects.

10.4   *Dependency injection*

Dependency injection is an important concept if you're building multiple clients for the app (for example, a web app and a Flutter app). It makes your code highly reusable and lets you share it across many platforms. If that sounds abstract, consider this: you can write server-side apps, web apps, and Flutter apps in Dart. There are, however, two different packages that Dart uses to make HTTP requests—one for web apps because they compile into JavaScript to run in the browser, and one for server-side and Flutter apps because they don't compile to JavaScript. So, if you have a Flutter app and a web app, the service that these two apps use to get the same data from Typicode is different.

Wouldn't it be nice if you could write controllers that didn't care about which platform is being used? By that I mean, wouldn't it be nice if the UI could just call `service.getTodos` but didn't really care what exactly the service is? That way, the web UI could call the same method as the Flutter UI, but the HTTP request that's made would be different. This concept is called *dependency injection*, as figure 10.7 illustrates. It's a way to share code between multiple apps (among other things).

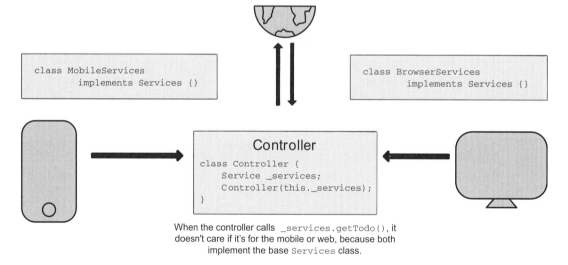

Figure 10.7   Dependency injection diagram

In the backend app I wrote for this chapter, I used dependency injection to "inject" the service dependency into the controller of the app. Notice that when fetching todos, the `_TodoPageState` object calls `widget.controller.fetchTodos`. And that method calls `services.getTodos`, and the `TodoController` is passed in a `Services` object. So, does the controller really care about *what* services are called? No. It only cares that it gets back a list of `Todo` objects when it calls `services.getTodos`.

If this is confusing, consider the `TodoController` for a moment. It declares a member with the line `final Services services`. But the lib/services/todos.dart file has three classes in it, as shown in the following listing.

Listing 10.18 Use abstract classes for dependency injection

```
abstract class Services {
  Future<List<Todo>> getTodos();
  Future<Todo> updateTodo(Todo todo);
  Future addTodo();
}

class HttpServices implements Services {
// ...

class FirebaseServices implements Services {
// ...
```

The first class is *abstract*. In some languages, this is similar to an interface. If you aren't familiar with interfaces, that's a class that you can't create instances of directly, but will keep other classes you create honest.

The following two classes *implement* the abstract class, effectively saying, "I am of type Service, but my methods have logic that may be different than other classes that implement Service."

To make that example concrete, let's look at the main.dart file. At the very top of the main function, you can inject the proper service into the controller, as shown in the next listing.

Listing 10.19 Using dependency injection

```
//backend/lib/main.dart

void main() async {
//  var services = HttpServices();
  var services = FirebaseServices();           ⟵  Create an instance of Services that's
  var controller = TodoController(services);   ⟵  specifically set up to use Firebase.
```

Create an instance of Services that's specifically set up to use Firebase.

Pass the Services object into the controller.

The point is that the controller doesn't care which instance of the Services class it gets, because it just calls Services.getTodos. Because the base Services class declares that it will have a function called getTodos, all classes that implement it are required to have that method and return the same type from those methods. So, the HttpServices and FirebaseServices classes will have a method called getTodos that returns a Future<List<Todo>>.

In real life, this example is somewhat contrived. It's unlikely that you'd have two different service implementations for the same client (such as a Flutter app), but you may have a different Services implementation for a web app and a Flutter app. Using dependency injection, both apps can use the same controller class, which means you don't have to rewrite the logic layer (the controller) of the app.

For a concrete example, I wrote a web app that uses the same models and controllers as the Flutter app. All this app does is fetch the todos when the app starts and prints them in the console. But the example shows how dependency injection is useful for multiple clients.

I created two new projects to make this happen: `shared`, which is where the shared controllers and models live, and `data_backend_web`, which is a bare-bones Dart web app. This isn't a book about writing web apps, so I'm just going to show the relevant code in the following listing. Recall that this is how the Flutter app is started up in the main.dart file.

Listing 10.20   Starting up the Flutter app

Create a new instance of FirebaseServices, which are specific to Flutter. These services live in the Flutter project.

Create a new instance of TodoController and pass it the services. This is a cross-platform class. It doesn't care what services it gets, just that it's some implementation of the Services class.

```
void main() async {
    var services = FirebaseServices();
    var controller = TodoController(services);

    runApp(TodoApp(controller: controller));
}
```

Run the app with the controller.

And the `FirebaseServices` class is created like this:

```
class FirebaseServices implements Services {
```

Recall that `implements` means that this class guarantees that it will have all the same methods that `Services` declares. This is how the app is certain that it can call `services.getTodos` and that method will exist and return the same type, regardless of what that method does. Then, in the shared project, the `WebHttp` services is implemented in the same way:

```
class WebHttp
 implements Services {
  Client client = Client();

  @override
  Future<List<Todo>> getTodos() async {
  // ...
```

The `Services` class is implemented to ensure that the `WebHttp` class can be used anywhere the `Services` class type is required. Finally, to drive it home, this is how you start the web app:

Import the shared library, which houses the shared code

Create a new instance of WebHttp services, which are specific to the web app.

Create a new instance of TodoController and pass it the services. This is a cross-platform class. It doesn't care what services it gets, just that it's some implementation of the Services class.

```
// data_backend_web/lib/main.dart
import 'package:shared/shared.dart';

void main() {
    var service = WebHttp();
    var controller = TodoController(service);

    runApp(controller);
}
```

Run the app with the controller.

```
runApp(TodoController controller) async {
  List<Todo> todos = await controller.services.getTodos();

  todos.forEach((Todo t) => print(t.toString()));
}
```

That's the whole example, and the power lies in the fact that you got to reuse code for models and controllers. In a robust app, this pays off quickly for a couple of reasons:

- Anytime there's a bug in the logic layer, fixing it once fixes it everywhere.
- Your clients remain consistent. When you add a new feature to the app, you only write it once, and then write the UI twice. The UI is generally less prone to bugs, so this is nice.
- Adding to the previous point, it kind of forces you to make your UI as "dumb" as possible, which makes it easier to reason about when there are bugs.

This is a powerful approach to sharing code with Dart between web apps and mobile apps (which is now possible in Dart thanks to Flutter). If you're building an app with multiple clients, this is an excellent way to guarantee all the apps are on the same page. At my day job, whenever we have a bug in our app, we can fix it once (usually in Flutter because the development environment is so wonderful), and it just works in both web and mobile. That saves a ton of time and resources.

Summary

- Google has provided packages for HTTP if you want to use a traditional backend.
- There's also Firebase packages, which let you use Firebase as a backend with ease. Firebase provides a *reactive*, NoSql database called Firestore, which is a great combination to use with Flutter.
- Breaking the controller logic out of your UI and making it a middleman between the UI and services makes your logic layer highly reusable.
- You can share code between a web app and mobile app using dependency injection.
- Regardless of the backend you're using, JSON serialization lets you gather data from external sources and turn it into proper Dart objects.
- JSON serialization can be done manually or with packages that generate code automatically.

Testing Flutter apps

This chapter covers

- Writing Dart unit tests
- Mocking HTTP calls
- Writing Flutter widget tests
- Writing Flutter integration tests with Flutter drive
- Accessibility widgets in Flutter

In the roughly 100 interviews I've endured in my life, one of the most common questions the interviewer asks is, "What kind of testing do you do at your current job?" Trying to mask my inadequacy with humor, and hoping that the interviewer will just forget they care about testing code and move on, I always say, "Not as much as we should." Which can be translated to "Not at all!" The only feeling of comfort I get from that is knowing that I'm not alone. (And, for the record, it's never worked.)

The reason they ask about that, I think, is because it's important, but often an afterthought. And that's what this final chapter is about: subjects that are important, but often forgotten. First, I want to talk about testing Flutter apps. Towards the end, I'll cover some built-in accessibility features in Flutter. You can think of this chapter as "things you should absolutely do for a production app, but probably aren't needed for projects that'll never leave your machine."

11.1 Tests in Flutter

Testing in Flutter can be split into three categories:

- *Dart unit tests*—When you need to test classes or functions, but there are no widgets involved. I'll use the mockito package for this to test HTTP calls.
- *Widget tests*—When you want to do simple tests on widgets.
- *Integration tests*—Tests that move through your app like a user would to make sure large features work, as well as provide performance feedback.

To run these tests, I'll continue to use the simple todo app from the last chapter. I understand the argument for testing a more robust app, but I think it's helpful to work with an app that won't bog you down in the source code. Figure 11.1 shows that app once again.

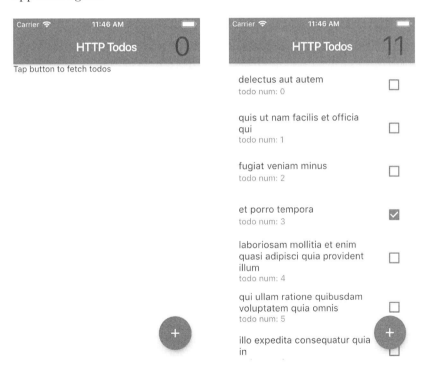

Figure 11.1   The todo app

11.1.1 Dart unit tests

The first set of tests have nothing to do with Flutter directly. You could test any Dart web app or server with the same approach. These unit tests are best used to test a single class or method. In the context of Flutter, you'll likely be testing controllers, blocs, models, or utility functions. Unit tests can also test dependencies using the mockito package. This package basically lets you create mock classes that call out to HTTP or any other external source. It's quite handy.

SETUP FOR DART UNIT TESTS

First, the proper dependencies need to be added to a test. For this section, two testing dependencies matter: test and mockito, as shown in this listing.

Listing 11.1   Todo app pubspec dependencies

```
// backend/pubspec.yaml
dev_dependencies:
  flutter_test:
    sdk: flutter
  flutter_driver:
    sdk: flutter
  build_runner: ^1.0.0
  json_serializable: ^2.0.0
  mockito: 4.0.0
  test: any
```

mockito allows you to mock tests.

test is the standard testing library for Dart.

After you've added these to the pubspec.yaml file and run flutter pub get, you can create the test file. The file should live in a directory called test in the root of your project:

```
| backend
├─ lib
├─ pubspec.lock
├─ pubspec.yaml
├─ test                    ←──  Add this folder and file.
|     ├─ dart_test.dart
```

That's all the setup you need to start writing tests.

THE CODE TO TEST

I purposefully made some functionality in this app more complicated than it needs to be for the sake of samples, so we can talk through some examples of the basic dart unit tests. The code will get more complicated and "correct" as we move through the chapter.

Figure 11.2 shows two views of the todo app. The feature that this code corresponds to is the Completed Todo counter in the app bar on the right-hand side of the figure.

Completed Todos count

Figure 11.2   Completed todos example

The state of that feature is controlled in the todos_controller.dart file by two classes: the controller itself and a class called `CompletedTodoCounter`. The second class is the contrived code, and what I want to test first. Here's the code we care about.

Listing 11.2 Testable code from the todos completed counter

```
// backend/lib/controllers/todo_controller.dart
class CompletedTodoCounter {
  int completed = 0;
  void increaseCounter() => completed++;
  void decreaseCounter() => completed--;
  void resetCounter() => completed = 0;
}

class TodoController {
  var counter = CompletedTodoCounter();

  // ... other class methods

  int getCompletedTodos() {
    counter.resetCounter();
    todos?.forEach((Todo t) {
      if (t.completed) {
        counter.increaseCounter();
      }
    });
    return counter.completed;
  }
}
```

This class provides a way to track the number of completed todos.

In the controller class, make a new instance of the counter.

Each time it's called, this method iterates through all the todos and finds those that are completed. It basically works by starting the counter over and recounting.

The reason this code is contrived is because there's way too much code to simply keep a count. But the reason I've done it this way will make sense when we move to using a testing library called mockito.

WRITING DART UNIT TESTS

Dart unit tests rely on three main functions from the test lib: `test`, `expect`, and `group`. The easiest way to explain how to write tests is to show some examples. This *isn't* the full example, but an example of a single test—the most basic test possible. If you've written tests in any other modern language, this will be pretty easy to read.

This test is basically saying, "Run a new test called `counter increases` and then test it by calling this function that I've provided. After creating the instance and calling `increaseCounter`, the `counter.completed` property should evaluate to 1."

Listing 11.3 Basic unit test in Dart

```
// backend/test/dart_test.dart
test("counter increases", () {

    final counter = CompletedTodoCounter();
```

All tests start by calling the test function, which takes a description as its first argument and a callback function as its second. The callback function is where you write the test.

We set up everything for the test, creating an instance of the CompletedTodoCounter.

```
    counter.increaseCounter();      ◁──── We need to call a function to test.

    expect(counter.completed, 1);   ◁─┐ Tests pass if their expect
// ...                                │ functions evaluate to true.
```

The expect function (figure 11.3) works by taking in an actual as the first argument, which is what you're testing, and a matcher, which is the expected outcome for the actual. If the two are the same, then the test will pass. Otherwise, expect will throw an error and fail the test.

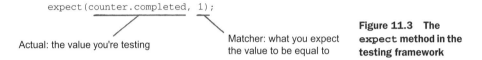

Actual: the value you're testing

Matcher: what you expect the value to be equal to

Figure 11.3 The expect method in the testing framework

Tests can be as complicated as you'd like, though. You can have multiple expect function calls in a single test. Consider this example where we're testing that the counter can do multiple actions and stay in sync.

Listing 11.4 Multiple expect calls in a test

```
// backend/test/dart_test.dart
test("counter increases and decreases", () {
    final counter = CompletedTodoCounter();

    counter.increaseCounter();
    expect(counter.completed, 1);        ◁─┐ If the first expect call fails, then the rest
                                            of the test doesn't matter. If it passes,
    counter.increaseCounter(); // +1        then the test will keep moving.
    counter.decreaseCounter(); // -1
    counter.increaseCounter(); // +1
    counter.increaseCounter(); // +1
    counter.decreaseCounter(); // -1     ◁─┐ If the second expect call passes, it will
    expect(counter.completed, 2);           terminate the test with a passing grade.
});
```

GROUPING MULTIPLE TESTS

If you have multiple tests that are testing the same function or class, you can group them together so they can use the same resources. The next listing shows the final example of basic Dart unit tests.

Listing 11.5 Full unit test example

Like all Dart programs, tests originate in the main function.

```
 ┌─▷ void main() {
        group(
            "counter keeps track of completed todos", () {   ◁─┐ A group function allows
                                                                multiple tests to use the
                                                                same resources.
```

```
          final counter = CompletedTodoCounter();

          test("counter increases and decreases", () {
            counter.increaseCounter();
            expect(counter.completed, 1);

            counter.increaseCounter(); // +1
            counter.decreaseCounter(); // -1
            counter.increaseCounter(); // +1
            counter.increaseCounter(); // +1
            counter.decreaseCounter(); // -1
            expect(counter.completed, 2);
          });

          test("counter resets to 0", () {
            counter.increaseCounter();
            counter.increaseCounter();
            counter.increaseCounter();
            counter.increaseCounter();

            counter.resetCounter();

            expect(counter.completed, 0);
          });
        });
}
```

This **CompletedTodoCounter** instance will be used in multiple tests.

This is the first test in the group, which uses the counter.

This test also uses the counter.

The advantage to using groups with many tests, rather than less tests with many `expect` calls, is that tests are more modular this way. Some tests can pass, and some can fail. In this example, it's reasonable that the `increaseCounter` and `decreaseCounter` methods work, but the `resetCounter` doesn't. Testing this way would catch that.

11.1.2 *Using mockito to test methods that need external dependencies*

When using HTTP in our test app, we want to make sure that the app behaves how we want, regardless of the response of the HTTP call. For example, maybe the API that we get todo data from is down and sending a 404 return message. That's a bummer, but there's nothing we can do about it. And we should plan on it happening from time to time. So, we can "mock" all the situations we are concerned about possibly occurring.

You can handle this by writing alternative mock versions of classes. Recall that the services in this app are all based on an abstract class called `Services`. You could create a new implementation of that class that doesn't do anything. I've actually done that for a later test. The mock-up looks like that shown in the following listing.

Listing 11.6 Mock services class

```
// backend/lib/controllers/todo_controller.dart
class MockServices implements Services {
    // ...
```

```
@override
Future<List<Todo>> getTodos() async {
  return [
    Todo(1, 1, "delectus aut autem", false),
    Todo(1, 2, "quis ut nam facilis et officia qui", false),
    Todo(1, 3, "fugiat veniam minus", false),
    Todo(1, 4, "et porro tempora", true),
    Todo(1, 8, "et porro tempora", true),
    Todo(1, 9, "et porro tempora", true),
    Todo(1, 10, "et porro tempora", true),
    Todo(1, 11, "et porro tempora", true),
    Todo(1, 12, "et porro tempora", true),
    Todo(1, 13, "et porro tempora", true),
    Todo(1, 14, "et porro tempora", true),
    Todo(1, 15, "et porro tempora", true),
    Todo(1, 16, "et porro tempora", true),
  ];
}
// ...
```

Rather than making an HTTP call, I can return some fake data. This is the same as the data we'd get back from the actual HTTP call to Typicode, hence the Latin.

That's great, but it can quickly become a burden if you have a big app with hundreds of services, and you need to write mock services for each one. That's where mockito comes in.

The point of mockito is to test that your app responds gracefully to external dependencies that it can't control. It provides a way to more easily test app functionality against a set of predictable external dependency behaviors. This removes some of the barriers that make testing a pain, thus encouraging more test writing!

We'll use it to mock the getTodos call on the services class. This is what the original getTodos method looks like (which we don't need to change; it's just a reminder).

Listing 11.7   `getTodos` makes an HTTP request

```
// backend/test/http_test.dart
Future<List<Todo>> getTodos(Client client) async {
  final response =
      await client.get('https://jsonplaceholder.typicode.com/todos');

  if (response.statusCode == 200) {
    var all = AllTodos.fromJson(json.decode(response.body));
    return all.todos;
  } else {
    throw Exception('Failed to load todos');
  }
}
```

Using the mockito package is easiest demonstrated with code. So take a look at the next listing and then I'll walk you through what's going on.

Listing 11.8 Using mockito to stub an HTTP call

```
// backend/test/http_test.dart
class MockClient extends Mock implements Client {}

void main() {
  group('getTodos', () {
    test('returns a list of todos if the http call completes', () async {
      final client = MockClient();
      when(client.get(
        'https://jsonplaceholder.typicode.com/todos')
      ).thenAnswer(
        (_) async => Response('[]', 200)
      );

      expect(
        await getTodos(client),
        isInstanceOf<List<Todo>>(),
      );
    });
```

Create a mock class of the HTTP client (from dart:http) by extending Mock and implementing Client.

Run tests as normal.

Create an instance of that mock client.

The when function from mockito basically stops the call from actually happening, so you can control the response.

thenAnswer takes a callback and returns whatever kind of response you'd like.

Now actually call that function that you want to test; mockito will stop the client.get () call because we told it to in the when function call.

A bulk of what's happening is in the when/thenAnswer call, so I'd like to break that down.

This test is going to call getTodos, but rather than passing in a real Client from the dart:http library, it's passing in a mock client. This mock client knows that it should fake whichever calls are made on it (*that we tell it to*) from the when function. As a reminder, the when function call looks like this:

```
when(client.get('https://jsonplaceholder.typicode.com/todos'))
        .thenAnswer((_) async => Response('[]', 200));
```

So, when the get method is called on the mocked Client class, it knows to return Response('[]', 200)); rather than actually making the HTTP call and responding. Pretty neat.

Here's another test that mocks a failed call:

Create the mock client.

```
// backend/test/http_test.dart
test('throws an exception if the http call completes with an error', () {
  final client = MockClient();

  when(client.get(
    'https://jsonplaceholder.typicode.com/todos')
  ).thenAnswer(
    (_) async => Response('Not Found', 404)
  );

  expect(getTodos(client), throwsException);
});
```

Tell mockito to look for calls to Client.get.

Respond with a failed HTTP response: 404 Not Found.

Test that the function throws an exception when the call fails.

The point of mockito is to test that your app responds *gracefully* to external dependencies that it can't control. It's a powerful tool to carry in your toolbelt.

11.1.3 *Flutter widget tests*

Widget tests in Flutter build on Dart unit tests. Rather than using the test package, however, you use the flutter_test package. The API is the same, but there are additional methods to test widgets and the UI. In general, the testing goes like this:

1 Tell the test which widget to use as the entry point. The test will build that widget and it's subtree.
2 Find widgets in that subtree.
3 Test that certain properties in this widget tree are true.

It isn't so different, but there are a couple of caveats and some new jargon you might need to learn. In this section, I'll first show you a code example of a widget test. And that will include some weird jargon that you probably won't know. That's okay, because this code example is just here to provide context. Then, the jargon will be easier to explain. But first, of course, we have to do some setup.

SET UP FLUTTER TESTS

The app is already structured to do tests, and there's only really one difference in the way you set up widget tests: add the right libraries to your pubspec.yaml file. Here's what that looks like:

```
// backend/pubspec.yaml
dev_dependencies:
  flutter_test:
    sdk: flutter
  flutter_driver:
    sdk: flutter
  build_runner: ^1.0.0
  json_serializable: ^2.0.0
  mockito: 4.0.0
  test: any
```

> **Import the flutter_test package, which you have to give an SDK. This is added to the pubspec file by default when you create a new Flutter project.**

That's all there is to setup this portion, actually.

WRITING WIDGET TESTS

First, take a look at an example in the next listing. This test ensures that there is a title in the `AppBar` of the widget.

Listing 11.9   Basic widget test function

Rather than test, call testWidgets; the callback is passed a WidgetTester.

```
// backend/test/widget_test.dart
  testWidgets(
    'App has a title', (WidgetTester tester) async {

      var services = MockServices();
```

> **I'm using the MockServices class from the lib/services/todos.dart file. It has nothing to do with the mockito package. We don't actually care about the services right now, but they're required to run the app.**

```
await tester.pumpWidget(
  TodoApp(controller: TodoController(services))
);

final titleFinder = find.text("HTTP Todos");
expect(titleFinder, findsOneWidget);

});
```

pumpWidget builds the widget you pass it and its subclasses. In this case, it's building the whole app because I've passed in the root widget of the app.

A big part of flutter_test is the Finder class, which is used to find specific widgets.

expect is the same, but when testing Flutter, you can use a number of built-in Matcher objects that are also a big part of testing widgets.

You can see that the general approach to writing tests is the same. The difference is that you have to use some flutter_test methods and objects to ensure the tests work. I'll walk through those here.

1   Finder objects—Finders are objects that scan the widget tree and find widgets by specific properties. The find object is a collection of many CommonFinders, including byText, byWidget, byKey, and byType (among others). You use these finders almost all the time. The find.byText call that I used in the previous test function literally searches for a widget with that exact text.

2   Matcher objects—Matchers are the same as they were in the unit tests. They provide a way to compare the *actual* case with what you expect. Because widgets are more complicated than simple values (like an int from the unit test example earlier in the chapter), the flutter_test library comes with a number of built-in matchers that do the hard work for you. The most common matchers are findsNothing, findsOneWidget, and findsNWidgets(int n). Testing widgets is largely about making sure they exist, which is where these come in.

3   WidgetTester class—The WidgetTester class is the base for all the flutter_test functionality. Its purpose is to interact with widgets the same way that users would. It can tap on widgets, drag and swipe on widgets, and insert text into text fields.

4   WidgetTester.pump (and similar methods)—There are a collection of methods that involve "pumping" the widget tester. The simplest way to describe these methods is that they call Widget.build. Anytime anything in the test imitates user interaction, you need to pump the app before doing anything else. This will make more sense when you see the following code listing.

With all that in mind, let me walk through that last code sample again.

Listing 11.10   Basic widget test function

```
// backend/test/widget_test.dart
  testWidgets(
    'App has a title', (WidgetTester tester) async {

    var services = MockServices();
```

The WidgetTester is needed for Flutter testing functionality.

```
await tester.pumpWidget(
  TodoApp(controller: TodoController(services)),
);
```

pumpWidget essentially calls
build on the widget it's passed.
It must be done before you
attempt to find or test anything.

```
final titleFinder = find.text("HTTP Todos");
expect(titleFinder, findsOneWidget);

});
```

find.text searches the widget tree
for a widget whose text is literally
HTTP Todos.

findOneWidget is a Matcher that checks for just that:
one widget in the tree that meets those parameters.

The long-short of it is that Flutter tests aren't much different than Dart unit tests, so
long as you know the API to interact with widgets. But the flutter_test package provides many more ways to interact with widgets. You can do things like tap on buttons,
drag on the screen, and input text into input fields.

Consider the todo app from this chapter and how it works. When you load the app,
it does nothing. But after tapping the FloatingActionButton, the app makes an
HTTP call to get some data, and then displays that data in the form of a todo list.

To test that this button makes a call and renders the list, we need to have the test
suite tap the FloatingActionButton. That's perfectly possible, and rather easy in
Flutter. This following listing shows how that works, as well as finding widgets by keys.

Listing 11.11   Finding and tapping on a button

```
// backend/test/widget_test.dart
testWidgets(
    'finds and taps the floating action button',
    (WidgetTester tester) async {
      var services = MockServices();
      await tester.pumpWidget(
        TodoApp(controller: TodoController(services))
      );

      Finder floatingActionButton =
        find.byKey(Key('get-todos-button'));

      await tester.tap(floatingActionButton);

      // rebuild the app
      await tester.pumpAndSettle(
        Duration(seconds: 2),
      );

      final firstTodoFinder =
        find.text("delectus aut autem");

      expect(firstTodoFinder, findsOneWidget);
});
```

tester.pumpWidget
builds the app.

You can find widgets by their unique
Key. This is the easiest way to handle
that, in my opinion, and I'll walk
through it in more depth later.

You can tap buttons by
using the tester.Tap button
and passing it a Finder.

This is the important part! You *must* re-pump the
app anytime you call a function that calls setState.
pumpAndSettle calls pump repeatedly for the
duration you pass in. Useful for asynchronous work.

I'm looking for a specific todo to make sure it exists. This works because
I know what the faked data is, so I can search for it specifically.

There are two things to note before I move on integration tests. First, finding elements by a key is easy, and what I recommend when you're looking for a single widget. In the previous example, I find the `FloatingActionButton` by its key. The code in the app that looks like this just has a simple `Key` on it, as shown in the next listing.

Listing 11.12   Finding widgets by keys in tests

```
// backend/lib/todo_page.dart -- line ~ 78
floatingActionButton: FloatingActionButton(
  key: Key("get-todos-button"),              ◁——  Any Key type will work. I'm
  onPressed: () => _getTodos(),                    just using the standard one
  child: Icon(Icons.add),                          here.
),

// And look for it with a test
// backend/test/widget_test.dart
testWidgets(
  'finds and taps the floating action button', (WidgetTester tester) async {
    var services = MockServices();
    await tester.pumpWidget(TodoApp(controller: TodoController(services)));
    Finder floatingActionButton =
        find.byKey(Key('get-todos-button'));   ◁—— Just make sure it's the String value.
```

That's pretty straightforward, I think. The other notable piece of the previous test is all the references to `pump`. There are two things to keep in mind:

- The widget you're testing must be wrapped in an `App` and `Scaffold`, because they provide objects like `MediaQuery` and other context to the test. This means you should be passing in the whole app when you "pump" it. If you don't want to pump a whole, giant app, you can make a tiny test app that wraps the widget you want to test in a `MaterialApp` and `Scaffold`.
- You have to pump the widget everytime you want `Widget.build` to be called! So after any tap or other interaction, you have to call `pump`. And after any call to `setState` in the your widgets, you have to `pump`!

These tests are ideal for simple widget tests, but can be cumbersome if you're trying to test a full UI workflow. Luckily, there are some nice tools you can use to write integration tests, because Flutter thought of everything.

11.1.4   *Flutter integration tests*

It's no secret by now that I'm a big fan of the problems that Flutter has solved for you. Integration testing is no exception. There's an integration test library built by the Flutter team that provides a nice way to run integration tests. It makes it easy to test how everything works together, and profiles the performance of your app.

This is done with the flutter_driver package. Tests with Flutter driver are written similarly to widget tests, but the package is really made to simulate a user. Driver tests actually run the app and then interact with it. You can watch it scroll through your app and tap buttons that you've described. If you've used something like Selenium Driver before, this is similar. If you haven't, prepare to be wowed.

SET UP FLUTTER DRIVER

The flutter_driver package is a bit pickier about setup than previous tests we've looked at. But it's still straightforward enough. First, of course, you need to import the package into your pubspec.yaml.

Listing 11.13   Todo app pubspec dependencies

```
// backend/pubspec.yaml
dev_dependencies:
  flutter_test:
    sdk: flutter
  flutter_driver:
    sdk: flutter
  build_runner: ^1.0.0
  json_serializable: ^2.0.0
  mockito: 4.0.0
  test: any
```

flutter_driver is the package you care about. It also takes an SDK.

You *must* import test. In past examples, test and flutter_test were basically interchangeable. But you cannot use any piece of the Flutter SDK in the same files as flutter_driver, so you need test here. It's okay to add flutter_test to your app's dependencies; just don't use it in the same file as your driver tests.

After you've imported those dependencies, you need to create the relevant files. The driver files should go in their own, separate directory from the rest of the tests. By convention, the directory is usually called test_driver. It's located in the root of the Flutter project.

Then you need to add two files: one to run the app and one to run the tests. Remember, the app actually runs when you use `flutter_driver`. It must be running in a different process, and therefore must be in a different file. This is what the project will end up looking like:

```
| backend
├── lib
├── pubspec.lock
├── pubspec.yaml
├── test
|    ├── dart_test.dart
|    ├── http_test.dart
|    ├── widget_test.dart
├── test_driver
|    ├── app.dart
|    └── app_test.dart
```

Add this folder and the two files in it.

The file that runs the app (app.dart) is only a few lines of code. The following listing shows what it looks like.

Listing 11.14   Set up the flutter_driver extension

```
// backend/test_drive/app_test.dart
import 'package:flutter_driver/driver_extension.dart';
import 'package:backend/main.dart' as app;
```

Import your app.

```
void main() {
  // This line enables the extension
  enableFlutterDriverExtension();    ◁——— Enable the extension.
  // run the app
  app.main();              ◁——— Run the app.
}
```

That's all there is to that file. Of course, in really complicated apps, you may have to do some setup in this file, like anything that needs to be preprocessed in the app.

Lastly, you have to have a device connected to run the app on. Whatever you usually use (iOS emulator, Android studio emulator, or an actual connected device) will do fine. But, the app literally runs, so it has to have a place to run.

WRITE TESTS FOR FLUTTER_DRIVER

The tests are in the test_app.dart file. Again, the tests aren't too different. You use Finders (though they're called slightly differently), Matchers, and the same expect calls. The difference mainly lies in the setup. You have access to special functions that are used to connect to the Flutter driver. The setup is shown in the next listing.

Listing 11.15 Writing flutter_driver integration tests

```
// backend/test_drive/app.dart
import 'package:flutter_driver/flutter_driver.dart';
import 'package:test/test.dart';              ◁————
```
Remember, you have to use the test package rather than the flutter_test package.

```
void main() {
  group("Todo App", () {
    final buttonFinder =
        find.byValueKey("get-todos-button");    ◁————
    final completedTodoCounter = find.byValueKey("counter");
    final listViewFinder = find.byValueKey("list-view");
    final lastTodoFinder = find.byValueKey("todo-19");
    final lastTodoSubtitleFinder = find.byValueKey('todo-19-subtitle');
```
Using the Finder is similar. Here, I'm finding many widgets by their key.

```
    FlutterDriver driver;      ◁————
```
Establish a reference to the FlutterDriver that you'll use like the WidgetTester class in the previous examples.

```
    // Connect to the Flutter driver before running any tests
    setUpAll(() async {              ◁————
      driver = await FlutterDriver.connect();
    });
```
Call driver.connect to setup the driver.

```
    // Close the connection to the driver after the tests have completed
    tearDownAll(() async {              ◁————
      if (driver != null) {
        driver.close();
      }
    });
```
You also must close the connection with driver.close or the processes will keep running in your app.

That's all there is to this setup. Basically, connect to the driver before you run the tests, and close the connection when you're done. Closing the connection effectively stops running the app. For the tests themselves, I decided to test two things. First, that FloatingActionButton can be tapped and will result in fetching todos, as seen in figure 11.4.

I'm testing that by checking the count of completed todos. (This only works because I know the test data. Otherwise, it wouldn't be safe to assume there are always more than 0 completed todos in the data set. But since I'm using a mock API, I know that the data is going to be the same every time.)

Figure 11.4   Completed todos in the todo app

Second, I'm testing to make sure that the list of todos scrolls, and that there are the number of items in the todo lists that I expect. This test is about showing two things: the power of flutter_driver (you can *watch* it scroll through your app) and how to use the flutter_driver package to profile your apps performance. I'll discuss that more in a bit.

This is what the tests look like that I wrote for the todo app:

```
//lib/test_drive/test_app.dart
test('taps fab button', () async {
    await driver.tap(buttonFinder);        // driver.tap replaces tester.tap.
    expect(
      await driver.getText(completedTodoCounter),
      isNot("0"),
    );
});                                        // driver.getText is similar. isNot is a Matcher that pretty much means !=.

test('can scroll to bottom', () async {
  final timeline =
    await driver.traceAction(() async {    // driver.scrollUntilVisible will do just that.
      await driver.scrollUntilVisible(
        listViewFinder,
        lastTodoFinder,
        dyScroll: -150.0,                  // lastTodoFinder finds the last todo. This argument is what you pass for the test to look for.
      );

  expect(
    await driver.getText(lastTodoSubtitleFinder),
    "todo num: 19",
  );
```

traceAction is used for profiling. More on this soon!

listViewFinder is a finder I wrote that finds the ListView in the app.

This is how many pixels the driver will scroll by *per action*. It'll scroll down 150 pixels and stop, search for the widget, and then 150 more if it doesn't find it, and so on. It's best if you don't put in a number that can be larger than the viewport of the device your app is running on.

There are basically three big differences in that test compared to the widget tests. First, `tester` is replaced with `driver`. But one or the other is the object you're using to access most of the test features.

The second is less subtle. The `scrollUntilVisible` method on driver is powerful! You actually can scroll with the normal flutter_test package, but it's not as "smart." `scrollUntilVisible` does much more for you. In the test example, the test will pass if it can tap the button, display some todos, and scroll down until it finds a todo with the Key `todo-19`. If there were 5,000 todos, it would be able to handle that, too. It just scrolls a bit, checks to see if the item is visible, and then continues. `scrollUntilVisible` is just one example of what flutter_driver can do. It makes it easy to simulate actual user usability.

The last big difference in this test (compared to widget tests) is the `driver.trace-Action` method. It's used to profile your app's performance, and I'll talk about that next.

11.1.5 *Performance profiling integration tests*

The reason that I specifically made a test that deals with scrolling is because scrolling is a costly task for a mobile app. While scrolling, the app is re-rendering several times per second. Flutter renders at 60 FPS (frames per second), if you're curious. When you're scrolling, your app is re-rendering the entire page over and over. It's an animation that's animated for you, which means that it's not too hard for scrolling to get "janky." flutter_driver provides a way to keep your app jank-free, via its built in performance profiling.

In a nutshell, you can tell your app to record performance metrics during any integration test, and it will give you the resulting data. The profiling is all about the UI itself, such as how smooth the animations are, what FPS the rendering is achieving, and so forth. You can use those results to try and pinpoint where your app's performance bottlenecks are, as they relate to the UI. (For example, if the data shows poor performance in a test that involves scrolling, perhaps the items in the scrollable are too costly to render).

Profiling the app with flutter_driver only really requires two quick steps. First, tell it what test to profile with the `traceAction` method. Then output the summary with an object called `TimelineSummary`. The test I showed you earlier (the scroll test) was actually incomplete. Here's the full snippet.

Listing 11.16 Profiling you app with flutter_driver

```
// backend/test_drive/app_test.dart
test('can scroll to bottom', () async {
  final timeline =
    await driver.traceAction(() async {
      await driver.scrollUntilVisible(
        listViewFinder,
        lastTodoFinder,
```

traceAction tells flutter_driver what to track. You pass your test in as a callback.

```
            dyScroll: -150.0,
      );
      expect(await driver.getText(lastTodoSubtitleFinder), "todo num: 19");
    });
    final summary =
      TimelineSummary.summarize(timeline);

    await summary.writeSummaryToFile(
      "scrolling_summary", pretty: true,
    );

    await summary.writeTimelineToFile(
      "scrolling_timeline",
    );

  });
```

> **TimelineSummary is the class that will parse all the data from traceAction and turn it into something digestible. We pass it the result of traceAction via the timeline variable.**

> **This method creates a new file that has all the data in it. The first argument (scrolling_summary) is the name you'd like to give the new file; pretty: true makes it readable by humans.**

writeTimelineToFile writes the whole timeline; it's way too much to read though, but it has its purpose (shown later).

This is all cool. Hopefully, we can all agree that it's neat that Flutter will profile your app for you. But reading the data is a different story. First, to actually run the test, do two steps:

1   Make sure you have a device running (the iOS emulator).
2   Run `flutter drive --target=test_driver/app.dart` in the root of your project.

This will take a minute because flutter_driver has to build and then run the app as you would when you run the app in development. Once the tests run, two files are generated, and both can be found in the build folder that's generated when you run a Flutter app. The first, backend/build/scrolling_summary.json, is full of JSON that gives some quick insights. Mine looks like this:

```
// backend/build/scrolling_summary.json
{
  "average_frame_build_time_millis": 4.57943661971831,
  "90th_percentile_frame_build_time_millis": 8.045,
  "99th_percentile_frame_build_time_millis": 10.86,
  "worst_frame_build_time_millis": 13.751,
  "missed_frame_build_budget_count": 0,
  "average_frame_rasterizer_time_millis": 2.4071690140845066,
  "90th_percentile_frame_rasterizer_time_millis": 2.85,
  "99th_percentile_frame_rasterizer_time_millis": 3.234,
  "worst_frame_rasterizer_time_millis": 3.551,
  "missed_frame_rasterizer_budget_count": 0,
  "frame_count": 71,
  // ...
```

To me, this is a little too much to digest. Those numbers really only have value when you've run many tests and can see the data points change over time. They don't have much context on their own. But you can see `missed_frame_build_budget_count`, which is 0. That's good. That means Flutter could handle every new frame it tried to render. However, there is an even more detailed set of data that will make this easier to digest. That's the scrolling_timeline.json file.

On it's own, it's a mess. It's so many numbers that it doesn't make any sense. But there's a tool inside Google's Chrome browser that can display this data in a graph. Digesting profiling data is beyond the scope of this book, but I will show you how to get there and share a few hot tips.

The tool that turns the data into graphs is free. And if you use the Chrome browser, you already have that tool. In the Chrome browser, you can go to the address `chrome://tracing/`. (Put that in the URL bar and navigate to the page.) What you'll see is shown in figure 11.5.

Load in a file.

Figure 11.5 Chrome profiling tool

Basically a blank screen! But on that screen, click the Load button and open the scrolling _timeline.json file. Now the data is loaded, and you'll see what's shown in figure 11.6.

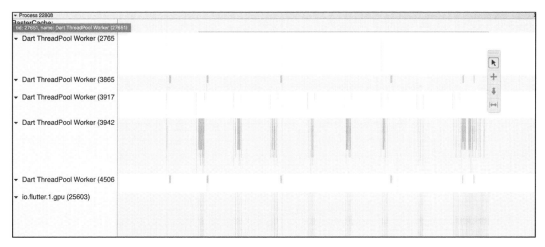

Figure 11.6 Profiler data visual

You can now see graphs. This graph reminds me of the Chrome dev tools Network tab, if you come from the web. Basically it allows you to zoom in on moments of time and see what's taking the most time for Flutter to handle (figure 11.7).

The data tells you exactly how long each process took, which gives you an idea of what you can whittle down. Again, these profiling tools are much more important with context. Trying to make sense of them in a test app won't be as useful as using them in real life. So with that in mind, I leave you knowing that the tools are there, and the next time you're building a Flutter app that seems janky, you know how to investigate it.

BlockScheduler::AssignEdgeWeights	0.037 ms	0.037 ms	0.001 ms 48
OptimizationPasses	133.588 ms	-1.704 ms	2.783 ms 48
CompileGraph	2.593 ms	2.593 ms	0.055 ms 47
FinalizeCompilation	4.185 ms	4.185 ms	0.089 ms 47
ComputeSSA	1.274 ms	1.274 ms	0.027 ms 48
ApplyICData	3.527 ms	3.527 ms	0.037 ms 95
TryOptimizePatterns	0.171 ms	0.171 ms	0.002 ms 95
SetOuterInliningId	0.020 ms	0.020 ms	0.000 ms 48
FlowGraphTypePropagator	36.899 ms	20.082 ms	0.038 ms 969
ApplyClassIds	0.691 ms	0.691 ms	0.007 ms 95
Inlining	65.029 ms	51.154 ms	1.355 ms 48
Canonicalize	4.594 ms	4.594 ms	0.015 ms 309
BranchSimplify	0.613 ms	0.613 ms	0.013 ms 46

Figure 11.7   Specific processes and their run times

11.2 Accessibility with the semantics widgets

In general, *accessibility* is about making sure your app is usable by *everyone*. The best example of this is color usage on screens. A lot of people are color-blind, and it's important that the colors you use in any Flutter app, web app, or literally anything else that humans have to read are readable by everyone, even if their vision is impaired; for instance, using heavy contrast between text and it's background.

This is a pretty short topic in Flutter because most of the principals and practices aren't specific to Flutter; for example, using images with high contrast or using large enough text. You could (and many people have) written full books about accessibility. I encourage you learn all that you can and use those practices. That said, Flutter does have one family of widgets that are specifically used for accessibility: the Semantics widgets.

Semantics widgets are used in the same way the alt property on the <a> tag in HTML is used. It provides information about what the app does and how it works. The Semantics widget annotates the widget tree with a description of its direct child. For example, you can use semantics to annotate a Button widget with what the button does. Or you can use it to annotate certain text that might be challenging for a visually-impaired person to read. This widget allows a screen reader to be able to decipher what's going on and report back to the user.

In Flutter, as we've learned, there are multiple trees that represent the app. This is how the Semantics widget works, too. There's (yet another) tree called the *semantics tree* that holds the semantics information for screen readers. Some of the work in building a good semantics tree is done for you, but you can also add to it yourself.

You add nodes to the semantics tree by simply wrapping widgets with a Semantics widget as a parent. Here's an example:

Semantics is a widget, like everything else.

```
Semantics(
    container: true,

    properties: SemanticsProperties(
```

If true, creates a new node in the semantics tree. You might not want it to be true if the node and it's parent are really one UI element (like a button and the text in it).

Properties give the semantics widget its power. There are many properties, but these represent a good number of them.

```
    button: true,
                                                    ◁─────   button should be true if the child is a
                                                             button; it tells screen readers if this is
    hint: "Performs action when pressed",   ◁───            an actionable component. There are
                                                             also properties like textField (for text)
    onTap: () => { ... },        ◁────                       and checked (for checkbox).
  ),
                                                     This hint is provided to screen
  child: Button(                                     readers so users know what
    // ...                                           the component does.
```

Then you just give it a   **onTap is one of many callbacks that can be**
child like anything else.   **passed that respond to actions that accessibility**
                                      tools (like screen readers) can make.

This is the bulk of what you need to keep in mind when it comes to using `Semantics` widgets. There are many, many properties on the widget. But the important thing to note here is that Flutter *does* consider accessibility and provides a way to make apps more accessible. You should *absolutely* use them to make your app production ready.

11.3 Next steps with Flutter

(Cue "You're Still the One" by Shania Twain on the jukebox.)

"Looks like we made it…"

(Credits roll…)

Welp, here we are. At the end of the book. And look how far you've come. As I'm writing this, I'm happy to say that there are some big, exciting things coming in the near future for Flutter. So, the journey isn't over (just yet).

In the meantime, I hope you'll continue to use Flutter and learn and maybe even contribute back to the community. I couldn't possibly cover everything in a single book, and it's so rapidly developing that I'd like to point out some of my favorite resources that I think are logical steps in learning more about Flutter:

- FlutterSamples.com—This site is a collection of Flutter apps that demonstrate different ways to approach the architecture of your Flutter app and its state. It includes sample apps that use blocs, Redux, inherited widgets, and more.
- *Accessibility Handbook*—This book (by O'Reilly Media) is nearly 10 years old, but it's still the go-to book for accessibility in websites. The same principals apply to mobile.
- Flutter's YouTube channel—The Flutter developer relations team puts *a lot* of work into learning materials and documentation. I think that's one of the things that makes Flutter such an amazing product. There are tons of helpful videos on all subjects from the official Flutter YouTube channel.
- CodeMagic—This is a CD/CI platform created specifically for Flutter. And it's easy to use. You can't beat that.

Finally, if you're really curious about the nitty-gritty computer-science-ish way that Flutter works under the hood, check out the article called "Inside Flutter" on Flutter's website. You'll find it at https://flutter.dev/docs/resources/inside-flutter.

Summary

- There are three ways to test Flutter code: Dart unit tests, widget tests, and integration tests.
- Unit tests are great for testing classes and functions.
- You can "mock" classes, especially useful for classes that make service calls, with the mockito library.
- Widget tests are best used to test specific widgets.
- Widget tests use `Matcher` and `Finder` objects to compare what you *expect* to happen and what actually happened.
- Integration tests can test how all the moving pieces of a feature work together. Integration tests in Flutter are done with the flutter_driver package.
- You can profile the performance of your app with integration tests.
- Tests written with flutter_driver are similar to widget tests. Both use the concept of "pumping" widgets to simulate an app being run.
- Accessibility is important in production apps.
- Flutter helps you write more accessible apps via the `Semantics` widget. Use it!

appendix A
Installation: Dart2

A.1 Installation: Dart2

In order to run Dart on your machine, you'll need to install the Dart SDK.

> **DART 2** The following instructions install Dart 2. This book will be using Dart 2; Dart 1 will not work! If you already have the Dart SDK on your machine, ensure that it's version 2.0.0 or greater.

Installing the Dart SDK is straightforward if you use the command line.

> **The command line**
>
> Many instructions in this book will involve running commands in your machine's command line. You don't need to be a command-line wizard to use this book. (I'm a big fan of GUIs and don't use the command line much.) Just know that anytime you see a line of code that starts with a $, it's a command for your terminal. In the following, ? is used to show the return value. For example, the command which dart in the OSX terminal returns the file path to your Dart SDK as shown here:
>
> ```
> $ which dart
> => /usr/local/bin/dart
> ```

Installation differs depending on what operating system you use.

A.1.1 Mac OS

If you're using a Mac, it's likely that you have a program called Homebrew on your computer. If not, you need to install it. Homebrew is a command-line program that lets you download and manage software packages from the terminal. We can install it easily from the command line. First, check to see if it's installed:

> **WARNING**   If you're copying and pasting command-line commands, be sure to remove the first $.

```
$ brew -v
```

If your terminal prints Homebrew 1.x.x, then you're good to go. Otherwise, you need to install Homebrew. You can find instructions for installing Homebrew via the command line at https://brew.sh. Homebrew will walk you through the steps in your terminal.

Second, install Dart SDK. Thanks to Homebrew, this is incredibly easy:

```
$ brew tap dart-lang/dart
$ brew install dart
```

Now, in your terminal, run this command to make sure everything is in its right place:

```
$ dart -v

=> Dart VM version: 2.x.x...
```

A.1.2   *Windows OS*

On Windows, the easiest way to install Dart is via the package manager, Chocolately. With Chocolatey on your machine, you simply have to run

```
C:\> choco install dart-sdk
```

A.1.3   *Linux*

The easiest way to install on Ubuntu is with this series of steps. Using all these commands will ensure that Dart automatically updates whenever the newest version is released.

For a one-time setup step

```
$ sudo apt-get update
$ sudo apt-get install apt-transport-https
$ sudo sh -c 'curl
➥ https://dl-ssl.google.com/linux/linux_signing_key.pub | apt-key add -'
$ sudo sh -c 'curl https://storage.googleapis.com/download.dartlang.org/
➥ linux/debian/dart_stable.list > /etc/apt/sources.list.d/dart_stable.list'
```

Now, install the Dart SDK:

```
$ sudo apt-get update
$ sudo apt-get install dart
```

A.2   *Installation: Flutter SDK*

Installing Flutter on your machine requires you to go to the Flutter web page to download a zip file of the SDK: https://flutter.dev/get-started/install/. From there, you can follow the instructions provided as they're extremely detailed. I'll provide the exact steps next, if you don't care about the details:

A.2.1 *Mac OS*

1 Download the SDK from https://flutter.dev/get-started/install/.

2 Extract the files in the proper place:

```
$ cd ~
$ unzip ~/Downloads/flutter_macos_v0.9.4-beta.zip
```

3 Add Flutter to your PATH temporarily:

```
$ export PATH=`pwd`/flutter/bin:$PATH
```

4 Open your bash_profile to update your PATH permanently:

```
$ cd ~
$ nano .bash_profile
```

5 Add this line to your bash_profile:

```
$ export PATH=$HOME/flutter/bin:$PATH
```

6 Run flutter doctor in your terminal.

   This is a nice command-line tool that tells you if you need anything else on your machine to run Flutter. Some of the tools are common (like Xcode and Android Studio), so I won't walk through every one. If you run flutter doctor, it'll tell you exactly what other tools you'll need to get your environment set up.

A.2.2 *Windows*

1 Download the SDK from https://flutter.dev/get-started/install/.

2 Extract the zip file and place the contained Flutter in the desired installation location for the Flutter SDK (for example, C:\src\flutter). Do not install Flutter in a directory like C:\Program Files\; that requires elevated privileges.

3 Locate the file flutter_console.bat inside the flutter directory and start it by double-clicking.

4 Add Flutter to your PATH if you like to use the command line. Go to Control Panel > User Accounts > User Accounts > Change my environment variables. Under User Variables, check if there is an entry called Path:
   – If the entry exists, append the full path to flutter\bin using ; as a separator from existing values.
   – If the entry does *not* exist, create a new user variable named Path, with the full path to flutter\bin as its value.

5 Reboot Windows to fully apply this change.

6   Run flutter doctor in your terminal.

This is a nice command-line tool that tells you if you need anything else on your machine to run Flutter. Some of the tools are common (like Xcode and Android Studio), so I won't walk through every one. If you run flutter doctor, it'll tell you exactly what other tools you'll need to get your environment set up.

A.2.3   Linux

1   Download the SDK from https://flutter.dev/get-started/install/.

2   Extract the files in the proper place:

```
$ cd ~/development
$ tar xf ~/Downloads/flutter_linux_v0.9.4-beta.tar.xz
```

3   Add Flutter to your PATH temporarily:

```
$ export PATH=`pwd`/flutter/bin:$PATH
```

4   Open your bash_profile to update your PATH permanently:

```
$ cd ~
$ nano .bash_profile
```

5   Add this line to your bash_profile:

```
$ export PATH=$HOME/development/flutter/bin:$PATH
```

6   Run flutter doctor in your terminal.

This is a nice command-line tool that tells you if you need anything else on your machine to run Flutter. Some of the tools are common (like Xcode and Android Studio), so I won't walk through every one. If you run flutter doctor, it'll tell you exactly what other tools you'll need to get your environment set up.

A.3   Tooling and a quick note on text editors

There are a lot of text editors in the world. And I'm sure they're all great. However, I'm a programmer and therefore opinionated (and correct), and you should use Intellij. But capitalism says that we're better off with many options. For Flutter use, I can only recommend these two text editors:

- VS Code
- JetBrains Intellij

Both of these editors have officially supported plugins for Dart.

VSCode is probably the best completely free IDE that exists. Every web developer on the planet is jumping ship to VSCode. It's the return of the IDE in the web world. And it's a fantastic option.

That said, Intellij is truly full-featured, and I recommend its use. An unfortunate part of writing code is that we also have to deal with managing a project, and an IDE like Intellij makes your life much easier on that front. Intellij Community Edition is free, and the Dart and Flutter features are fully supported in the free version.

One of the greatest things about the Dart community is that it is ... err ... *concise*, compared to other languages used to write web apps that I will not name here. Thanks to these IDE plugins and other tooling, you don't have to mess with linters, formatters, or any of that. If you use the plugins, all that comes for free. In Dart, there's one way to do it: the right way. I'm kidding (kind of).

Before moving on to the next section, you should install one of these two editors, as well as the Dart plugin.

A.4 *DartPad*

You don't have to do any setup or installation right now, because for this example, you can use DartPad. DartPad is a browser-based text editor that lets you write and run Dart, HTML, and CSS. Find it at https://dartpad.dartlang.org/.

DartPad is a pretty valuable tool for testing little bits of logic. It's worth bookmarking in your browser and using as a tool when you're trying to iterate quickly with Dart snippets.

appendix B
The Pub package manager

Pub is Dart's package manager. It's where you pull in open-sourced libraries, as well as your own. Most packages you'll ever use are at https://pub.dartlang.org/. Here you'll find packages published by the Flutter and Dart teams, as well as Dart community members.

Dart has a concise community. In some other languages, like JavaScript or Java, there are about 45 to 445 libraries for every possible problem you come across in your code. In Dart, the community seems to favor contributing to current packages over publishing new ones—"a rising tide lifts all boats" kind of thing. This saves time and energy and will leave you confident in the packages you're using.

You use the packages on Pub by declaring which ones you'd like to use in a file called pubspec.yaml. All Dart applications *must* have a pubspec file, and it must be in the root of the project. When you run or build any Dart app, this is the first thing the engine looks for.

A fresh pubspec.yaml file looks like this:

```
name: my_dart_app
description: An absolute bare-bones dart app.
# version: 1.0.0
# homepage: https://www.example.com
# author: eric <email@example.com>
environment:
sdk: '>=2.0.0 <3.0.0'
# dependencies:
# path: ^1.4.1
dev_dependencies:
  build_runner: ^0.10.0
  build_web_compilers: ^0.4.0
```

The top section describes the project's metadata.

The environment describes which version of Dart you're using.

Dependencies are where you tell Dart to pull in other packages, as well as dev_dependencies.[1]

---

[1] dev_dependencies are usually concerned with running your app on your machine for development, but aren't used when you build an app because they aren't needed.

B.1 Hosted packages and versioning with Pub

Each dependency hosted on the Pub website follows the same structure: `title: version`. There are special characters, like the ^, which describe a range of versions. The robust way to describe a version is by using comparison operators, such as

```
sdk: '>=2.0.0 <3.0.0'
```

This basically says, "Give me the newest version from 2.0.0 to 3.0.0, but not including 3.0.0."

For Pub hosted packages, you can also use the caret (^) syntax to define a range. For example, `path: ^1.4.1` is the same as saying, "Give me the newest version that is guaranteed to be backwards compatible to 1.4.1."

> **WARNING** If you're using the > character in your pubspec, the line containing the > must be in quotes. Without quotes, it will be read as YAML syntax and break everything.

B.2 Using packages on your machine or from GitHub

Finally, you can use packages that aren't hosted on Pub. This is good if you're developing a package or don't want to open source your package.

B.2.1 Git

To use packages from Git, import packages similarly to the following code example in your pubspec.yaml file:

```
dependencies:
  cool_package:
    git: git://github.com/cool_company/cool_packages.git
```

Or you can use a specific branch of the Git repo:

```
dependencies:
  kittens:
    git:
      url: git://github.com/munificent/kittens.git
      ref: some-branch
```

And you can use subfolders of a repo (useful if you have mono-repo-style projects):

```
dependencies:
  kittens:
    git:
      url: git://github.com/munificent/cats.git
      path: path/to/kittens
```

B.2.2 Local packages

You can tell Pub where to find a package on your machine with `path`, like this:

```
dependencies:
  cool_local_package:
    path: /Users/me/cool_local_package
```

B.3 Using the packages

In any case, using packages in your Dart code is always the same. To use the library from `cool_package`, import it at the top of your Dart file by telling it the entry point of the package. Generally, the entry point file will mimic the name of the whole package. For example

```
import "package:cool_package/cool_package.dart";
```

appendix C
Flutter for web developers

The Flutter documentation has a *fantastic* page about coming from the web, so for this appendix, I'd like to touch on some of the most common questions and concerns web developers new to Flutter ask. I'll structure this as a series of questions and answers.

I suggest you read the opening chapter (or two) before reading this—even if you're super familiar with JavaScript and have never seen a line of Flutter code. A lot of the jargon in this section is Flutter-specific.

Also, there is a lot you *won't* find here. For example, animations. Animations are a big part of writing UIs and can be challenging. But there's an entire chapter in this book about animations in Flutter. This document is more about pointing you in the right direction because all the information you want is in the chapters of this book.

C.1   *The good news first*

The good news is twofold. First, Flutter is heavily influenced by ReactJS. If you're coming from the modern web, the paradigm is very similar. Second, the entire Dart language fits semantically inside JavaScript. So there aren't really any "gotchas." Other than working with classes and typing, the two languages are similar.

And finally, I'm a web developer. I'm not an iOS or Android developer. So I can give you the best of my knowledge and my personal struggles going from web to Flutter. The poor souls that are reading iOS for Flutter and Android for Flutter will probably be left wanting.

The big difference between web development and Flutter development is that *everything* is Dart code. There is no markup language (like HTML) or styling language (like CSS). It's all just in-line Dart. In the JS community, everyone is fighting about CSS-in-JS, and in the Flutter world, we aren't even writing HTML. It's cool.

With that in mind, this part of the book is all about the HTML and CSS equivalents in Flutter. You shouldn't be concerned with JavaScript because that's similar. And there is no DOM on mobile, so there's no need to talk about handlers.

C.2   *How is layout handled in Flutter? Is there a flexbox equivalent?*

Yes! There is a flexbox equivalent. In fact, by default, you'll almost certainly be using Flex in your Flutter app. Flutter ships with a ton of layout widgets, including Row and Column, which enforce Flex rules on their own. When using those widgets, you can tell their children how to lay out using the properties from justify-content and others that you're already used to. The following listing shows an example.

Listing 3.1   The Column widget in the counter app

```
// Column widget example
body: new Center(                                    Column is aptly named. It lays out
  child: new Column(                                 all its children in a vertical fashion.
    mainAxisAlignment: MainAxisAlignment.center,     This alignment property is
    children: <Widget>[                              similar to flexbox in CSS. It
      new Text(                                       tells Flutter how to lay out
        'You have pushed the button this many times:', the Column children in
      ),                                              relationship to each other.
      new Text(
        '$_counter',
      ),
    ],
    // ...
```

The Row widget behaves like the Column widget, but on a horizontal axis. Finally, in addition to Center, you can use the following properties on MainAxisAlignment:

- Start
- End
- Center
- SpaceAround
- SpaceBetween
- SpaceEvenly

For an in-depth look at Row and Column, read chapter 2.

C.3   *What about using an absolute position?*

To specify an absolute position for a widget as x-y coordinates, nest it in a Positioned widget that is itself nested in a Stack widget. Positioned gives you access to properties like top, left, right, and bottom, similar to CSS. Here's an example:

```
// Stack and Positioned          All children of a Stack can be positioned.
Stack(
  children: [                     This widget is basically saying
    Positioned(                   position:absolute in CSS.
      child: Text("Lorem ipsum"),
```

```
    left: 24.0,
    top: 24.0,
  ),
  Text("Not positioned"),
 ],
),
```

> **Any child of a stack that isn't positioned is laid out like it would be in a Column (or Row if you change the main axis to horizontal).**

For an in-depth look at `Row` and `Column`, read chapter 2. For an in-depth look at `Positioned`, check out chapter 4.

C.4 What about the basics: Borders, padding, margin, and color?

Like everything else in Flutter, these are handled with widgets. You can add padding to any widget by wrapping it in `Padding`:

```
Padding(
  padding: const EdgeInsets.all(16.0),
  child: Text("Wrap me up"),
),
```

> **You can add padding around every edge this way, or use EdgeInsets.only(top: 8.0) to add padding to specific sides.**

You can also add `padding` with a `Container`. The `Container` widget is a "convenience" widget that provides a whole slew of properties that you would otherwise get from individual widgets (like the padding widget), which solely add single properties to their children. You will likely get a lot of use out of the `Container` widget. It can be used to set padding, margin, background colors, borders, border-radius, width, height, box-shadows, and the list goes on.

C.5 Manipulating text style

You change text via a `TextStyle` widget. This widget can be given as an argument to `Text` widgets, and it'll allow you to set things like `fontSize`, `fontWeight`, and `fontFamily` and `color`. Here's an example:

```
// TextStyle example
Text(
  "Lorem ipsum",
  style: TextStyle(
    color: Colors.white,
    fontSize: 24.0,
    fontWeight: FontWeight.w900,
    letterSpacing: 4.0,
  ),
),
// ...
```

C.6 Global styles

In addition to global CSS declarations, there's a `Theme` widget in Flutter. `Theme` can be used to set all kinds of styles that'll apply everywhere. Specifically, you'll use it to set color options and text options, like font family. An entire section of chapter 4 is about the `Theme` widget.

appendix D
Flutter for iOS developers

The Flutter documentation has a *fantastic* page about iOS, and I am *not* an iOS expert. So, for this appendix, I'd like to touch on some of the most common questions iOS developers new to Flutter ask, as well as how you can make an app that's familiar to iOS users. I'll structure this as a series of questions and answers.

I suggest you read the opening chapter (or two) before reading this appendix—even if you're super familiar with iOS and have never seen a line of Flutter code. A lot of the jargon in this section is Flutter-specific.

Also, there is a lot you *won't* find here. For example, animations. Animations are a big part of writing UIs and can be challenging. But there's an entire chapter in this book about animations in Flutter. This document is more about pointing you in the right direction, because all the information you want is in the chapters of this book.

D.1 What's the equivalent of UIView in Flutter?

In iOS, you create your UI with view objects that are instances of `UIView`. In Flutter, everything is a widget, and that's the closest comparison to a `UIView`. They aren't exactly the same because they handle more, but they are used to construct UIs. For our intent and purpose, they're close enough. So, if widgets are UIViews, what are the differences?

First, widgets are *immutable*. They're light-weight blueprints for the UI that are destroyed as soon as they need to be changed. Every time the configuration or state of a widget changes, Flutter redraws the relevant widget tree. But widgets are just descriptions for actual elements and don't get drawn to the screen directly.

Also, because of the immutability, a widget doesn't change its child widgets. Rather than saying, "Hey, UI element, remove child ABC and replace it with XYZ," you just redraw the UI element with the child XYZ.

NOTE Widgets and updating the view are explained in detail in chapters 1 and 3.

D.2   What's the paradigm or mental model difference?

The biggest difference between writing a Flutter app and an iOS one is that Flutter uses composition and reactive-style programming to make handling your UI state simple. You, the developer, don't have to be concerned with mutating the UI state because it's handled by the framework internally. This is mostly due to the fact that the UI is described by widgets.

Widgets aren't UI elements themselves, but rather they're *blueprints* for true elements. And you use widgets to describe the current view. As your app's state changes, and the screen needs to re-render, the framework is just rendering the current widget tree, and it knows how to transition the UI as it changes.

You don't have to tell the UI explicitly to remove elements from the screen and add new ones. You just say, "Hey Flutter, this is what my widget tree looks like. And when that button is pressed, it'll look like this." Flutter knows how to make that transition happen. This is called *reactive programming*.

Secondly, in iOS you often extend UIView or other UI classes to create your views. Flutter uses *composition* instead. All of your widgets are tiny, modular views that are pieced together, similar to a markup language like HTML. This makes your views highly reusable.

NOTE Composition is discussed quite a bit in chapter 2.

D.3   Can I build an app that uses iOS design patterns?

Yes! Quite easily, actually. Flutter, by default, ships with tons of widgets. Many of them follow Material guidelines, the Google design system. But there's a whole package, called Cupertino, that ships with the SDK, which includes tons of iOS style widgets. Here's a few:

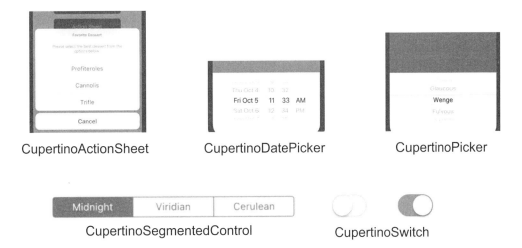

CupertinoActionSheet   CupertinoDatePicker   CupertinoPicker

CupertinoSegmentedControl   CupertinoSwitch

D.4   How to I make complex layouts like UITableView?

In iOS, you can show a list of elements in either a UITableView or UICollectionView. In Flutter, this can be done with ListView widgets, GridView widgets, and Table widgets.

The ListView widget is specifically a great example of Flutter versus iOS. Unlike iOS, there's no need to determine the number of rows or the size of the cells up front. Due partially to the *immutability* of widgets, you simply pass a list of widgets to a ListView and it just works.

D.5   What's similar to Storyboard?

In short, nothing. Everything is a widget, including the app structure and layouts themselves. You use widgets to add padding to other widgets, rather than setting constraints in the Storyboard.

D.6   How do you draw to the screen?

In iOS, you can use CoreGraphics to draw on the screen. Flutter has something similar-ish called Canvas. It's similar to the HTML canvas. You draw to the canvas, which is housed by a widget, using the CustomPainter class, which you use to run your algorithm that paints lines and shapes to the screen. There's a big section on this in chapter 6 of this book.

D.7   How do I add dependencies (like Cocoa Pods)?

Dependencies are added via a YAML (Ain't Markup Language) file called pubspec .yaml in the root of your project. This is similar to a Podfile in iOS. The pubspec file uses Dart's Pub package manager to declare and fetch dependencies. This same file can also be used to tell your app about assets like images and fonts.

NOTE   See the Pub package manager appendix to learn more.

D.8   How do I interact with the device and use native APIs?

Perhaps the biggest difference between native mobile development and Flutter development is that Flutter doesn't have direct access to the devices underlying SDK. Your Flutter app actually is hosted in a ViewController on iOS, but you can't communicate with it directly.

Flutter solved this problem by creating *platform channels*, which can communicate with the ViewController. According to the docs, "Platform channels are essentially an asynchronous messaging mechanism that bridges the Dart code with the host View-Controller and the iOS framework it runs on. You can use platform channels to execute a method on the native side, or to retrieve some data from the device's sensors, for example."

Most platform channel work would be included in your app as a plugin that encapsulates the native code and the Dart code, and exposes the Dart API. You can write your own plugins to do this, which basically consists of writing iOS native code, because the Dart code is generally quite simple. This isn't necessary, though, because there are already a ton of plugins provided by the Pub package manager that communicate with native APIs. These are some examples:

- `image_picker` to access the camera
- `geolocator` to access the GPS sensor

NOTE See the Pub package manager appendix to learn more.

D.9 *Is there an equivalent to CoreData?*

Not exactly. But CoreData in iOS is actually just a thin wrapper over an SQL database. There is a Flutter package, called SQFLite, that you can use to mimic this functionality.

appendix E
Flutter for
Android developers

The Flutter documentation has a *fantastic* page about Android, and I am *not* an Android expert. So, for this appendix, I'd like to touch on some of the most common questions Android developers new to Flutter ask. I'll structure this as a series of questions and answers.

I suggest you read the opening chapter (or two) before reading this appendix—even if you're super familiar with Android and have never seen a line of Flutter code. A lot of the jargon in this section is Flutter-specific.

Also, there is a lot you *won't* find here. For example, animations. Animations are a big part of writing UIs and can be challenging. But there's an entire chapter in this book about animations in Flutter. This document is more about pointing you in the right direction, because all the information you want is in the chapters of this book.

E.1 What's the equivalent of a view in Flutter?

In Android, you create all your UI elements with views. In Flutter, everything is a widget, and that's the closest comparison to a view. (Widgets aren't exactly the same as views, because they also handle more than just UI, but widgets are used to construct UI of mobile apps also.) For our intent and purpose, they're close enough. So, if widgets are views, what are the differences?

First, widgets are *immutable*. They're light-weight blueprints for the UI that are destroyed as soon as they need to be changed. Every time the configuration or state of a widget changes, Flutter redraws the relevant widget tree. But widgets are just descriptions for actual elements and don't get drawn to the screen directly.

Also, because of the immutability, a widget doesn't change its child widgets. There is no equivalent to addChild() or removeChild(). Rather than saying, "Hey,

UI element, remove child ABC and replace it with XYZ," you just redraw the UI element with the child XYZ.

> **NOTE** Widgets and updating the "view" are explained in detail in chapters 1 and 3.

E.2 What's the paradigm or mental model difference?

The biggest difference between writing a Flutter app and an Android one is that Flutter uses composition and reactive-style programming to make handling your UI state simple. You, the developer, don't have to be concerned with mutating the UI state because it's handled by the framework internally. This is mostly due to the fact that the UI is described by widgets.

Widgets aren't UI elements themselves, but rather they're *blueprints* for true elements. And you use widgets to describe the current view. As your app's state changes, and the screen needs to re-render, the framework is just rendering the current widget tree, and it knows how to transition the UI as it changes.

You don't have to tell the UI explicitly to remove elements from the screen and add new ones. You just say, "Hey Flutter, this is what my widget tree looks like. And, when that button is pressed, it'll look like this." Flutter knows how to make that transition happen. This is called *reactive programming*.

Secondly, in Android, you often extend or subclass `View` to create your views. Flutter uses *composition* instead. All of your widgets are tiny, modular views that are pieced together, similar to a markup language like HTML. This makes your views highly reusable.

> **NOTE** Composition is discussed quite a bit in chapter 2.

E.3 Where's the XML layout file?

In short, you don't write markup anymore. Everything is Dart code. Everything is a widget, including the app structure and layouts themselves. You use widgets to build the *widget tree*, which handles styles, layout, and structure (among other things).

E.4 How do I draw to the screen?

Flutter has an API based on the same rendering engine as Android; it's also called `Canvas`. You draw to the canvas, which is housed by a widget, using the `CustomPainter` class that you use to run your algorithm. This paints lines and shapes to the screen. There's a big section on this in chapter 6 of this book, but in general, the Flutter canvas should feel very familiar to Android developers.

E.5 What's the equivalent of an intent in Flutter?

In short, nothing. Flutter doesn't really have a concept of activities. Rather, you navigate between screens using a navigator and routes. It's much closer to routing on the web.

E.6   *What's the equivalent of runOnUiThread() in Flutter?*

The closest equivalent is `Isolates` in Dart. But they aren't quite the same because Dart is single-threaded and event-loop driven. There is no UI thread, and there is no need to run UI in a different thread.

   You can use `Isolate` objects to perform heavy computation that won't block the event loop, but it isn't necessary for the UI. At my day job, we have multiple web and mobile clients written in Dart, and I don't think we use a single `Isolate`. Rather, you can use Dart's asynchronous features to run code to perform async work.

> **NOTE**   Chapter 9 is all about async Dart and Flutter.

E.7   *What's the equivalent of a Gradle file? How do I add dependencies?*

Dependencies are added via a YAML (Ain't Markup Language) file called pubspec .yaml in the root of your project. This is similar to a gradle file in Android. The pubspec file uses Dart's Pub package manager to declare and fetch dependencies. This same file can also be used to tell your app about assets like images and fonts.

> **NOTE**   See the Pub package manager appendix to learn more.

E.8   *What's the equivalent of a LinearLayout? What about ScrollView?*

All layout building is done with widgets. Flutter provides a ton of widgets right out of the box. I don't think you'd ever have to write a custom layout widget because there are already so many. Specifically, you can use a `Row` or `Column` widget instead of `LinearLayout`. And the standard scrolling widget in Flutter is called `ListView`.

> **NOTE**   Rows and columns are discussed in chapter 3 of this book. Scrolling is discussed in several places in the book, but specifically in chapter 9.

E.9   *How do I access shared preferences or SQLite?*

In Android, you can store a small collection of key-value pairs using the SharedPreferences API. In Flutter, access this functionality using the Shared_Preferences plugin. This plugin wraps the functionality of both Shared Preferences and NSUserDefaults (the iOS equivalent).

   In Android, you use SQLite to store structured data that you can query using SQL. In Flutter, access this functionality using the SQFlite plugin.

index